CELLULOID CLASSICISM

[CELLULOID CLASSICISM]

EARLY TAMIL CINEMA AND THE MAKING OF MODERN BHARATANĀṬYAM

HARI KRISHNAN

WESLEYAN UNIVERSITY PRESS

Middletown, Connecticut

Wesleyan University Press
Middletown, CT 06459
www.wesleyan.edu/wespress

Manufactured in the United States of America

Typeset in Utopia by Tseng Information Systems, Inc.

Library of Congress Cataloging-in-Publication Data available upon request

Hardcover ISBN: 978-0-8195-7886-0
Paperback ISBN: 978-0-8195-7887-7
Ebook ISBN: 978-0-8195-7888-4

5 4 3 2 1

CONTENTS

NOTE ON TRANSLITERATION AND SPELLING

In this book, I have used standard Tamil transliteration (following the University of Madras's *Tamil Lexicon*) for all words and text from Tamil sources. Words from Telugu sources or of Sanskrit origin also appear in standard transliteration, with *ĕ* and *ŏ* representing short vowels in Telugu.

The names of films are usually spelled as they appear in English-language sources, often advertisements or film credits (for example, *Thyagabhoomi*, not *Tiyākapūmi*). In instances where I have not found English representations of these words, I have transliterated them following the *Tamil Lexicon*. Where English equivalents or translations for the film names are provided in the credits of the film or film advertisements (for example, as is the case with the 1948 film *Vedhala Ulagam*, which was marketed in English as *Demon World*), I have used those translations. In other cases, I have translated the titles myself. Place names, regardless of their appearance, are spelled using their contemporary "official" spellings (Thanjavur, not Tañcāvūr or Tañjāvūr, and Vazhuvoor, not Vaḻuvūr).

With the names of twentieth-century people, for the most part I have followed the standard practice of phonetic spelling adopted in the modern Tamil context (Sundaram, not Cuntaram; Muthuswamy, not Muttucāmi or Muttucuvāmi). The names of some early twentieth-century and all nineteenth-century people are usually spelled using standard Tamil transliteration, since most of these were imported from Tamil-language sources (Kurucāmitās, not Gurusāmidās).

ACKNOWLEDGMENTS

This book began around 2002, when I was introduced to the former dancer-actress, Padmini Ramachandran (1932–2006). Over the course of a number of years, I engaged in conversations with Padmini, whom I affectionately referred to as "Pappimā," at her home in New Jersey, and enjoyed her ever-warm hospitality. We spoke at length about Bharatanāṭyam, the cinema, and their deeply interconnected place in her life. This work owes much to my informal conversations with Padmini. Had she still been alive, it would have been a very different work, with her clearly at its center.

The material that is at the heart of this book was found largely in two major archival collections. I would like to express my profound gratitude to S. V. Jayababu, a private collector and film aficionado in Chennai, whose astounding collection of materials and meticulous curatorial skills have been central to this work. I would also like to thank G. Sundar and the staff of the Roja Muthiah Research Library in Chennai for their help in locating and copying a vast number of archival sources for me.

In the period 2012–14, I was fortunate to be able to conduct interviews with a number of artists in South India. Some of the most moving experiences over the course of this project came from my interviews with the former actress-dancers Thanjavur Kuchalakumari, L. Vijayalakshmi, and the late Pillaiyarchetty Bhakthavatsalam Naidu Rajeevalochana (known in films as Rajasulochana). I am deeply grateful to these women for very generously sharing aspects of their professional and personal lives with me. In particular, Kuchalakumari continues to be a respected confidante and source of inspiration. While much of this material did not make it into the final version of the book, I would like to acknowledge the Chennai- and Bangalore-based dancers who very graciously gave of their time for interviews related to this project: the late Udupi Laxminarayan, Sudharani Raghupathy, Nandini Ramani, the late Maya Rao, Anita Ratnam,

Malavika Sarukkai, Radhika Shurajit (with Churchill Pandian), Padma Subrahmanyam, Alarmel Valli, and Lakshmi Viswanathan.

I have also had the great pleasure of extended conversations with eminent film historians and scholars on the subject of dance in the Tamil cinema. I am grateful to Theodore Baskaran, Madabhushi Rangadorai (who writes under the penname Randor Guy), and V. A. K. Ranga Rao. As always, I am grateful to B. M. Sundaram, whose wisdom has guided all of my work on Bharatanāṭyam history.

I must express my profound gratitude to Suzanna Tamminen and Wesleyan University Press. Suzanna's vision for publishing cutting-edge dance research is inspiring to say the least, and I am grateful that my book is being published by Wesleyan.

This book began as a dissertation at Texas Woman's University, and I would like to thank two inspirational professors—Penny Hanstein and Linda Caldwell—who mentored me for a number of years and transformed my perspective on interdisciplinary research. Linda Caldwell in particular was a formidable and nurturing presence throughout my years as a doctoral student. I express my gratitude to Rosemary Candelario for all her guidance and patience, and to Mark Kessler for being on my dissertation committee. I would also like to thank dear friends in my PhD cohort for their long-standing support and camaraderie, especially Julie Mulvihill, Wanda Ebright, and Ilana Morgan. I also remember with great fondness and gratitude my undergraduate professors in South Asian studies—Brenda Cantelo, Robert Hueckstedt, and Klaus Klostermaier—who set me on the path of academic inquiry.

I would also like to thank my colleagues in the Dance Department at Wesleyan University for their support and faith in me for over almost two decades—Pedro Alejandro, who continues to inspire me as both an artist and scholar; and my dearest friends and closest colleagues, Patricia Beaman, Katja Kolcio, Susan Lourie, Iddrisu Saaka, Nicole Stanton, and the one and only Michele Olerud. I'd also like to thank John Elmore at Wesleyan for his help with the technical and aesthetic dimensions of many of the images that appear in the book.

In the wider contexts of South Asian studies and dance studies, I must thank a number of colleagues whose work has played a very significant part in my own thinking about issues related to Bharatanāṭyam. Many of these people have also been friends and interlocutors for a number of years—Matthew Allen, Ananya Chatterjea, Ann David, Andrée Grau,

Usha Iyer, Saskia Kersenboom, Avanthi Meduri, Srividya Natarajan, Janet O'Shea, Indira Viswanathan Peterson, Rumya Putcha, Katyanani Thota, Archana Venkatesan, and Amanda Weidman.

I would also like to thank my close friends and the members of my support network who are spread across India, Singapore, Canada, and the United States—Srividya Natarajan, V. Balakrishnan, Shana Hillman, Nalin Bisnath, Yashoda Thakore, and Muni. My gratitude goes out to Nada Ristisch for her warmth, discerning artistic eye, generosity, support, and constant faith in my work over the years.

Much of my own sensitivity toward the material in this book has been conditioned by my training as a performer of Bharatanāṭyam dance. I would like to acknowledge a number of dance masters and performers from the traditional community of *devadāsīs* and *naṭṭuvaṉārs*, who have shaped my understanding of Bharatanāṭyam from both deeply embodied and political points of view—my beloved and formidable guru, K. P. Kittappa Pillai of Thanjavur, Pandanallur M. Gopalakrishnan, K. Chandrasekaran, Viralimalai Muttukkannammal, P. R. Thilagam, Thanjavur Rajalakshmi, and Vaideeswarankoyil Kanakambujam.

This book would not have been possible without the input of my long-term collaborator who has been like a brother to me, Davesh Soneji of the University of Pennsylvania. Our long years of friendship have included in-depth conversations about the politics and social histories of Indian dance, extensive collaborative ethnography with hereditary dance communities in remote parts of South India, and much more. We have been involved in so much collaboration over the past several years—from research, dissemination, and publishing to performance—that it is hard to capture its scope in words. This book has benefited greatly from Davesh's critical eye, his intense scholarly rigor, and his careful and always insightful advice.

The love of my life, Rex, whose nurturing and unconditional love has sustained me emotionally for the past twenty years, has ensured that this book saw the light of day. Rex has been my champion and was always there to lift me up and cheer me on. His endless faith and confidence have been crucial to my getting through the long and often emotionally taxing work of writing.

Finally, I am indebted to my beloved parents, Vimala Krishnan and K. R. Krishnan, who have supported my artistic and scholarly interests ever since I was a teenager and took my first steps in dance. I am particularly indebted to my mother, who has given up so much to ensure that I could pursue my academic and artistic education in North America. I owe so much in my life, including the completion of this book, to the years of hardship my mother has endured only to invest in my well-being. I dedicate this work to her.

INTRODUCTION
On Convergent Histories

Bharatanāṭyam dance wouldn't be what it is today without the cinema. Do you really think it would be popular like this without the impact of our film dance? Just look at both (pāru) and observe them carefully (kavaṉi).

PADMINI RAMACHANDRAN

In 2005, the dancer-actress Padmini Ramachandran (1932–2006) encouraged me to "look and observe" how two of the most affectively and politically charged cultural forms of modern South India—Tamil cinema and Bharatanāṭyam dance—share complex and closely intertwined histories.[1] This book is about the entangled emergence of these two modern art forms from the 1930s to the 1950s, decades that were marked by distinctly new, intermedial modes of cultural production in cosmopolitan Madras. This project rethinks received histories of modern Bharatanāṭyam by arguing that cinema, in all its technological, moral, and visual complexities, heavily and irrevocably influences iterations of this so-called classical dance. Bringing archival research into conversation with choreographic analysis and ethnographic work with film performers and Bharatanāṭyam dancers, this book addresses key questions about the exchange of knowledge between cinematic and stage versions of Bharatanāṭyam in the first half of the twentieth century. It includes deliberations on subjects such as participation of women from the *devadāsī* (courtesan) community in the cinema, the period of the urban reinvention of dance from the standpoint of cinematic history, the impact of the forces of cultural nationalism and regionalism, and the making of new aesthetic vocabularies and techniques for Bharatanāṭyam in the cinema. The work concludes with notes on the persistence of cinema and Bharatanāṭyam as ever-entangled vernacular idioms in the global age of the late twentieth and early twenty-first centuries. Taken together, the materials presented in this book provide a detailed cultural history that draws lateral, paravisual linkages between the production and circulation of Tamil cinema and Bharatanāṭyam dance.

INTERMEDIAL AND INTEROCULAR CULTURES IN EARLY TWENTIETH-CENTURY SOUTH INDIA

Much of this project is concerned with intersections—historical, aesthetic, political, and social—between new cultural forms as they circulated in early twentieth-century South India. I argue that these new, intersectional epistemes are based on new ways of seeing and reading that cannot be understood without reference to new technologies of interfacing with the visual world in colonial South Asia. Photography and the cinema were the harbingers of this new visual world. But at the heart of this book is a historical inquiry into the social history of individuals and collectivities involved in the making of both Bharatanāṭyam and the early Tamil cinema. Indeed, as the visual anthropologist Christopher Pinney has recently argued, "[social h]istory is intimately related to the visual and the performative" (2014, 115). This social history, however, can emerge only from the "rhizomatic" and lateral linkages that I draw between printed texts and images, live performances, and cinematic representations. I take my cue from the work of Kajri Jain, a visual anthropologist of South Asia who invokes Gilles Deleuze and Félix Guattari in thinking about the "rhizomatic" nature of popular cinema in South Asia. She writes:

> I approach the commercial cinema as a node in what Gilles Deleuze and Félix Guattari (1977, 1987) call a rhizomatic network, whose ceaseless proliferations make various kinds of lateral linkages across heterogeneous categories. The strength of a rhizomatic approach is that it allows us to simultaneously hold in view different registers of efficacy. . . Most analyses of visual culture emphasize the effects and affects that flow from the meanings of objects or from their work of representation; . . . however, I want to foreground those that flow from their production and circulation, from the networks they inscribe (local, national, and transnational), and the forms of sociality and mobilty they enable. (Jain 2005, 72–73).

Closely linked to this concept of the "rhizomatic" and lateral linkages across visual registers in modern South Asia is the idea of "interocularity" or the "interocular field" as a key signpost of public culture. The term was first used by the cultural anthropologists Arjun Appadurai and Carol Breckenridge, who concede that "the socializing and regulating of the public gaze is to some degree affected by the experiences of the other sites. The interweaving of ocular experiences, which also subsumes the substantive transfer of meanings, scripts, and symbols from one site to another (in surprising ways), is a critical feature of public culture in contemporary India" (Appadurai and Breckenridge 1995, 12). In his discussion of the emergence of the chromolithograph in South Asia, Pinney brings Appadurai and Breckenridge's notion of interocularity to bear on the modern arts in South Asia, arguing that it is intermedial conversations across both visual and performative genres that produced cultures of viewing and consumption in modern South Asia: "Chromolithography was created and consumed within a wider visual culture in which there was a continual slippage between genres. The conversation between the idioms of chromolithography, theatre and photography in late nineteenth- and early twentieth-century India created mutually reinforcing expectations. These different visual fields crossed each other through processes of 'inter-ocularity'—a visual inter-referencing and citation that mirrors the more familiar process of 'inter-textuality'" (Pinney 2004, 34–35).

In this book, I demonstrate how the emegence of Bharatanāṭyam as a modern cultural artifact cannot be dissociated from a wider interocular and intermedial field that fuels the consumption practices and aesthetic taste habits of the Indian middle class in the twentieth cenutry. The wider interocular field in which Bharatanāṭyam resides includes the printed book and print culture more generally, the modern Tamil theatre (later known as *icai nāṭakam* [musical drama], which has its origins in the hybrid theatre form often called Parsi theatre, discussed below), as well as the early Tamil cinema. Figure I.1a illustrates how visual and performative themes circulate through these intermedial conversations. On the left is a famous painting by Raja Ravi Varma (1848–1906) titled *Vishwamitra and Menaka*" (1890). Ravi Varma, a self-taught artist from Kerala, has been described as embodying the "paradoxical ideology of the Indian renaissance, at once traditionalist and modern" (Kapur 2000, 145). Ravi Varma art was among the most widely circulated in India in the late nineteenth and early twentieth centuries, and his hybrid, realist aesthetic was redistributed in a range of cultural forms and practices—including

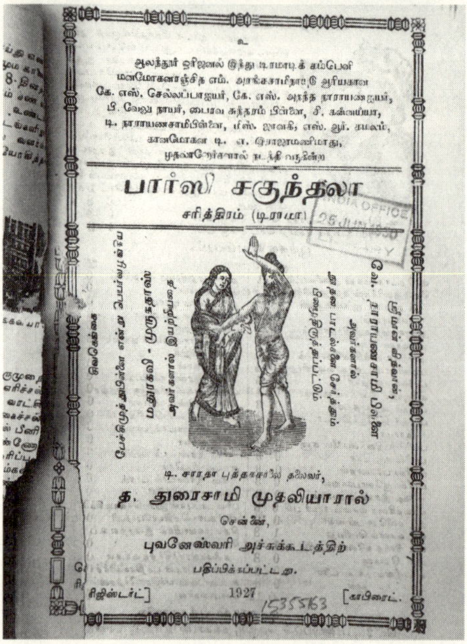

Figure I.1 a, b, c. The frontispiece from the Tamil Parsi theatre play, Pārsi Cakuntalā *(center, 1927, © British Library Board, pTam.D.2657) and an advertisement for the Tamil film* Viswamitra *(right, 1936, private collection of S. V. Jayababu), based on the famous painting* Vishwamitra and Menaka *by Raja Ravi Varma (left).*

printed chromolithographs, books, and performances.[2] *Vishwamitra and Menaka* depicts a mythic narrative in which the sage Viśvāmitra rejects the daughter (named Śakuntalā) born from his union with the celestial courtesan Menakā. The story of Śakuntalā was extremely popular in both Indian and European Orientalist representations of literature and drama for centuries (Thapar 2011). In figure I.1b, at the center, the image is reproduced on the frontispiece of the script for a Tamil play *Pārsi Cakuntalā Carittiram Ṭirāmā* (The life of Śakuntalā, in the Parsi drama style) from 1927, and just under a decade later, the same image is reproduced by the bodies of the actors M. K. Gopala Ayyangar and Rajasundari Bai in one of the earliest Tamil sound films, *Viswamitra* (1936; figure I.1c).

On the one hand, these three images clearly position the cinema as a site of culmination and of cultural bricolage, in which accretions showing the influence of text and print culture and the new theatre can clearly be seen. On the other hand, these images also demonstrate that popular culture in South India in the early twentieth century was fundamentally intermedial, characterized by a flow of cultural knowledge between medial forms. The most concrete illustration of this intermedial cultural flow is that in the cinema houses of Madras in the 1930s and 1940s, cinema screenings were supplemented by live performances in a range of musical and dance styles, including courtesan dance, Western dance, and eventually the reinvented Bharatanāṭyam (Hughes forthcoming; this point is discussed further in chapter 2). In this work, I apply intermedial modalities to thinking about how Bharatanāṭyam was reconceived, disseminated, and consumed as a new cultural practice. Indeed, if we are to understand Bharatanāṭyam's complexities as a reinvented form, we cannot forget that the cinema was a very large component of the interocular and intermedial matrix in which it was born.

FILM AS FOIL: BHARATANĀṬYAM AND THE LIMITS OF THE CLASSICISM

In bringing Bharatanāṭyam into dialogue with cinematic history, I hope to convincingly demonstrate that taken together, these forms signfy a sphere of culture that might better be seen as popular rather than classical. In their introduction to a volume titled *Fingerprinting Popular Culture: The Mythic and Iconic in Indian Cinema*, the cultural historians Vinay Lal and Ashis Nandy see Indian cinema as the site for confrontations and negotiations between the various signposts of Indian modernity: "Popular culture, especially popular cinema, now began to look like a crucial battle ground where the battles between the old and the new, the traditional and modern, the global and the local were being fought through the renegotiation of myth and fantasy life" (Lal and Nandy 2007, xxiv).

I would argue that Bharatanāṭyam—in its post-1930s avatar as a middle-class, semiprofessional practice—is imbricated in the same sets of questions and contestations. As we will see below, the "renegotation of myth and fantasy life" was a central component of Bharatanāṭyam's emergence as an urban, devotional, and Sanskritized cultural practice. The language of classicism was first applied to Bharatanāṭyam only during the process of its reinvention at the hands of the English-educated Brahmin elites in Madras in the 1930s. In their brilliant introduction to a volume titled *Performing Pasts: Reinventing the Arts in Modern South India*, the cultural historians Indira Peterson and Davesh Soneji remark on the social complexities of the creation of "the classical" in South India in this period: "From the reformist/revivialist perspective, the dance and music of hereditary and other traditional communities were secret, idiosyncratic, heterogenous, unscientific, non-canonical, hybrid, vernacular, and non-modern. They were transmitted and performed through oral, caste-based, and practice-centred processes. The new classical arts, on the other hand, would be based on 'ancient' yet suitably reformed, modernized textual and theoretical canons, and the performers would be modern professionals, untained by caste associations and non-scientific methods" (Peterson and Soneji 2008, 7).

The classical performing arts as they are constructed by Indian elites and the bureaucratic machinery of the nation-state exist in opposition to the popular arts, a category that by the 1940s almost exclusively referred to the cinema. One of the major contributions of this book is to think about the complex spaces of social and aesthetic intersectionality that Bharatanāṭyam occupies. Its contrived classicism, based largely on the grafting of Orientalist discoveries of Sanskritic knowledge systems onto a vernacular dance culture, takes root in opposition to the popular cinema, yet cinematic iterations of Bharatanāṭyam often construct the dance as timelessly classical or distinct from other forms of dance and somatic expression. This, I argue, produced deeply affective and long-standing aesthetic parameters that remain in both today's Tamil cinema and today's performances of Bharatanāṭyam. Essentially this book tells the story of Bharatanāṭyam's transformation in the first half of the twentieth century by thinking about the cinema and the urban stage as laboratories of culture. The unique use of the classical to refer to Bharatanāṭyam, this book argues, simply cannot be understood without reference to the dance's early filmic instantiations—hence the title of this book, *Celluloid Classicism.*

Moreover, the story of Bharatanāṭyam's emergence as nationalist art form in the 1930s cannot be separated from the wider political debate on caste and social mobility that framed nationalist modernity in South India. Tamil cinema too, as the film historian Theodore Baskaran (1981), M. S. S. Pandian (1996 and 2007), and others have demonstrated, emerged from a frame of non-Brahmin political assertion in this period. In this book, I emphasize the fact that representations of dance in the cinema enable slippages, in terms of both mobility and oppression, under caste hierarchy. Dance in the cinema produces a seemingly naturalized and ancient aesthetic regime for modern Bharatanāṭyam, and it also involves a range of actors who represent themselves (and are represented) along lines of difference (based on caste, class, and gender) yet are homogenized through discourses of nationalism and Tamil regionalism.[3] Chapter 3 explores this complex relationships among early film dance, caste, regional Tamil politics, and Indian nationalism in greater depth.

MODERN TAMIL DRAMA AS INTERMEDIARY BETWEEN BHARATANĀṬYAM AND THE TAMIL CINEMA

A major gap in the social history of Bharatanāṭyam has been the lack of attention paid to the central role of the emergence of the modern Tamil drama tradition, variously known as *icai nāṭakam* ("musical drama"), *tamiḻ nāṭakam* (Tamil drama), boys' company drama, and special *nāṭakam* (Araṅkacāmi 1989; Kiruṣṇamūrtti 1979; Mangai and Arasu 2009; Perumal 1977, 1981, and 1988; Seizer 2005; Sugimoto 2008; Veṅkaṭarāmaṉ 2001). The modern Tamil drama represented an intermediary and socially liminal space that enabled the flow of professional and semiprofessional actors into the emerging Tamil cinema and also enabled women from *devadāsī* backgrounds to enter the world of the professional theatre and, by extension, the early Tamil cinema. Tamil drama is born of the interface between old forms of Tamil theatre (known variously as *kūttu, terukkūttu,* or *kaṭṭaikkūttu*; see de Bruin 1999) that essentially consisted of songs interpreted through gesture, strung together with spoken dialogue, and a new hybrid form of colonial theatre, usually called the Parsi theatre (Gupt 2005; Hansen 1999, 2001, 2003, 2009, 2011, and 2018). This was a form of popular drama that grew out of colonial theatrical techniques and modern adaptations of Shakespearean performance by Britons in South Asia in the mid-nineteenth century. When these practices were taken up by natives, initially by the Gujarati-speaking Parsi community in the Bombay Presidency, and indigenized (through the use of Indian narratives and scripts in Indian languages), they came to be known as the Parsi theatre. Parsi theatre companies such as the Victoria Parsi Theatrical Company (established in 1868 by K. N. Kabra) toured large parts of India and Southeast Asia, giving major performances in Madras in the 1880s.[4] These performances inspired Tamil amateur and semiprofessional dramaturges and literary aficionados to create new forms of Tamil theatre that drew both content and technique from the Parsi theatre but also retained aspects of performance (such as the gestural interpretation of text [*abhinaya*] and *rāga*-based music) from older traditions like the *kūttu* theatre and even courtesan dance. Hundreds of new Tamil dramas were composed between the 1870s and the 1930s, spanning a range of historical, pseudohistorical, mythological, and (later) social themes. As this tradition became increasingly popular, the writers or dramaturges Caṅkaratās Cuvāmikaḷ (1867–1932) and Pammal Campanta Mutaliyār (1873–1964) came to be heralded as the pillars of the form. They composed new and highly innovative scripts for performance, even when they drew upon older themes, including mythological ones (for example, figure I.2 shows the cover of the first print edition of Cuvāmikaḷ's play based on the mythological narrative of the child devotee Prahlāda). The new Tamil theatre was a space of intercaste interaction and even included women performers from the *devadāsī* community.[5] Indeed, as early as 1876, *devadāsī* dancers were involved in modern Tamil theatrical productions in Madras.[6]

Film historians (Baskaran 1981, 1996, and 2009; Guy 1997; and others) have long noted the formative influence of the modern Tamil drama on early cinema. However, this matrix of drama and early cinema has never been considered with reference to the emergence of modern Bharatanāṭyam or classical (Karṇāṭak) music. Many of the actors, techniques, and narratives of modern Tamil theatre were brought into the cinema, and some of these crossed over into representations of Bharatanāṭyam on

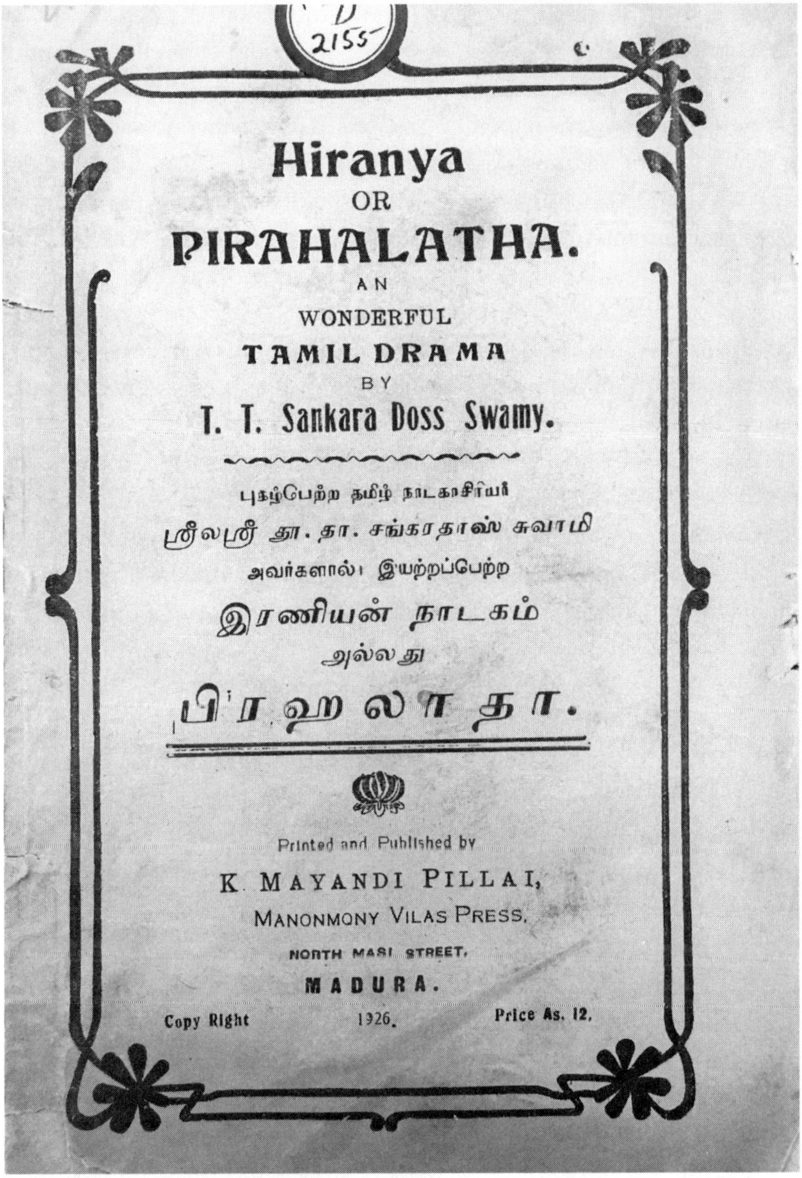

Figure I.2. The cover of the play Iraṇiyaṉ Nāṭakam allatu Pirahalātā *by Caṅkaratās Cuvāmikaḷ, published in Madurai in 1926 (© British Library Board, pTam.D.2155).*

both stage and screen. The biggest female stars of the early Tamil cinema, for example, came from *devadāsī* backgrounds but entered the cinema only after they had become established performers in the networks of the emerging Tamil drama, a point discussed in greater detail in chapter 1.

Moreover, music remained at the heart of the modern Tamil drama, which eventually was known as *icai nāṭakam*, just as it did in Tamil cinema. From the time of the earliest South Indian talkie, *Kalidas* (The poet Kālīdāsa; 1931), music and dance have occupied a central place in the aesthetic vocabulary of cinema in this region. *Kalidas* included songs from the emerging classical canon of Karṇāṭak music (including songs attributed to the composer Tyāgarāja [1767–1847]) as well as popular Tamil nationalist songs.[7] Thus, the discussion of the intermedial nature of the intertwined histories of cinema and dance goes beyond the histories of just these two forms to include the world of Tamil theatre, music history, and print culture. In this book, I adopt a multisited and polyvocal historical approach, in which conversations on dance history are linked to discussions of larger sets of cultural practices and broader cultural histories.

WRITING "FILM DANCE": SOUTH ASIA AND BEYOND

Recent studies of dance and visual media in Western cultural contexts have included exceptional theoretically oriented works such as Douglas Rosenberg's *Screendance: Inscribing the Ephemeral Image* (2012), which focuses on the tensions between dance as an ephemeral form and film as a fixed idiom and draws on both historical and contemporary works that exemplify aspects of this tension. Rosenberg's work explores both the possibilities and the limits that emerge from celluloid and digital iterations of the dancing body in Euro-American contexts. Studies of dance in the cinema itself are relatively few and far between. One of the major works in this vein is Sherril Dodd's *Dance on Screen: Genres and Media from Hollywood to Experimental Art* (2001), which focuses on representations of dance in a range of cinematic genres—from mainstream popular film to the avant-garde cinema of the 1990s. More recently, Erin Brannigan's *DanceFilm: Choreography and the Moving Image* (2011) is a fascinating study of what she calls "dancefilm," or representations of the choreographic in film. Her book may be one of the most comprehensive studies of dance in popular cinema from the beginning of the medium into the twenty-first century. Drawing insights from both cinema studies and dance studies, Brannigan argues that dancefilm expresses choreographic sensibilities that are unique to this idiom. Dance on film produces its own affective and somatic vocabularies, constituting what she calls a "polyaesthetic field" (Brannigan 2011, 194).

Closer to my field of study, however, are works that deal specifically with representations of dance in South Asian cinema. Unfortunately, these also have been very few in number.[8] A few significant studies of dance and music in Hindi (Bollywood) cinema have appeared recently, such as the volume edited by Sangita Gopal and Sujata Moorti titled *Global Bollywood: Travels of Hindi Song and Dance* (2008), but these categorically exclude discussions of South Indian cinema. An exceptional work on dance in the Hindi cinema is Usha Iyer's unpublished dissertation titled "Film Dance, Female Stardom, and the Production of Gender in Popular Hindi Cinema" (2014), which weaves together many of the issues of the issues that I discuss here—albeit from the standpoint of Hindi popular cinema. In my view, Iyer's work represents some of the finest scholarship on dance and the popular cinema in South Asia and reveals the deep intellectual potential that social history of the cinema can offer to both South Asian studies and dance studies. Works on dance and cinema in northern India include an essay by Amita Nijhawan (2009) that focused on themes of sexuality, desire, and transgression in Bollywood dance sequences, while the work of Ann David (2007 and 2010) and Sangita Shresthova (2011) has explored the transnational migration of forms of popular Hindi cinema dance in the United Kingdom, Nepal, and the United States. Most recently, Pallabi Chakravorty's book *This Is How We Dance Now: Performance in the Age of Bollywood and Reality Shows* (2017) examines cultures of dance—especially dance derived from a Bollywood dance aesthetic—in the postliberalization age, as they travel through new pedagogical and performative iterations such as television reality shows, film-dance institutions, and social media.

Finally, two recent doctoral dissertations deal with dance and the South Indian cinema, but these focus on Telugu cinema and the dance form known as Kūcipūḍi. The first is Rumya Sree Putcha's dissertation titled "Revisiting the Classical: A Critical History of Kuchipudi Dance" (2011), and the second is Katyayani Sree Thota's dissertation titled "Stage to Screen, and Back: A Study of the Dialogue between Kuchipudi and Telugu Cinema" (2016).[9] Both of these projects have much in common with mine. Putcha's work examines how instantiations of dance in the cinema contributed to the formation of a regional or nationalized art form of Kūcipūḍi, eclipsing other popular performance traditions that could have vied with it for the status of the "classical dance" of Andhra Pradesh. Putcha also demonstrates how Kūcipūḍi dance was undergoing a massive aesthetic overhaul in Madras just as cinematic and staged performances of it were being innovatively showcased for the first time. Thota's excellent work also dwells on how cinematic iterations of Kūcipūḍi contribute to its sedimentation as the "classical dance" of Andhra Pradesh in the national imaginary, and she provides detailed life narratives and choreographic analysis of the makers of this kind of dance. Finally, I should also mention a blog called *Cinema Nritya* that is run by the dance enthusiast Cassidy Behling (2013a, 2013b, and 2015) and focuses on Indian traditions in the cinema. Needless to say, the blog has a number of entries that address some of subjects covered in this book, but these entries lack the scholarly apparatuses and larger critical historical and theoretical perspectives that are at the heart of this project.

English-language scholarship on Tamil cinema at first glance appears to be vast, and a significant number of works address the impact of Tamil cinema on contemporary politics in South India. These include the works of Theodore Baskaran (1981, 1996, and 2009), M. S. S. Pandian (1996 and 2007), and a number of others.[10] Two other significant earlier works were Stephen Hughes's unpublished dissertation on the history of early South Indian cinema (1996) and Sara Dickey's unpublished dissertation (1993) that focused on the reception of Tamil cinema by lower-middle-class audiences in Tamilnadu. It may be Hughes (2002, 2007, 2010, 2014, and forthcoming) who has given us some of the richest and most detailed cultural histories of the early Tamil cinema to date. In 2008, Routledge published the first scholarly anthology on Tamil cinema, edited by Selvaraj Velayutham and titled *Tamil Cinema: The Cultural Politics of India's Other Film Industry*. This book provides an overview of the history and distinctive characteristics of Tamil cinema, and the individual essays examine themes such as gender, religion, class, caste, fandom, cinematic genre, the politics of identity, and diaspora. Throughout, the book cogently links cinematic history to broader social, political, and cultural history in Tamil-speaking India. Since then, a number of excellent studies on the history and anthropology of Tamil cinema have emerged, including the work of Preminda Jacob (2008) on Tamil film advertisements, the outstanding work of Swarnavel Eswaran Pillai (2015) on Madras film production studios, and the anthropological studies by Anand Pandian (2015) and Constantine Nakassis (2016) on contemporary Tamil film-making and consumption, to name a few. Excellent recent works by Amanda Weidman (2012a and 2012b) have explored questions of voice, gender, and embodiment in Tamil cinema music, while Kiranmayi Indraganti's *Her Majestic Voice* (2016) explores the history of female "playback" singing in the Telugu cinema, with some implications for the study of similar issues in Tamil cinema.

Much of my thinking about Bharatanāṭyam as a historical form draws on the work of Avanthi Meduri (1996), Matthew Harp Allen (1997), Janet O'Shea (2007), Indira Peterson and Davesh Soneji (2008), and Soneji (2010a and 2012). In their pathbreaking writings on Bharatanāṭyam, these authors have radically altered earlier, nationalist-inflected received histories. My earlier published work (Krishnan 2008 and 2009) has been produced in conversation with this collective of revisionist scholars of Bharatanāṭyam, who have given us a critically engaged and nuanced scholarly discourse that embeds Bharatanāṭyam's history in the context of larger issues related to nation, body, sexuality, and politics in South India.

CINEMA EPHEMERA: PRINT MATERIAL AS TEXTUAL ARCHIVE

Much of the original data for this project come from what I call cinema ephemera—that is, print materials from the 1930s to the 1950s in two genres: cinema songbooks and magazines, almost all exclusively written in the Tamil language. Cinema songbooks (see, for example, figure I.3) are texts related to a large cottage industry of popular publishing in the form of low-priced chapbooks that sought to bring Tamil literature to the masses. In his monumental work on Tamil print culture titled *The Province of the Book*, the historian A. R. Venkatachalapathy has demonstrated how cinema songbooks appeared at the end of several decades of popular chapbook printing through a certain class of publications known in Tamil as *gujili* (*kucili*).[11] These popular chapbooks, sold for the equivalent of a few cents (for example, one anna, six paisa, or nine paisa), were hawked at crossroads and town markets. In chapter 2, I examine one of these chapbooks from 1937, a kind of moral tract on the dangers of the cinema, authored by K. Kurucāmitās, a Tamil poet from the town of Kumbhakonam. Venkatachalapathy notes that while popular publishing and popular bazaar literature did not disappear in Tamil India after

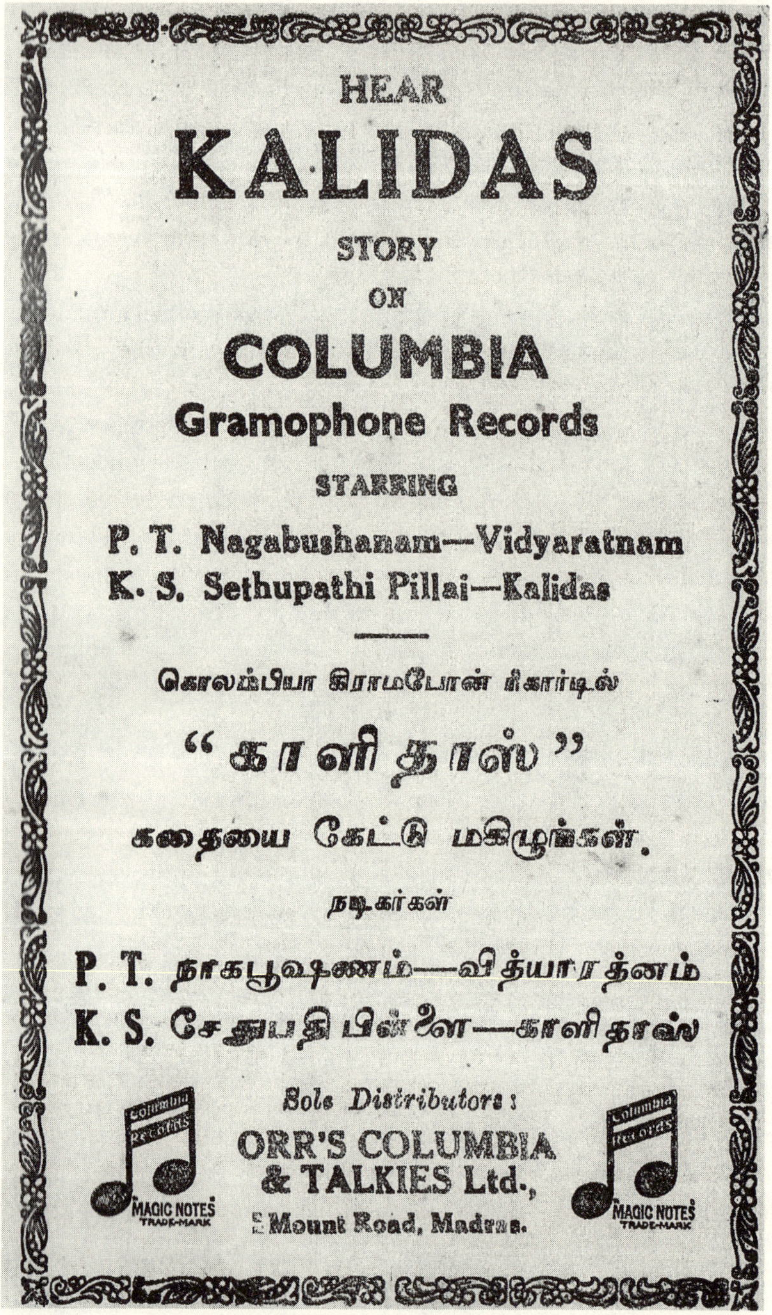

Figure I.3. A page from the songbook of the first South Indian talkie, Kalidas *(Kālīdāsa [a poet]; 1931), advertising the gramophone record by Columbia that accompanied the film. Private collection of S. V. Jayabau.*

the 1930s, much of its energies were redirected into "cinema songbooks, wherein the lyrics of popular cinema are reduced to print" (Venkatachalapathy 2012, 167). These songbooks are crucial to my work. They give us access to texts for music and dance, often in the absence of aural or visual traces. This is particularly important given the emphasis on text and poetry in traditional forms of dance and dance music in South India. The text in many ways literally orients the presentation of the dance. Indeed, we could think about courtesan dance in South India as a tradition of performed commentary on poems composed for this purpose. We will see how important texts are in both staged and cinematic versions of Bharatanāṭyam dance throughout this book, and in chapter five in particular I will explore how a vast amount of the genre's repertoire is framed textually.

Typically, songbooks have been understood as modes through which audiences could access the lyrics of songs, to recall them after viewing the film. In that sense, the songbook worked in tandem with the gramophone record, as we see in figure I.3, where the songbook for the earliest South Indian talkie, *Kalidas* (1931), advertises the gramophone record for the film, encouraging readers to hear it. This movement across reading, hearing, and seeing the film or its ephemera takes us back to the centrality of intermedial modes of experience to cultural production and consumption in this period. Indeed, in this example, intermedial sensory engagement and mobility were encouraged by the producers of culture: the text had to be read, the songs heard, and the film seen.

Songbooks evolved in structure and content from the 1930s to the 1950s. The earliest songbooks featured a cover page, usually showing a still from the film, and then presented the texts of the songs featured in the film, with headings that indicated which character performed the song and usually the name of the *rāga* (tonal scale) of the song. The back cover usually featured advertisements of other publications by the press that printed the songbook. However, songbooks of the early 1940s also contained a list of the cast and crew, usually called *naṭikarkaḷ* (actors), often with a separate list for female performers called *naṭikaikaḷ* (actresses). Increasingly, songbooks also included a roughly page-long synopsis of the plot of the film, called *kataic curukkam* (gist of the story). By the mid-1940s, some songbooks were bilingual, containing the synopsis in both Tamil and English, with important sections of the credits—such as the names of the director and the production studio—also

Figure I.4. Cover of the songbook for the film Ekampavāṇaṉ *(1947), starring P. A. Ranganayaki, with dances by Kamala. Private collection of S. V. Jayababu.*

appearing in English. This is the space where, by the 1940s, credits for dance were often found. The back covers of the songbooks increasingly featured advertisements for forthcoming films, often those produced by the same studio. By the 1950s, the songbook had reached its maturity, containing numerous photographs from the film and detailed production credits (figure I.4).

Another major source consists of Tamil film magazines. These began to circulate in the 1930s, and by the late 1940s they had become the major vehicle for information about Tamil film production and consumption practices. In a fascinating essay titled "Emotion, Identity and the Female Subject: Tamil Women's Magazines in Colonial India, 1890–1940" (2003), the historian Mytheli Sreenivas establishes that Tamil popular magazines were central to the formation of new modes of subjectivity for an emerging middle class. Indeed, these magazines not only produced new reading publics, but when it came to discourse on the arts and cinema, they also helped create new modes of consuming and understanding visual and performative cultures. The deep and long-standing relationship between the publics of magazine reading and cinema can most clearly be seen in the fact that one of the most popular Tamil magazines, *Āṉanta Vikaṭaṉ*, was initially published in 1928 and successfully promoted by Subramaniam Sreenivasan (1904–69; more popularly known as S. S. Vasan), a journalist who went on to become one of South India's most famous film producers and directors and the owner of Madras's largest production studios, Gemini.[12] Tamil film magazines performed a kind of commentarial role. They often combined notes on film production, biographical narratives about actors, and information about the musical dimensions of films. Indeed, the name of one of the most popular such magazines—*Kuṇṭūci* (needle), established in the late 1930s—refers to the work of such texts, that sewed together various strands of cultural production in this period.[13] By far the most successful of such magazines was *Pēcum Paṭam* (Talking pictures), which was founded by the film journalist T. V. Ramnoth in the 1930s and was so popular that it was eventually published out in Telugu and English versions, titled *Cinema Rangam* and *PicturePost* respectively.[14]

Film magazines from this period until the 1950s, like songbooks, serve as windows to films that have become otherwise invisible. Prints for many of the Tamil films I examine in this book are not available, so print material provides the only historical traces of them. A case in point is the film *Nāṭṭiyarāṇi* (Queen of dance, 1949; figure I.5), which is a relatively late film but nonetheless no longer exists. The songbook and advertisements for the film survive, and the photographs in the advertisements give us the only visual clues about the film. It was a quasi-historical film in which a milkmaid turned dancer named Śāntalā marries a king of the medieval Hoysala dynasty, and becomes queen of the city of Belur.[15] The print materials tell us that both the actresses B. S. Saroja (b. 1922) and Vasundhara Devi (1917–88, mother of the star dancer-actress Vyjayanthimala (b. 1933), who is discussed below) starred in the film, and that it included other dances by the sisters Lalitha and Padmini. The vernacular magazine thus offers a kind of antidote—albeit a limited one—to the fleeting nature of the material dimensions of the early Tamil cinema.

Figure I.5. Poster for Naṭṭiyarāṇṇi (Queen of dance, 1949), in Kuṇṭūci *(August 1949, 7). Roja Muthiah Research Library.*

Figure I.6. The cover of Āṭal Pāṭal *(*Āṇṭu Malar *1936). Roja Muthiah Research Library.*

Magazines such as these, I would argue, are part of a print culture that constitutes a new kind of public space in which the arts take on a new meaning, and are consciously brought into inter-medial conversations. Magazines such as *Āṭal-Pāṭal* (Dance and song), for example, carry news stories about the latest films but also about figures like Rukmini Arundale (1904–86) and E. Krishna Iyer (1897–1968), both key figures in the nationalist reinvention of the arts in modern South India; articles about local stage performances of Bharatanāṭyam, such as debut performances (*araṅkēṟṟams*) of young female dance students); features about female morality; and notes on the technique of Bharatanāṭyam dance (figure I.6).[16] By the 1940s, other magazines like *Kuṇṭūci* were running large regular features with titles like "Naṭaṉam Āṭiṉar" (They danced)—referring to the famous song *naṭaṉam āṭiṉār* (He danced) (figure I.7) that will be discussed in detail in chapter 5—and featuring news about and profiles from the world of live performances of Bharatanāṭyam in Madras. The magazines thus produce for their audiences the overlap-

நடனம் ஆடினர்

நவம்பர் 9-ம் தேதியன்று ரஸிக ரஞ்சனி சபையில் ஸ்ரீமதி உஷா தேவியின் நடனக் கச்சேரி நடைபெற்றது. "வர்ணம்", "தில்லானா" இவைகளில் ஜதித் தொகுப்புகள் அழகாக அமைக்கப்பட்டிருந்தன. ஆனால், சொற்கட்டுகளை சொல்லும்போது இசையோடு ஒட்டாமல், 'கரடு முரடா'க இருப்பதுபோல் தோன்றிற்று. சிக்கல் மிகுந்த அந்த வேகமான அடவுகளை ஆடுகையில் பல இடங்களில் கைகளின் அசைவுகள் பூரணமாக இல்லாமல் இருந்தன.

பதங்களில் விந்யாசம் கற்பனை நிரம்பியிருந்தது, "சிந்தையறிந்து", "தாயே யசோதா" முதலிய பதங்களில் அபிநயம் குறிப்பிடத்தக்க வகையில் இருந்தன. "தந்தை தாய்", "மதுரா நகரிலோ", மற்றும் சில பதங்களில் ஆங்கிகம் தொடர்பு இல்லாமல் இருந்ததால் அபிநயம் என்னவோபோல் 'சப்'பென்று இருந்தது. இசையோடு கூடிய ஒத்திகைக் குறைவால் இப் பிழைகள் ஏற்பட்டிருக்கலாம். அன்றைய நடனத்தில் சுத்தமான தாளக் கட்டும், துடிப்பான வெட்டுகளும் குறிப்பிடத் தக்க அம்சங்களாகும்.

சில பதங்களை பாடிய வி. சுப்புலக்ஷ்மியின் பாட்டை விட நட்டுவனார்கள் மட்டுமே பாடிய பாட்டுகள் இனிமையாக இருந்தன. பந்தநல்லூர் மீனாக்ஷிசுந்தரம் பிள்ளையின் சிஷ்யையான உஷாதேவியின் நடனத்திற்கு, அன்று பி. எஸ். ஸ்வாமிநாதனும் தஞ்சை எம். அருணாசலமும் நட்டுவாங்கம் செய்தனர்.

ஸ்ரீ கச்சாலீஸ்வரர் கான சபையில் சென்ற மாதம் 22-ம் தேதியன்று குமாரி சுசீலாவின் நடனக் கச்சேரி சென்னை கோகலே ஹாலில் நடைபெற்றது. அன்று, சாஸ்திரீயமான நடன நிகழ்ச்சிகளை விட குறத்தி, மார்வாரி, ஜிப்ஸி போன்ற கிராமிய நடனங்களே பிரமாதமாக அமைந்திருந்தன. பதங்களில் அநேக இடங்களில் பாவப் பொருத்தம் இல்லாமலிருந்தது. பத விந்யாசம் சரியாக அமையாததால் இந்தப் பிழைகள் நேர்ந்திருக்கின்றன. பதங்களில் அநுபாவங்களான இயக்கங்கள் சரியாக இருந்தும். வார்த்தைகளின் பொருளையுணர்ந்த சாத்விக பாவங்கள் அமையாததால் ரஸானந்தம் மட்டுப்பட்டிருந்தது. மணிபுரி நடனங்களிலுள்ளதைப் போல, ஆங்கிக விதிகளை அவ்வளவாக கவனிக்காமல், அநுபாவம் என்பதை மாத்திரம் மனதில் கொண்டு பரந்து ஆடியதால், சாஸ்திரீய நடனங்களில் அழகு குறைந்திருந்தது. ஓரியன்டல் நடனங்களையே முழுக் கச்சேரியாக இவர் ஆடினால் ரஸிகர்கள் பெரிதும் விரும்பிப் பாராட்டுவர்.

"எவ்வேட நேனு" என்ற க்ஷேத்ரக்ஞரின் பதம் அன்றையக் கச்சேரியில் விசேஷமான அம்சமாகும். நட்டுவனார் கோபாலகிருஷ்ணன் அன்றைய தினம் பின்னணி கீதங்கள் பாடினார்.

சிறுமி சாருபாலா

இந்தியன் பைன் ஆர்ட்ஸ் ஸொஸைட்டியின் ஆதரவில் கோகலே மண்டபத்தில் அடுத்த நாளன்று குமாரி சாருபாலாவின் நடனக் கச்சேரி நடைபெற்றது. கம்ப ராமாயணத்தில் பாலகாண்டத்திலிருந்து எடுக்கப்பட்ட இரண்டு பாடல்களை 'வர்ண'மாக அமைத்து ஆடியது அன்றையக் கச்சேரியில் விறுவிறுப்பும் அழகும் நிறைந்த அம்சமாக விளங்கியது. கண்ணனை உண்மைச் சேவகனாகவும், உயிர்த் தோழனாகவும், மதி மந்திரியாகவும், பல கோணங்களில் வைத்து அன்பு சொரி

75

Figure I.7. Kuṇṭūci *eventually runs a column called "Naṭaṉam Āṭiṉar" (They danced), which features news and profiles from the world of stage performances of Bharatanāṭyam in Madras. Roja Muthiah Research Library.*

ping worlds of dance and cinema and facilitate movement between these spheres of cultural production and consumption. It is also significant that unlike many newspapers, the magazines circulated at the local, sub-national level. In these vernacular writings, we can trace histories that would otherwise remain hidden in the nationalizing discourse about the arts that began to emerge in India in the 1930s. Individual life histories and narratives in particular appear almost exclusively in these vernacular magazines.[17]

This book consists of five major chapters, followed by a coda that brings some of the work's historical discussions to bear on the enduring presence of Bharatanāṭyam's "celluloid classicism" into the present. Chapter 1 is about how, when, and why courtesan performers (*devadāsīs*) enter the South Indian cinema—and how they were able to sustain viable careers for a short while, until they were eclipsed by women of higher caste and class backgrounds. This chapter also highlights the deep imbrication of South Indian cinema with Tamil popular drama (known as *icai nāṭakam*) and accounts for the presence of *devadāsī* women in this matrix. Even though the first South Indian talkie featured a non-*devadāsī* woman as its heroine, women from *devadāsī* communities populated the bulk of films in Tamil and Telugu produced between 1937 and 1950. The chapter provides, among other things, a sketch of the life of S. D. Subbulakshmi (b. 1917; not to be confused with the singer M. S. Subbulakshmi), a *devadāsī* actress from the town of Srivaikuntam who became the "second wife" of early Tamil cinema's most celebrated director, K. Subrahmanyam (1904–71) and, with him, was responsible for setting up, around 1945, one of Madras's earliest dance schools, Natana Kala Seva. This morphed into Nrithyodaya, currently headed by Subrahmanyam's daughter, the dancer Padma Subrahmanyam (b. 1943). The chapter concludes with a detailed ethnographic portrait of T. D. Kuchalakumari (b. 1937), a former actress whose ancestors performed dance at the Tanjore court during the reign of the Queen Kamakshi Amba Bai Saheb (d. 1892) and at the public festivals of the Bṛhadīśvara temple. Kuchalakumari's aunts, cousins, and nieces continue to be involved in the cinema, and in an unapologetic manner she traces her family's journey from Tanjore's *devadāsī* community to the world of today's cinema.

The second chapter focuses on rereading the so-called revival or reinvention of Bharatanāṭyam in the 1930s through the lens of cinematic history. It charts the participation of the major actors in that reinvention—figures like Rukmini Arundale and E. Krishna Iyer—in the world of Tamil cinema, arguing that the emergence of Tamil cinema and the reinvention of Bharatanāṭyam were projects that shared semantic, performative, and poltical affinities. The chapter also includes an analysis of the extant visual and written traces of the first film in India about dance, *Jalaja* (1938), in which the *devadāsī* artist Kumbhakonam Bhanumathi played the lead character. The chapter ends with reflections on how dance in the cinema allows us to map shifting notions of the morality of Bharatanāṭyam and how the cross-pollination of screen and stage versions of Bharatanāṭyam radically shifts standard narratives about dance in this period.

While chapter 2 focuses on the ultra-elite activities related to dance and cinema of figures affiliated with organizations such as the Madras Music Academy and the Theosophical Society, chapter 3 moves into the realm of new instantiations of popular culture that brought some of the elite's activities to a broad range of audiences beginning in the 1930s. Indeed, the major argument of this chapter is that it is the work of cinema—particularly the nationalist cinema that featured directors such as Subrahmanyam and later actresses such as Kamala Lakshman and Padmini Ramachandran—that is responsible for the popularity of reinvented Bharatanāṭyam. This popularity also brought with it new forms of public somatic morality, resignifications of the body that were in dialogue with antinautch politics and the anticinema movement (which included figures like Mohandas K. Gandhi [1869–1948]). This chapter also examines the incorporation of figures like Gandhi and the Tamil poet Subrahmaniya Bharati into the vocabulary of Bharatanāṭyam because of cinema, and the creation of new ways of seeing dance as embodied national heritage on screen. The end of the chapter focuses on the movement of dance into the living rooms of Madras's elite through the cinema, in a radical expansion of the dance's overall cultural presence. By casting dance as compatible with conjugal life and domesticity, this chapter argues, the cinema of the 1940s and 1950s articulates a new moral vision for dance in South India. In some senses, these popular and nationalist-inflected articulations of form, allegory, and technique eclipsed the elite projects of reinvention that were staged in 1930s Madras. The chapter thus maps the emergence of Bharatanāṭyam's somewhat awkward self-representation as classical yet popular dance.

Chapter 4 begins by shifting the focus to men in the *devadāsī* community who commonly took on the professional or semiprofessional role of dance master (*naṭṭuvaṉār*). One of the major arguments of the chapter is about the financial opportunity that both cinema and reinvented Bharatanāṭyam afforded men from this community at a time when professional opportunities for women were fast disappearing. As early as the late 1930s, dance sequences in South India required dance masters, and some men from the community benefited tremendously. Their work in the cinema also enabled these men to participate in the world of modern urban performances of Bharatanāṭyam on Madras stages. A large portion of the chapter is devoted to the life and labor of Vazhuvoor Ramaiah Pillai (1910–91), an iconic choreographer for the early cinema and Madras's new stage performances of Bharatanāṭyam from the 1930s to the 1960s. Ramaiah Pillai's aesthetic sensibilities not only set the standard for representations of Bharatanāṭyam-style dances on screen, but they also filtered back into stage performances in Madras. Indeed, Pillai's prime disciple, Kamala Lakshman, seamlessly moved between stage and screen, and the interocular dynamism of Pillai's choreographies for Lakshman was appreciated and deeply internalized by audiences for decades. In addition to Ramaiah Pillai, the chapter also discusses five other men from the *devadāsī* and *naṭṭuvaṉār* community who became renowned choreographers in the cinema and attracted a range of students, many from abroad, who wanted to learn Bharatanāṭyam from them. The chapter concludes with an ethnographic portrait of one of the earliest nonhereditary dance masters of the South Indian cinema, Udupi Laxminarayan (1926–2015), whose work began to appear in the 1940s and whose legacy as a choreographer and teacher is represented on the global stage by his male student, the award-winning film dancer and choreographer Prabhu Deva (b. 1973).

Chapter 5 presents details about how dance—in terms of its aesthetics, technique, and repertoire—is irrevocably transformed through its encounter with cinema. This chapter traces how traditional *devadāsī* dance genres like the Tamil *padam*, an erotic love song, are represented and transformed in the cinema. It analyzes the way that melody (*rāga*), rhythm (*tāla*), and movement techniques are deployed in genres like *padam*, but also in other genres from the courtly *devadāsī* dance reperoire like *jatisvaram* and *tillāṉā* that find their way into the cinema. In some senses, the early cinema also offers a way of documenting older dance techniques and repertory that have disappeared from today's

Bharatanāṭyam but remain captured on film from the 1930s. The chapter also examines how slippages between idioms were integral to the making of both film and stage versions of Bharatanāṭyam in this period. The chapter unpacks these slippages by pointing to the creation of new types of dance that were the products of the encounter between cinema and stage, such as the snake dance (*pāmpu naṭaṉam*) and the dance of Śiva (*naṭaṉam āṭiṉār*). These new forms breathe a different aesthetic life into the idiom of Bharatanāṭyam and become representative of it as a whole in the mid-twentieth century.

The coda dwells on the pedagogical resonances that cinematic representations of Bharatanāṭyam had for middle-class audiences in this period. Print material from the 1940s and 1950s evinces a clear connection between the culture of cinema dance and pedagogy about the classical. Film magazines contain spreads that outline, for example, the meaning of hand gestures (*muttiraikaḷ*), as well as advertisements for the *araṅkēṟṟams* of young, upper-class amateur dancers, side by side with articles about dance in the cinema, cinema advertisements, and notes about classical dance. This collapsing of pedagogy and publicity for screen and stage dance, the coda argues, gives rise to urban cults of celebrity. As the idea of the dancer-actress comes to full fruition in the 1950s, with the popularity of figures such as Kamala Lakshman, Padmini Ramachandran, Vyjayanthimala, Jayalalitha, and others, Bharatanāṭyam comes to permanently inhabit the space of a celluloid classicism in ever-expanding ways.

In an effort to chart a more robust critical history of Bharatanāṭyam, this book tries to show how the category of the classical itself cannot be understood without reference to cultural iterations in the cinema. This study reminds us that that the discursive and social fields within which new critical histories of Bharatanāṭyam have been located were equally visual and paravisual fields of knowing and being. As a synthetic artifact of the modern world, Bharatanāṭyam appears to seamlessly reintegrate disparate and sometimes conflicting representations of its pasts. The unique theatrical modernism that Bharatanāṭyam embodies today—wrought as it has been by the complex politics of gender, class, caste, and religious nationalism—is rooted in both a semiotics and a history of the early South Indian cinema.

[1]

THE *DEVADĀSĪ* COMMUNITY AND THE CINEMATIC IMAGINATION

Politics, Participation, and Representation

My five-year-old daughter acted in my film . . . and when I needed help, my wife too acted in female parts. . . . God willing, if one day these prostitutes can be removed and replaced with women from good families, our studios will no longer be compared to whore houses and the prestige of filmmakers and their teams will be salvaged.

DHUNDIRAJ GOVIND PHALKE, *quoted in* Mrinal Pande, "Moving beyond Themselves"

Of course, all that [the traditional lifestyle of women from devadasi communities] has changed now. The films and theatres have opened up a paying career for them which, while bettering their material prospects, has slowly undermined their old traditional outlook and relative morality. Now, they do not hesitate to change hands or run amok among the idle rich and gay bachelors. But there are among them devadasis who stick to their old customs and ways of living and who still cling to one man for a number of years, and to that small band of cultured devadasis Balasaraswati belongs.

G. VENKATACHALAM, *Dance in India*

The anti-*devadāsī* legal interventions of the late 1920s in colonial Madras coincide not only with the reinvention of dance at the hands of upper-caste urban elites, but also with the diverse possibilities opened up by mass cinematic production in India. The powerful matrix of cultural modernity represented by the making of a new national dance tradition and the new medial form of cinema afforded women from *devadāsī* communities short-lived (but sometimes significant) professional promise, even as anti-*devadāsī* legislation simultaneously curtailed other social and economic prospects. This chapter is about the cultural labor of women from *devadāsī* backgrounds in the early Tamil cinema, and also about representations of such women and their work in the film media of early Madras. Indeed, prior to the late 1930s, nearly all female performers in the cinema came from this community, and certainly their presence—albeit dwindling, only to eventually be eclipsed by largely Brahmin women—remained central to film production in Madras until the 1970s. While recently scholars such as Davesh Soneji (2012) and Sundar Kaali (2013) have pointed to the significance of women from this community as the first actresses of Tamil and Telugu cinema, in this chapter I provide the life histories of individual actresses based on archival and ethnographical material. I locate the resonances and dissonances that the lives of actresses have with their cinematic roles, against the backdrop of the larger historical, social, and political implications of representations of the *devadāsī* community. In that sense, this chapter (like chapter four, on *naṭṭuvaṉār*) might well be thought of as a kind of prosopography in critical historical perspective.[1] The life narratives presented in this chapter (based largely on archival material) demonstrate the ways in which labor, morality, and aesthetics were intertwined in the experiences of *devadāsī* women who participated in the early Tamil cinema.

LOCATING *DEVADĀSĪ* PERFORMANCE PRACTICES IN THE MADRAS PRESIDENCY IN THE LATE NINETEENTH AND EARLY TWENTIETH CENTURIES

Before the so-called dance revival in the 1930s, Bharatanāṭyam dance was the exclusive hereditary professional practice of communities of courtesans referred to in colonial discourse by the Sanskrit term *devadāsī* (servant of god).[2] These women performed music and dance in courts, occasionally in temples, and at private events in the homes of the social and political elites. These women were referred to in colonial discourse as temple prostitutes or temple dancers, and we know that their artistic, sexual, and social labor extended far beyond the highly romanticized space of the Hindu temple, and that their nonconjugal sexuality differed in form and function from that of the sex worker in colonial South India (Soneji 2012).

In South India in the eighteenth and nineteenth centuries, *devadāsī* performance practices were located largely at three sites: courts (which included the zamindaris [little kingdoms], feudal courts set up by landowning elites), temples (most of which were financed by courts and zamindaris), and inside the homes of urban elites (usually upper-caste men, who in the colonial period were afforded a great amount of civic power in Madras by the colonial government).[3] The bulk of the *devadāsīs'* income came from the funds generated by their performances of dance and music, gifts of cash and jewelry given to them by their patrons and sexual partners, and a system of land tenure known as *ināmdāri* (or *inām*) in which they received tax-free land from temples (or the courts that managed the temples) in return for dedicating women from their families to these institutions through a ritual known as *poṭṭukkaṭṭutal* ("tying the *poṭṭu* pendant"), which marked women as nonconjugal courtesans.

By the end of the nineteenth century, a number of prominent *devadāsī* families had moved from towns and villages in the Tamil- and Telugu-speaking regions of the Madras Presidency to Madras itself, which had become a major hub in the new colonial economy. Soneji has suggested that the rise in demand for private salon performances (known in colonial parlance as nautch performances) provided opportunities for professional musicians and dancers in the city, even as these very performances came under moral and eventually legal scrutiny within a century or so of their origin. Soneji has also suggested that these types of performances, including those of a similar nature taking place in courts such as those at Tanjore and Pudukkottai, may have come into being as an emulation of (and a result of the demand for) nautch performances by courtesans in Calcutta, who were patronized by both European officials and native elites (Soneji 2012, 64). While many scholars have focused on the famous family of T. Balasaraswati (1918–84), whose great-great-grandmother Kamakshi (1810–90) moved from Tanjore to Madras around 1857, there are numerous other examples of migration to Madras. Toward the end of this chapter I focus on the film star Kuchalakumari (b. 1937), whose great-great-grandmother Tanjore Bhavani (dates unknown) also moved from Tanjore to Madras to pursue opportunities as a professional musician and dancer. Madras offered new possibilities to professional women artists, including exposure to the emerging fields of Tamil and Telugu drama, gramophone recording, and eventually cinema.

REFORM AND SOCIAL RUPTURE IN *DEVADĀSĪ* COMMUNITIES

Beginning in approximately the middle of the nineteenth century, a movement to dislodge hereditary professional women artists from the public sphere using public debate and eventually legal intervention, reached its apex with the passing of the Madras *Devadāsī* (Prevention of Dedication) Act in 1947, just months after India attained independence. In Madras, much of this movement was directed specifically toward the *devadāsī* communities of the region, which included professional performers who spoke Tamil, Telugu, and Kannada.[4] For almost a century, social reformers and Indian nationalists engaged in voluble debates about the social and legal status and future of professional female musicians and dancers. Even as standard scholarly representations of *devadāsī* reform characterize it as a project that was completed with the 1947 act, for individuals in these communities today, the experience of living through and with reform has left many loose ends. Thus, while *devadāsī* dance was reworked by E. Krishna Iyer, Rukmini Arundale, and others in a class- and caste-bound framework (a process discussed in detail in chapter 2) beginning in the 1930s, women from *devadāsī* communities have never been able to participate successfully in the professional practice of dance in postcolonial India.[5]

While I will not repeat the whole history of social reform in the *devadāsī* community here, a task that has most eloquently and recently been undertaken by Soneji (2012), I would like to highlight some chronological signposts that are relevant for the study of the interface between women in the *devadāsī* community and the early Tamil cinema. First, it is significant that the first legal intervention against the community—namely, the resolution proposed to the Madras Legislative Assembly on November 4, 1927, by Dr. Muthulakshmi Reddy that urged "the Government to undertake legislation to put a stop to the practice of dedication of young girls and young women to Hindu temples for immoral purposes" (quoted in Soneji 2012, 121)—generated a tremendous amount of public debate on the legal and moral status of women from these communities. As Soneji has shown in his analysis of documents from Reddy's archive, this debate was complex and included a range of voices, including those of the *devadāsīs* that were raised in protest. These legal interventions coincided not only with the reinvention of dance by upper-caste urban elites, but also with the diverse possibilities opened up by cinematic production in India. The powerful matrix of cultural modernity represented by the making of a new national dance tradition and the new medial form of cinema afforded women from *devadāsī* communities short-lived (but sometimes significant) professional promise, even as anti-*devadāsī* legislation simultaneously curtailed their prospects. Second, such interventions were paired with the emergence of non-Brahmin political assertion through the Self-Respect Movement, engineered by the radical political thinker and leader E. V. Ramasami Naicker (1879–1973; also known as Periyar).[6] As Soneji has shown (2012, 143–50), anti-*devadāsī* legislation worked in favor of men in the community, who often rose to great professional heights as women's labour was rendered increasingly invisible in the early decades of the twentieth century. The entrance of men from *devadāsī* communities into the political world of non-Brahmin assertion in the public sphere produced a long-lasting connection not only between the world of cinema and Tamil politics, but also between the new face of the *devadāsī* community in public modernity and Tamil politics.[7] This new face of the community was a distinctly masculine and patrilineal one. As result of anti-*devadāsī* legislation, men reinvented themselves by creating a new caste identity, calling themselves *icai vēḷāḷars* ("cultivators of music"). This identity linked them to the world of cultural production, placing them in the respectable caste status of *vēḷāḷars*, a mid-caste agricultural community, and simultaneously removed the titular, social, and cultural female presence that had been yoked to their self-representation. Together, these two residual effects of anti-*devadāsī* legislation—the production of a new cultural matrix and the political assertion of men from the community—were key aspects in the making of the Tamil cinema. On the one hand, women from *devadāsī* families were encouraged to participate in the cultural labor of the cinema in its early decades. On the other hand, men from the community became involved in a new political assertion in which cinema played a central role, and as scriptwriters for many of the earliest explicitly political Tamil films, individuals such as C. N. Annadurai (1909–69; chief minister of Tamilnadu in the 1960s) created a permanent nexus between the political and the cinematic in modern Tamilnadu (Baskaran 1981; Irschick 1986; Soneji 2012).

DIGLOSSIA: TAMIL- AND TELUGU-SPEAKING COURTESAN COMMUNITIES IN THE EARLY CINEMA

It is significant that the Madras legal interventions were aimed at both Tamil- and Telugu-speaking courtesans, a fact that is made explicit in the language of the 1947 act that listed epithets for *devadāsīs* that came mostly from Telugu linguistic contexts.[8] The legislation drew upon colonial geopolitical configurations (such as that of the Madras Presidency) to construct a unified sign of a South Indian *devadāsī* culture. Vernacular traditions, especially those of naming (such as the use of the Telugu term *kalāvantulu* or the Tamil *tēvaraṭiyāḷ*), now collided with the strictures of the state and law, which brought all of these together under the universalized category of *devadāsī*. However, it is true that Tamil- and Telugu-speaking courtesan communities have shared histories and that flows of repertoire, technique, and bodies across these linguistic registers were a key feature of courtesan performance traditions throughout South India.

Similarly, the earliest instantiations of a distinctly South Indian cinema, in the form of the first talkies, were aimed at the linguistically *diglossic* (if not multilingual) Tamil-Telugu audiences of the Madras Presidency.[9] Films like the first talkie, *Kalidas* (Kālīdāsa [a poet]; 1931) contained dialogue in both Tamil and Telugu (and even small portions in Hindi), and actors in the early cinema thus came from both the Tamil- and Telugu-speaking districts of the Madras Presidency.[10] With the political and cultural push toward increased linguistic differentiation close to the time of Indian independence, Tamil and Telugu cinema had emerged as somewhat distinct entities by the 1940s, but they continued to share common aesthetic registers, production networks and apparatuses, and even actors and audiences. Thus, women from the Telugu *kalāvantula* courtesan community were key players in both acting and the emerging playback singing in Tamil cinema between the 1930s and the 1950s.[11] As with many Tamil-speaking actresses, the early *kalāvantula* actresses often came into the cinema through the world of popular Telugu drama.[12] The most significant early actress from the *kalāvantula* community to perform in the Tamil cinema was Pasupuleti Kannamba (1911–64), who acted in numerous Telugu and Tamil films, married the drama performer Kadaru Nagabhushanam in 1941, and established the film production company called Rajarajeswari Films. Most notably, Kannamba acted in the film *Kannagi* (Heroine of the Tamil epic *Cilappatikāram*; 1942), one of the earliest films for which the *naṭṭuvaṉār* Vazhuvoor Ramiah Pillai was the choreographer (figure 1.1a). Another significant figure was Rushyendramani (1917–2002), an actress who performed originally in Kommuri Pattabhiramaiah's drama company called Lakshmi Vilasa Nataka Sabha and later in the Rajarajeswari Nataka Mandali, run by Kannamba and Nagabhushanam. Rushyendramani's first film was the Telugu *Sri Krishna Tulabharam* (The weighing scales of Kṛṣṇa), produced by Rajarao Naidu

Figure 1.1 a, b. Left: The cover of the songbook for Kannagi *(1942), featuring Pasupuleti Kannamba. Right: Anjali Devi in the pose of the god Śiva-Naṭarāja in a still from the Tamil film* Maṅkaiyarkkaraci *(1949).* Kuṇṭūci, *August 1949, 43. Private collection of S. V. Jayababu.*

in 1935, and she began acting in Tamil films in the early 1950s. Perhaps the most popular actress who crossed the Tamil-Telugu cinematic worlds in modern memory was Anjali Devi (1929–2014), who became famous as an actress and dancer, and was known for her bold cinematic presence (figure 1.1b). She was born into a *kalāvantula* household in the town of Peddapuram, in the Godavari district of the Madras Presidency. Like Kannamba, she began as a drama performer in the East Godavari region, and entered the cinema as a child actor in 1936. She went on to act in a number of significant Telugu and Tamil films. In 1949, Devi partnered with the leading male actor of this period, Akkineni Nageswara Rao (1924–2014), to create a production company called Aswini Pictures, and in 1951—with her musician husband, Adi Narayana Rao—she established her own studio, called Anjali Pictures (S. Srinivas 2013, 82).

The dual presence of Tamil *devadāsīs* in Telugu cinema and Telugu *kalāvantulu* in Tamil cinema reflected a wider and older pattern of the circulation of technique and repertoire across these communities throughout the eighteenth and nineteenth centuries, as Soneji (2012) has shown. At the end of this chapter we will see how the preeminent Tamil *devadāsī* family with an intergenerational involvement with the South Indian cinema—namely, that of Tanjore Bhavani—adopted girls from Telugu *kalāvantula* families, and trained them in forms of music and dance as a way of grooming them for careers in the cinema.

THE TROPE OF THE *DEVADĀSĪ*: VERNACULAR LITERATURE, TAMIL DRAMA, AND EARLY FILM AS INTERTEXTUAL MEDIA

Representations of *devadāsīs* circulate widely in the Madras Presidency through a dense and complex world of intertextual and intermedial forms. Soneji has very effectively demonstrated how the *devadāsī* as literary trope has been present in South India since the seventeenth century in certain Tamil literary genres (such as the *viralivițutūtu* ["messenger poem of the female bard"]). In these poems, composed largely under courtly patronage, *devadāsīs* emerge as socially maligned figures who dupe innocent men, ensnaring them in sexual and economic traps. Soneji (2012, 84–95) posits that these literary texts undergird representations of *devadāsīs* that begin to emerge in the new literary world of print in nineteenth-century Madras. I would extend Soneji's argument to include not only poems and novels from the late nineteenth and early twentieth centuries, but also Tamil social dramas and eventually scripts for the early cinema. The relation between cinema and drama as literature is especially important here, for as we will see, scripts for early cinema drew extensively from the popular dramas that were circulating in print between the 1880s and the late 1930s. This certainly is an area that requires further systematic research. In this section, I would like to simply point to the fact that *devadāsī* labor flowed through a range of medial spaces, and discursive or narrative constructions of *devadāsīs*, often pejorative or deeply stereotyped, followed women into all of these spaces.

The Tamil popular theatre of the late nineteenth and early twentieth centuries represented a kind of aesthetic bricolage, drawing from multiple sources, ranging from older forms of Tamil theatre (*kūttu*, also known as *terukkūttu* or *kațțaikkūttu*) to Victorian-inspired Parsi theatre.[13] This hybridized theatre that eventually came to be known in Tamilnadu as *icai nāțakam* or sometimes special *nāțakam* (explained below) was organized in the form of professional or semiprofessional companies, often called boys' companies because they consisted largely of young male actors.[14] The most significant figure in the formation of this tradition was Caṅkaratās Cuvāmikaḷ (1867–1922), who wrote, produced, and acted in a number of early *icai nāṭakam* performances and was the teacher of and mentor to a generation of actors—some of whom went on to be become stars of the Tamil cinema.[15] Cuvāmikaḷ was also a musician, and he composed the music for his own plays. Modern Tamil theatre matured in the hands of Pammal Campanta Mutaliyār (1873–1964), founder of the famous Suguna Vilasa Sabha theatre company in Madras.

The themes of *icai nāṭakam* plays included *devadāsī* characters. Often these representations in the plays drew from earlier Tamil literary contexts (such as the *viraliviṭutūtu* discussed above). The literary historian Sascha Ebeling (forthcoming) examines one such early drama about *devadāsīs* that moves through the realm of popular dramatic print texts and cinema and was the subject of a public obscenity debate, largely because of its protagonist's relationship with the *devadāsī* character. The drama—*Ṭampācārivilācam* (Dalliances of a dandy), by Caitāpuram Kācivicuvanāta Mutaliyār (1806–71)—draws on many themes found in early *viraliviṭutūtu* texts (figure 1.2a). The plot essentially is about a married man named Ṭampācāri who falls in love with a *devadāsī* named Mataṉacuntari and leaves his wife for her. She fleeces him of all his wealth, and soon he is reduced to the status of a beggar. Mataṉacuntari rejects him, and he goes back to his faithful wife who has been waiting for him to return. Through the intervention and grace of the god Śiva, Ṭampācāri finds the inheritance his father had left for him and is able to pay off his debts. The story has a happily ever after ending in which Ṭampācāri finds peace in conjugal life. The play was produced as a film by A. C. Maruthachalam Chettiar in 1935, with the non-*devadāsī* actress Saraswathi Bai playing Mataṉacuntari, under the title *Dumbachary or the Ideal Wife* (figure 1.2b).

A similar narrative was used in 1877 in another drama, *Piratāpacantira Vilācam* (The dalliances of Piratāpacantira; 1877).[16] The drama, which contained phrases and even sentences in English, was intended to warn young men against indulging in relationships with *devadāsīs*. The English preface by Pi. Vi. Irāmacāmi Rāju notes, for example, that "this play is written to reform those young men, who, instead of learning the good aspects of Western culture, like civility and a hygienic way of living

Figure 1.2 a, b. Left: The cover of the second printed edition (1871) of the Tamil play Ṭampācārivilācam, *by Caitāpuram Kācivicuvanāta Mutaliyār, first published in 1861. Roja Muthiah Research Library. Right: Poster for the Tamil film* Ṭampācāri allatu Uttama Maṉaivi, *rendered in English as* Dumbachary or the Ideal Wife *(1935). Private collection of S. V. Jayababu.*

and respect for women, only imbibe the bad aspects of their social living like partying and expensive habits" (1877, 2). It is clear that dramas like this—and, by extension, films like *Dumbachary*—have a didactic moral orientation.

Representations in the cinema also attempt to excavate *devadāsī* figures from mythical or literary contexts. In many of these representations, narratives hark back to a supposed golden age in which *devadāsīs* represented chastity and high morality, as opposed to those in the present, who are framed in what Soneji has termed a "narrative of degeneration" (2012, 6; see also 6–12).[17] I would like to turn to one such example, even though many such representations are common in the 1940s. I have chosen this example because the actress playing the *devadāsī* is T. R. Rajakumari, herself a descendant of the famed *devadāsī* Tanjore Bhavani

Figure 1.3. The cover of the songbook of Krishna Bhakthi *(*Kiruṣṇapakti*, Devotion to Kṛṣṇa; 1949), with an image of the actress T. R. Rajakumari. Private collection of S. V. Jayababu.*

(whose lineage is discussed in detail below in this chapter). The film, called *Krishna Bhakthi* (Devotion to Kṛṣṇa; 1949) draws its narrative from a curious mélange of sources (figure 1.3). The film historian Randor Guy (2008b) claims that the assistant director of the film, S. Ramanathan, was inspired to center the narrative on a figure inspired by the controversial Russian mystic Grigori Rasputin, whom he learned about through an English translation of a French novel called *The Monk*. The film is essentially about the liberation of a singer and orator who is an ascetic devoted the god Kṛṣṇa, and his love for the chaste courtesan named Devakumāri. In the sequence I examine here, the protagonist (known as a *harikathā bhāgavatar*) is performing devotional musical storytelling (known as *harikathā* or *kathākālakṣepam*) at a temple. He begins by singing about how chaste married women are able to attain liberation (*mokṣa*) because of the powers of their devotion to their husbands and families. He is then prodded by his disciple to talk about the moral and soteriological status of *devadāsīs*, who are not family women. The *bhāgavatar* then proceeds to narrate the story of a mythical *devadāsī* named Ceṅkamalam ("red lotus") who, unlike many *devadāsīs*, was honorable.[18] The entire sequence unfolds as a lesson in morality to a young *devadāsī* named Devakumāri, played by Rajakumari, who listens to the *bhāgavatar*'s oratory from a distance.

Devotee: Revered teacher, your servant has a question.

Teacher [named K. R. Ramasami, played by P. U. Chinnappa]: Ask, please ask. It's my duty to clear the doubts of devotees like you.

Devotee: The sermon about chastity makes sense with regards to family women (*kulastrīkaḷ*). But, those women from the clan of the *devadāsīs* (*tāci kulam*) who make a living as "women of pleasure" (*vilaimātarkaḷ*), do they have any chance of attaining salvation?

Teacher: Oh Kṛṣṇa! Kṛṣṇa! Why did you utter that word "*vilaimātarkaḷ*"? Oh Lord! Why does that word have to fall upon my ears? [singing] Don't ever say that word, my dear disciple. It's a great sin. When we are born, is there ever caste difference (*kula pētam*)? Speaking ill about women is just evil. Hari! Hari! These words [are] abhorrent to my ears. [talking] Listen, dear disciple. People seem to have forgotten who the real *devadāsīs* are! Women who perform service to god are *devadāsīs*. They themselves seem to have forgotten their birthright. To whom are they servants (*tāci*)? Certainly not to men (*nara maṉitaṉ*). They were called *devadāsīs* because they performed service to gods. But because lust-filled men manipulated them, the great *devadāsīs* who should have been venerated by everyone, were reduced by society to what you call them today, "women of pleasure" (*vilaimātarkaḷ*). Unfortunate, so very unfortunate! Don't ever put that ill-fated word in my ears. [singing] A woman born as a *devadāsī* should be like Ceṅkamalam, who did not sell her body, did not desire wealth, and did not desire sex. And since she only served god, she received salvation (*mōṭcam*). Only such a person is a *true devadāsī*.

Disciple: My Lord, who is this Ceṅkamalam? It would be instructional if you told us about her.

Teacher: Dear devotees, in the age known as Dvāpara, in the holy city of Śrīraṅgam, there lived a *devadāsī* named Ceṅkamalam. She had great faith in the power of her devotion. She was the auspicious one (*mahārāci*), unequaled in the arts of dance and music. That was the *devadāsī* named Ceṅkamalam. Beauty! Beauty! What a beauty she was! Even the local king lusted for her. Ceṅkamalam's mother also tried to force her to give in to his lustful desires. But did Ceṅkamalam give in? No, never! She said, "I will never be a slave to any king. I will be a slave only to Lord Kṛṣṇa."

[singing] Even though she was possessed of such beauty and so talented, she said she would only be a slave to Lord Kṛṣṇa! She rejected the lustful ways of the ordinary "women of pleasure" but was duped by a holy man. The holy man raped her. He told the king that if Ceṅkamalam was in love with him, she should marry him. The king was shocked, and declared: "Oh pure and chaste Ceṅkamalam, become the spiritual disciple of Paramatattaṉ Vipracīṉai Pākavatar. Become his apprentice and serve him well." Ceṅkamalam did just that and attained salvation!

[The camera then shifts to show the corner where a *devadāsī* named Devakumāri and her mother are standing]

Devakumāri's mother [to Devakumāri, who has been silently listening to the sermon]: What's wrong with you? You're so still. Won't the king be waiting for you?

Devakumāri (played Rajakumari): Wait mother. . . . What wise, true words.

Teacher: Hence, a *devadāsī* is not one who marries the man she thinks about and falls in love with. She is one who sees god through art. She does not desire married life even if it is with a great king. A true *devadāsī* is one who performs devotional service to god (*pākavata cēvai*) for her entire life.

Devakumāri: True! True!

Kaali (2013) has discussed the film *Chintamani/Bilwamangal* (1937) in great detail, and the representation of the courtesan character here reifies the same images of *devadāsīs* that we encountered in the print texts of early popular Tamil drama (figure 1.4). The film *Chintamani/Bilwamangal* is also a modern act of hagiographic retrieval and representation. It is the story of the thirteenth-century saint Līlāśuka Bilvamaṅgala

Figure 1.4. Advertisement for the film Chintamani/Bilwamangal *(1937), the story of Līlāśuka Bilvamaṅgala, the author of the Sanskrit work* Kṛṣṇakarṇāmṛtam, *who is infatuated by the courtesan Cintāmaṇī. Collection of the author.*

Figure 1.5. Advertisement for the film Devadasi *(1948), directed by Manik Lal Tandon, starring T. A. Mathuram and N. S. Krishnan. Private collection of S. V. Jayababu.*

(author of a famous Sanskrit devotional text called *Kṛṣṇakarṇāmṛtam*), read through the lens of texts like the nineteenth-century *Ṭampācārivilācam*. The saint, like the "dandy" of *Ṭampācārivilācam*, is infatuated by a courtesan named Cintāmaṇī. She is represented as a dancing courtesan, very much along the lines of *devadāsīs* of the late nineteenth century. Such anachronistic readings of courtesans in South India's cultural history are found in many early Tamil films (for example, *Kannagi*, mentioned above in this chapter, represents the courtesan character Mātavi in the fifth- or sixth-century Tamil epic *Cilappatikāram* as if she were a nineteenth-century *devadāsī*). What I wish to highlight here is how the figure of the nineteenth-century *devadāsī* is ubiquitous in the early cinema, standing in for courtesan figures from distant historical contexts.

This takes us to one final example, a film titled *Devadasi* (1948), which took three years to produce and starred the actress Leela, about whom not much is known (figure 1.5). The film also featured comedic dance sequences by T. A. Mathuram (1918–74). Although both archival and contemporary sources talk about her as being from a family of artists or entertainers, it is almost certain that she came from a *devadāsī* family. In an article for the *Hindu* in 2008, Guy summarizes the plot of this film (which he retrieved from a print source that is no longer available) as follows (no print of the film exists):

> *Devadasi* narrated the story of an economically weak girl begging on the streets and picked up by a smart devadasi woman.... She changes the girl's name to Devakunjari ... and trains her in Bharathanatyam and other dance forms. Many wealthy people fall for the charms of the dancer, but the greedy foster mother looks for the big fish—such as the king himself, who falls in love with her. However, the dancer falls in love with his friend, which complicates matters.... Soon the king takes to spirituality and so does [Devakunjari's] lover, who marries [her].... However, both are unable to forget the dancer, and [they] wage a battle of minds. Their spiritual guru tries to change their minds but not with much success. Finally, the dancer, by now deeply religious, surrenders herself to the Lord, and vanishes from their midst. (Guy 2013)

Guy claims that this narrative was inspired by the 1890 French novel *Thaïs*, by Anatole France, which is about the fourth-century Roman Egyptian female saint Thaïs—often described as a repentant courtesan in Catholic hagiography. According to Guy, this novel was the basis of a Bengali novel that inspired the Hindi film *Chitralekha*, which was first made in 1941 and then remade by the same filmmaker in 1964. Guy believes that the script for the film *Devadasi*, written by B. S. Ramaiah, was based partly on the 1941 version of *Chitralekha*. It is clear from Guy's description that this film uses the old trope of the courtesan as temptress. However, it also sublimates *devadāsī* sexuality, shifting it to the realm of devotion and the grace of god. We saw this kind of image in the film *Krishna Bhakthi*, discussed above in this chapter. This representation thus also connects itself to the golden age narratives about *devadāsīs*, who in the ancient past were pure and led pious devotional lives, only becoming morally degenerate in the modern age. The invocation of the golden age was key to both the antinautch movement and the cultural nationalism of the dance revival in the 1930s. We will return to this golden age representation of Bharatanāṭyam's past in the following chapter. For now, it is sufficient to note that the only extant early film to carry the title *Devadasi* uses this kind of representation. The bold title of the film may have made producers and distributors nervous, since the word "*devadāsī*" had become taboo and potentially volatile in Madras in the 1940s, following the antinautch movement.

AXES OF INVISIBILITY: ARCHIVAL SILENCE AND WOMEN ACTRESSES FROM *DEVADĀSĪ* COMMUNITIES

Much of this chapter involves a retrieval of the narratives of *devadāsī* women's professional lives through the use of archival materials. Both absences and presences of *devadāsīs* in the textual archive produce a kind of historical messiness; in many ways, they make desirable, definitive outcomes impossible. For example, rarely do archival sources use terms like "*devadāsī*." They gloss over such sites of public discomfort by using somewhat slippery language such as "traditional artist" or in Tamil, phrases like *icai kuṭumpattil vantavaṅkaḷ* ("descended from a music family"). On the one hand, information about some *devadāsī* artists abounds in archival sources. For example, Rajakumari, discussed in detail below, appears in hundreds of sources that comment on her beauty, and she was at the top of what Neepa Majumdar has termed the "hierarchy of female stardom" in early Indian cinema (2009, 93; see also 93–122). On the other hand, archival sources offer only traces of women who never became stars and remained marginal, yet recognizable to mass audiences. A case in point is P. S. Gnanambal (dates unknown), who acted in a handful of early Tamil films including *Dhruva Charithram* (The story of the devotee Dhruva; 1935). All we know about her is that she acted in drama companies and was from a traditional music background—which allows us to infer that she was from the *devadāsī* community. A single portrait of her exists, published in 1936 (figure 1.6), and in it we can see that she has received medals for her performance skills and pinned them to her sari. It was a common practice for *devadāsī* performers to display such medals in this manner.

In other cases, women from the *devadāsī* community slip into conjugality—"passing," as Soneji puts it (2012, 157), as non-*devadāsī* women. The professional and personal complexities of such reconstitutions are perhaps most evident in the famous example of M. S. Subbulakshmi (1916–2004), discussed in greater detail in chapter 3. But a more directly pertinent example is that of K. Rukmani (1929–2007; also known as Baby Rukmani or Kumari Rukmani) (figure 1.7). Like Subbulakshmi, Rukmani

Figure 1.6. Portrait of P. S. Gnanambal (1936), Āṭal Pāṭal *(*Āṇṭu Malar *1936), 36.*

was born to a mother who was a performer of music and dance in Madras in the early twentieth century. Rukmani's mother was named Nungambakkam Janaki (dates unknown), and she was originally from Thanjavur. Janaki also acted in just one film, the third Tamil talkie, *Harishchandra* (Hariścandra [a king]; 1932), in which Rukmani also made her debut as a child artist. Rukmani went on act in a number of popular films, including *Sri Valli* (The goddess Vaḷḷi; 1945), in which she performed a dance piece in the *tillāṉā* genre choreographed by Ramaiah Pillai. While working on the film *Lavangi* (Lavaṅgī [a courtesan]; 1946), she married the film's chief actor, director, and producer, Y. V. Rao (1903–73), who divorced his first wife Rajam to be with Rukmani. The couple's daughter is the actress known as Lakshmi (R. Venkatalakshmi, b. 1952) who was popular in the 1970s and 1980s. Lakshmi's daughter Aishwarya (b. 1971) is an actress in Tamil, Telugu, and Malayalam films. Even though Rukmani performed in more than a hundred films in Tamil, Telugu, and Hindi, much of her stardom came from her association with Rao and later from her work as a producer of two Hindi films. Of course, Rukmani was a star in the sense that she appears to have appealed to mass audiences, but her star

Figure 1.7. Baby Rukmani in a still from the film Bhagya Leela *(1938).* Āṭal Pāṭal *(*Āṇṭu Malar *1938), 62. Courtesy of the Roja Muthiah Research Library.*

status—and her presence in the archive—depended to some degree on what Majumdar calls "displacements" of identity (2009, 12).[19]

For the most part, the stars of Tamil cinema who were from the *devadāsī* community, such as the women discussed below in this chapter, have long-standing and narrativized presence in the archive. But I would like to point here to the some of the dangers of what Anjali Arondekar calls the "seductions of recovery and access" (2009, 18). Even in the case of women such as Rajakumari, whose professional lives are annotated in the archives, presentations of the complexities of these lives are full of gaps. In the sections that follow, therefore, I am not making claims about archival truth, insularity, or epistemic totality. However, archival fragments do nevertheless make it possible for us to reimagine the place of *devadāsī* women in the public life of Madras in the early decades of the twentieth century.

POLYMORPHOUS PERFORMANCE: MUSIC, DANCE, AND CINEMA IN THE LIFE OF S. D. SUBBULAKSHMI

The movement of women from *devadāsī* communities into the emerging world of cinema was a complex process that forces us to reconsider

Figure 1.8 a, b. Left: Portrait of S. D. Subbulakshmi in Āṭal Pāṭal *(*Āṇṭu Malar *1936, 51). Roja Muthiah Research Library. Right: S. D. Subbulakshmi on the cover of* Āṭal Pāṭal *(*Āṇṭu Malar *1938). Courtesy of the Roja Muthiah Research Library.*

received ideas about the centers and peripheries of cultural production in Madras in the 1930s and 1940s. On the one hand, it is certainly true that women from *devadāsī* communities remained somewhat on the peripheries of all of the cultural worlds they inhabited in the first half of the twentieth century, including music, dance, gramophone recording, drama, and cinema. On the other hand, it is also true that in some exceptional cases, women from *devadāsī* communities were able to help make and manage the early cinema, even as they remained on the peripheries of other cultural forms. This type of movement through multiple medial and aesthetic forms, which I call a kind of polymorphous engagement with performance in the new twentieth-century public sphere, is perhaps best exemplified in the case of the virtually forgotten S. D. Subbulakshmi (1917–87; also known as SDS; figures 1.8a and 1.8b), not to be confused with the famous singer M. S. Subbulakshmi. Subbulakshmi's life illustrates how *devadāsīs* who were engaged with the emerging world of modern Tamil drama could easily slip into the cinema and achieve a degree of fame in this context. Subbulakshmi is unique in that she became a second wife to South India's most important film director in this period, Krishnaswami Subrahmanyam (1904–71), who lived (and produced children) with both his Brahmin wife and his *devadāsī* wife, much in the manner of the earlier forms of institutionalized concubinage that defined the social organization of *devadāsī* communities in Tamil- and Telugu-speaking South India. Moreover, Subbulakshmi's life is intimately linked to both live and radio performances of devotional music (in the genre known as *harikathā* or *kathākālakṣepam*), which she was famous for in Madras well into the 1950s and 1960s. In the section that follows, I construct her life from the archive (relying primarily on a document composed in 1952) in an attempt to map the complexities of *devadāsī* women's polymorphous performance careers and their imbrication in multiple medial and aesthetic forms in the first half of the twentieth century.[20]

Subbulakshmi was born in the town of Srivaikuntam (in today's Thoothukudi district) on December 5, 1917. Her father, Doraiswamy Pillai, was an actor in a popular Tamil theatre (*nāṭakam*) company called the Dantimukhananda Hall Boys' Company. Her mother, Janaki Ammal, was a professional dancer within the *devadāsī* community. Her maternal grandmother, Muttulakshmi Ammal, was among the earliest women to perform a type of devotional music called *harikathā* or *kathākālaksepam*.[21] Subbulakshmi's father had joined the Dantimukhananda Company when she was just two years old, so she was largely raised by her mother. When she was five, Subbulakshmi was enrolled in public school. When she was eight, her mother made arrangements for her to be trained in dance and music. Her dance teacher was a *naṭṭuvaṉār* named S. Swaminatha Pillai, who was also her mother's teacher. There are a number of anecdotes in the archive about her early life that show her early passion for performance. The following is related to her childhood interest in the theatre:

> As she was being trained in dance, the famous Kannaiya [Drama] Company was touring Tirunelveli and the nearby villages. Everyone was talking about how wonderful this theatre company was. So Subbulakshmi and her mother traveled [from Srivaikuntam] to Tirunelveli to watch the play. Subbulakshmi was amazed with

> the quality of acting in this company. She was determined to act in these kinds of plays. Even without her mother's knowledge, as an 8-year old, she boldly went up to Kannaiya [the company's director] himself, begging him to let her join his company. Kannaiya saw her bright eager face and asked why she wanted to act. He told her his company did not accept female actors but said he had always wanted a daughter, and she should give up the desire to act and become his adopted daughter instead. Subbulakshmi refused and with great sadness returned home because all she wanted to do was to act on stage. ("Es. Ṭi. Cuppulakṣmi" 1952, 66)

Around age eight or nine, Subbulakshmi acted in her first role in a play staged by the Dantimukhananda Hall Boys' Company, the same company for which her father worked. For unknown reasons, six months after her first performance as a child actor, she and her father stopped working for this company, and the entire family relocated to the city of Madurai. There, she was contracted to perform in what were known as special *nāṭakams*, in which each actor was hired individually—or "specially"—for each performance, as opposed to the company-based *icai nāṭakam*, in which drama companies were commissioned by patrons to enact plays (Seizer 2005, 26–28). It is in the context of acting in these special *nāṭakams* that Subbulakshmi became very famous in Madurai. When she was twelve, she was honored in a public ceremony in Madurai, at which she was awarded a medal for her acting skills. When she was sixteen, she went to Sri Lanka (then Ceylon) to act and also performed concerts of *kathākālakṣepam* there. By the time she was fifteen, she had acted alongside the greatest male drama artists of Tamil India, including S. V. Subbiah Bhagavathar and M. K. Thyagaraja Bhagavathar (1910–59; also known as MKT), as well as the actress K. P. Sundarambal.

Subbulakshmi's engagements with music also ran deep. Her father knew how to play the harmonium, and she learned the basics of this instrument and vocal music for *nāṭakam* performances from him. At the age of thirteen, she began giving performances of *kathākālakṣepam* in Ramanathapuram, having learnt this didactic storytelling musical form from her maternal grandmother. Later she performed in Sri Lanka again, and in a few other cities in India such as Delhi and Calcutta. Furthermore, "in 1932, just before she acted in [her first film] *Pavalakkodi*, she performed *kathākālakṣepam* for the marriage [reception] of [the emi-

Figure 1.9. S. D. Subbulakshmi performs kathākālakṣepam *in Madras in the late 1950s. Private collection of S. V. Jayababu.*

nent actor] M. K. Thyagaraja Bhagavathar in Trichy" ("Kuḻantaikaḷē Periyavarkaḷāka Ākiṟārkaḷ" 1936). Music was a constant presence in Subbulakshmi's life. Even long after her cinematic acting career came to a close in the 1950s, she continued to give performances of *kathākālakṣepam* in Madras, well into her forties and fifties (figure 1.9).

Until she was seventeen, Subbulakshmi continued to act in the popular Tamil theatre. She was often paired with the actor M. K. Thyagaraja Bhagavathar, who would eventually become a superstar of the early Tamil cinema. Their most popular production was a Tamil play titled *Pavaḷakkoṭi* (The coral queen), about the love between Arjuna, the hero of the Hindu epic *Mahābhārata*, and a princess from a coral island. They toured in this play all over the southern part of the Madras Presidency. Once in 1934, when they were performing it in the town of Karaikkudi, S. M. Lakshmana Chettiar (a businessman turned producer, also known as Lena Chettiar) and his friend K. Subrahmanyam (a former lawyer), who had just formed the studio called Meenakshi Cinetone were in the audience. They immediately decided to transform the play into a film, and offered Thyagaraja Bhagavathar and Subbulakshmi the lead roles. The film version of the play, *Pavalakkodi* (1934), was shot entirely in Madras and was a huge box office success.[22]

Figure 1.10. The director K. Subrahmanyam on the set of the film Seva Sadanam *(House of service; 1938), which was the debut film for the actress-singer M. S. Subbulakshmi (far left). Also seen here are his eldest daughter Lalitha (a child of his first wife) and S. D. Subbulakshmi (his second wife; far right).* Kuṇṭūci, *December 1952, 67.*

Subbulakshmi was contracted to act in two other Tamil films, both shot in Calcutta and directed by Subrahmanyam, *Naveena Sarangadhara* (The new *Sāraṅgadhara*; 1936) and *Usha Kalyanam* (The wedding of Uṣā; 1936). Through this period, Subbulakshmi and Subrahmanyam fell in love (figure 1.10). Subrahmanyam was already married to a woman named Meenakshi, whom he had married in a traditional Brahmin child marriage when she was nine years old.[23] The relationship between Subbulakshmi and Subrahmanyam became so intense that just before the completion of the filming of *Usha Kalyanam*, on September 13, 1935,they were married in a civil ceremony in Calcutta. Subbulakshmi thus became Subrahmanyam's "second wife" in a mode that resonated with earlier relations of concubinage between Brahmin men and *devadāsīs*. On the same day, they formed a new production company called the Madras United Arts Corporation (MUAC).

Over the next decade, MUAC produced a number of films, some of which starred Subbulakshmi. The films included *Bhakta Kuchela* (The

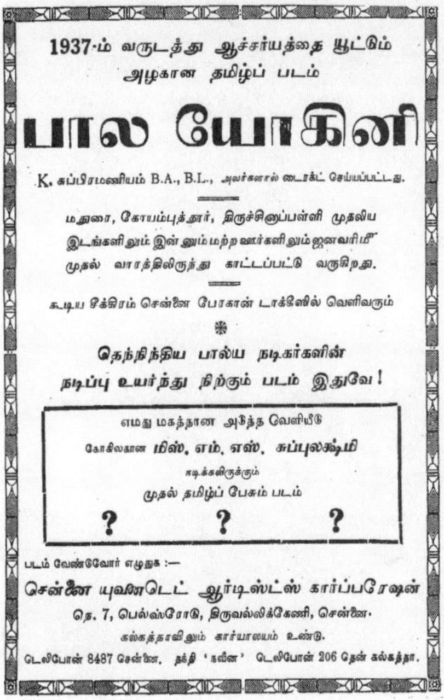

Figure 1.11 a, b. Posters for the MUAC films Balayogini *(1937) and* Seva Sadanam *(1938) in* Aṭal Pāṭal (Aṇṭu Malar *1936, 8, and 1938, 12). Courtesy of the Roja Muthiah Research Library.*

devotee Kucela; 1936); *Balayogini* (The girl *yogini*; 1937) (figure 1.11a); *Mr. Ammanji* (1937), which was a comedy featuring a song in "playback" by Subbulakshmi); *Seva Sadanam* (The House of service; 1938), which was the debut film for the actress-singer M. S. Subbulakshmi (figure 1.11b); *Thyagabhoomi* (The land of sacrifice; 1939); *Anantha Sayanam* (The lord who reclines on the serpent; 1942); and *Mana Samrakshanam* (The protection of honor; 1945). This last film marked the end of the professional collaboration between Subrahmanyam and Subbulakshmi.

In the early 1940s, with the encouragement of Subrahmanyam, Subbulakshmi formed a dance group called Natana Kala Seva ("Service to the art of dance") and toured extensively throughout Tamilnadu. By this time, reinvented Bharatanāṭyam had already made its mark in Madras, due to the activities of Rukmini Arundale and the International Academy for the Arts (later renamed Kalakshetra), and one of the key markers of the reinvented form was the new idiom of the dance drama (discussed in greater detail in the following chapter). One of the first productions of

Figure 1.12. An image from the 1942 dance drama Pārijātāpaharaṇam *produced by the dance troupe Natana Kala Seva, featuring S. D. Subbulakshmi as the god Kṛṣṇa, second from the left (Kannan and Kannan 2004, 22).*

Natana Kala Seva was the dance drama titled *Pārijātāpaharaṇam*, based on the narrative of the god Kṛṣṇa stealing the celestial *pārijāta* tree to present his wife, Satyabhāmā, with the flower of the tree (figure 1.12). In this production, Subbulakshmi played the male role of Kṛṣṇa, as she had done in some of her hit films, such as *Bhakta Kuchela*.

In 1942, Subrahmanyam founded a dance school in which students would be taught dance for free. Separate from Natana Kala Seva, this was called Nrithyodaya ("the dawn of dance"). Subbulakshmi ran this dance school for two years, a fact that is not mentioned in other accounts of the school's early years (such as Kannan and Kannan 2004). Subrahmanyam's involvement with the nationalist politics of dance runs deep, as we will see in chapter 3. For example, in 1945 he began work on an epic film about dance titled *Narttaṉa Muraḷi* (The dancing flute) that he eventually shelved. The dancer Padma Subrahmanyam—Subrahmanyam's daughter with his first wife, Meenakshi—is the current director of Nrithyodaya, which has grown into a large transnational dance institution.

There is little archival information about Subbulakshmi's life after the early 1940s. In 1943, she gave birth to a son named Ramachandran (also known as Ramji), and she did not act in films until she appeared in one titled *Panam* (Money; 1950)—her first film that was not directed by her husband. She later played small supporting roles in the films *Andaman Kaithi* (The prisoner on the Andaman Islands; 1952) and *Manamagal* (The bride; 1951), by which time a new generation of upper-caste female artists had begun to populate the world of Tamil cinema. In the mid-1950s she returned to the world of the Tamil drama, where her career had begun: "Lately she also has been thrilling her stage fans too. After a seven-year gap in acting as a pair, it is wonderful to note that Subbulakshmi and M. K. Thyagaraja Bhagavathar have reunited as a pair on stage and are acting in plays now. They have been presenting in the play *Pavalakkoṭi* in Nagappattinam, Mukkoodal and Chennai" ("Es. Ṭi. Cuppulakṣmi" 1952, 70).

Subbulakshmi died in 1987, leaving behind rich and varied contributions to cultural production in modern South India. A professional musician, theater artist, dancer, dance teacher, and cinema actress, she should have been included in mainstream nationalist-oriented histories of the arts in twentieth-century India. The question of her invisibility, despite her marriage to one of India's most renowned upper-caste filmmakers, raises the question of stigma and its effects on the lives of women from *devadāsī* communities. That stigma that persists today for many women in the community (Soneji 2012). One archival source, for example, ends by dwelling on Subbulakshmi's exceptional moral standing despite her background: "When one sees Subbulakshmi, one does not see the usual traits attributed to an ordinary woman from the film world, but instead one sees the sophisticated attributes of a woman from a good family. Isn't she preserving her integrity, dignity and self-respect very well?" ("Kuḻantaikaḷē Periyavarkaḷāka Ākiṟārkaḷ" 1936).

Here the "woman from the film world" is contrasted with the "woman from a good family" (*uyar kuṭumpa strī*), and it is clear that the reference to the cinema is a euphemistic way of invoking the *devadāsī* community. A similar kind of discomfort and silence exists about Subbulakshmi even within her own family. For example, her stepdaughter, Padma Subrahmanyam, had the following to say about her:

> If there was one field where caste difference was not observed, it was in the world of dance and music. If anybody tells you other-

> wise, do not believe them. I have grown up in that atmosphere and so for me, caste is no barrier. In fact, S. D. Subbulakshmi is my stepmother and we will always acknowledge this no matter what. . . . My mother and she were best friends and were like sisters. They both died within sixteen hours of each other. I lost both my mothers within sixteen hours in 1987. Two wives dying at the same time is unheard of. My mother would always praise S. D. Subbulakshmi. Both of them adored each other. . . . More importantly than introducing *devadāsīs* into films, my father also made a bald old Brahmin widow act in the film *Seva Sadanam*. That was how revolutionary he was.[24]

In these comments, Subbulakshmi's *devadāsī* background is glossed over in favor of a kind of normalized reading of her identity and her relationship to Subrahmanyam's father. But this normalization is also clearly uncomfortable for Subrahmanyam, a fact that we see in the final sentence—in which the question of *devadāsī* participation in the cinema is trumped by a statement about how representing orthodox Brahmin widows with shaved heads on screen was much more of a social achievement for her father.

Taken together, these aporetic perspectives about Subbulakshmi reveal the complexities of representing *devadāsī* women's professional lives in the postreform period. Relatively speaking, Subbulakshmi's career was at the successful end of the spectrum when it comes to thinking about the postreform lives of individuals from the community. Yet as we have seen toward the end of this section, the relative professional success is met with silence, awkwardness, and prickliness in the context of public acknowledgments of *devadāsī* identity.

GRAMOPHONE, CINEMA, AND STAGE: THE FAMILY OF THIRUVIDAIMARUDUR BHAVANI

The intermedial performance lives of women from *devadāsī* families at the beginning of the twentieth century, and indeed the complexity of such artistic flows can be mapped through the life narratives of the women over the generations. In this section, I present two case studies, both of which focus on matriarchs with the same name, Bhavani. The first, and less complex, family is that of Thiruvidaimarudur Bhavani (1876–1932); the second is that of Tanjore Bhavani (dates unknown). In both cases, women whose families were involved in traditional courtly, salon, and temple-based performance practices shifted their participation to the emerging new media, including the popular Tamil drama, gramophone recording, and cinema. I have been fortunate to meet and interview the last women artists in both these families, and in the descriptions that follow, I attempt to bring some historical details to bear on the forms of artistic production in which these women participated.

I begin with Thiruvidaimarudur Bhavani, who is at the top of a *devadāsī* family tree that extends over several generations of multimedial artists. Bhavani was born in the town of Thiruvidaimarudur, about fifty kilometers from Thanjavur (Tanjore). This town was famous for the small palace built by the Marāṭhā ruler Amar Singh (also known as Amarasiṃha, r. 1793–98), which hosted performances by courtesan troupes, and also for the old Mahāliṅgasvāmi temple dedicated to the god Śiva, where courtesan troupes were hired to perform for festival events. Bhavani was born into a *devadāsī* family here, and while not much is known about her early life, we do know that she studied vocal music with a Brahmin musician named Thiruvisainallur Narayanasvami Ayyar (Sundaram 2003, 197). At some point in her life, she seems to have moved to the Kanchipuram or Madras area, a fact that can be discerned from the way she is acknowledged in her early gramophone recordings, as "Miss Bhavani—Conjeevaram [Kanchipuram] (Thiruvadamaradur)." By the first couple of years of the twentieth century, Bhavani was making recordings for HMV's 10-inch "e" suffix series and its 12-inch "f" suffix series (Kinnear 1994, 214–15 and 227–28). Her recordings include Telugu devotional songs and *kīrtanas*, as well as *padams* (courtesan songs), mainly in Tamil.[25]

Bhavani had a sister named Rukmini who was a professional dancer. Almost nothing is known about her other than that a painting based on a photograph of her was made to adorn the walls of a pavilion in the Śiva temple in the village of Konerirajapuram in 1923, for the temple's major reconsecration ceremony (*kumbhābhiṣekam*). In the painting Rukmini's dance troupe (*mēḷam*) appears to be giving gifts to a gathering of colonial officers (figure 1.13). It is likely that the image of Rukmini that this painting was based upon (which can no longer be traced) was simply a portrait, and that the additional figures—such as the colonial officers—were added to the image by the painter.[26] Bhavani and Rukmini had a cousin named Krishnamma (the daughter of their aunt), who was

Figure 1.13. A painting based on a photograph of Thiruvidaimarudur Rukmini on the wall of a pavilion (maṇḍapa) *of the Śiva temple at Konerirajapuram. The painting was completed in August 1923. Collection of the author.*

a dancer (Sundaram 2003, 197). Not much is known about Krishnamma except that her daughter, Nīlāmpāḷ, who was also a dancer, trained with a dance master named Thiruvidaimarudur Cuppayya Naṭṭuvaṉār and was regularly hired to dance in the Mahāliṅgasvāmi temple.

Nīlāmpāḷ's eldest daughter, Rajalakshmi, was born on November 30, 1916 (figure 1.14). She began her dance training at the age of seven with Cuppayya Naṭṭuvaṉār, her mother's dance master. Unlike most women in the *devadāsī* community, her *araṅkēṟṟam* took place at the rather late age of thirty. But even before her debut as a professional dancer, Rajalakshmi was approached by production agencies to act in films. Her first role was a very minor one as the goddess Kālī in the film *Kalamegam* (Kalamegham [a poet]; 1940), which was produced by Sri Dhandayuthapani Films and Salem Mohini Pictures and directed by Ellis R. Dungan (1909–2001), an American director.

She acted in a few Tamil films in the 1940s, including *Satimurali* (The chaste woman; 1940), *Tilottamma* ("Tilottamā [a celestial courtesan]; 1940) and *Karaikkal Ammaiyar* ("Kāraikkāl Ammaiyār [a Tamil Śaiva

Figure 1.14. Thiruvidaimarudur N. Rajalakshmi performs abhinaya *in conversation with the author, Coimbatore, December 2006. Photograph by the author.*

poet]; 1943). There were two films in which she played significant roles: *Chokhamelar* (1942), based on the life of the fourteenth-century Marathi saint Cokhāmeḷa, and the courtly drama *Divan Bahudur* (The honorable minister; 1943). By the end of the 1940s, it was clear to Rajalakshmi that she could not make a successful career for herself in the cinema. Disenchanted by the competitive world of cinema, she attempted to resume a career as a professional dancer in the Thanjavur region. Between 1943 and 1968, she gave performances, even though such opportunities were increasingly limited for women from the *devadāsī* community. Her performances largely took place in smaller towns and cities, such as Thanjavur, Trichy, and Kumbhakonam, and she most often performed as a soloist. However, she sometimes danced with a partner from the *devadāsī* community, Tirubhuvanam Jayalakshmi (Sundaram 2003, 198). During this period, she also attempted to teach dance under the aegis of a cultural organization called Neyveli Kaveri Sangam, but this too turned out to be a fairly peripheral and economically unviable enterprise for her. In the 1980s, she was invited to teach dance to the daughter of a temple

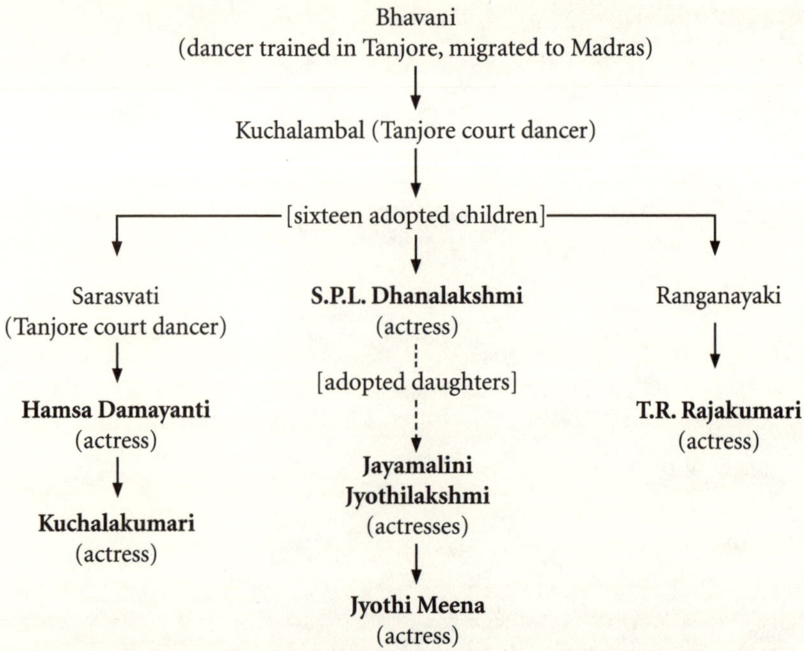

Figure 1.15. Descendants of Tanjore Bhavani. The names of women who performed in the cinema are indicated in bold.

trustee in the city of Coimbatore and decided to settle there permanently with her son and a daughter. Her story illustrates the complex ways in which the intergenerational participation of women from *devadāsī* backgrounds across multiple genres and medial forms is actually a central feature of the genealogies of many *devadāsī* families in modern South India.

TANJORE BHAVANI'S DESCENDANTS AND THE TAMIL CINEMA

The deep and long-standing effects that the cinema had on the lives of women from *devadāsī* communities can perhaps best be illustrated by the second family that has had multigenerational and multimedial relationships with the arts, including the cinema. This is the family represented by the matriarch Tanjore Bhavani, who moved to Madras from Tanjore with her *naṭṭuvaṉār*-teacher, Capāpati (1836–94), the son of Civāṉantam (1808–63) of the famous Tanjore Quartet—a family of court *naṭṭuvaṉārs* of Tanjore during the reign of King Serfoji II (1777–32) (figure 1.15). According to the historian B. M. Sundaram, because of her move to Madras, which was also known as Chennai or Chennapattanam, Bhavani was known to locals in Tanjore as Pattanattammal ("lady from Chennapattanam") and her house in Tanjore was known as *paṭṭaṇattammāḷ vīṭu* ("house of the lady from Chennapattanam") (Sundaram 2003, 78–79). Despite the fact that she was living in Madras, Bhavani maintained close relations with Tanjore, and her daughter Kuchalambal and adopted granddaughter Sarasvati continued to dance at the Tanjore court untilthe reign of Tanjore's last rulers, Queen Kamakshi Amba Bai Saheb (d. 1892) and Princess Vijayamohana Mukta Bai Saheb (r. 1846–85) as well as at the public festivals of Tanjore's Bṛhadīśvara temple.

T. R. Rajakumari

Rajakumari (born Thanjavur Ranganayaki Rajayi) was born on May 5, 1922, in Thanjavur to Ranganayaki, one of the five daughters of Kuchalambal. She attended the Veeraraghava Secondary School in Thanjavur. For some reason, she dropped out during her third year of high school. Her youngest aunt, S. P. L. Dhanalakshmi (dates unknown), learned music from a male Brahmin musician named Umayalpuram Kalyanarama Ayyar and began giving concerts at the age of thirteen. She also diversified her musical practice and by performing *kathākālakṣepam*. In 1935, Dhanalakshmi had the opportunity to act in the film *Parvati Parinayam* (The wedding of Pārvatī), produced by National Movietone. With the support of her aunt, young Rajayi moved to Madras permanently in 1938. She would later act with her aunt in a mythological film titled *Prabhavathi* (Effulgent lady; 1942) (figure 1.16). Dhanalakshmi arranged for Rajayi to break into the film world, and her first film was *Kumara Kulottungan* (Prince Kulōttuṅka; 1939), produced by Deccan Cinetone, in which she played the heroine opposite the actor C. D. Kannabiran. Rajakumari was also trained in music by Kunnakkudi Venkatarama Ayyar (dates unknown), a Brahmin musician who composed music for many early Tamil films from the late 1930s to the mid-1950s.[27] This unsuccessful film was followed by two other films by which time Rajayi had been renamed Rajakumari. She played the heroine in both of these films, *Mantiravāti* (The magician; 1941) and *Suryaputri* (Daughter of the sun; 1940), in which she acted alongside the stars K. R. Selvam, M. S. Sundaribai and Kothamangalam Subbu.

Rajakumari's rise to stardom has been attributed to her interface with the Indian director K. Subrahmanyam (Guy 1997, 255), even though she

Figure 1.16. An advertisement for the film Prabhavathi *(1942), which featured both S. P. L. Dhanalakshmi and her niece T. R. Rajakumari. Private collection of S. V. Jayababu.*

had already worked with the American director Ellis Dungan, who directed her earlier film *Suryaputri*. Subrahmanyam cast Rajakumari in his film *Kacha Devayani* (Kaca and Devayāni; 1941) which was inspired by the success of a Telugu film of the same name made in 1938 by B. V. Ramanandam.[28] Guy claims that "even though *Kacha Devayani* was her third film . . . it was released first. It was for this reason that K. Subramaniam [*sic*] claimed that it was he who first discovered Rajakumari" (1997, 255). This claim is difficult to verify, since most film magazines claim her earlier films were in fact released on time. Nevertheless, it is clear that *Kacha Devayani* became a major hit and earned much acclaim. Following its success , Rajakumari was chosen by Modern Theatres to be the heroine two films, *Sati Sukanya* (The chaste woman Sukanyā) and *Manonmani* (Jewel of the mind), both made in 1942.

Another huge turning point came the following year, when S. M. Sriramulu Naidu of Pakshiraja Films and Central Studios chose Rajakumari to star in *Sivakavi* (Śivakavi [a poet]; 1943), pairing her with the rising musician and film star M. K. Thyagaraja Bhagavathar. The film featured one of the early songs in Tamil cinema in praise of dance, *Kavalayai tīrppatu nāṭṭiyakalaiyē* (The art of dance removes all sorrows).[29] This film was also a major hit, and the pairing of Rajakumari with Thyagaraja Bhagavathar MKT was understood to be at the core of its commercial success.

The following year, the two were paired again in Sunder Rao Nadkarni's *Haridas* (Haridās [a poet]; 1944). In this film, Rajakumari plays the role of a *devadāsī* who attempts to seduce and dupe the pious hero, a plot similar to the early literary and dramatic texts discussed above in this chapter. Among the most well-known scenes in the film is the song "*Manmatalīlaiyin̲ ven̲r̲ār untō*" (Who can match you in the sports of the god of love?), in which Rajakumari dances to this very intimate erotic lyric that mirrors *padams* or *jāvaḷis* from the traditional courtesan dance repertoire. The song also features a sequence in which Rajakumari blows MKT a kiss (discussed in detail in chapter 5) along with other acts of intimacy that were considered somewhat scandalous at the time.[30] It is also significant that Rajakumari did not learn dance until she entered the cinema, and it appears that *Sivakavi* is the first film in which she performs dance. The sequences discussed here (and in *Haridas*) were choreographed by the *naṭṭuvan̲ār* Ramaiah Pillai (figure 1.17). As Guy notes, *Sivakavi* "created history, with its record 114-week run in one the-

Figure 1.17. Vazhuvoor Ramaiah Pillai choreographing on Rajakumari on the set of Sivakavi (1943). From Suresh Balakrishnan's Bagavather: His Life and Times *(2010).*

atre [Sun Theatre] in Madras, a record for regional language film which remains unequalled even after half a century" (1997, 256).

Rajakumari's next big success came four years later, in *Chandralekha* (1948), a major production of Gemini Studios (figure 1.18). The film took five years to complete and was made in both Tamil and Hindi.[31] *Chandralekha*'s fantasy dance sequences played a major part in the film's commercial success. One of the most memorable sequences features Rajakumari performing a kind of Oriental dance on top of giant drums lined up along the set. This piece was choreographed by a man named Jaya Sankar (about whom very little is known), and it cost 500,000 rupees to shoot (Dhananjayan 2014, 74). The Hindi version allowed Rajakumari to showcase her skill in that language (she sang her own songs and spoke her own lines).

Following *Chandralekha*, Rajakumari acted in a number of films: *Krishna Bhakthi* (Devotion to Kṛṣṇa; 1948), *Pavalakkodi* (Red coral; 1949), *Idhaya Geetham* (Song from the heart; 1950), *Vijayakumari* (Woman victor; 1950), *Vanasundari* (Forest beauty; 1951), *Amarakavi* (The immortal poet; 1952), *En Veedu* (My home; 1953), and *Pudhumai Pithan* (The new madman; 1957). In the mid-1950s, she and her brother, T. R. Ramachandran (better known as T. R. Ramanna) formed a production com-

Figure 1.18. The cover of Pēcum Paṭam *(*Cittirai Malar*, 1948) featuring Rajakumari in the Tamil version of* Chandralekha *(1948). Private collection of S. V. Jayababu.*

pany called R. R. Pictures.[32] The company produced a number of significant films in which Rajakumari acted, including *Gulebakavali* (The flower of Bakāvali; 1955), in which she was paired with the emerging superstar M. G. Ramachandran, and *Paasam* (Noose; 1962). In 1963, she had a minor role in her final film, *Vanambadi* (Nightingale; 1963), and there is little information about the rest of her life.

Almost nothing is known about Rajakumari's private life, either, and this is perhaps one of the largest archival gaps in the social history of film actresses in South India. It is certain, however, that—like her mother—she never married, and the two women lived together in a house Rajakumari she built in Madras in the early 1950s.[33] Around the same time, Rajakumari also built a movie theatre called Rajakumari Theatre, which provided a substantial income to her and her mother.

Yet the stardom that Rajakumari had achieved by the 1950s can be seen in a number of adoring features on her that were published in the late 1940s and early 1950s. The following is an excerpt from one such feature, titled "A Life Portrait of T. R. Rajakumari" and written by Sampath Kumar for *Pēcum Paṭam*:

> She is blessed with an attractive figure, great height and beautiful speech. Rajakumari and her mother believe in traditional customs and practices. Rajakumari is very religious. She has built a little temple in her bungalow. She is also a reserved person, keeping her conversation with others limited. To maintain her strength and figure, she regularly does physical exercises. She adores her family. She also has pet dogs, which she loves. She is fearless. She bravely has acted holding live snakes in her hands in her films like *Sukanya* [*Sati Sukanya*, 1943]. She is also an avid reader and is well versed in written and spoken Hindi. She lives in style and has employed [former soldiers from Nepal as guards] at her bungalow. (1951, 57)

T. Kuchalakumari

T. Kuchalakumari (b. 1937) is the granddaughter of Sarasvati, another of Kuchalambal's adopted children. Like her mother Kuchalambal, Sarasvati was trained as a court dancer for the Tanjore palace, where she served as an official concubine to the royal house. These concubines had the Marathi honorific title *bāī* ("respected lady") attached to their name and lived in purdah, a practice known locally as *kośa* (the term used by Kuchalambal's descendants). Not much is known about Sarasvati's life except that she had a *katti kalyāṇam* ("sword marriage," a ritual that marked a woman as a palace concubine) to one of the Marāṭhā nobles of the palace and became one of his concubines after he saw her perform at a festival at the Puṉṉainallūr Māriyammaṉ temple in Tanjore.[34]

Sarasvati's daughter was named Hamsa Damayanti, and she was also trained in dance in Tanjore. She moved to Madras five months after giving birth to Kuchalakumari, to seek opportunities in the emerging cinema industry following the success of her adoptive aunt, S. P. L. Dhanalakshmi. Damayanti's most popular role was in the mythological film *Bhookailas* (*Pūkailās allatu Maṇṭōtari Pariṇayam* [Heaven on earth, or the wedding of Maṇḍodarī; 1938]). She played the female lead, Maṇḍodarī, the wife of the demon Rāvaṇa from the epic narrative *Rāmāyaṇa*. She also played the lead in *Manimekalai* (*Maṇimēkalai* [a Tamil epic]; 1940) and acted in a number of other films, including *Parvathi Kalyanam* (The wedding of Pārvatī; 1942), *Gangavathar* (Descent of the river Gaṅgā;

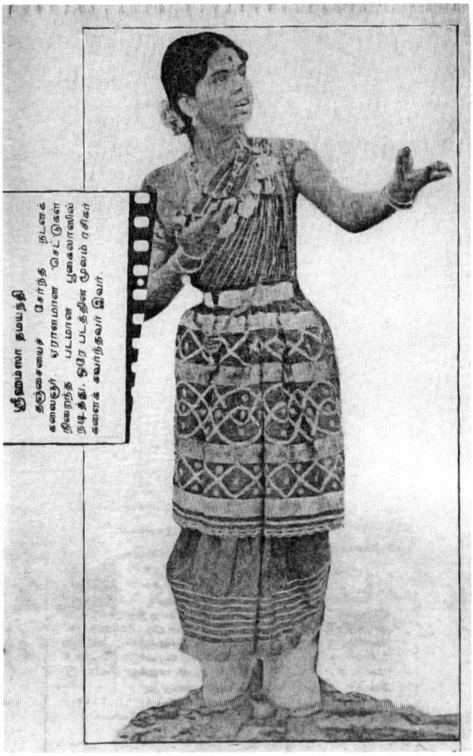

Figure 1.19. A very rare image of Hamsa Damayanti, the mother of Kuchalakumari, dressed to perform traditional devadāsī dance in Madras. Citrā *magazine (date unknown). Private collection of S. V. Jayababu.*

1942), and *Vikata Yogi* (The crooked yogi; 1946). A single dancing image exists of her, as a performer of *devadāsī* dance, likely before her cinema career (figure 1.19).

Damayanti had two children, Kuchalakumari and a son named Kamalasekhar. Kuchalakumari represents the final phase of possibilities of serious involvement in the cinema by women from *devadāsī* communities. Unlike her mother and one of her aunts (S. P. L. Dhanalakshmi), she entered the cinema in the late 1940s and early 1950s, a time when upper-caste women had already gained a strong foothold in Tamil cinema. Kuchalakumari never became a star, as her aunt Rajakumari did (she was called "South India's Dream Girl" [Guy 1997, 56]), nor did she successfully integrate herself into the mechanics of film production like Subbulakshmi or her own aunt Dhanalakshmi, who married the producer S. M. Letchumanan Chettiar (Lena Chettiar, founder of the production company called Krishna Pictures). Kuchalakumari's interface with the cinema was thus clearly more peripheral. She played mainly supporting

Figure 1.20. The author with Kuchalakumari, Chennai, December 17, 2012. Photograph by the author.

roles and often appeared in scenes involving dance. Another major difference between her and the previous generation of *devadāsī* performers is that all of her training in dance came from postreinvention Madras. That is, she was trained in dance not within the *devadāsī* community (by her mother or grandmother, for example) but by the new urban pedagogy of Bharatanāṭyam that was aimed specifically at middle-class, upper-caste, non-*devadāsī* female performers. She was trained by Ramaiah Pillai (discussed in greater detail in chapters 3 and 4), a *naṭṭuvaṉār* who had reinvented the aesthetics of Bharatanāṭyam performance in a radical manner.

In December 2012, I was fortunate to be able to interview Kuchalakumari about her early life, film career, and her thoughts on the relationship between Bharatanāṭyam as it is performed on stage and in the cinema (figure 1.20).[35] I have chosen to present her life narrative largely in her own words, rather than search for information about it in archival sources. Kuchalakumari's bold and honest statements about her family and professional life provide a rare subjective account by a member of this generation of the *devadāsī* community. I begin with some of her thoughts on her ancestry and the community in general:

> We are all born and raised in Tanjore. I was named after our family deity, the goddess Kucalāmpāḷ, and this was also the name of my great-grandmother.[36] Two of her daughters were trained as professional dancers, and she ensured that they danced at the Bṛhadīśvara temple in Tanjore. Her other daughters were vocalists and *kathākālakṣepam* artists, and her sons were musicians, drummers, and players of the *vīṇā* [a stringed instrument]. Once, when my grandmother Sarasvati was performing at the Puṉṉainallūr Māriyammaṉ temple, a Marāṭhā nobleman saw her and fell in love with her, and at that point kept her in the palace in seclusion (*kośa*). Even if she would come to visit us at the family home, she would come on a palanquin in seclusion. She also never danced after she married this nobleman. My mother did not live in the palace, but she would visit. Our house in Tanjore was large, with lots of relatives living together in a "joint family" structure. Some of my grandmother's siblings were professionals. One of her brothers was a subregistrar [the chief official of one of Tanjore district's subdivisions], and another taught music to people like M. K. Thyagaraja Bhagavathar, and he was also a [district] collector. We owned houses in Tanjore district. . . . [By the time I was born], one of our family homes in Tanjore was given to the bank, another house near the Bṛhadīśvara temple was sold off, and hence there was only house left. Then many of my relatives died, and most of the male family members got married and settled down.
>
> I was born in 1937 in Tanjore. I remember my grandmother well. My mother relocated to Chennai because of her involvement with cinema. When she came to Madras, a producer saw her and offered her opportunities to act. I was a five-month-old child when I came to Madras with my mother, and my grandmother had died by then. My mother's aunt was S. P. L. Dhanalakshmi, who was a great singer and was also involved in films. My mother and my aunt learned Karṇāṭak vocal music in Madras from Kunrakkudi Vaidyanatha Iyer [1935–2008], and their *araṅkēṟṟam* was held in Vadapalani [a suburb of Madras]. They gave music concerts together, and I was inspired by their music and would dance to it as a very young

child. They also both began their film careers at Pragathi Studios in Madras near Greenways Road.[37]

Kuchalakumari discussed the idea of dance in the cinema and on the stages of Madras in the middle of the twentieth century. She often gave stage performances, and she spoke with great enthusiasm about her training:

> My mother's cousin was T. R. Rajakumari. . . Rajakumari was not a formally trained dancer. She worked with the young Vazhuvoor Ramaiah Pillai, who was just coming up as a dance choreographer in the film industry. [In the family] only I trained formally as a classical Bharatanāṭyam dancer. My cousins were Jyothilakshmi and Jayamalini, who were the adopted daughters of S. P. L. Dhanalakshmi, and it was only after I began dancing that they began training in dance. My interest in dance began at a very young age. I use to play [gramophone] records and improvise some kind of dance. At that time, my audiences were our house cook and servants! I would invite them to watch me dance. Along with film dance, I also performed extensively on stage. . . . I often danced a full suite of Bharatanāṭyam—*alārippu, jatisvaram, śabdam, varṇam, naṭaṉam āṭiṉār, tillāṉā* and the snake dance (*nātar muṭimēl irukkum*)—all items that my dance master Vazhuvoor Ramaiah Pillai taught me. I began learning from Ramaiah Pillai when I was six years old. He would come to my house every day to teach me. I also learned from one Chellappa [Chokkalingam?] Nattuvanar of Pandanallur. They were good friends. Later I trained with [Pillai's student] M. S. Ramaswami Pillai of Mayavaram.

She was conscious of the similarities and differences between her performances on stage in Madras and her representations of Bharatanāṭyam in the cinema. She described the rigor and professionalism with which she would approach stage performances of Bharatanāṭyam:

> There *is* a difference between between Bharatanāṭyam on stage and in the cinema. On stage, one has to be very careful because it's live. If you make any mistakes, the audience will know it. All your movements have to perfect, and only then can the audience appreciate your dancing. On stage, the applause and admiration of the audience are very encouraging for the artist. This is has always

been a great source of encouragement for me. No matter how many films I have done, I've always enjoyed stage performances more, and I've danced live within Tamil Nadu, Andhra, and Karnataka. I've even performed [Bharatanāṭyam at] village shows, large public halls (*sabhas*), charity shows, government-sponsored shows, and marriage shows (*kalyāṇakkaccērikaḷ*).

We would always take our "music party" [orchestra] with us. Our shows were billed as "Kuchalakumari and Party." We also brought other dancers with us, because if there was only a solo dancer, we felt the audience would get bored. So, for example, in a stage performance of [the long repertory piece called] *varṇam,* I would dance first, and then two other girls would dance for a while, and then I'd come back on stage again. During a three-hour stage performance, we would dance about fourteen pieces! Ramaiah Pillai would always perform *naṭṭuvāṅkam* [recite the vocalized rhythms and play the cymbals to keep the rhythm] for us. His assistants Ramaswami, P. S. Gopalakrishnan, K. J. Sarasa, and Radhakrishnan were the ones directing our rehearsals, giving us corrections. They would also give private classes. The actress Sukumari [cousin of the actress Padmini Ramachandran] used to dance in my troupe. We used to do "dance ballets" [dance dramas in the new idiom made popular by Arundale], too. After 1972, I used to do shows in which my dancing was accompanied by *nāgasvaram* ["sound of serpents"; an instrument like an oboe with a double reed] music. I was the first one to do this! I was actually inspired by the film *Thillana Mohanambal* [1968; about the love between a *devadāsī* and a *nāgasvaram* musician] to do this.

By contrast, Kuchalakumari's thoughts on dancing in films shows her awareness of the complexities of camera technique, choreography, and space. Indeed, she was the only dancer with whom I conducted ethnographic work who commented on these themes:

In films, it's as if we are dancing for the camera. That is, the dance is specifically tailor-made for close-ups and long shots, so the visual focus is not on the whole body but rather on isolated parts of the face, feet, and torso. There are many takes for each sequence, and this can get really grueling! Although many of the dance movements could be the same whether it's on stage or in the films, we have to remember that there is a larger narrative in the films in which the dance is nested. So for example, in addition to the choreography of the body, there is also sometimes a subtle interface that the dancer makes with other members of the cast while she is dancing. This interaction between the dancer and others adds another layer of complexity to dancing in films.

Kuchalakumari narrates her life history almost exclusively with reference to dance. It becomes clear that her engagements with film dance are significant signposts not only in her career, but also in terms of her aesthetic enjoyment of dance:

> A producer named Somasundaram from Jupiter Pictures saw me and invited me to act and dance in the films when I was six years old. He said there was a film in which he felt I could play a small role. This was a role as the daughter of P. U. Chinnappa and Kannambal. The tile of this film was *Mahamaya* [Great illusion] made in 1943. This was my first film.... The first film in which I performed a dance was *Krishna Bhakthi* [Devotion to Kṛṣṇa], with Ramaiah Pillai's choreography. At that time, he was the dance master in several films for Krishna Pictures. K. N. Dandayudhapani Pillai [1921–74] came onto [the] scene a little later. In the film *Manamagal,* there is a famous song, "*Nalla peṇmaṇi*" (She is a jewel among women) that I am very proud of.[38] The choreography is by K. N. Dandayudhapani Pillai. N. S. Krishnan [the director and producer of the film] loved my dancing and was eager to have me dance in the film. The lyrics of that song are packed with so many good moral messages about how a married woman should act and how she should behave. Even today, this song is played at many weddings.... This continues to be my favorite cinema dance sequence! Jayalalitha Jayaram [1948–2016; a famous actress and former chief minister of Tamilnadu] used to tell me that it was because of this song that she fell in love with dance and was inspired to learn Bharatanāṭyam! I also loved performing the romantic *padam*-like song, "*Āḷayiṉ caṅkē nī ūtāyō*" (Sound the conch shell of humanity) in the movie *Ratha Kanneer* [Tears of blood; 1954].
>
> One of my hit dance songs is the dance competition sequence from *Konjum Salangai* [A little jingle of the dancing bells; 1962] with Kamala Lakshman. My character's name was Kāmavalli. This

was such a lavish, expensive song sequence, which took months to film. It was in full technicolor, and there were so many lights on the film set. Sometimes the lightbulbs would break because of the high intensity, and we would have to shoot the scene again. The combination of the severe hot lights and makeup actually damaged my skin! Kamala was my senior and I admired her a lot. . . . We both learned dance from Vazhuvoor Ramaiah Pillai. . . . I have worked with so many film dance masters—Ramaiah Pillai, K. N. Dandayudhapani Pillai, Vempati Pedda Satyam, Vempati Chinna Satyam, Sohan Lal, and Hira Lal.

Like her aunt Rajakumari and so many women from the *devadāsī* community who entered the cinema, Kuchalakumari never married. She evinced a deep understanding of the *devadāsī* aspect of her own identity and unabashedly and proudly reminisced about this:

I feel the films have not represented my *devadāsī paramparai* [heritage] well at all. I feel sad about that. You must understand that for us dancers, the *devadāsī paramparai* means *tēvaraṭiyāḷ* [those who are slaves of god]. The art we perform is divine. We tie the *poṭṭu*. I personally have not had it tied, but my mother and aunts have all tied the *poṭṭu* at the Bṛhadīśvara temple [in Thanjavur]. They were all considered *nityasumaṅgalī* [ever auspicious]. The *poṭṭu* pendant was first tied to a *katti* [dagger] and then tied upon them. This *katti kalyāṇam* ritual consecrated them as part of the *devadāsī paramparai*. The government unfortunately brought a law that prohibited this, and we lost our respect then. . . . The initial we all take before our given names is "T," which means Thanjavur, and this is used by all the ladies in our families [married women take their husband's first initial, but this is not the case in *devadāsī* communities]. Educated people would know the difference between us and others. Only ignorant, uncultured people would say bad things about our communities. This is so wrong, you know! How dare they speak ill of us without the right knowledge and understanding of who we are! Wrong is wrong! There are all kinds of *devadāsīs*, from Tamilnadu to Andhra to Karnataka. There were also such women in the north. After the legislation, women from my generation used to get married off to men from our own community. But women still faced stigma. I remember [the actress and niece of the *naṭṭuvaṉār*

> K. N. Dandayudhapani Pillai] Sripriya's mother, Girija, who is also from our community, used to scold people who spoke ill of our community. She would say, "How dare they criticize us?" . . . I am a very audacious person. I did not get married intentionally because I solely focused on my profession. My work ethic means everything to me. I used to work so hard! So much stage dance and film work. Lots of sweat!

S. P. L. Dhanalakshmi and Her Adopted Daughters Jayamalini and Jyothilakshmi

In an attempt to map some of the complexities of the realities of *devadāsī* women in the cinema, I conclude this chapter with the generation of women in this family who immediately followed Kuchalakumari. She had left the cinema world by the mid-1960s, while the women I discuss here, T. Jyothilakshmi (1948–2016) and T. Jayamalini (b. 1958), made their way into the cinema in the 1970s and 1980s, a time when hardly any women from the *devadāsī* community were visibly involved in the cinema. Perhaps as a result of the repopulation of the cinema by upper-caste women, Jyothilakshmi and Jayamalini made their careers not as lead actresses, like the women in their family who preceded them, but worked on the fringes of South Indian cinema, largely typecast as what are known as "item dancers" in today's Bollywood jargon (figures 1.21a and 1.21b). They represent, as one writer put it in a recent obituary for Jyothilakshmi, the "subalterns of the [South Indian] film world" (Chakravarthy 2016), and though they had somewhat active careers in the echelons of what came to be known as Tamil and Telugu B films, even in those contexts, they could hardly be considered feted women actors. Both Jyothilakshmi and Jayamalini were adopted by Dhanalakshmi, who was herself one of the sixteen adopted children of Kuchalambal. Dhanalakshmi married the wealthy film producer Lena Chettiar and had stopped acting in the cinema by the 1950s. It is unclear exactly how or when Jyothilakshmi and Jayamalini were adopted by Dhanalakshmi, but we know that they were born in Sullurpeta, near the town of Nellore, in the Telugu-speaking region around Madras. Through interventions made by Dhanalakshmi, Rajakumari, and apparently also Kuchalakumari, both Jyothilakshmi and Jayamalini were trained in Bharatanāṭyam, first by Vazhuvoor Ramaiah Pillai and then by one of his students, S. K. Kameswaran (1929–2007) (figure 1.22).[39]

Figure 1.21 a, b. Jyothilakshmi (left) and Jayamalini (right) in "item dances" from Telugu films from the 1970s. Private collection of S. V. Jayababu.

Figure 1.22. Jayamalini (third from left) with S. K. Kameswaran, following one of her Bharatanāṭyam performances in Madras, c. 1975. Private collection of S. V. Jayababu.

Figure 1.23. Jyothilakshmi and Jayamalini perform on the set of a Telugu film in the 1970s. Private collection of S. V. Jayababu.

Very occasionally, but significantly, the kinds of dances performed by actresses like Jyothilakshmi and Jayamalini—known as "record dances" or "cabaret dances"—were brought into dialogue with the choreographic syntax and visual cultures of Bharatanāṭyam. In figure 1.23, for example, from an unidentified Telugu film, Jyothilakshmi and Jayamalini are dressed in versions of the reinvented Bharatanāṭyam costume and are posing holding the gesture known as *alapadma* ("lotus").

Traces of Bharatanāṭyam thus come to occupy even the landscape of the the highly sexualized and distinctly male spectatorial spaces of these film sequences. From the standpoint of most elites who perform classical Bharatanāṭyam on the stages of Chennai and beyond, these dances—and, by extension, performers like Jyothilakshmi and Jayamalini—represent for the degeneration of Bharatanāṭyam through the cinema and are understood as a kind of blemish on a sacred tradition. These notions, scripted in tandem with the moral registers of the dance revival, extend these registers into the realm of cinema. They also serve to reinforce caste-based hierarchies that once again, as during the reinvention of the 1930s, push *devadāsī* performers to the farthest edges of cultural production and labor in the contemporary world.

[2]

THE OCULAR POLITICS OF MAKING MODERN BHARATANĀṬYAM

I had to try to make something new—not with the idea of making it look new, but with the idea of making it look old.
RUKMINI ARUNDALE "My Experiments with Dance"

The parallel and symbiotic evolution of the South Indian cinema and the reinvented, urban practice of Bharatanāṭyam dance that began to circulate among the middle class in the late 1930s owes much to ocular acts of making meaning. This chapter maps the trajectories of the major actors of the reinvention—figures like Rukmini Arundale and E. Krishna Iyer—noting their complex and deeply imbricated relationships with the Tamil cinema. The chapter also includes an analysis of the extant traces of the first film in India about dance, *Jalaja* (1938), in which the *devadāsī* artist Kumbhakonam Bhanumathi played the lead character. The chapter ends with reflections on how cinema dance allows us to map shifting notions of the morality of Bharatanāṭyam dance, and how a focus on the cross-pollination of cinematic and stage versions of Bharatanāṭyam radically transforms standard narratives about dance in this period. I contend that the production and consumption of these cultural forms involved the same actors and were directed toward the same audiences. Just as dance moved into the realm of respectability when it was no longer associated with the *devadāsī*-courtesan community and its social and moral world, so in the late 1930s, the initial elite disapproval of the cinema began to disappear as the cinema world was repopulated by "respectable" individuals. As M. S. S. Pandian puts it, the Tamil elite "realised, within years of the arrival of the talkie that [the] cinephobic mode of engagement with the cinema was inadequate" (1996, 952). Thus by the 1930s, we see the metamorphosis of cinema into a respectable medium appropriated by the middle class.

In attempting to inject a historical consciousness of the cinema into a critical study of the reinvention of Bharatanāṭyam, I take seriously Gilles Deleuze's insistence that we view cinema not as a language but as "signaletic material (*matière signalétique*)" (1989, 29). From a Deleuzian standpoint, cinema's affective and political power resides in this matrix, which includes features that are "sensory (visual and sound), kinetic, intensive, affective, rhythmic, tonal and even verbal" (ibid.). In our case, the "signaletic materials" of Bharatanāṭyam's stage and cinematic versions are inextricably intertwined. In this chapter, I unpack the ways in which visual, sonic, social, and discursive practices mark a way of knowing the new Bharatanāṭyam in the 1930s and 1940s. Indeed, as we will see toward the end of this chapter, the shared histories of the urban, reinvented Bharatanāṭyam and the early Tamil cinema point to the social and affective powers of interocularity in the nation's new cultural imaginary.

RUKMINI ARUNDALE, THEOSOPHICAL OCCULTISM, AND THE SPIRIT OF BHARATANĀṬYAM'S PAST

The reinvention of Bharatanāṭyam in the 1930s by elites in Madras is a now a thoroughly grounded and well-established signpost of critical histories of the dance. Dance scholars and ethnomusicologists such as Avanthi Meduri (1996), Matthew Allen (1997), and Janet O'Shea (2007), as well as anthropologists and social historians such as Amrit Srinivasan (1984) and Davesh Soneji (2010a and 2012), have contributed to our understanding of this very significant period in the dance's history. I do not wish to rehearse this history here. However, below I will briefly summarize the work of Rukmini Arundale from a critical standpoint in order to contextualize some of my own arguments about this period that follow.

Arundale was born in Madurai to *smārta* Brahmin parents, Neelakanta Sastri and Seshammal. After retiring from the Madras Public Works Department, where he had worked as an engineer, Arundale's father bought a home in Adyar, a suburb of Madras where the Theosophical Society had established its international headquarters in 1883 under the guidance of the Russian spiritualist Helena Petrovna Blavatsky (1831–91) and the American Henry Steel Olcott (1832–1907). It is important to remember that religion is a hybrid phenomenon in Theosophy, which is a form of Orientalist occultism that synthesized elements of Christian gnostic mysticism and Neoplatonism with secret languages, levels of initiation, and elements of upper-caste philosophical Vedantic Hinduism and Indo-Tibetan and Sinhalese Buddhism.[1] Urban Tamil- and Telugu-speaking Brahmins in Madras, such as Arundale's father, were drawn to the unique blend of old and new spirituality in Theosophy, as well as its clearly visible role as a hub for an emerging internationalism and cosmopolitanism in Madras. At the age of sixteen, Rukmini was married to George Sydney Arundale (1878–1945), the third president of the Theosophical Society. In 1928, at the age of twenty-four, Rukmini was appointed to the messianic role of "World Mother" by Annie Besant (1847–1933), the leader of the Theosophical Society and President of the Indian National Congress. Aundale became a kind of visionary heir to the society, and also had the honorific title Devi ("goddess") permanently bestowed upon her. In their capacity as figureheads of the Theosophical Society, Rukmini and George Arundale traveled around the world, and it was in this capacity that Rukmini was exposed to the emerging, fashionable Euro-American Oriental dance and also to Russian ballet, through the figure of prima ballerina Anna Pavlova (1881–1931), who befriended the couple. Rukmini Arundale took lessons in ballet from Cleo Nordi (1899–1983), who danced with Pavlova, and also later performed experiments with Oriental dance—including choreographing a play produced by the Theosophical Society called *The Light of Asia* (based on Edwin Arnold's book of the same name about the life of Gautama Buddha) in 1934.

In 1933, Arundale was invited by Krishna Iyer to witness a dance performance by two women from the *devadāsī* community that was sponsored by the Madras Music Academy, an elite institution founded in conjunction with the Indian National Congress. The two dancers whom Arundale saw perform there were Tiruvalapputtur Rajalakshmi (1900–69) and Jeevaratnam (1905–33), daughters of the very famous dancer Tiruvalapputtur Kalyani (1873–1958) and students of Pandanallur Meenakshisundaram Pillai (1869–1954), a descendant of the famous Tanjore Quartet dance masters of the nineteenth century (figure 2.1). For over a year after that performance, Arundale looked for dance masters to teacher her, and she eventually settled on Pillai himself—who after nearly a year was convinced to accept her as his student. In 1935, after six

Figure 2.1. Tiruvalapputtur Rajalakshmi and Jeevaratnam (both in the center), with Tiruvalapputtur Pakkirisvami, a clarinet player (far left), and the dance master Tiruvalapputtur Svaminatha Nattuvanar (far right). This photo was taken following their performance at the Madras Music Academy in January 1933. Photograph from the collection of B. M. Sundaram.

months of training, she decided to give her first public performance as part of the diamond jubilee celebrations of the Theosophical Society. Her teacher was not convinced that she was ready to perform on stage and refused to oversee the performance, sending his son-in-law in his place.

This performance was somewhat controversial, for no Brahmin woman in recent memory had performed the dance of the *devadāsīs*, yet it also held out tremendous possibilities for cultural elites and cultural nationalists, who saw in the dance a possible new heritage symbol. However, this performance was a highly altered version of the dance—from both visual and epistemic perspectives—as we shall see below. Arundale had radically revised the presentation and content of the dance, and she had made this conscious intervention because "some of the dances were quite vulgar and so I wanted to avoid such things" (quoted in Ramani 2003, 61). This new dance was aimed at an audience that included both the upper-caste intelligentsia of Madras and the conglomerate international bourgeoisie represented by the Theosophists.[2] While the colonial modernity represented by many *devadāsī* dance practices in the early twentieth century was eschewed by Arundale, her position within the colonial-hybrid matrix of the Theosophical Society and its links to elite Indian nationalism (particularly via the figures of Annie Besant and George Arundale) cannot be ignored. It is from within this matrix of power that Arundale's taste (that is, her aesthetic reforms of *devadāsī* dance) was able to command nationwide authority and legitimacy by the 1940s. In 1936, Arundale established the International Academy for the Arts, with the institutional support of the Theosophical Society—which was renamed Kalakshetra ("temple of the arts") by the Sanskritist P. S. Subrahmanya Sastri (1890–1978) in 1938.

OPTICS, ILLUSION, AND ALLEGORY

As we saw in the epigraph at the beginning of this chapter, the visuality of the dance practice of Bharatanāṭyam—the way it looks—was at the very heart of its reinvention. Embedded in the realm of the visual were all of the moral, historical, and aesthetic valences that cultural elites wanted scripted into the form in its new middle-class, Brahminic avatar. The most significant transformations ushered in by the new practitioners of Bharatanāṭyam, most significantly Arundale herself, thus involved radical interventions in the optics of the form. Most performances of Bharatanāṭyam in the late nineteenth and early twentieth centuries took place either in private salon settings or wedding celebrations or in public spaces such as the pavilions of temples during Hindu festivals. Additionally, as Soneji (2012) has noted, markers of colonial modernity had come to characterize these performance practices, and the use of Western instruments (such as the clarinet and violin) to accompany the dance, as well as the use of the English language, northern Indian (Hindustāni) music and culturally hybrid forms of attire, had become systemically woven into the dance (figure 2.2). Indeed, Western dress and Western musical forms (such as the *noṭṭusvaram* inspired by a Western marching and drinking tune and discussed by Soneji [2012, 184–87]) had become integral elements of the complex matrix of dance, music, and drama that women from *devadāsī* communities were involved in as professional artists at the time. It was precisely these aspects of *devadāsī* engagement with the hybrid modern that urban, nationalist revivalists took issue with in the 1930s and 1940s. For individuals such as Arundale, these fea-

Figure 2.2. "Rangapushpa" Chitra, a famous performer from the kalāvantula-courtesan community, danced in the court of the nizam of Hyderabad in the very early twentieth century. Here she is seen wearing tights and slippers and dancing with a tambourine, likely to a Hindustāni tune. Collection of Davesh Soneji.

tures were at odds with the reclamation and resignification of the pure, precolonial glory of India: "It must be understood that the present solo recital of Bharata Natya used to be called Sadir Kacheri which had its own associations because of which I preferred to call my recitals Bharata Natya recitals.... I have known these [Sadir Kacheri] recitals with Hindustani songs & even English notes. The Hindustani songs were always of a cheap variety" (Arundale n.d.b, 13).[3]

Indeed, for Arundale, *devadāsī* performance represented a kind of foil to her own ideas about the classical. The hybrid performance styles of *devadāsīs* were not only seen as degenerate forms of an imagined classical past, but they were also clearly classified as lowbrow forms of art that sharply contrasted with Arundale's project of creating a classical cultural vocabulary for the nation. Implicit in these class-based discourses about cultural production (seen in the use of terms like "cheap" in the quote above) were ideological moves that discredited the livelihood and aesthetic sensibilities of traditional performers. They clearly reveal that the reinvention was not about democratizing the arts; it instead created what Anna Morcom has termed "cultures of exclusion" (2013) in Indian dance.

Arundale's position within the ultracosmopolitan Theosophical Society, with its deep Orientalism, shaped a series of taste habits and aesthetic sensibilities that have become commonsensical in the production and consumption of today's Bharatanāṭyam. Perhaps most importantly, these shifts signify broader concerns about the nature, form, and purpose of Bharatanāṭyam, which in its new configuration has what Arundale, in the shadow of Theosophy, calls an "essence" or "spirit." In an undated lecture delivered at Kalakshetra, Arundale expresses the essentially "spiritual" nature of her Bharatanāṭyam by contrasting its hermetic "purity" with the profane, secular world: "From time to time people have invented new gestures to express new ideas. However, I hope that new gestures will not be made to represent this present material world of money, motorcars, horns, jazz. If you depart from the purely imaginative, the mystical, the religious, you depart from the very spirit of Indian dance" (Arundale, n.d.a, 26).

In the sections that follow, I trace Arundale's enunciation of the religious essence of Bharatanāṭyam through the radicalization of the visuals of dance. That is, I argue that the three major ocular interventions of temple stage, dress, and narrativization are the sites where the transformation of the dance took place, and where Arundale located the perceived antiquity and religiosity of the dance. However, it is also in these transformations that we are able to clearly see the interdependence of the new dance and its representation and staging in the cinema. In each of the three sites, Bharatanāṭyam is simultaneously scripted as an ancient, spiritual, and national dance, both on stage and on screen.

Allegory: The Temple Stage

In a fascinating essay titled "Temple Stage as Historical Allegory in Bharatanāṭyam," Avanthi Meduri draws our attention to the fact that Arundale's interventions constituted "a modern visual and spectatorial epistemology for classical Bharatanāṭyam in the world at large" (2008, 156):

> Rukmini Devi mounted the icon of Shiva/Nataraja, the presiding deity of the *Natyashastra*, on a pedestal and placed him on one corner of the Western proscenium. She seated her guru and his musical ensemble along the wings . . . and designed a temple-stage using temple backdrops and front curtains, with traditional imagery from the [Hindu] temple. She then lit what I describe as her temple-stage constellation, comprising the three historical symbols of god, guru, and temple, with an electrical moving spotlight imported from British stagecraft. By staging Bharatanāṭyam allegorically, with the help of historical symbols from history and antiquity, and dancing reflexively within this symbolic worldview, Rukmini Devi emerged as the first urban dancer allegorist and dancer-historian of Bharatanāṭyam. Urban dancers, trained both within Kalakshetra and outside in the broader mainstream practice, used Rukmini Devi's temple-stage setting to visualize their Bharatanāṭyam recitals. (ibid., 134)

I take seriously Meduri's claim that the god (Śiva-Naṭarāja), the guru, and the temple served as epistemic framing devices for Arundale's new dance, and that these are enduring, even authoritative, features of the contemporary practice of the dance.[4] I would argue, however, that the sedimentation of these iconic emblems in the popular practice of Bharatanāṭyam can be almost exclusively attributed to the dance's dialogue with early South Indian cinema. The role of the icon of Śiva-Naṭarāja is discussed below. Here I would like to briefly mention the temple backdrop and other optics of illusion (such as dress and narrativization) that were central to Arundale's restaging of Bharatanāṭyam.

The question of the significance of understandings of the Hindu temple under colonialism cannot be divorced from Orientalist fascinations with the temple as an iconic index of Hindu morality. While early pre-British forms of colonialism dwelled on the exotic and heathen aspects of Hindu temples, by the time of the mature phase of British Orientalism in the nineteenth century, the Madras School of Orientalism in particular was highlighting the historical, cultural, aesthetic, and civilizational significance of temples (Trautmann 2009). From a literary standpoint, we have texts like the 1836 *Hindoo Temples and Palaces at Madura*, by the poet and novelist Letitia Elizabeth Landon (1802–8), which focuses on the Hindu temple as a site of both romantic beauty and

Figure 2.3. "The Bayadères, or Dancing Girls of India" by N. Whittich (1838). A drawing of the performance by the troupe from Thiruvahindrapuram at the Adelphi in London in 1838. The temple backdrop is clearly visible in this drawing. From Bor (2007, 64).

cultural excess (Fernandez 2005). However, the idea of the Hindu temple as a backdrop was certainly not an invention of Arundale's. Forms of Indian dance had been staged against temple backdrops for European and Euro-American audiences for a hundred years before Arundale did so in 1937. In 1838, a troupe of five *devadāsī* dancers and three musicians was taken from the town of Thiruvahindrapuram in South India to Europe by the French impresario E. C. Tardivel. As Joep Bor has demonstrated, when they performed at the Adelphi Theatre in London, for example, they were inserted into prefabricated narratives such as *The Robing of Vishnu* or *The Hindoo Widow* that reinforced European audiences' received narratives about women, religion, and morality in India in the nineteenth century: "The Indian dancers showed up in the second piece, a one-act burletta called *The Law of Brahma* or *The Hindoo Widow*. . . . They were drawn to the front of the stage 'upon a moving platform.' Sitting with flywhisks in their hands 'around a statue of Vishnu, in the interior of a temple, they [were] performing the important duty of fanning the image'" (2007, 62). These dancers inevitably performed against backdrops that vaguely resembled European cathedrals or Oriental pagodas (figure 2.3). It is a matter of speculation as to whether the Thiruvahindrapuram *devadāsīs* would even have known that their dances (which were

*Figure 2.4. "Ruth St. Denis with native Hindus in Radha" (1908). New York Public Library for the Performing Arts, *MGZEB (Denishawn, no. 60).*

from the courtly repertoire of the Tanjore region) were being framed by Orientalist metanarratives such as that of suttee.[5] Of course, this staging of real *devadāsīs* in 1830s Europe is based on over three centuries of theatrical representation of Indian temple dancers in a host of German, Italian, French, and Russian plays, operas, and ballets.[6]

Aside from these early representations, the temple stage as backdrop for Indian (or at least Indian-inspired) dance surfaces in the Oriental dances of Euro-American dancers such as Ruth St. Denis (1879–1968), La Meri (1898–1988; born Russell Meriwether Hughes), and Ragini Devi (1897–1982; born Esther Luella Sherman). As early as 1908, the American dancer Ruth St. Denis was staging her versions of Oriental dance, inspired by Indian ideas and aesthetics against backdrops meant to resemble Hindu temples, and with "native Hindus" playing the roles of musicians and temple priests (figure 2.4).

Arundale's temple backdrops thus are part of a long chronology of optic fascination with Hindu temples and the visual imbrications of temples and the history of dance in India. According to Meduri, Arundale's temple backdrop was first staged at her public recital at the Madras Museum theatre in 1937. Alex Elmore, a theosophist in Madras and a close associate of Arundale, wrote a review of that performance in a magazine called the *Young Theosophist,* in which he commented: "The stage was set to suggest a South Indian temple with four large granite pillars and a temple tower in the background. Into this setting came Rukmini Devi in an exquisite red and gold costume with jewels and a beautiful gold and jeweled belt which gave her the appearance of an ancient bronze statue come to life and color. This effect was never lost and in fact gained when she danced.... One was made happy and taken into a world where happiness and divinity were in the very air one breathed" (quoted in Meduri 2008, 143).

Arundale wrote about how she perceived the role of temples in the history of Bharatanāṭyam. She understood Bharatanāṭyam as fundamentally a sacred or temple dance, which justified many of her interventions. For her, the end of dancing in temples due to antinautch legislation representsed a cultural loss, and she hoped that one day the dance would be brought back to its perceived roots as a ritual dance form:

> At that time Bharata Natyam was called Sadir and there were many bad associations connected with that Sadir. It had acquired a very bad reputation because of the lives of the dancers themselves who were not all they should have been. But I felt there was something marvelous in the art which should not be lost. At that time, in fact, there was a campaign to discontinue the dance in the temples. The result was that it was prohibited in the temples and this situation continues even now. I hope a time will come when the dance will find a home in the temple again, at least as far as the Upacharas—the religious aspects—are concerned. (1958a, 60)

Implicit in Arundale's restaging of the dance against a temple backdrop is the idea of cultural retrieval. For Arundale, the temple signifies a lost golden age for Bharatanāṭyam.

> *Sringara* or love can be portrayed in its most beautiful aspect, as I am sure, for example, was meant by the great [poet] Kshetragna whose songs are among the most beautiful ever composed for the dance. At the same time *sringara* can become coarse and vulgar. India's gift [to the world] is spirituality and when some dancers forsook the idea of dancing to the Deity in the temple and began to dance to the ruler or patron, then the dance became personal and

gradually deteriorated to such an extent that it came to be considered a degrading thing to see or learn. (1948, 20–21)

Her narrative resists the courtly origins of Bharatanāṭyam, the very-form she had learned from Pillai. Instead, she felt that the form had its origins in temples and that it was *devadāsī* performers who denigrated the form by making it into an erotic, courtly practice in praise of "the ruler or patron." For Arundale, the socioeconomic reality of cultural production and patronage—indeed, even the survival of the dance—was replaced by idealized, transcendent notions of a timeless classicism. As we will see later, the class-based implications of this notion of classicism loom large in the decades that follow the reinvention in the 1930s.

Dressing the Part

In Arundale's writings, costumes turn out to be a major concern. The costume is an index of a wider and deeper concern about the dance's moral and aesthetic status. Indeed, Arundale sometimes found it difficult to separate morality from aesthetics. In several instances, she makes a point of stating that the redesigning of the clothes worn for the performance of contemporary Bharatanāṭyam was one of her key contributions. She thinks of the saris and accoutrements worn by *devadāsīs* as having "no aesthetic sense," and hence she reformed the visual landscape of the dance through alterations:

> There was no aesthetic sense evident anywhere outside the actual dance. The jewelry was very beautiful, but the kinds of costumes that were used—the saris for example—were very cheap tinsely stuff that did not match the dance and were, according to me, too showy. The *pyjamas* [leggings] that were worn, the Victorian style of *cholis* [bodices]—they all seemed to me to be a mixture of many different civilizations. All these I felt required thought, and after thought, appropriate change. I had to try to make something new—not with the idea of making it look new, but with the idea of making it look old. In other words, create costumes that were in the spirit of what our people wore thousands of years ago. This was not very easy. It was not easy to get help from the sculptures because they are clothed only below the waist! Therefore we had to think creatively in order to catch the old spirit. Gradually I evolved my

Figure 2.5. Rukmini Arundale with the seamstress "Madame Cazan," c. 1939. Image from the Theosophical Society Archives, Chennai (Ramani 2003, 49).

> costume, and those used in Kalakshetra are based on my original design. (1958a, 62)

As we saw with the temple backdrop, a key concern is the concept of Indian purity. The hybrid costume that reflects the accretions of cultural encounters in South India is unsuitable for a classicism that is meant to represent the spirit of India's people. Somewhat ironically, the costume that would come to represent this spirit was designed by Mary Elmore and a woman referred to as "Madame Cazan," both European, and executed through distinctly colonial technologies of tailoring (figure 2.5). The result was the now well-known Bharatanāṭyam costume inspired by temple sculpture (figures 2.6a and 2.6b), which has become the standard representation in nearly all performances of Bharatanāṭyam today. Arundale wrote: "Generally, no attention was paid to stage presentation. . . . I wanted to change all that. . . . I designed my own costumes. Madame Cazan who was good at tailoring and Mary Elmore helped me to put my ideas into proper shape. Conrad Woldringh, a remarkable young musician, who was a wonderful technician on stage, Alex Elmore who was a lighting expert, all of them did a marvelous job even with the limited equipment we had. All these things made a profound impact and pre-

Figure 2.6 a, b. Early costumes codesigned by Mary Elmore and "Madame Cazan," c. 1935. Images from the Theosophical Society Archives, Chennai (Ramani 2003, 100).

sented the despised Sadir in an entirely new form" (quoted in Ramani 2003, 45).

Arundale's resistance to traces of colonial modernity could be staged only through the power of the distinctly modern and cosmopolitan space that she inhabited as "World Mother" of the Theosophical Society. As we see in the passage above, Arundale expended tremendous effort on the optics of the restaging of Bharatanāṭyam. These changes endured, perhaps because they represented not only a new epistemology, but also a new moral order for the dance.

It is significant that these changes were very quickly absorbed by the early Tamil cinema. Until the late 1930s, women performers in the cinema wore costumes that resembled those worn by popular *icai nāṭakam* drama performers, which themselves were inspired by those of the colonial Parsi theatre. The costumes included crowns and jewelry made of brass and aluminum and saris made of cotton and sometimes synthetics—especially what was known as "imitation silk" (rayon).[7] By the early to mid-1940s, these older-style costumes had been replaced by the iconic Bharatanāṭyam costume invented by Arundale's associates.

In the world of post-1940 cinema, this costume was used not just in representations related to dance—it also became the standard costume of the mythological cinema. To this day, all cinematic (and television) representations of Hindu deities, particularly goddesses, in almost every region of India have them wearing the stitched Arundale-inspired Bharatanāṭyam costume. The enduring presence of the costume and its wider links to the representations of things considered sacred takes us to the final visual transformation of the dance—namely, the rendering of the form as both narrative and spectacle.

Narrativization, Mythology, and Spectacle

Perhaps the most obvious parallel between the reinvented Bharatanāṭyam and cinema is the emphasis they both place on religious narrative. As Randor Guy (1997) and Theodore Baskaran (1996 and 2009) have demonstrated, the successes of early cinema did not rely on realism but, in the South Indian context, on the popularity of Indian (usually Hindu) mythology. That is, popular culture, shaped largely by theatre and cinema in the 1920s and 1930s, relied almost entirely on the iteration of known mythological narratives that were accessible to the masses. It is thus not a stretch to see how the popularity of the reinvented Bharatanāṭyam logically followed suit. The dance drama idiom promoted by Arundale in the early 1940s had a deep and long-lasting impact on the future of Bharatanāṭyam. Beginning in 1947, Arundale turned her focus from the reformation of solo Bharatanāṭyam to the production of multidancer dance dramas. As many scholars have noted, these drew from the Western idiom of the ballet as well as from Indian forms of theatre such as Kathakaḷi of Kerala and the Bhāgavata Mēḷa Nāṭaka of Tanjore district (Meduri 1996; Allen 1997; O'Shea 2007).[8] However, a major piece of the puzzle is missing in these characterizations of how Arundale's dance-drama idiom emerged, and this has to do with the staging of the dance drama in a manner parallel to the genre of early mythological cinema.

The dance-drama idiom used the vocabulary of Bharatanāṭyam to tell stories from Hindu epics and other religious narratives. In other words, it was like a mythological film brought onto the stage. The audiences who witnessed the emergence of the new Bharatanāṭyam dance-drama form in the 1940s were the same audiences who were the primary consumers of mythological cinema in that period.

Arundale's first dance drama was staged in 1944. While this was a *ku-*

ṟavañci drama, discussed further in chapter 5, it is significant that Arundale had produced a number of mythological dramas for the Theosophical Society in the early 1930s, including *The Light of Asia*, *Bhisma* (The story of the patriarch of the epic *Mahābhārata*), *Kuchela Vratam* (The vow of Kṛṣṇa's devotee Kucela), and *Karaikkal Ammaiyar* (The story of the female Śaiva saint Kāraikkāl Ammaiyār). The first non-*kuṟavañci* drama produced at Kalakshetra was *Kumarasambhavam* (1947), based on the Sanskrit play of the same name attributed to the poet Kālīdāsa. The play tells the story of the birth of the god Kumāra, also known as Kārttikeya or Murukaṉ, son of Śiva. In the period 1933–46, three Tamil films had already been produced on this theme. While I do not aim to draw a one-to-one correspondence between Arundale's dance dramas and Tamil films, it is significant, as we see in the table 2.1, that the themes that Arundale chose for her dance presentations had their counterparts in the Tamil cinema of the 1930s and 1940s. However, I would like to emphasize that this only highlights the significance of interocular and intermedial consumption practices in early twentieth-century Madras. Granted, these themes were also common to *icai nāṭakam* (for example, the narratives of Damayantī and Āṇṭāḷ), and others were traditional plays in the Bhāgavata Mēḷa Nāṭaka genre of Tanjore (Rukmāṅgada, Uṣā Pariṇayam, Rukmiṇī Kalyāṇam, and Dhruva Caritram). Nonetheless, Arundale's careful curation and re-presentation of these narratives to Madras audiences at a time when they were circulating through the medium of cinema is significant.

Narrative and spectacle, at least from the consumer's standpoint, were part of a common culture of interocularity, and narrative frameworks were shared across visual specters and vocabularies, as we see in table 2.1. It is also significant that there are a number of crossover factors in this intermedial world of dance and early cinema. I would like to briefly discuss one of these factors here—namely, the sonic element—through the figure of the Brahmin musician Papanasam Sivan (1890–1973). Sivan was a traditionally trained musician before he moved to Madras in 1933. In that year, he was hired to compose music for the film *Seetha Kalyanam* (1934) through his contact with producer G. K. Seshagiri (discussed below in this chapter), and months later Arundale hired him as the music teacher at the Besant Theosophical School.[9] In 1939, owing to increasing pressure and demand from the film world, he left the school. It

TABLE 2.1.
Parallel themes in the dance-dramas of Rukmini Arundale and some early Tamil films

ARUNDALE DANCE DRAMA	RELEVANT EARLY TAMIL FILMS
Kumarasambhavam (1947)	*Sri Valli* (1933), *Kanda Leela* (1938), and *Sri Murugan* (1946)
Ramayana suite: *Sita Swayamvaram* (1955), *Sri Rama Vanagamanam* (1960), *Paduka Pattabhishekam* (1960), *Sabari Moksham* (1965), *Choodamani Pradanam* (1968), and *Maha Pattabhishekam* (1969)	*Ramayanam* (1932), *Seetha Kalyanam* (1934), *Lava Kusa* (1934), *Lanka Dahanam* (1935), *Sati Ahalya* (1937), *Kambar* (1938), *Rama Nama Mahimai* (1939), *Seethapaharanam* (1939), *Seetha Jananam* or *Vedavati* (1941), *Valmeeki* (1946), and *Sampoorna Ramayanam* (1958)
Rukmangada Charitram (1959)	*Mohini Rukmangada* (1935) and *Rukmangada* (1947)
Geeta Govinda (1959)	*Bhakta Jayadevar* (1937)
Usha Parinayam (1959)	*Usha Kalyanam* (1936)
Andal Charitram (1961)	*Andal Tirukalyanam* (1937) and *Sri Andal* (1948)
Kannappar Kuravanji (1962)	*Kannappa Nayanar* (1938)
Rukmini Kalyanam (1964)	*Rukmini Kalyanam* (1936)
Shakuntalam (1967)	*Sakuntala* (1934) and *Sakuntalai* (1940)
Dhruva Charitram (1971)	*Dhruva Charitram* (1935)
Kuchelopakhayanam (1972)	*Bhakta Kuchela* (1936)
Matsya Kurma Avataram (1974)	*Dasavataram* (1934)
Meenakshi Vijayam (1977)	*Meenakshi Kalyanam* (1940)
Damayanti Swayamvaram (1978)	*Nala Damayanti* (1935)
Meera of Mewar (1984)	*Meera Bai* (1936), *Bhakta Meera* (1938), and *Meera* (1945)

is significant that while he taught there, he continued to compose music for a number of Tamil films that shared themes with Arundale's dance dramas, such as *Bhakta Kuchela* (1936). Arundale's version of this narrative about Kucela, a devotee of the god Kṛṣṇa, was made into the Sanskrit dance drama *Kuchelopakhayanam* in 1972.[10] In 1961, he returned to collaborate with Arundale, when he composed the music for Kalakshetra's dance drama *Andal Charitram*, about the early medieval Tamil female saint and poet Āṇṭāḷ. He also composed music for Arundale's *Kannappar Kuravanji* (1962) and *Shakuntalam* (1967; with Turaiyur Rajagopala Sarma).[11] By this time, Sivan's musical style had become somewhat fixed, and his music seamlessly provided a sonic crossover between the tunes (*meṭṭu*) used in mythologically themed films for which he was the composer and the songs he composed for these dance dramas.[12]

It is significant that the dance-drama idiom very quickly became a staple in the burgeoning local Madras dance schools for middle-class young women, such as the Saraswathi Gana Nilayam (established in 1939 by the dancer K. Lalitha), and Nrithyodaya (established under the name Natana Kala Seva by the film director K. Subrahmanyam in 1941). Schools such as these shifted their focus to the production of these dance dramas not only because they were thought to impart culture to young people in a manner that the traditional courtesan repertoire could not, but also because of their value as spectacle. The appeal of these presentations, often described using the English terms "ballet" or "dance-ballet," was confirmed by the former actress Rajasulochana (1935–2013), who trained at the Saraswathi Gana Nilayam in her youth: "Dance ballets are the best way to make people appreciate classical dance. Dance ballets are basically entertaining for audiences (*jaṉa-rañjakam*). This kind of presentation guarantees audience appreciation, as opposed to other kinds of dance presentation" (pers. comm. Chennai, December 26, 2012). It is this doubling of moral pedagogy and spectacle that, as we have seen above, was at the heart of the reinvention of Bharatanāṭyam. Madras audiences' desire to witness such spectacular stagings of Hindu mythology were undoubtedly conditioned by the ubiquity and mass circulation of Tamil films, which by the 1930s and 1940s were among the few cultural forms to attract both mixed-gender and mixed-caste audiences (Baskaran 1996).

SHIFTING TOWARD THE LENS: THE SOUTH INDIAN DANCE REVIVAL AND CINEMA

Moral anxieties about the cinema were rampant throughout India during the 1920s and 1930s, and while the nationalist movement opened up possibilities for the creation, dissemination, and consumption of new forms of mass culture, key figures of the movement, including Mohandas K. Gandhi, vehemently objected to the cinematic medium on moral grounds. Indeed, in 1942, when asked what would happen if he supported the cinema, Gandhi replied, "I should lose my caste, my Mahatmaship" (quoted in Mukhopadhyay 2011, 425) In a fascinating recent essay, Urvi Mukhopadhyay demonstrated that despite Gandhi's condemnation of the early Indian cinema, filmmakers actively allied themselves with the projects of Gandhian nationalism, and nationalist celebrations of Indian (Hindu) history thus came to permeate the cinema of the 1920s and 1930s

Figure 2.7. The cover of Kaliyukattil Naṭaṉamiṭum Ṭākkīs Paritāpac Cintu *(Song of suffering about the talkies of the Kaliyuga) by K. Kurucāmitās. © British Library Board, pTam.B.7514.*

(ibid.). Chapter 3 mentions this point in its discussion of dance and nationalism in the South Indian cinema of the 1940s and 1950s.

Here, however, I would like to turn to the fact that in the Madras Presidency, articulations of the dangers of cinema and dance were ubiquitous. A good example comes from the work of K. Kurucāmitās, a Tamil poet from the town of Kumbhakonam in the Tanjore district.[13] In 1937, he published a seven-page Tamil song in the *cintu* genre called *Kaliyukattil Naṭaṉamiṭum Ṭākkīs Paritāpac Cintu* (Song of suffering about the talkies of the Kaliyuga) on the dangers of his "younger brothers (*tampikaḷ*)" watching "talkies in the evening" (figure 2.7). For the poet, the advent of the cinema represents a disintegration of the Hindu moral order (*dharma*) in the most degenerate of all ages in the Hindu cyclical calendar, the Kaliyuga. The song is written in the four-line meter known as *venpā*. The first few verses are:

1. The plight of India's people is pathetic. Brothers, it's just not right! They spend all the money they've earned during the day on talkies at night.
2. Gone are the days of adorning the body with jewels, in the evening it is only talkies! People are possessed, as if by the demons who reside in sacred fig trees.
3. It's a bad time. There is no rain, no harvest. It's bad time. Why go to the talkies?
4. Men just don't go to work anymore, they sleep until well after dawn! They pawn their wives' saris, just to go watch the talkies! (Kurucāmitās 1937, 1)

It is not surprising that six years later, the same author composed a set of similar songs titled *Meṭrācai Viṭṭu Nāṭṭipurattukku Oṭṭam Piṭitta Tācikaḷ Taṇkappāṭṭu* (Songs about the *dāsīs* who left Madras and ran away to the villages), a collection of insulting songs aimed at women from *devadāsī* communities who, the author claims, are running back to their villages from Madras because of the impending anti-*devadāsī* legislation. The text is full of images of women suffering from painful venereal disease and repeated slurs and insults. As Soneji has shown, this highly misogynistic and casteist work and earlier works like it "facilitated new urban representations of *devadāsīs* as worthy targets of moral and aesthetic reform" (2012, 93–94.).

RUKMINI ARUNDALE IN THE TAMIL CINEMA

In 1936, Rukmini Arundale established the International Academy for the Arts, later renamed Kalakshetra. That same year saw the production of the film *Raja Desingh*,[14] starring T. K. Sundarappa (figure 2.8). The film was based on the famous story of the eighteenth-century Raja Tej Singh of Senji, about whom the historian Sanjay Subrahmanyam has written at length.[15] The film surprisingly featured three dances by Rukmini Arundale—who otherwise, like Gandhi, disparaged the cinematic medium. In the late 1950s, long after the film had disappeared from memory (for reasons discussed below), Arundale reflected on cinema and dance:

> The problem of the cinema is peculiar. The film engages a traditionally trained musician or dancer but very soon these change into a new type. The Indian film has now created a type of music and dance which we can definitely call cinema music and cinema

Figure 2.8. Poster for the Tamil film Raja Desingh *(1936), produced by Rajeswari Talkies. The poster specifically advertises the live performance of "Classical Baratha Natya* [sic]*" by Rukmini Devi and a speech by George Arundale. Courtesy of the Roja Muthiah Research Library.*

> dance. The classical way must be jealously [*sic*] preserved if it is to be presented on the stage because it is easily seen that once an artist is engaged on the films, he or she cannot completely go back to the traditional way; at least not easily, just as the milk that is once curdled can never again be turned into fresh milk. (1958b, 88–89)

She also wrote: "In our country over and above the different types of dance forms such as Kathakali, Manipuri, Kathak and Bharatanatyam, there is a new type of dance and music, which, for want of any other descriptive title, is classified as cinema art. I have no objection to a new type but when in this so-called new dance there is no originality at all except in the distortion of pure and classical forms such as Bharatanatyam,

I feel unhappy and think it is a tragedy. Such vulgarisation does neither the dance nor the cinema any good" (Arundale 1959, 42–43).

In these remarks, film dance is pitted against the "pure and classical" Bharatanāṭyam. In the first passage, trained musicians and dancers who cross over into the world of cinema perform an irrevocable act—they can never be "fresh milk" again, in Arundale's analogy. As in many of her pronouncements on prerevival forms of dance practiced by *devadāsī* women, she uses language that usually combines moral and aesthetic judgment. Film dance—on account of its hybridity and cultural bricolage, like the older forms of *devadāsī* dance—is thus cast by Arundale as a "distortion" of the imaginary "purity" of something marked as "classical," as a "vulgarisation" of "the traditional way."

It is commonly believed that the Arundales paid the film's producers to buy all copies of *Raja Desingh*, which were subsequently intentionally destroyed to conceal the fact that Arundale had participated in the popular cinema. In the words of the film dance historian V. A. K. Ranga Rao,"Rukmini Devi Arundale's public stance was against cinema but she herself performed in a Tamil film called *Raja Desingh*. After the movie was made, she herself paid the producer to buy the film back" (pers. comm., Chennai, August 22, 2012).

Let us now briefly turn to the substantive portion of Arundale's involvement with the film *Raja Desingh*. To begin with, it had a live performance component. As Stephen Hughes has shown, cinema initially came to Madras "as a kind of European entertainment using the same local venues as the European variety circuit. . . . [The] shows conformed to a variety format and they frequently mixed films with other kinds of live performances" (2010b, 147). Hughes continues:

> Contrary to our contemporary expectations that stage performance and film screenings were separate media practices that happen at different venues at different times for different audiences, cinema and dance performance had from the late nineteenth century had an ongoing mixed media relationship. From the earliest film shows at the end of the nineteenth century, exhibitors had used a format that combined live stage acts, musical accompaniment and films. This continued to be the norm in South India for roughly the first two decades of the cinema. The touring entertainment companies from Europe, the US and Australia that had visited Madras

as part of a global circuit used a wide variety of different performance genres and formats including the circus, fairground, variety shows and comic opera. . . . Amongst all these attractions it was very common for dance to be featured as the primary attraction. (forthcoming)

Hughes goes to great length to draw attention to the fact that cinema houses in Madras in the 1920s (and even earlier) were sites of multimedial performance and laboratories for new cultures of interocularity. Eminent female performers—mostly from courtesan backgrounds, such as Gauhar Jan of Calcutta (1873–1930) and Bajjar Battoo of Lahore—performed *abhinaya* in Madras's cinema houses, for example (ibid.). Arundale's participation in this film extended beyond the recorded versions of her dance that were captured on film, including a live performance on certain days when the film was screened. On these days, commentary about the dance was provided, presumably in English, by George Arundale, who was the world president of the Theosophical Society. While the film reels no longer exist, the synopsis and songbook of the film do (figure 2.9).

From the songbook, we learn that Rukmini performed three pieces, all of which are from the courtesan repertoire. The section containing the songs strangely ends with a photo of Rukmini in a costume in North Indian style (perhaps reflective of the theme of the film) (figure 2.10). The first piece was an interpretation of a song in the Tamil *padam* genre, *Pataṟi varukutu* (My heart trembles) in the *rāga* Kāmbodhi, in which the heroine addresses the god Murukaṉ as her beloved (figure 2.11).[16] A translation of the song as it appears in the film (only one verse, or *caraṇam,* was used) is as follows:

Pallavi: My heart is trembling, clinging, clasping, melting
. . . [G]o and tell him, *aṭi* (friend)!
Anupallavi: This Vēlavar [Murukaṉ] who dwells in Paḻaṉi, the place that has no equal
I have kept him within my heart; what is happening? The god of love arrows in my
Breast make me swoon—go and bring my lord Murukaṉ to me.
Caraṇam: Come, *aṭi,* bring my lord Murukaṉ to me.
To play with me . . . getting together . . . embracing and loving.

Figure 2.9. The cover of the songbook for Raja Desingh *(1936). Private collection of S. V. Jayababu.*

He will sing Kāmpōti *rāga*, and he'll sprinkle magic powder
[*māyappoṭi*] right on me.
Go, *aṭi*! Is there any equal to him? He took my hand, he gave me a
ruby.
Seeking him, sing his favorite beautifully worded *padam* for him
And without delaying or quarreling, come running and bring him
to me![17]

The second piece was centered on abstract dance and rhythm, a *jati-svaram* (in the *rāga* Sāveri) attributed to the famous nineteenth-century dance masters known as the Tanjore Quartet. This piece remains a staple composition for students at Kalakshetra, and nothing is said about it apart from its having the title *svaram* ("notes") in the songbook for *Raja Desingh*. The final piece was a *padam* in the Telugu language, *Sariga koṅgu* in the *rāga* Curuṭṭi by an unknown poet, in which the god Kṛṣṇa of Mannargudi is the beloved. Only two lines of the poem are included in the songbook, and my translation follows them:

Figure 2.10. A photo captioned "The world-renowned Rukmini Devi of Adyar: the best form of Bharatanāṭyam will be showcased" from the songbook for Raja Desingh *(1936). Private collection of S. V. Jayababu.*

Sariga koṅgu musugu dānitō vāḍu
saiga jēsinadi kaṇṭinē
tirigi tirigi jūcukoni sogasugā
devuḍaina mannāru raṅguḍu
He makes signs to her
Under the veil of her sari
That handsome Lord Mannāru Raṅga [Kṛṣṇa]
Repeatedly turns to glance at her. (*Raja Desingh* songbook, 1936)

Both of these *padams* were taught to Arundale by Mylapore Gauri Ammal (1892–1971), a famous *devadāsī* artist of Madras who for a very brief period was hired to teach at Kalakshetra. However, it seems that Rukmini often rejected these interpretations of *abhinaya*, and she wrote that after her first performance in 1935, she transformed the *abhinaya* for nearly all of the lyric-based repertoire she had learnt. It might be safe to assume that these public performances in 1936 featured the infamous

ஸ்ரீ ருக்மணி தேவியின்

பரத நாட்டியப் பாட்டுகள்.

ராகம்—காம்போதி. தாளம்—சதுஸ்ரஜாதி ரூபகம்.

பதரி வருகு துருகு தென்னாவி
பதைக்குதே வகை சொல்லடி—
சற்று நில்லடி—மனங் கல்லோடி—அடி
தளுக்கு குலுக்கு மினுக் கென்னபோடி. (பதரி

அநுபல்லவி.

எதிரில்லாத பழனி வேலவரிடத்தினுர
த்தில் கருத்தை வைத்தபின் ஏது மதன்
கணை மார்பில் சோருதே
எந்தன் துரை கந்தசாமியைக் கூட்டிவா.

சரணம்.

வாடி எந்தன் வடிவேலரைக் கூட்டிவா
கூடி மருவிக்குலாவி விளையாட
பாடுவார் காம்போதி மாயப்பொடி
போடுவார்—எந்தன்மீது, போடி
அவரைப் போல் ஈடு ஜோடுண்டோடி,
பிடித்தார், எந்தன் கை கொடுத்தார்
மாணிக்கம், நாடியவர் கேட்ட செஞ்
சொற்பதம் பாடி, மோடி செய்யாமலே
தேடி அழைத்து வா,

ஸ்வரம்.

1) ச்ா ரி ஸ்தாப மகரிச நிதஸரி பபதரிஸ்ா

2) ச்ாரிக் ஸ்க்ரிஸ் நிதபம பதச் நிதபமகரி
சரிஸதரீஸ் பமயப நிதரிஸ்ா
நிதபம பதஸ்.

Figure 2.11. "Paṭaṟi varukutu" *(My heart trembles), in "Śrī rukmaṇi tēviyiṉ parata nāṭṭiyap pāṭṭukaḷ" (Sri Rukmini Devi's Bharata Nāṭya songs), from the songbook for the film* Raja Desingh. *The song is in the* rāga *Kāmbodhi. Private collection of S. V. Jayababu.*

"cleaned up" *abhinaya*, devoid of erotic references, which would have allowed Arundale and her husband to present their reinvented art to new (that is, nontheosophical) audiences in cinema houses. The Irishman George Arundale's authoritative voice would no doubt have echoed the highly transcendental interpretation that the Theosophists had brought to Indian dance long before Rukmini Arundale had performed it.

While not much is known about the reception of her dancing in *Raja Desingh*, the event certainly created both a new kind of public presence for Arundale and self-conscious reflections on dance among producers and consumers of cinema. On April 4, 1936, for example, the popular film magazine *Silver Screen* featured an article titled "Dance in the Talkies" that specifically referred to Arundale's dance in *Raja Desingh* as a major intervention:

> In the world of today's Tamil talkies, one cannot find any film without dances. Whether the dances have a connection to the story or whether they are disconnected from the story, it would be difficult to appreciate films without dance. It could be a dance when the heroine is crying about being separated from her beloved Lord. The next scene could be a dance where she is dancing in scantily clad clothing sometimes by herself or sometimes with a group of other women, where they dance in a vulgar (*āpācam*) manner. In my English publication, I wrote an article about this. I saw many ladies dancing and acting in such a vulgar way. These dances were mostly influenced by westernized dances (*mēlnāṭu naṭaṉaṅkaḷ*). When one sees these dances, one certainly wonders, "Does one really need such a color film?"
>
> Because of this vulgarity, the records that would be made by the Sangeetha Company did not come out. One does feel disappointed about this at all.
>
> The wife of the leader of the Theosophical Society, Dr. Arundale, Sri Rukmini Arundale, has been contracted to dance in a film by Rajeswari Talkies. This is truly an extremely admirable moment. In South India, where the nation has been given a second life and there is a renaissance, Bharatanāṭyam is front and center. Regarding Bharatanāṭyam, readers would be familiar with the famous 1932 debate between Dr. Muthulakshmi Reddy and Sriman E. Krishna Iyer. When she said, "Due to the evil ways of the *devadāsīs*, their

> dance is definitely not longer necessary," Iyer responds by saying "the arts must flourish and the *devadāsīs'* lifestyle (*tācikaḷ vaḻkkai muṟai*) must be remedied."
>
> At this time, our sisters from upper-class families (*uyar kuṭumpattu cakōtarikaḷ*), must come forward to dance and also act in films. This will be good for the arts. More specifically, dance in a film by a world-teacher like Dr. Arundale's wife will certainly not only increase the profile of India's arts around the world, but it will also increase the respectability of Bharatanāṭyam. The film company should be praised. ("Dance in the Talkies," 1936)

It is significant that the writer invokes the revival of dance with an eye to the public debates on *devadāsī* morality and the figure of Reddy. Again, the purity of revived forms of Indian dance is contrasted with dance that contains Western influence and thus perceived as "vulgar." Arundale is championed as an exemplary figure for the future of the dance, which the author hopes will survive through the bodies of "sisters from upper-class families." The presence of Arundale's dance in the cinema will have a global impact on perceptions of Indian culture, the author says, and will also "increase the respectability of Bharatanāṭyam."

E. KRISHNA IYER AND THE TAMIL CINEMA

Even before Arundale's rescue efforts, another figure, the *smārta* Brahmin lawyer and music and theatre enthusiast Krishna Iyer, had already made significant interventions in staging *devadāsī* dance in Madras for urban elites. Krishna Iyer was born on August 9, 1897, in a Tamil Brahmin family in the village of Brahmadesam, which is in today's Tirunelveli district. He received his bachelor of arts degree from the renowned Madras Christian College in 1918, and in 1921 he went to Trivandrum to study law. He practiced as a lawyer at the Madras High Court until 1943. Krishna Iyer was an active member of the Indian National Congress in the 1930s (in 1932 he participated in Gandhi's Salt March). In the 1930s he also joined Madras's premier theatrical company, Suguna Vilasa Sabha (established by Pammal Campanta Mutaliyār), and in preparation for the dance sequences in his plays, he learned the basics of Bharatanāṭyam from a *devadāsī* performer named Madhurantakam Jagadambal (1873–1943).[18] He also was very active in the Music Academy, where he served as secretary for a number of years, and it was he who sent a personal invitation to Arundale to attend the recital by the *devadāsīs* Rajalakshmi and Jeevaratnam in 1933. When Reddy introduced her abolition bill in the Madras Legislative Assembly in 1927, Krishna Iyer was among those who opposed her, arguing that the art of dance must be preserved by *devadāsīs* until it could be fully transferred to women from respectable families. It is important to note that Krishna Iyer did not empathize with women from *devadāsī* communities as some modern historians claim; rather, he saw them as vessels of cultural "stuff" that must be mined by "better persons," as shown in a letter he wrote to a newspaper in response to Reddy's proposal to the Legislative Assembly:

> Thanks to the great impetus recently given to the development of Music proper by the Music Academy, the Annamalai College of Music and in a halting manner the University of Madras as well, something is being done in that direction. I do not know whether the anti-nautch people are aware of the efforts made by the Music Academy to provide facilities in public and private functions to bring out the talents of elderly respectable women—and half a dozen of them are now found to possess talents developed almost to the professional standard. The anti-nautch people who have tried to kill the Art, have a heavy responsibility on them to make sufficient arrangements to resuscitate the Art and to put it on a proper basis.
>
> For my part, it is no question of Art at the expense of morality, or even positive encouragement of the present day nautch girls as a class and never a justification for the perpetuation of the Devadasi class as such. The Heavens would not fall and morality would in no way be jeopardised if one or two cases of very good Art is reluctantly tolerated in exceptional instances—without the associated vice—*as a matter of temporary evil necessary, pending the coming up of better persons*. And exceptions are recognised by the Doctor [Reddy] as well. (Krishna Iyer 1932; emphasis added)

Krishna Iyer's response also makes clear the doubled and intertwined discourses of respectability of the cinema and the art of the *devadāsīs*:

> With regard to the Cinema: A certain respectable film company desirous of producing at least one Tamil talkie of a high standard is on the look out for cultured and respectable actors and actresses and

> has requested me to help in their search. The company is willing to provide the necessary facilities and safeguards to make the players feel at home without any violence to their sentiments of a higher nature. I have mooted the matter to some respectable high-placed ladies. As yet, no one has come forward. Will the enthusiastic Doctor and her friends move in the matter and help in a desirable reform to rescue art from unworthy hands? (ibid.)

Krishna Iyer championed the repopulation of the fields of both dance and cinema by non-*devadāsī* women. He understood *devadāsīs* as reservoirs of a knowledge system that could and must be grafted onto the bodies of respectable non-*devadāsī* women. In a 1948 article titled "Renaissance of Indian Dance and Its Architects," he reflected on the reinvention of Bharatanāṭyam and its repopulation by respectable women, unabashedly taking credit for engineering this process: "With all these, Bharata Natya was still in the hands of exponents of the old professional class, with all its possible and lurking dangers as pointed out by social reformers. The efforts of the present writer were turned towards steadily taking it out of their hands and introducing it among cultured, family women of respectable classes" (1948, 24).

Krishna Iyer performed dance in at least one film, acted in a couple of others, and was a scouting agent for still others. In 1939 the popular film magazine *Minnoli* published a short biography of him (figure 2.12. The two accompanying photographs were from the 1939 film *Cairantiri*, in which Krishna Iyer acted—playing both the ever-masculine role of Arjuna, one of the heroes of the epic *Mahābhārata*, and the role of Bṛhannalā, Arjuna in the guise of an effeminate dance teacher. The famous photograph of Krishna Iyer in the second role, which has been reprinted hundreds of times in publications on Bharatanāṭyam, has often been thought to have been taken during one of his stage performances, but in fact it is a still from the film. In the advertisement for *Cairantiri* (Kīcakavatam) there is also mention of Krishna Iyer's performing a *tillāṉā* (figure 2.13). Again, the juxtaposition of the *Mahābhārata* narrative of Arjuna-Bṛhannalā with the courtly *tillāṉā* dance augments the scripting of a new, religious genealogy for Bharatanāṭyam. And once again, it is the medium of cinema that enables the articulation and circulation of this genealogy.

ஸ்ரீ. ஈ. கிருஷ்ணய்யர்

ஸ்ரீ. ஈ. கிருஷ்ணய்யர், பி. ஏ., பி.எல்., பட்டம் பெற்ற ஒரு வக்கீலாவார். மற்றும் அவர் ஒரு கலைப்பித்தர் ; தீவிர தேசத்தொண்டர், அவர் ஆரம்பத்தில் சுகுணவிலாஸ சபா, செகரெடேரியட் பார்டி முதலியவைகளில் ஸ்த்ரீ வேஷங்களிலும், புருஷ வேஷங்களிலும் சுமார் 10 வருஷகாலம் நடித்து நல்ல புகழ் பெற்றார். 1930-ல் சத்தியாக்கிரஹப் போரில் ஈடுபட்டுச் சிறை சென்றார். அந்தக் காலத்தில், அவர் மிருச்சகடியில் வசந்தசேனையாகவும், இரு சகோதரிகளில் லீலாவதியாகவும், கபீர் தாஸில் அவரது மனைவி லாயாகவும், ஹாம்லெட்டில் ஜெர்ட்ரூட்டாகவும் நடிப்பதில் மிகப் புகழ் பெற்றிருந்தார். நாடக மேடையில் நடித்து வருகையில் அவர் பரத நாட்டியத்தைப் பயின்றார். சிறிது காலத்திற்கெல்லாம் அவ்வுயரிய கலைப்பித்தராகவே மாறிவிட்டார். அந்த நாள் முதல் இன்று வரை இக்கலையை உன்னத ஸ்தானம் பெறச் செய்வதற்கு அவர் அரும்பாடுபட்டு பிரசாரம் செய்து வந்திருப்பது பாராட்டத்தக்கதாகும்.

சைரந்திரியில்
அர்ஜுனன் வேஷத்தில்

சங்கீதத்திலும் ஸ்ரீ. கிருஷ்ணய்யருக்கு நல்ல தேர்ச்சி உண்டு, சங்கீத வித்வத் சபையை ஆரம்பித்து வைப்பதற்குக் காரணமாயிருந்தவர்களில் இவரும் ஒருவராவார். பத்திரிகைகளில் சங்கீதம, நாட்டியம், நாடகம் இவைகளைப் பற்றி யெல்லாம் பல கட்டுரைகளை எழுதியிருக்கிறார். "சங்கீதப் பிரமுகர்கள்" என்ற தலைப்பில் அவர் எழுதிய கட்டுரைகள் மிகப் பாராட்டப்பட்டன.

அவருக்கு சினிமாவில் நடிக்கவேண்டு மென்ற அவா சில வருஷங்களாகவே இருந்தும், சினிமா தற்போதுள்ள நிலைமையில் அதன் மூலம் கலையை விருத்திசெய்ய முடியாது என்ற எண்ணத்துடன் இத்தொழிலில் இறங்காமலிருந்தார். ஆனால் ராய் சகோதரிகளும், சைரந்திரி பட முதலாளிகளும் அவரை விடாப்பிடியாய் சினிமாவிற்குக் கொண்டு வந்துவிட்டது சந்தோஷிக்கத்தக்க விஷயமாகும், இப்படத்தில் இவர் தம் வாழ்க்கை லக்ஷியத்தில் ஓரளவு வெற்றியும் பெற்றிருக்கிறார். ஆகவே, அவர் மற்றும் பல படங்களில் தம் திறமையை வெளியிட இசைவாரென்று எதிர்பார்க்கிறோம்.

சைரந்திரியில்
பிருஹன்னளா வேஷத்தில்

Figure 2.12. "Sri Ī. Kirusṇayyar," an article about Krishna Iyer in the film magazine Minnoli *(1939). These photographs are actually stills from the film* Cairantiri. *Courtesy of the Roja Muthiah Research Library.*

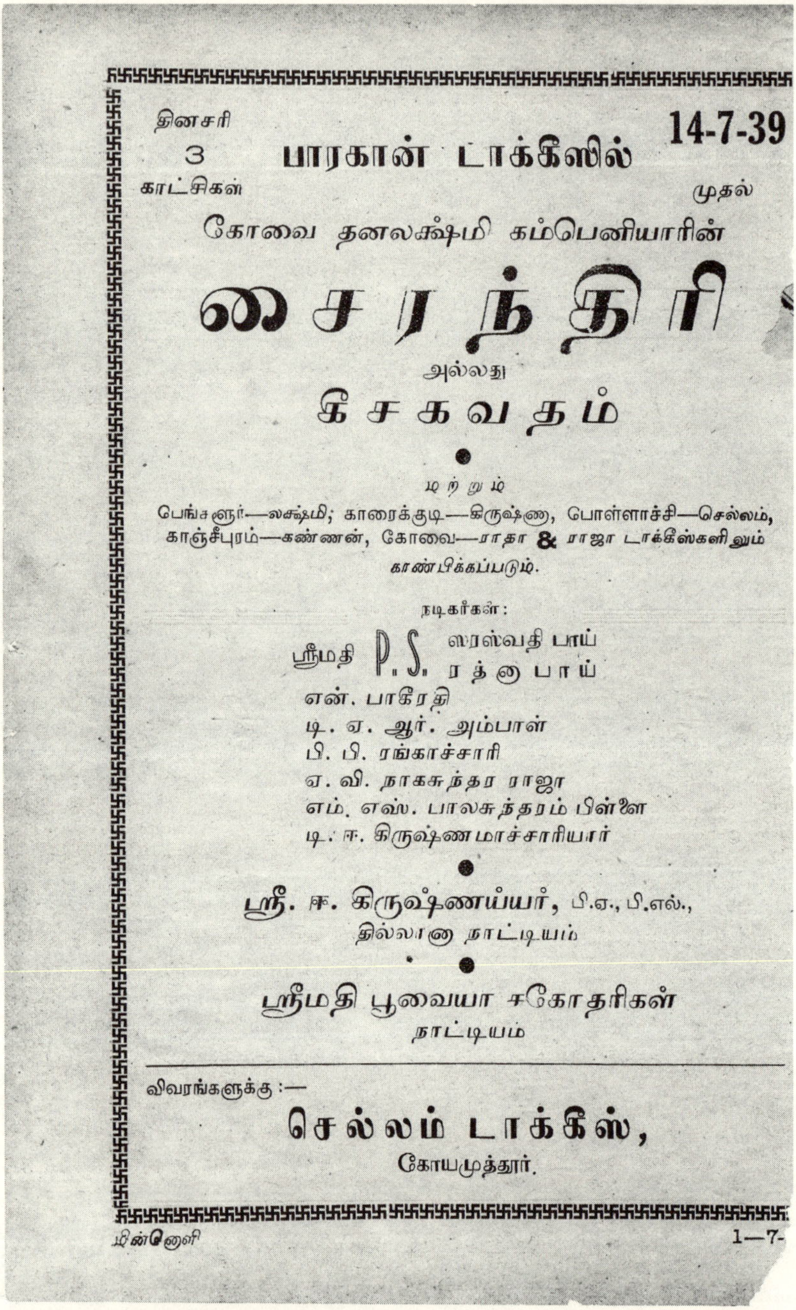

Figure 2.13. An advertisement for the screening of the film Cairantiri *(Kīcakavatam) (1939), with a* tillāṉā *dance by Krishna Iyer foregrounded as a special feature. Courtesy of the Roja Muthiah Research Library.*

REPRESENTATIONS OF ART, ARTIST, AND NATION: THE FIRST FILM ABOUT DANCE

As we have seen above, the 1930s represented a crucial period for Bharatanāṭyam dance in Madras. The Madras Music Academy, established in 1928, featured a dance recital by Rajalakshmi and Jeevaratnam on March 15, 1931, followed by another on January 1, 1933. Arundale presented her first recital at the Theosophical Society's diamond jubilee celebrations in 1935, and in 1936 she established the International Academy for the Arts, later renamed Kalakshetra. In addition to these well-known signs of Bharatanāṭyam's reinvention in Madras are several other narratives of the dance from the 1930s that have been rendered invisible in standard histories of the form. This period is also significant in terms of the history of Indian cinema, for it was when the first full-length feature film about dance—the Tamil film *Jalaja* (1938)—was produced in South India. Dance in the cinema took on a uniquely self-reflexive representation, and the discourses that resulted resonate deeply with narratives and positionalities that emerged as Bharatanāṭyam became a public form in Madras.

A key moment that I wish to highlight here is the period between 1936 and 1938. By this time, even though Arundale had performed her reinvented version of the dance, performances by women within the *devadāsī* community continued, and the narrative that follows shows how this kind of dance found its way into cosmopolitan, and even early global, circuits of cultural production and the new medial form of the cinema. At this time, a group of women from the *devadāsī* community in the town of Kumbhakonam were learning and performing dance. They came from a distinguished lineage of female performers in the Thanjavur region, and a whole generation of cousins was trained by the *naṭṭuvaṉār* Papanasam Vadivelu Pillai (1884–1937).[19] Prominent among these women were Kumbhakonam Varalakshmi (1910–37) and her cousins, the Saranayaki sisters (dates unknown) and Pattammal sisters (dates unknown) (figures 2.14a and 2.14b). Another cousin was Kumbhakonam Bhanumathi (1922–2003), who trained with the same *naṭṭuvaṉār*. Varalakshmi and Saranayaki had been performing in public as a duo in and around Kumbhakonam, and they were invited by the Music Academy to dance in Madras on December 28, 1933. But soon after Bhanumathi came on the scene, she quickly replaced Saranayaki in the duo dance presentations.

Srimathi PATTU of Kumbakonam
PATTU and SARANAYAGI formed a pair
Guru Papanasam Vadivelu Nattuvanar

Figure 2.14 a, b. Left, front row, left to right: Kumbhakonam Varalakshmi; another relative, Sulochana; Kumbhakonam Bhanumathi; and Kumbhakonam Pattammal. In the back (left to right) are Saranayaki and an unnamed cousin. Photograph courtesy B. M. Sundaram. Right: Kumbhakonam Pattammal in a dance pose. Collection of the author.

Varalakshmi and Bhanumathi performed as a duo at the Music Academy on December 31, 1934, and December 27, 1936.

Possibly through their acquaintance with Krishna Iyer, who was one of the secretaries of the Madras Music Academy, Bhanumathi and Varalakshmi were brought into contact with an impresario and film producer named G. K. Seshagiri—son of the famous Sanskrit scholar S. Kuppuswami Sastri (1880–1943)—who managed the Renaissance Theatre, an arts organization that regularly staged performances of drama and dance, and screened films at large public venues like the Victoria Public Hall and Gokhale Hall in Madras.[20] In 1936, La Meri—the American dancer who would later be known as the "Queen of Ethnic Dance"—arrived in Madras after learning some Kandiyan dance in Colombo, Sri Lanka (Venkateswaran 2005, 14). La Meri wrote a book titled *The Gesture Language of the Hindu Dance* (1941), which contained a foreword by the Orientalist and art historian Ananda Kentish Coomaraswamy (1877–

1947), and with Ruth St. Denis founded the first school of Indian dance in America (the School of Natya, in New York City) in May 1940 (ibid., 40 and 106). La Meri also collaborated with the Indian Burmese dancer Ram Gopal (1912–2003) for a brief period. Seshagiri invited La Meri to a performance of Varalakshmi and Bhanumathi at the Music Academy (figures 2.15a and 2.15b). Deeply moved by their performance, La Meri decided she wanted to learn the dance, so Seshagiri introduced her to Vadivelu Pillai, the teacher of the Bhanumathi and Varalakshmi. She trained with him for about three months (ibid., 15).

At the end of this period, Seshagiri staged a performance under the aegis of the Renaissance Theatre titled "The Celebrated International Dancer La Meri and the Brilliant Bharata Natya Artists of South India Varalakshmi and Bhanumathi." A single copy of the souvenir program for this performance is available at the New York Public Library, which houses an extensive archive related to La Meri's performance career.[21] The program does not provide dates, but a Tamil magazine article reveals that there were two performances, on February 1 and 3, 1937 (*Āṉanta Vikaṭaṉ* 1937). The program is full of advertisements for South Indian talkies, interspersed between long descriptions (and, in the case of the Bharatanāṭyam repertoire, translations) of the songs of the dance pieces being performed.[22] In any case, it is significant that this performance was clearly intended for cosmopolitan audiences in Madras, with La Meri's dances (labeled "Interpretive Dances" and "Racial Dances") juxtaposed with dances by Varalakshmi and Bhanumathi (always labeled "Bharata Natya"). La Meri performed pieces like "Caprice Viennoise" and "Adoration of the Virgin" under the heading "Interpretive Dances" and "North American (Red Indian) Hoop" and "Spanish Goyesca" under "Racial Dances." She also brought Bharatanāṭyam into the latter category, as this section ended with her performing an excerpt of the *varṇam* (in the *rāga* Śaṅkarābharaṇam) that she had just learned from Vadivelu Pillai. In this unique juxtaposition of forms, La Meri is simultaneously scripted as the embodiment of both an international aesthetic and Bharatanāṭyam. According to the program, "La Meri is a celebrated International Dancer; she has come to India to study types of Indian Dance. And *Bharata Natya* has known no devotee, more ardent, more sincere; it is the privilege of the Renaissance Theatre, again, to present her along with Varalakshmi and Bhanumathi, two of our own talented artists amid ideal conditions, new stage-mountings, appropriate light-effects; a splendid

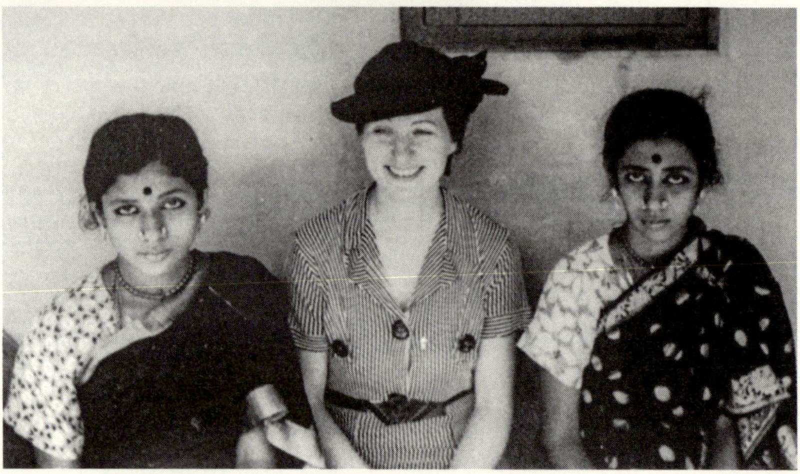

Figure 2.15 a, b. Left: La Meri with G. K. Seshagiri and "Kalyan Sundaram" (A. N. Kalyanasundaram Iyer), who eventually married Bhanumathi, in Madras, 1937. Below: La Meri with Bhanumathi and Varalakshmi (Venkateswaran 2005, 14–15).

display combining the inventiveness and fluidity of western dancing with the peculiar grace and unique expressiveness of *Bharata Natya*."[23] Varalakshmi and Bhanumathi performed an entire concert suite of Bharatanāṭyam courtly compositions.[24]

The performance with La Meri gave Varalakshmi and Bhanumathi considerable visibility among Madras's cosmopolitan elite audiences. It

Figure 2.16. Manjeri S. Isvaran, author of the short story "No Ankletbells for Her" (1949), Script writer and assistant director of the film Jalaja. *Photograph from the frontispiece of the book* No Ankletbells for Her *published by Mitra, Madras (1949).*

was around the time of this performance that Varalakshmi was hired by Seshagiri to act in a film he wanted to produce in Tamil about the life of a Bharatanāṭyam dancer. The film's story, a fictional account of a young woman from a *devadāsī* background, was written by Seshagiri, the Sanskritist Venkataraman Raghavan (a prize student of Seshagiri's father, who was very active in writing about dance in this period and was also on the board of the Madras Music Academy),[25] and a writer named Manjeri S. Isvaran (figure 2.16), who had just written the program notes for La Meri's Madras performance. Isvaran, who was a close associate of Seshagiri, later wrote an English short story about a young (non-*devadāsī*) girl's desire to learn dance, likely inspired by his early experiments writing for *Jalaja*, titled "No Ankletbells for Her."[26]

Many of the people who collaborated on the performance by La Meri, Bhanumathi, and Varalakshmi also worked on the film. In addition to Seshagiri's and Isvaran's participation in writing the script, the music for the film was composed by A. N. Kalyanasundaram Iyer (figure 2.15b) who also helped with the La Meri show, and eventually married Bhanumathi.[27] Seshagiri played the role of Rajagopalan, the hero of the film, and he hired Varalakshmi to play the part of Jalaja, the main female protagonist. Shooting began in 1937 in Bombay, and tragically, on Novem-

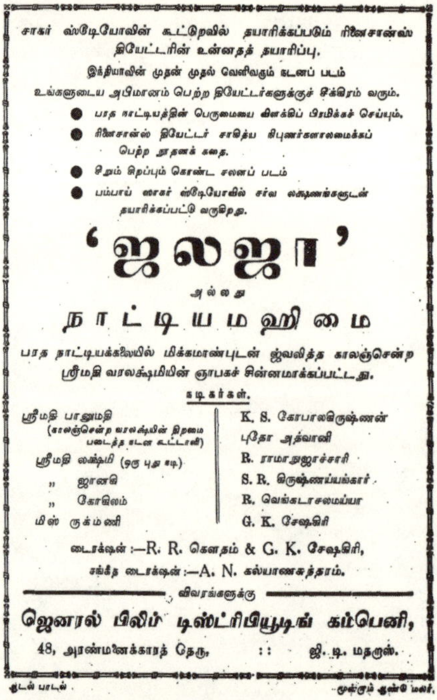

Figure 2.17 a, b. Left: Advertisement for Jalaja *(1938),* Āṭal Pāṭal (Āṇṭu Malar *1938), 7. Right: Advertisement for* Jalaja, *source unknown. Private collection of S. V. Jayababu.*

ber 3, Varalakshmi died there at the age of nineteen (Sundaram 2003, 41). Bhanumathi was asked to replace her in the role of Jalaja, which she did.

The film's full title in Tamil was *Jalajā allatu Nāṭṭiya Mahimai* (Jalaja, or the greatness of dance), and it is clear from the title that the film's agenda was to bring a vision of dance and its newly encoded symbolic meanings to a wider audience. One advertisement in the magazine *Āṭal Pāṭal* makes it clear that the film is simply about the "greatness of Bharatanāṭyam (*paratanāṭṭiyatiṉ perumai*)" (*Āṭal Pāṭal* 1938.) (figure 2.17a; see also figure 2.17b).

Unfortunately, no prints of the film have survived. However, I have found a copy of the songbook (figure 2.18) and some publicity materials for the film. The songbook includes a rather lengthy synopsis of the film in English, which is certainly the most detailed account we have of the plot, and I reproduced the synopsis in its entirety in the appendix.

The plot of the film reflects a number of tropes about Bharatanāṭyam and its social history that had already crystallized in the public imagination by the late 1930s, including those about the centrality of the god

Figure 2.18. Advertisement for the gramophone record of the film from the songbook for Jalaja *(1938), clearly indicating that the film was produced by the Renaissance Theatre in Madras. Private collection of S. V. Jayababu.*

Śiva-Naṭarāja as the god of dance and the patron deity of dancers, the old trope of the money-hungry *devadāsī*-courtesan and her mother (discussed in the previous chapter), and the idea that *devadāsīs* need to be "purified by association with elite men to have a public presence (as would become the case for the singer and actress M. S. Subbulakshmi). Also, the film dramatizes the old trope of the tension between the wife and the courtesan, except that in this case the modern wife yearns to know the courtesan's art—which in the film she cannot seem to master. Indeed, the images of modern Indian women are presented in the form of a dichotomy between tradition and modernity. Lalita, the modern wife, is an educated, urban woman who can drive a car, whereas Jalaja, the *devadāsī* from a temple to Śiva in a South Indian village, represents the piety and naivety of traditional India, a remnant of the past that has been lost in modernity. At the climax of the film, it is dance that mediates this tension, literally calming the madness of Lalita. In that sense, Jalaja's dance is not only morally pure but also has a superhuman or otherworldly quality, that of transcendence—a trope that was used throughout the period of Bharatanāṭyam's reinvention. The concluding scene of the film, in which Jalaja "stands in adoration before the image of Lord Nataraja"[28] simply confirms the film's message about the links between the practice of dance and religion, a message that Arundale couched in the language of a thoroughly Indianized Theosophy, while others such as Coomaraswamy and Krishna Iyer articulated it through the foregrounding of canonical upper-caste Sanskrit textual traditions (*śāstra*) related to philosophy and aesthetics.

The moral register of the film is consistently foregrounded in almost all the available sources. Bharatanāṭyam is a dance that transforms women's own awareness and inculcates idealized notions of what it means to be a woman. Another advertisement from the magazine *Silver Screen i*n 1938, for example, begins with the following line:"Music (*pāṭṭu*) is essential for all girls (*peṇkaḷ*), but it is dance (*āṭṭam*) that improves all feminine traits (*peṇmai*)."[29]

By the 1930s, music had already come to be seen as a relatively acceptable and respectable pastime for non-*devadāsī* women, largely because of its associations with Indian nationalism and Gandhian politics (Weidman 2006; Soneji 2012). Dance, on the other hand, was still lurking in the shadows of *devadāsī* reform and the ultra elite cultural projects of figures such as Arundale. Although it would take at least another decade for Bharatanāṭyam to become a popular cultural form, Seshagiri and the others involved in *Jalaja* likely saw the new medial form of cinema as a suitable mode for amplifying the public discourses around dance in the 1930s that had already been set into motion by the Madras Music Academy and Arundale.

A film about dance, *Jalaja* contained eight songs, almost all of which were presented as dance numbers. The songbook also contains an advertisement for the gramophone record of the film's songs (figure 2.18) and notes that Bhanumathi sang for most of the songs herself.[30] Indeed, this is a major marketing feature for HMV, which produced the record. It is only in the Tamil songbook for the film that one Es. Caṅmukam is listed in the credits as "*naṭṭuvaṉār.*" Since Varalakshmi and Bhanumathi's teacher Vadivelu Pillai died in September 1937, it would be safe to assume that he did not choreograph the dance sequences for the film. Instead, the person mentioned is probably Shanmukasundara Nattuvanar of Thiruppanandal, in Thanjavur district, who was a close associate of Vadivelu Pillai—not much else is known about Shanmukasundara (B. M. Sundaram, pers. comm., Chennai, August 27, 2012). The texts of the songs are probably the best indications of how dance was represented in the film. It is significant that no items from the traditional courtesan repertoire appeared in the film—that is, none of the recognizable genres of the repertoire (*alārippu, jatisvaram, śabdam, varṇam*, and so on) are present in the songbook. Instead, *devadāsī* dance is for the most part recast as devotional dance, and the dances appear encased in generic musical forms (known in concert music as *kīrtana* or *kṛti*). Let us begin with one such piece from the film:

Pallavi: God of the Blissful Dance, consort of the Goddess Beautiful as Desire!
Don't you have compassion on a poor soul like me?
Anupallavi: Destroyer of the demon Tripura, please protect me!
Supreme Soul! Please save me!
Caraṇam: Lord of Citamparam who performs the *tāṇṭavam* dance!
Please rule over me and relieve my uneasiness. (*Jalaja* songbook, 1938)

This is a devotional song that Jalaja sings to the god Śiva-Naṭarāja. It includes a number of epithets of the god (such as God of the Blissful Dance [*āṉantanaṭēca*] and Destroyer of the Demon Tripura [*tiripurān-taka*]) and also contains references to the localized lore of the Chidambaram temple in Tamilnadu, the cultic center of Tamil Śaivism, where Śiva is worshipped as Naṭarāja. These descriptive features are formulaic aspects of devotional poetry in South India, and the poem represents a plea on the part of the devotee who has been separated from the god. One can see how such a piece would lend itself to interpretation through gesture, mimicking the symbols invoked by the descriptions. Also, as we will see below, the interpretation of *kīrtanas* in modern Bharatanāṭyam became a trend in stage performances of Bharatanāṭyam and the cinema beginning in the 1940s, and songs dedicated to the newfound patron deity of Indian dance, Śiva-Naṭarāja, became something of a staple in the repertoire of the newly reinvented dance. Another song, very similar in content, may suggest ever so subtly a style that resonates with the Tamil *padam* genre (Allen 1992), which was a staple in the repertoire of Varalakshmi and Bhanumathi. According to the songbook, it was sung in the film by both the characters Lalita and Jalaja and is in the *rāga* Khamās:

Pallavi: Why hasn't your compassion (*tayavu*) descended?
Tell me, what kind of a secret is this?

Anupallavi: Great Nourisher, dancing in the golden hall (*tillai ponnampalattē āṭi*),
You have enslaved me (*aṭimai koṇṭa*) at such a tender age, my great king (*aracē*)!
Caraṇam: You have patiently borne my sins (*piḻai*) in the past, so please continue.
Only you know my troubles and can take them away.
Dancing God (*naṭēcaṉē*)! Once you have shown your compassion and ruled over me, make sure no one speaks ill of my clan (*kulam*). (*Jalaja* songbook, 1938)

There is a certain self-reflexivity at work in this poem. The woman who sings the song has been "enslaved" by Śiva since a young age—perhaps a reference to the fact that the character of Jalaja is a *devadāsī* who, after undergoing the courtesan initiation ritual of *poṭṭukkaṭṭutal* in his temple, is considered a slave (*aṭimai*) or courtesan (*kaṇikai*) of Śiva. More importantly, the final line of the song—"make sure no one speaks ill of my clan"—has two meanings. It refers to Lalita's need to protect her family's reputation because of Jalaja's intrusion into her family life, and it refers to the stigma Jalaja faces because she is a *devadāsī*, which makes her particularly vulnerable. In both cases, once again, morality—sexual morality in particular—is involved. The film's ultimate resolution of the issue of Jalaja's sexual morality is to allow it to dissipate into a space of transcendence, and hence in *Jalaja*, we see how the invocation of religion clearly made Bharatanāṭyam's past respectable.

We have no information about how *Jalaja* fared in the box office other than some anecdotal news of its poor performance (Pattabhi Raman 1992, 27). However, regardless of the success of the film, it provides us with new perspectives on thinking about the ways in which Bharatanāṭyam was circulating in the period immediately following the work of the Music Academy and Arundale. The global forces influencing the form—which, as we have seen, included not only the Theosophical Society's international network, but also key figures from the world of American dance—enabled new histories and imaginaries of the dance to emerge, while simultaneously rendering invisible earlier hereditary traditions and individuals. In that sense, there is of course some poignancy to Bhanumathi's playing a *devadāsī* character, whose transcendental disappearance at the end of the film suggests the widespread disappearance of *devadāsī* women from the world of public dance performance in this period.[31] The figure of Lalita—a married, urban, and definitely modern woman who wishes to try her hand at this art—foreshadows the eclipse of *devadāsī* performers by women who were part of the modern, conjugal economy of Madras. And that economy also turned what had been a professional practice into something performed by amateurs, for women like Lalita did not intend to take up the practice professionally but rather only as a hobby. As we will see below in this chapter, the entrance of Bharatanāṭyam into the emerging middle-class domicile dovetails with the reformulation of conjugal life and the household under social reform movements and Gandhian nationalism.

SCREENING RESPECTABILITY: FILMS INDEX THE TRANSITION FROM TĒVAṬIYĀR-NĀṬYAM TO BHARATANĀṬYAM

The Tamil film *Sabhapathy* (Lord of the hall; 1941), a social drama produced by AVM Studios and directed by A. V. Meyappan and A. T. Krishnaswami, contains a short dialogue that help us map perceptions of the public transformation of Bharatanāṭyam in the late 1930s and early 1940s. Dialogues such as these demonstrate the degree to which the interventions of figures like Arundale and Krishna Iyer trickled down to the public. However elite their projects may have been, those interventions rapidly led to profound transformations of dance in the public sphere. The dialogue takes place just before Sivakami—the heroine of the film, played by the actress R. Padma (from a *devadāsī* family herself and related to the dancing duo Sayi and Subbulakshmi, discussed in chapter 4), performs a song in the *padam* genre.[32] Two elderly women (the heroine's mother and mother-in-law) are talking about the heroine's interest in dance:

> Mother-in-law: What's going on [with your daughter]? Why is she dancing the dance of the courtesans (*tēvaṭiyāl kaccēri*)?[33]
>
> Mother: Oh God! In this Kaliyuga [the most degenerate age of the Hindu calendar], there are so many new things taking place! Even in schools today, there is a new dance called Bharatanāṭyam, which students are required to learn.
>
> Mother-in-law: Yes, yes.
>
> Mother: My daughter seems to be very talented in this [dance] and has received many medals. A performance has been arranged as

part of the war effort at our collector's bungalow. That is why she is practicing.

Mother-in-law: Oh, I see. My son also loves dance and music (*āṭṭam pāṭṭam*). Last month, as part of the war effort, he staged a play as his contribution.

Mother: Oh, I am so glad. I know there some people who do not like this.

The shifting moral and aesthetic valence of Bharatanāṭyam dance is palpable in the public sphere, and there is no doubt that the cinema—perhaps even more so in films like *Jalaja*—played no small part in both the construction and the dissemination of Bharatanāṭyam's respectability and popularity. As early as 1936, the Tamil magazine *Āṭal Pāṭal* (Dance and song; originally a column in the magazine *Āṉanta Vikaṭaṉ*) featured a story about Bharatanāṭyam's unprecedented popularity and acknowledged that the presence of dance in the cinema represented a new, yet crucial, dimension:

> Something amazing has happened to Bharatanāṭyam! North India and North Indian dancers have been giving much respect to Bharatanāṭyam. Art aficionados will take great pleasure in the fact that women who are in a very high position in society like Srimati Rukmini Arundale have taken to the art and are practicing it. Some of these dancers have been integrated into talking pictures. The films we see these days also showcase Bharatanāṭyam recitals (*kaccēri*) and enhance the greatness of our country and its heritage. Even though the physical rigor and rhythmic complexity involved has many students struggling to learn this dance, many experts are of the belief that with hard work, they will be able to overcome [this] and shine [in the world of dance]. In fact, the newspapers have expressed several opinions about this and I am not sure if people have arrived at any consensus. Once opinions are expressed, then we can start debating the merits and demerits of the physical rigor of Bharatanāṭyam. Lastly, it is gratifying and joyful to see many people taking up Bharatanāṭyam as a full-time profession. (*Āṭal Pāṭ* 1936, 20–21)

I would like to conclude this section with some thoughts on how the interocular world of Madras in the 1930s and 1940s affected the category of the classical and all of the moral, aesthetic, and class-centered complexities it implies. On the one hand, cinema became the perfect "other" of what in the 1930s was emerging as classical music and dance in Madras—that is, classical music and dance were created in opposition to the vulgarity and popular nature of cinematic music and dance. This was certainly a view held by most members of the cultural elite in Madras until recently, and it is one of the reasons why studying film dance in particular was discouraged among students of the classical dance traditions. On the other hand, it is clear that cinema effectively created the idea of the classical dance. Its visual boundaries and extremes were depicted only in the cinema. As we will see later, explicit articulations of classical dance in films—often choreographed by *naṭṭuvaṉār*—became the aesthetic frame of reference for staged versions of Bharatanāṭyam. In a slightly older and perhaps unjustly disregarded essay titled "Tamil Cultural Elites and Cinema: Outline of an Argument," Pandian discusses cinema as a site of "intertextual excess" (1996, 950). This might be a useful way of thinking specifically about the imbrications of cinema and Bharatanāṭyam discussed in this chapter. It is this intertextual and interocular legibility that enables slippages between the forms. To this end, Arundale's desire to make dance look old might be thought of as a kind of illusory strategy, much in the way that cinema attempts to construct and order reality through various levels of illusory strategy. I would argue that the staging of religious sentiment (*bhakti*) and the perceived ritualization of such staging certainly belong to the realm of illusory strategy, as much as the new-yet-old costumes and temple stage do. The questions of who speaks, and to whom, are equally complex, for Bharatanāṭyam's social history over the past hundred years has been inextricably tied to questions of power. It is within this complex matrix of power and powerlessness, presence and absence, and speaking and silence that the making of Bharatanāṭyam's classical avatar must be understood, a fact made evident through Bharatanāṭyam's continual winding through the early Tamil cinema.

[3]

CINEMA, DANCE, AND BOURGEOIS NATIONALISM

Mediated Morality, Classicism, and the State in Modern South India

By now, critical historical work on Bharatanāṭyam has established the complexity of nationalist registers upon which the dance was reimagined, restaged, and reembodied by urban elites in Madras between the 1930s and 1950s.[1] This critical turn in understanding the making of the classical as a bourgeois project of nationalist modernity has forced us to reconsider both the social and moral consequences of art making and the caste- and class-driven aesthetic sensibilities that govern practices like today's Bharatanāṭyam. In this chapter, I hope to contribute to the arc of this critical turn by demonstrating how cinematic representations of Bharatanāṭyam were the major vehicle through which the nationalist dimensions of the bourgeois classicization project were actualized. That is, while cultural nationalists such as Rukmini Arundale, the Sanskrit scholar V. Raghavan, and the lawyer E. Krishna Iyer were discursively couching Bharatanāṭyam in an elitist nationalist telos, the cinema performed the work of taking this discourse to the masses, and ocular cultures more generally were the vehicles used to stage cultural nationalism in South Asia.

In this chapter I examine the ways in which the image field of Bharatanāṭyam in both its staged and cinematic forms was a cultural product, an "imagined community" (Anderson 1983) that stages a peculiar set of collective national symbolisms. To a large degree, religious nationalism in India has enveloped Bharatanāṭyam, creating a discourse of neoconservativism and figural religious excess that occluded the dance form's social history and yoked the art form to new narratives of patriotic piety and modern Hindu devotionalism. As a medium constructed under the gaze of nationalism from the 1930s to the 1960s, modern Bharatanāṭyam cannot but lead to the inertia of radicalized forms of Hindu self-assertion (Hindutva) in the public sphere today.

The neoconservativism engendered by contemporary Bharatanāṭyam also harks back to the socially and discursively constructed links between nation and woman in the 1920s and 1930s, so it is not surprising that women's sexual morality occupies center stage here. As we have seen above, anxieties about women's chastity and sexual purity constitute a cornerstone of the whole debate about dance in modern India—as well as the debate about the cinema as a national medial form. This is illustrated in an unsigned article from 1938 titled "Kuṭumpa Stirikaḷum Ciṉimāvum" (Family women and cinema). The author presents cinema as a career option for "respectable" (that is, noncourtesan, upper-class, and upper-caste) women, in the Gandhian spirit of encouraging women to work for the betterment of the nation:

> In North India, when films first came about, some of the roles of women were played by men (*strī vēṣam*). For example, these include the films of Phalke, like *[Shri] Krishna Janma*, and those on the theme of the sports of Krishna (*kiruṣṇa-līlai*) and Madan company's *Pati Bhakti* [Devotion to the husband], where the roles of women were played by men. But since these cross-dressing portrayals were not working for the general public, women came forward to act in films. Even when the silent movie was transformed into the talkie, many women came forward to act and still continue acting. Many of the women seem to be family women (*kuṭumpa strīkaḷ*). I am not sure if it was because of newspaper reports that said good women should not act in cinema, but recently the Parsi community made a big deal out of not allowing their women to act in films. But that proved to be counterproductive.
>
> In our South India, it seems that every minute there are so many Tamil films being produced. There seem to be many family women acting in these films as well. They seem to appreciate the inherent beauty of the art of cinema and seem to be ready to want to partake of this craft. But there are still newspapers that continuously

> and firmly decree that family women should be banned from acting in films, and if they do so, it will affect their chastity (*kaṟpu*) and their family lives will also be adversely affected. But even after such negative and fearmongering writing, our women are not hiding in fear and shying away from acting in films.
>
> However, there are other more progressive newspapers in our land of Bhārat [India] that proclaim women are very strong and have destroyed their subservience, empowering themselves with knowledge and acquiring knowledge of *caṅkītam* [music and dance]. They are now seen in public spaces, taking up roles of leadership in government, courts of law, giving public speeches and participating in salt marches, resilient as heroic mothers (*vīrattāy*). Therefore, acting in films is not an issue, and it is clear that it will not compromise women's family life.
>
> They realize the beauty of good cinema will give rise to devotion (*bhakti*), knowledge and values. They also realize that cinema is not a space that gives rise to prostitution (*vipacāram*). The films that really touch people will always involve the cooperation of a sophisticated and well-behaved director, a dignified producer and responsible and intelligent actors. Only those directors and producers who are full of "animal lust" (*kēvalam miruka iccai*) compromise the chastity and respectability of family women. ("Kuṭumpa Stirikaḷum Ciṉimāvum" 1938)

In this chapter, I examine how the forces of various kinds of Indian nationalism affected representations of dance in the cinema, and the effects such representations had on stage performances of Bharatanāṭyam between the late 1930s and 1950s. The first half of the chapter focuses on threads of Gandhian nationalism and the vernacular Tamil Indianism in the dance-related cinema work of some prominent writers and film directors. The second half of the chapter specifically examines morality and the pedagogic dimensions of the gendered discourse of Bharatanāṭyam on screen, focusing on how Bharatanāṭyam's unique classicism, which I term "celluloid classicism," cannot be understood without reference to the central places of nation and nationalism, morality, and religion in its earliest instantiations as a modern cultural form.

GANDHIAN NATIONALISM, CINEMA, AND THE ARTS

I would like to begin with the figure of Mohandas K. Gandhi, since Gandhian politics became so deeply rooted in the Madras Presidency between the 1920s and 1940s and, as I hope to demonstrate below, became the anchor for the distinctly Brahmanic bourgeois cultural nationalism that framed the emergence of Karṇāṭak music and Bharatanāṭyam dance as classical arts in the twentieth century. Gandhi's relationship with the arts, and cinema in particular, is very complex. He was at the heart of the *devadāsī* abolition debates of the late 1920s. Davesh Soneji's recent work (2010b and 2012) has demonstrated the extent to which Gandhi was invested in wider discussions about morality and womanhood in colonial South India and Ceylon, and in both places *devadāsī* women became the ground upon which he staged such discourses for well over a decade. As Soneji shows (2012, 133), Gandhi's preoccupation with the supposed moral deficiency of the nonconjugal sexuality of *devadāsī* women meant that he could not accommodate them in his anticolonial political struggle (despite their desire to join him), nor could he view them as suitable citizens of the postcolonial nation. And it is the trace of suspicion of the moral dimensions of the performing arts that follows in his deliberations on the cinema.

As the historian Urvi Mukhopadhyay has argued in a recent essay, Gandhi's antagonistic relationship with the cinematic medium was full of contradictions not only about the medial form, but about modernity itself:

> An ambiguity emerged when despite his strong reservations against modernity, which he had often equated with his political position of being anti-colonial/anti-capitalistic, Gandhi in his campaigns used modern and somewhat cutting-edge technologies of his time, such as railways, microphones and, of course, the printing press, to address his followers across the country. At the same time, his position visibly hardened when it came to the question of the cinematic medium. Gandhi never acknowledged the cinematic medium as an emerging popular and effective means of mass communication. When in 1927 the Indian Cinematograph Committee approached him for his opinion about the state of Indian films along with a

questionnaire, Gandhi showed his disdain for the medium by calling cinema a "sinful technology." (2011, 418)

The notion of the "sinful" nature of cinema, as we have seen in chapter 2, also became a major trope in Tamil vernacular writing. Gandhi's thoughts on the dubious morality of by the cinema thus take on powerful, albeit overridden, resonances. Take for example, his famous words to the Indian Cinematograph Committee of 1927: "I have never been to a cinema. But even to an outsider, the evil that it has done and is doing is patent. The good, if it has done any at all, remains to be proved" (quoted in Dwyer 2011, 349). Gandhi remained skeptical of the cinema's morality, even as dozens of films were being made about him during his own lifetime. As Theodore Baskaran has noted (1981, 200n49), between 1930 and 1932, the state archive records show that thirteen documentaries about Gandhi, mostly produced in Madras, were banned. So while Gandhi disliked the film medium, it is clear that large numbers of people—perhaps especially in South India—were eager to gather information about him through that medium.

While Gandhi was averse to new medial forms, the one cultural form that remained central in his political imaginary was music. In contrast to dance, which was explicitly connected to courtesan communities in both North and South India, music by the 1920s had already moved beyond the field of courtesan cultural production and into the hands of nonhereditary nationalist practitioners. For example, Vishnu Digambar Paluskar (1872–1931), the Marathi Brahmin music reformer who started one of the earliest systemic nationalization projects for music in northern India—namely, the founding of the Gandharva Mahavidyalaya (a school for classical music) in 1901 in Lahore—joined Gandhi. In 1921 Paluskar performed the famous devotional song (*bhajan*) *Raghupati rāghav rājārām* (King Rāma, scion of the Raghu clan) at a rally in Ahmedabad for Gandhi, and the song subsequently became one of Gandhian nationalism's most cherished anthems and, by extension, a kind of "national song" (Bakhle 2005, 165). The affective potential of music in its various forms was a cornerstone of Indian nationalism in the early decades of the twentieth century, even as forms of music—such as those of hereditary lower-caste and other minority musicians—were simultaneously severely censured, appropriated, and even criminalized.

Far more straightforward was the question of institutional forms and practices related to music in Madras. The Madras Music Academy, discussed at length above, emerged directly out of the Indian National Congress (INC). In 1927, the INC held a meeting in Madras at which S. Satyamurthi (1887–1943), a famous Brahmin lawyer and member of the Madras Legislative Assembly, requested that the INC organize an All-India Music Conference to coincide with its annual meeting. In December of that year such a conference was held, and it was suggested that the INC support the creation of an institution for music in Madras. The Madras Music Academy was formally inaugurated on August 18, 1928, by the eminent Brahmin politician and lawyer Sir C. P. Ramaswami Aiyer (1879–1966).[2] As we have seen, this organization that clearly had its roots in the type of cultural nationalism represented and used by Gandhi and the INC had significant consequences for Bharatanāṭyam dance in the post-1930s period.

"BHĀRATI NĀṬYAM" AND BHARATANĀṬYAM: THE POET SUBRAMANIYA BHARATI'S IMPACT ON DANCE AND CINEMA

It would be very difficult to move forward in our discussion of dance and nationalism in 1930s Madras without addressing the question of Tamil politics and the ways in which regional identity politics flowed into the realm of popular culture. In the section that follows, I track the representation of nation and region in Tamil cinema and Bharatanāṭyam through the performance of choreographed versions of the works of the Tamil nationalist poet C. Subramaniya Bharati (1882–1921). Bharati's poetry was a foundation of much of modern Bharatanāṭyam dance in its emerging phase precisely because it addressed the issues of nation, religion, gender, and caste that were so central to the discursive and somatic reinvention of the dance. Bharati's songs are complex from this standpoint. They express strong anticolonial nationalist sentiment, harking back to an imagined notion of the nation as goddess (Bhārata Mātā), yet they also address social issues such as women's education. In this section, I make connections between the new medial appropriations of Bharati's poetry in Madras and the politics of both the nation (India) and he region (Tamilnadu) that were at their height in the 1930s.

The discovery and enunciation of the Dravidian and Indo-Aryan language groups in the nineteenth century (Trautmann 2006) gave rise to a distinct political force in the Tamil-speaking regions of India that is often glossed by the term "Dravidianism." It is significant, however, that Dravidianism is not a homogeneous or monolithic category. In her definitive work on Tamil language politics titled *Passions of the Tongue: Language Devotion in Tamil India, 1891–1970* (1997), the historian Sumathi Ramaswamy addresses the complex politics of *tamiḻpaṟṟu* ("devotion to the Tamil language") in the period we are examining here. She establishes that Tamil nationalisms around 1920 were multiple and heteroglossic.

From Ramaswamy's work emerges an analysis of three ideological streams that approached Tamil language and civilization from varying perspectives. Each of these ideologies were politicized and exerted considerable influence in the public sphere. As we will see below, each had a unique perspective on Tamilnadu's relationship to the rest of India at a time when questions of anticolonial nationalism were paramount. The adherents of the first stream were those whom Ramaswamy glosses as "neo-Śaivas," who dwelled on the inherent divinity of the Tamil language, drawing their inspiration from Śaiva religious reforms that stressed the important of recovering a pure Tamil religion that was devoid of Sanskrit or Aryan influence. The historian Ravi Vaithees (2015) has recently written a masterful work on Maṟaimalai Aṭikaḷ (1876–1950), one of the chief ideologues of neo-Śaivism. The adherents of the second stream were those Ramaswamy calls the classicists—who, following the work of European Orientalists who had recently discovered Tamil texts, used Tamil as a marker of civilizational glory, an ancient language on a par with Sanskrit, Greek, and Latin. The classicists differed from European Orientalists, most of whom saw Tamil as a vernacular language, ands sought to establish it as a classical language (*uyartaṉic cemmoḻi*). The adherents of the third stream, the group most relevant to our discussion of Bharati, were the Indianists, who framed their love of Tamil in terms of their love of India, often invoking the idea of a mother tongue and the nation as mother in the same breath. As Ramaswamy puts it, "negotiating gingerly between . . . the shoals of pride in the nation (*tēṣāpimāṉam*) and pride in their language (*pāṣāpimāṉam*), Indianism reminded Tamil speakers that the liberation of Tamil would have to proceed in tandem with the liberation of India" (1997, 48). It is noteworthy that the members of this group largely came from upper-caste (often Brahmin) backgrounds and often allied themselves with pan-Indian Gandhian or INC politics by the 1920s and 1930s, unlike the neo-Śaivas and classicists—who identified with regional politics and were largely non-Brahmin. Moreover, Ramaswamy notes how some Indianists cast doubts on the discourses of pure

Dravidianism put forth by the classicists and argued that there "was always a place for Sanskrit" in Tamil civilization (ibid., 49).

Bharati is perhaps the best exemplar of this final category. Bharati was born into a Tamil Brahmin family on December 11, 1882, in the town of Ettayapuram, near the city of Tirunelveli. He was married at the age of fourteen to Chellamma, a girl who was seven—according to the custom of child marriage in Tamil Brahmin families. Bharati was educated in Varanasi, where he learned Sanskrit, Hindi, and English, and after returning to Madras, he became assistant editor of the Tamil newspaper *Cutēcamittiraṉ*. He joined the INC and, along with figures like Bal Gangadhar Tilak (1856–1920; also known as Lokmanya Tilak) and Aurobindo Ghose (1872–1950), supported its militant wing. In 1908, faced with the threat of arrest, he fled to the French state of Pondicherry, where he produced his most creative poetic and political works. In 1918, he reentered India and was arrested and jailed for several weeks, until he was released through the intervention of Annie Besant. Throughout his life, he was in touch with a wider, pan-Indian nationalist network.[3] Bal Gangadhar Tilak, Aurobindo Ghose, Gandhi, and Sister Nivedita (born Margaret Noble, a Western disciple of the protonationalist leader Swami Vivekananda) were all associates of his, and he produced some of the earliest Tamil translations of their speeches. He died unexpectedly in Madras in 1921, at the age of thirty-nine.[4]

Even though Bharati did not live long enough to see his poems enter the world of cinema, they were among the most ubiquitous lyrics for songs to appear in the early Tamil cinema. Bharati's poetry, which circulated through the very dense nationalist networks that used both print culture and performance, also became part of the signaletic vocabulary of Tamil cinema within just four years of its earliest instantiation (table 3.1).[5]

The first known Tamil film to include the songs of Bharati is *Menaka* (The heavenly courtesan Menakā, 1935). The poem chosen for use in it wais *Vāḻka nirantaram vāḻka tamiḻ moḻi* (Prosper forever, may the Tamil language prosper), a lyric that places the politics of Tamil language devotion in a wider pan-Indian notion of civilizational grandeur. In this early phase, the poems of Bharati appear alongside a host of other songs that profess Gandhian or Indianist nationalism.[6]

Unlike the earlier films, the film *Nam Iruvar* (We two; 1947) was marketed as a film that featured the works of Bharati. Thus one advertise-

TABLE 3.1.

Some of the earliest films to incorporate the poems of Subramaniya Bharati

YEAR	FILM	POEM	COMPOSER
1935	*Menaka*	"Vāḻka nirantaram vāḻka tamiḻ moḻi"	T. K. Muthuswamy
1940	*Uttama Puthiran*	"Ceṅtamiḻnāṭṭenum pōtinilē"	S. Velsamy
1947	*Nam Iruvar*	"Āṭuvōmē paḷḷu pāṭuvōmē" and "Veṟṟiyeṭṭu tikkum"	R. Sudarsanam
1948	*Vedhala Ulagam*	"Ōṭi vilayāṭu pāppa," "Tūṇḍir puḻuviṉai pōl," "Vacam ulla pūparipēnē," "Koṇṭu kuliviṉai pōl," and "Tīrāṭṭa vilayāṭu piḷḷai"	R. Sudarsanam
1949	*Vazhkai*	"Pārata camutāyam vāḻkavē"	R. Sudarsanam

ment explicitly announces: "Coming! Bharathi in Talkie! Hear the National Songs of the Immortal Poet in AVM Productions' *We Two*." *Nam Iruvar* will be discussed in greater detail below in this chapter, when we turn our attention to the figure of the Brahmin dancer-actress Kamala Lakshman. For now, I would like to focus on another concrete example of the integration of Bharati's poems into Bharatanāṭyam from an archival source dated 1939. This is a spread in the Tamil magazine called *Hanumāṉ*, featuring the *devadāsī* dancer turned actress T. M. Pattammal (dates unknown) in an article titled "Bhārati Nāṭyam" (*pārati nāṭṭiyam*), a pun on the term "Bharatanāṭyam" (figures 3.1a and 3.1b).

Pattammal came from a *devadāsī* community in the town of Thirukkazhukundram. She learned dance from Thirukkazhukundram Turaicāmi Naṭṭuvaṉār (dates unknown), who also taught Vazhuvoor Ramaiah Pillai—who in turn later took Pattammal as his first student (Sundaram 2002, 235). It is not clear how she entered the cinema, but she acted in at least two films in 1939, *Jothi* (Flame) and *Maya Macchindra* (Matsyendranātha the magician)—inspired by the Hindi and Marathi film of the same name produced in 1932, one of the first Indian films to use special effects.[7] The poem by Bharati that Pattammal dances in the magazine spread is in the genre of *kiḻi-pāṭṭu* ("songs to the parrot"), in which the lovelorn heroine speaks to a parrot, a symbol of erotic love. She asks the parrot to act as a messenger (*dūta* or *tūtaṉ*) to her beloved. In the spread, Pattammal is depicted in a set of photographs that use gesture to depict moments in the poem. In one shot, which represents the line in which the god Śiva is invoked, Pattammal dresses as Śiva and assumes the pose of Śiva-Naṭarāja. This poem may be one of those to which Bharati as-

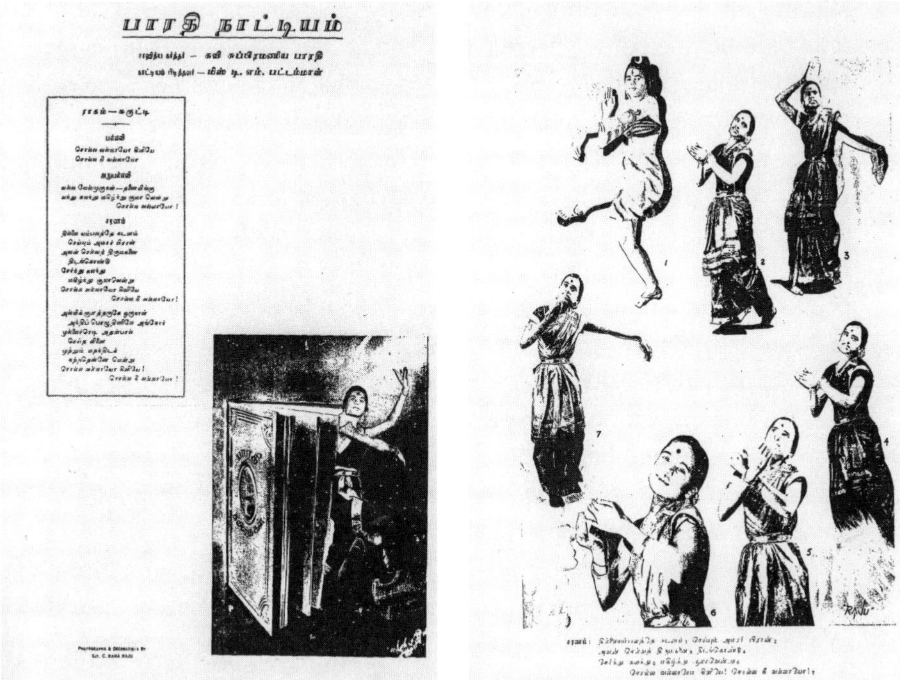

Figure 3.1, a, b. Two pages from a four-page spread showing T. M. Pattammal dancing to the Bharati poem Colla vallāyō kiḻiyē *(Will you be able to tell, my bird?)* *(*"Pārati nāṭṭiyam" *1939, 44 and 46). Courtesy of the Roja Muthiah Research Library.*

signed a *rāga*, since the *rāga* Curuṭṭi is listed in the spread and this is the way the song is rendered in all concerts of Karṇāṭak vocal music today. The text of the poem, as it is reproduced in the spread, is as follows:

> *Pallavi*: Will you be able to tell him, O *kiḻi*, will you be able to tell?
> *Anupallavi*: Ask the Lord Murukaṉ holding the lance, to come and talk to all of us.
> *Caraṇams*: Ask the darling son of the Lord who dances in Cidambaram (Śiva-Naṭarāja), to come here, join us, and be filled with joy.
>
> How could he have completely forgotten what happened that day at dusk near the water lily pond amid the jasmine plants there?
>
> Ask him to recall the beautiful words he spoke while we were walking hand in hand in the desert, while he uttered an oath to me, with his lance as witness. ("*Pārati nāṭṭiya*." 1939, 44–45)

Many of Bharati's other poems, such as the very famous *Ciṉṉañciṟu kiḻiyē* (Darling little parrot), were performed first in the cinema and later adapted to stage performances of music and Bharatanāṭyam. *Ciṉṉañciṟu kiḻiyē* was first featured in the 1951 film *Manamagal* (The bride)—which among other things, was the debut film for the dancer-actress Padmini, discussed in greater detail below in this chapter. In the film, the song is rendered by the playback vocalists M. L. Vasanthakumari (1928–1990; from the *devadāsī* community) and V. N. Sundaram. Although these poems are not nationalistic in their content, the fact that they are works of Bharati—and explicitly identified as such—drew audiences into this realm of the political through their aesthetic and affect. Bharati's poems are thus imbued with nationalist significance both because of their authoriship and their allegorical or symbolic value as women's songs or *bhakti* (devotional) poetry, two key modes in which the literary manifestations of nationalism in South India thrived.

The presence of Bharati's poems in the Bharatanāṭyam and Tamil cinema of the early twentieth century indicate bourgeois nationalism's role in the crafting of both of these medial forms. The gendered focus on the idea of woman as nation, the sexual morality of female citizens of the nation, and female education anchors Bharatanāṭyam and the early Tamil cinema in the larger political debates and frameworks of middle-class nationalism in India in this period.

THE BOURGEOIS PEN: DANCE IN THE WRITER'S IMAGINATION, GANDHIAN NATIONALISM, AND THE CASE OF KALKI

The early Tamil cinema also cannot be divorced from the writing of another major bourgeois nationalist figure, Ramaswamy Aiyer Krishnamurthy (1899–1954), who wrote under the pen name Kalki. Kalki is significant for our study because he, like K. Subrahmanyam and other members of the Brahmin elite in Madras, was at the epicenter of a new form of cultural nationalism that was staged through various media. Functioning primarily as a writer, Kalki influenced popular print culture, and his work entered the modern Tamil theatre and cinema and even stage performances of Bharatanāṭyam. Kalki is also significant because Gandhian nationalism—and Indian nationalism more generally—was mobilized in Tamilnadu through his intermedial interventions, much as it was through K. Subrahmanyam's films.

According to Akhila Ramnarayan, Kalki was born in the village of Puttamangalam in Thanjavur district, and early in his life he met Gandhi and later the Gandhian politician C. Rajagopalachari (1878–1972; also known as Rajaji), both of whom deeply inspired him. In 1923 he moved to Madras, where he began writing for the Tamil literary magazine *Navasakti* (Ramnarayan 2006, 73). He also translated Gandhi's autobiography into Tamil under the title *Cattiya Cōtaṉai* and was heavily involved in the production of anticolonial literature that drew heavily on the idioms of Gandhian nationalism. A large part of Kalki's popularity as a writer and political commentator came from the fact that his writing crossed genres and forms. Ramnarayan writes: "A multi-faceted writer who took on each aspect of the nationalist challenge to British rule, Kalki employed different pen-names (ten in all) under which he successfully experimented with different genres for popular magazines: he wrote fiction as Kalki, nonfiction as Raki, and reviewed the arts under the pseudonym Karnatakam. The pseudonyms afforded [Kalki] Krsnamurti the opportunity to perform a variety of identities for his audiences" (ibid.,8). He wrote extensively for one of the most widely read middle-class Tamil magazines, *Āṉanta Vikaṭaṉ*, and in 1941, together with T. Sadasivam, the husband of the *devadāsī* artist M. S. Subbulakshmi, he founded one of the most widely circulated magazines in the history of Tamil print, called *Kalki*.[8] Start-up funds for the magazine were raised through screenings of the film *Savitri* (1941), in which Subbulakshmi reluctantly played the role of the mythical male sage Nārada (ibid., 77).

Not only did Kalki write serialized novels and reviews of stage Bharatanāṭyam performances, but he was also actively involved in the world of the early Tamil cinema, even before he started *Kalki*. In the late 1930s, he wrote a serialized novel that was published in the magazine *Anaṉta Vikaṭaṉ*, called *Tiyākapūmi* (Land of sacrifice), which had questions about Brahmin identity, untouchability, and anticolonial nationalism at its heart. In 1939, the owner of *Āṉanta Vikaṭaṉ* magazine, S. S. Vasan (1904–69), decided to finance and distribute a film version of the novel, with K. Subrahmanyam as director. The musician Papanasam Sivan played the male lead, while Subrahmanyam's second wife, S. D. Subbulakshmi (discussed at length in chapter 1) played the female lead. After running for twenty-two weeks, the film was banned by the British government in India for its alleged anticolonial and pro-INC stance.[9] Kalki's next major venture into the world of cinema was writing the script for the film *Meera* (1945), about the sixteenth-century Rajasthani female saint Mīrābāī.[10] In addition to the script, he wrote many of the lyrics of the songs for the film. The film was produced by Kalki's magazine partner, Sadasivam, and featured Sadasivam's wife M. S. Subbulakshmi in the title role. The film was directed by the American filmmaker Ellis Dungan and was so popular that two years later it was partly remade, partly dubbed into Hindi, and rereleased nationally. Kalki's novel *Kalvaṉiṉ Kātali* (The thief's lover), which originally appeared as a serialized novel in *Āṉanta Vikaṭaṉ* in 1935, was later made into a Tamil film of the same name (*Kalavanin Kathali*, 1955).

Kalki's proximity to the projects of Brahmin cultural custodianship in the twentieth century is perhaps most clearly demonstrated in his celebrations of the postrevival Bharatanāṭyam in Madras and his incorporation of themes related to dance and music into his own work.[11] In 1944, Kalki wrote one of his monumental novels, *Civakāmiyiṉ Capatam* (The oath of Civakāmi), a historical romance about the seventh-century Tamil king Narasiṃhavarman and a fictional courtesan named Civakāmi.[12] By the time he wrotes this novel, Kalki was already something of a literary celebrity in the world of the early Tamil cinema, and his thoughts immediately turned to making the novel into a film. He apparently approached Arundale about playing the role of Civakāmi. Ramnarayan reports what happened:

> Kalki asked Rukmini Devi Arundale, a controversial practitioner of south Indian dance who founded her own dance academy Kalakshetra in 1936, to play the character of Civakami on film. . . . In invoking this figure, Kalki's sole aim appears to be the valorization of the form itself for his target audience, largely brahminical and middle-class. In 1936, Kalki wrote a glowing review of a performance by Rukmini Devi Arundale held at the Theosophical Society in Madras, exclaiming: "When Srimati Rukmini Devi Arundale took the stage, for one second, one wondered whether the performance was set in the heavens. . . . To gain greatness in a chosen art form is not just a matter of pride in its achievement nor the desire to achieve perfection. Each and every art form has some aspects that cannot be learned through diligence, [aspects] that are instinctively known. Rukmini Devi has been endowed with this intrinsic ability in the realm of dance." (qtd. in Sunda 366). Having established Arundale's closeness to divinity, a kind of eulogizing

that repeatedly accompanies Civakami's performance in the novel, Kalki remarks approvingly: "Her attire and ornaments were tastefully chosen, befitting the occasion. The costume and ornamentation was in accordance with the ancient traditions of the Tamil people; however, the new was intermingled with the old. . . [Her costume] was comfortable enough for dance moves, yet when you observed her in motion, it seemed as though a figurine carved by a sculptor in ancient times had come to life" (qtd. in Sunda 366–67). This type of rapturous effusion combines neatly with Kalki's tutelary agenda in the representation of the female artist, something we see frequently in descriptions of Civakami's performances in the novel. Kalki is here a strong advocate of innovations in costuming and performance that he naturalizes as "tasteful," appropriate, and pleasing to the eye, aesthetic and moral categories acceptable to the brahmin palate. (Ramnarayan 2006, 87–88)

Ramnarayan also relates an incident in which Kalki reluctantly went to watch a dance performance by T. Balasaraswati at a wedding in Madras, after which he was convinced of the superiority of Bharatanāṭyam over new medial forms such as the modern cinema, even while he located the dance in the emerging intermedial cultural world of 1930s Madras. At the same time, he cast Balasaraswati as an exceptional *devadāsī* artist, enabling him to carefully maneuver around the moral implications of his watching a performance of *devadāsī* dance:

The descendant of a centuries-old musical and performance lineage patronized by the Tanjore court, Balasaraswati first performed in Kalki's presence at a wedding. Kalki and T. K.C. went to see her unwillingly. . . . At the time, T. K. C. and Kalki opposed this dance form. They were shocked that it was being performed at a wedding. However, after the kutcheri [concert] they changed their views. After witnessing the kinds of shastras [texts] and traditions contained in the art, they said, 'This art form, with its rich evocations of rasa, has evolved out of the most elevated creative realms; along with the aesthetic response it generates, it is capable of eliciting emotions relating to the divine in the most sophisticated manner' (qtd. in Sunda 364). Kalki writes of the same performance in 1933: "When I watched Veenai Dhanammal's granddaughter Balasaraswati dance . . . I realized that she was one performer in Tamilnad who had extraordinary ability. . . . In modern times, when comparing [this art to] western cinema and talkies and the kinds of dancing we view in them, it is obvious that Bharata Natyam easily outclasses the rest" (qtd. in Sunda 365). (Ramnarayan 2006, 90)

In the figure of Kalki, we see one concrete example of the emergence of a distinctly Tamil Brahmin cultural nationalism, in which Brahmins are understood almost exclusively as custodians and brokers of the arts. This kind of bourgeois Brahmanic nationalism became the long-standing and paradigmatic framework in which the arts were understood, institutionalized, and consumed for much of the twentieth and early twenty-first centuries.

K. SUBRAHMANYAM AS FILMMAKER AND PATRON OF DANCE

We have already discussed some aspects of the life of K. Subrahmanyam in chapter 1, where his "second wife"—S. D. Subbulakshmi, from the *devadāsī* community—was also introduced. In the section that follows, however, I would like to elaborate on Subrahmanyam's engagement with nationalism through the cinema and dance.[13] Subrahmanyam was born on April 20, 1904, in the village of Papanasam, near the town of Kumbhakonam, to the eminent Brahmin lawyer C. S. Krishnaswamy Iyer and his wife, Venkatalakshmi. As a child he studied the Brahmin ritual theatre form known as Bhāgavata Mēḷa Nāṭaka.[14] I do not wish to provide his whole life story here (that can be found in Rangarajan 2005 and Kannan and Kannan 2004, 28–32). Instead, I would like to focus on two important aspects of his work as a filmmaker: his involvement in the production of films focused on nationalism and issues of social reform; and his unfinished project *Narttaṉa Muraḷi* (1945), a film about dance, and its consequences for the institutionalization of dance in Madras.

Subrahmanyam gave up a potential career in law after earning a law degree at the Madras Law College to take up a position as assistant director to Raja Sandow (1895–1943) on some of the earliest silent films produced in South India, in the 1930s. Subrahmanyam had come into his own by the late 1930s, when he made films on somewhat unconventional themes such as *Balayogini* (The ascetic girl child; 1937), which offered commentary on caste discrimination, child marriage, and the treatment of widows (Baskaran 1981, 131–32). One of Subrahmanyam's monumental films was

Seva Sadanam (House of service; 1938). This was based on a Hindi novel by Munshi Premchand called *Sevāsadan* (1918), which was subsequently translated and serialized for publication in Vasan's *Āna̱nta Vikaṭa̱n*.[15] In 1938, Subrahmanyam bought the rights to the film from Vasan for 4,000 rupees, which was, at that time, the highest amount ever paid in South India for rights to any work of fiction (S. Pillai 2015, 152). However, Subrahmanyam's best-known and most feted film was inspired by Kalki's novel of the same name, *Thyagabhoomi* (Land of sacrifice; 1939). This film drew heavily on Gandhian nationalist ideology and also addressed issues related to discrimination against Dalits. The protagonist is a Brahmin reformer named Sambhu Sastri (played by the Brahmin musician Papanasam Sivan) who is called "the Gandhi of Tamilnadu" in the film (Baskaran 1981, 138). He is depicted as a musician who goes to Madras in search of a job as a music teacher, while his granddaughter is depicted as a child dancer. The film affirms the links between music, dance, Brahmins, Gandhian notions of the utopic nation-state, and upper-caste religion. Throughout the film, Sambhu Sastri's Gandhian project of reform receives divine approval from a goddess called Ambikā in the film. In the words of Baskaran, "as a filmmaker conscious of the religious and social background of his audience, Subrahmanyam established his credibility by affirming his faith in God and religion. Moreover, the anti-caste appeal of the film gained greater impact from the fact that most of the team who worked on the film were Brahmins" (ibid., 138). Subrahmanyam's cinematic interventions, widely understood as social breakthroughs, thus cannot be divorced from their location in the project of bourgeois cultural nationalism and the heavily Brahmin-inflected contours of this project in 1930s Madras.

It is against this backdrop that I would like to shift our focus to Subrahmanyam's relationship to dance, specifically by discussing an unfinished film called *Narttaṉa Muraḷi* (The dancing flute; 1945). Like the film *Jalaja* (1938), discussed in chapter 1, *Narttaṉa Muraḷi* would have been one of the earliest films entirely about dance. Unlike *Jalaja*, however, *Narttaṉa Muraḷi* emerged at a time when not only was Bharatanāṭyam becoming a respectable pastime for young upper-caste women, but also its symbolic framework had been fully reworked, and Bharatanāṭyam had undoubtedly become India's national dance form. In *Jalaja*, the central role played by religion in representations of Bharatanāṭyam was evident: in the final scene, the *devadāsī* heroine sublimates her identity into that of the dancing god Śiva-Naṭarāja. *Narttaṉa Muraḷi* affirms a similar representation. This film is actually a cluster of mythological narratives about the god Kṛṣṇa, represented through the various classical dance styles of India. By 1945 when Subrahmanyam conceived of this project, Bharatanāṭyam, Kathak, Maṇipūri, and Kathakaḷi had all been marked by the term "classical," having been brought into the ambit of the cultural discourse of a national cultural revival. Subrahmanyam thus envisaged *Narttaṉa Muraḷi* as a film that would bring all of these dance forms into dialogue, in a move that paralleled the state's philosophy of national integration that came to occupy center stage in the period of Nehruvian nationalism from the late 1940s onward (see, for example, Parekh 1991).[16]

As we have seen above, Subrahmanyam's ties to dance and music were quite tight, and they were also key elements of his personal life, including his own training in Bhāgavata Mēḷa Nāṭaka as a child, and his intimate relationship with the *devadāsī* artist S. D. Subbulakshmi. The film *Narttaṉa Muraḷi* also represents a somewhat mature phase in the classicization of the arts. By this time, Kalakshetra had been established in Madras, dance was being taught at a number of private institutions across India, and state-sponsored patronage of the arts was clearly on the horizon. Subrahmanyam was involved in such state-sponsored cultural activities after 1947.[17]

Archival references to *Narttaṉa Muraḷi* are few and far between, unlike those to *Jalaja*. I have been able to locate only one advertisement for the film (figure 3.2), and to my knowledge, no songbook for the film exists. I draw, therefore, on conversations with Subrahmanyam's daughter, Padma, for information about the film.

Padma Subrahmanyam clearly understands her father as a cultural nationalist and presents him as a steward of "the essence of Indian culture, which for him meant the classical arts" (interview by the author, Chennai, December 23, 2012). She outlined how her father aligned classical dances from various regions of India with various scenes in the film *Narttaṉa Muraḷi*. From the standpoint of Bharatanāṭyam's twentieth-century history, this move brought Bharatanāṭyam into conversation with other dance forms and reinforced the new narrative of the pan-Indian nature of the performing arts, enabling Bharatanāṭyam to converse—through new institutions and visual representations—with other regional cultures of India:

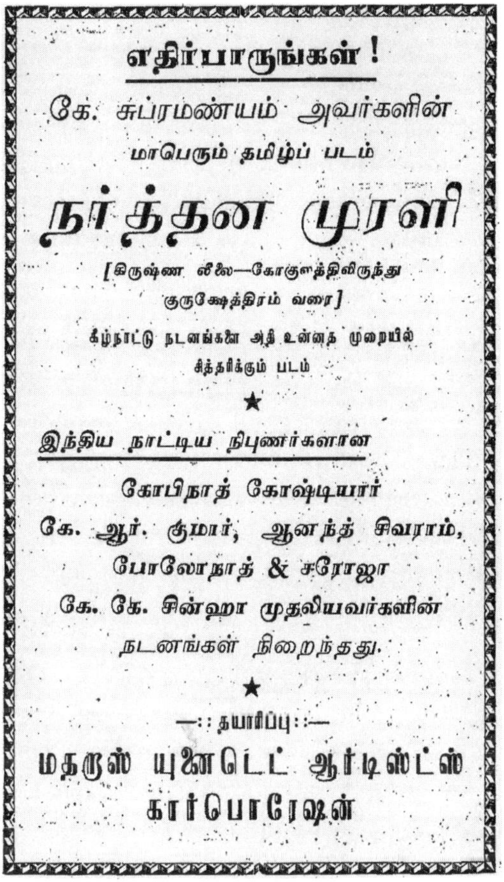

Figure 3.2. Advertisement for the film Narttaṉa Muraḷi *(The dancing flute), directed by K. Subrahmanyam (*Pēcum Paṭam, *March 1945, 6). Private collection of S. V. Jayababu.*

He was a revolutionary—he spoke against caste and child marriage and also spoke about supporting the freedom and liberation of women and other socially relevant issues. But he was very sensitive and conscious about the essence of Indian culture, which for him meant the classical arts. He wanted to produce and direct a full dance film called *Narttaṉa Muraḷi*. They rehearsed for one year. This was supposed to be one of the first films entirely about dance, and [it] was to be made simultaneously in Tamil and Hindi, from Madras. He conceived [of] the movie with various episodes from Kṛṣṇa's life being interpreted through the various classical dance styles of India. So, for example, the lullaby for Kṛṣṇa was supposed to be in the Maṇipuri dance style, whereas the episode of his liberating the demoness Pūtanā was supposed to be in Kathakaḷi style.

One hundred dancers were trained by six or seven dance teachers for a year. The teachers and choreographers for the film included Vazhuvoor Ramaiah Pillai and Kuttralam Ganesan Pillai for Bharatanāṭyam, Guru Gopinath for Kathakaḷi, Guru Kamini Kumar Sinha for Rabindra Nṛtya, Kumaran Aasan for folk dance, and Guru Gadhak and Guru Bhola Nath Sharma for Kathak. All these masters were brought to Madras. *Narttaṉa Muraḷi* was quite an ambitious project!

My father was a genius. I feel his artistic impulses came from a young age. As a child, he had learned [the ritual theatre form known as] Bhāgavata Mēḷa Nāṭaka. My father's native village was Papanasam, and the next village was Melattur. He had learned from a great guru from Melattur by the name of Kinjin Kondandarama Iyer. My grandfather Krishnaswamy was a leading lawyer but also had a theatre background. In fact, because of his association with the staging of Shakespearean plays, and his skill in performing female roles, he used to be called "Portia" Krishnaswamy! I think my father comes from great stock and has great "artistic DNA"! (interview by the author, Chennai, December 23, 2012)

Subrahmanyam also told me how the shelving of the *Narttaṉa Muraḷi* was inadvertently the reason for the birth of the dance school created by her father, which she now heads:

Narttaṉa Muraḷi was not produced because World War II broke out and film was not available. Chennai had to evacuated. There was a bombing. The music was done by a variety of composers including a man named Parthasarathy Iyengar (for the Bharatanāṭyam pieces) and Moti Babu (for the Hindustani part), and the lyrics were composed in both Tamil and Hindi. My father had his film company called Madras United Artists Corporation [MUAC]. Even before All India Radio had a *vādya vṛṅda* [orchestra], my father had a classical Karṇāṭak *vādya vṛṅda*, from the 1930s until the war broke out, consisting of thirty musicians. The musicians were all on the payroll of MUAC, which also cut records. The rehearsals used to take place on Kutcheri Road. When the government declared that Madras had to be evacuated, he told his musicians to return to their villages. My father himself was thinking going back to his native village Papanasam or my mother's native place, Nagapattinam. All his artists and technicians said, "We'll all stay with you, we won't leave you." He was very paternal in nature, truly loving with no axe to grind. So over two hundred people went with him to his village, and they were all living together. He made them start teaching music and dance to the people in the village. And that's how my school, Nrithyodaya, was born. When he returned to Madras, he established Nrithyodaya here. He made it so that students could learn dance for free. At that time, in 1942, he thought training in Bharatanāṭyam was becoming too expensive, so he wanted it to be taught for free! Can you imagine? (interview by the author, Chennai, December 23, 2012)

Finally, Subrahmanyam told me about the afterlives of the incomplete film *Narttaṉa Muraḷi*, reporting that the famous dancers from Kerala known as the Travancore Sisters—Lalitha (1930–82), Padmini (1932–2006), and Ragini (1937–76)—began to use the soundtrack of the film in their own stage performances of Bharatanāṭyam dance dramas during the 1950s: "So *Narttaṉa Muraḷi* was never made. There were posters, though, and the movie was advertised. Our school had a performing wing called 'Natana Kala Seva.' It was in that institution that the sisters Lalitha, Padmini, and Ragini were constantly featured. They used all the songs from *Narttaṉa Muraḷi* for their own performances. Their dance dramas 'Krishna Tulabharam' and 'Parijatapaharanam' featured music and lyrics from my father's unmade film *Narttaṉa Muraḷi*. So although the film was never released, thanks to the trio, its songs and music continued to live on the proscenium stage" (interview by the author, Chennai, December 23, 2012).

Other elements of *Narttaṉa Muraḷi* also survived in one of K. Subrahmanyam's last films, *Geetha Gandhi* (Song of Gandhi; 1949). This film featured his daughter Padma playing the role of Kṛṣṇa at the age of five and melded aspects of Hindu mythology with Gandhian nationalism, a strategy that would become a mainstay of popular Bharatanāṭyam in the decades that followed. Fortunately, the songbook for *Geetha Gandhi* still exists (figure 3.3), and it shows that two choreographers for the film—Pandit Bholanath Sharma and Ghadak—were scheduled to choreograph *Narttaṉa Muraḷi*. Another *naṭṭuvaṉār* is listed only as Muttucuvāmi, which refers to V. S. Muthuswami Pillai (1921–92; discussed in

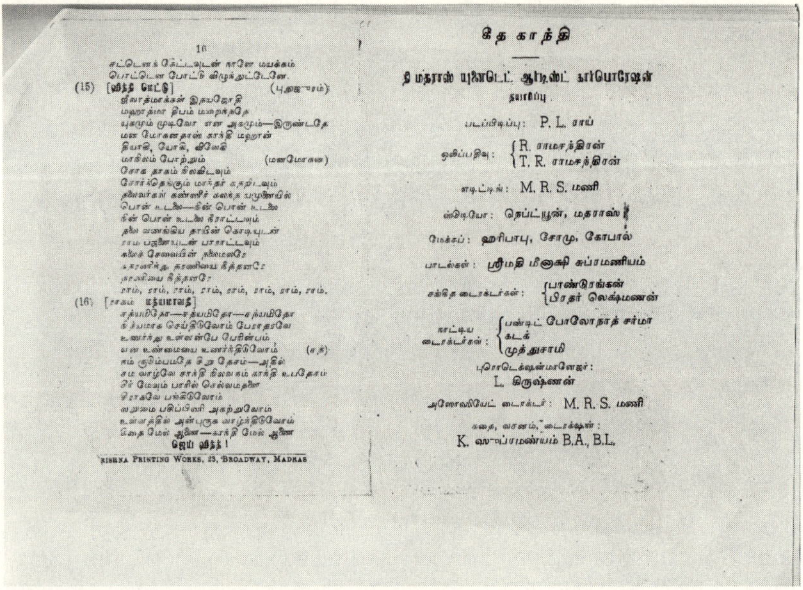

கீத காந்தி

தி மதராஸ் யுனைடெட் ஆர்டிஸ்ட் கார்பொரேஷன்
தயாரிப்பு

படப்பிடிப்பு: P. L. ராய்

ஒலிப்பதிவு: R. ராமசந்திரன், T. R. ராமசந்திரன்

எடிட்டிங்: M. R. S. மணி

ஸ்டுடியோ: நெப்ட்யூன், மதராஸ்

மேக்கப்: ஹரிபாபு, சோமு, கோபால்

பாடல்கள்: ஸ்ரீமதி மீனாக்ஷி சுப்ரமணியம்

சங்கீத டைரக்டர்கள்: பாண்டுரங்கன், பிரதர் லெக்ஷ்மணன்

நாட்டிய டைரக்டர்கள்: பண்டிட் போலோநாத் சர்மா, கடக், முத்துசாமி

புரொடெக்ஷன் மானேஜர்: L. கிருஷ்ணன்

அஸோஸியேட் டைரக்டர்: M. R. S. மணி

கதை, வசனம், டைரக்ஷன்: K. ஸுப்ரமண்யம் B.A., B.L.

ஜெய் ஹிந்த் !

KRISHNA PRINTING WORKS, 23, BROADWAY, MADRAS

Figure 3.3. The opening pages of the songbook for Geetha Gandhi *(*Kīta Kānti*, Song of Gandhi, 1949), presenting the names of choreographers and the nationalist chant "Jai Hind"* (jēy hint)*. Private collection of S. V. Jayababu.*

greater detail in chapter 4). The songbook also is peppered with nationalist slogans such as *Jai Hind* (Victory to India).

Subrahmanyam's life shows how Gandhian nationalism, dance, and the institutionalization of dance and dance pedagogy were linked through the culture of cinema making. Ironically, his legacy did not live through the cinema but survives most potently through the dance career of his daughter Padma who blends forms of Hindu nationalism with dance and a new vision of Bharatanāṭyam's pasts that is rooted in Sanskrit texts, Brahminic Hinduism, and the idea of a Hindu nation.[18]

HOME, NATION, AND RELIGION: KAMALA AND THE MAKING OF BHARATANĀṬYAM AS A POPULAR VISUAL ICON

As we have already seen, by the end of the 1930s, dance had entered the visual space of the cinema in an almost ubiquitous and seamless manner. If the seeds of nationalism were sewn through dance in films like *Jalaja* and the early films of Subrahmanyam in the 1930s, the 1940s marked the entrance on the scene of Kamala Lakshman (b. 1934, popularly known simply as Kamala), and her dance repopulated the aesthetic canvas of Bharatanāṭyam. Her dance was markedly different from its predecessors—athleticized and virtuosic in a new way. Perhaps more importantly, however, Kamala's dance was inextricably yoked to representations of home and nation in obvious ways. In the section that follows, I track a few of her many representations of Bharatanāṭyam on screen to illustrate how the new form of Bharatanāṭyam that she came to represent had nationalist strings attached. That is, it could not be understood without the discursive and performative scaffolding of nation, womanhood, and religion that undergirded the new avatar of the dance form.

Figures such as Kamala served not only to visually relocate the dance in a mythical cultural imagination that displaced the dance's real social historical connections to the courtesan community, but they also enforced a division into two social groups of the women who were performing dance in the 1930s and 1940s. In the North Indian context, Usha Iyer has referred to this bifurcation as the performative "spaces of the Bai and the Devi" (Iyer 2014, 132), with the term *bāī* ("lady") referring to courtesans and the title *devī* ("goddess") being self-consciously appended to the names of noncourtesan performers in the twentieth century as a sign of respectability. Iyer uses *devī* to refer to figures such as Vyjayanthimala who were part of the earliest generation of upper-caste dancing actresses from South India to perform in the Hindi cinema. In South India, Kamala undoubtedly occupies such a role. Her cosmopolitan Brahmin identity, coupled with her apprenticeship under the *naṭṭuvaṉār* Vazhuvoor Ramaiah Pillai, set the aesthetic standard for staged performances of Bharatanāṭyam in Madras. It was her work, not that of Rukmini Arundale and Madras's intellectual elites, that persistently straddled the stage and cinema and brought Bharatanāṭyam to South India's middle class in the 1940s. In that sense Kamala has become an iconic figure in received histories of both cinema and reinvented Bharatanāṭyam.[19]

Kamala's debut in cinema was as a child actress in *Valibar Sangam* (The youth association; 1938), in which she performed a single dance. Meanwhile, at the Madras Music Academy (an institution that thought of itself as an organ of the Congress Party), a handful of *devadāsīs* were performing in public as part of that institution's attempts to prevent the baby from being thrown out with the bathwater—that is, saving Bharatanāṭyam from *devadāsīs*, whose lifestyles were simultaneously being criminalized by the Madras Legislative Assembly. The same year that *Valibar Sangam* was released, a *devadāsī* named Balachandra performed at the Music Academy. In this visual and performative public space of urban consumption—perhaps even more forcefully than in the legal debates around *devadāsī* reform—the tensions related to women's sexuality, domesticity, caste, and aesthetics were clearly foregrounded.

Kamala was born into a Tamil Brahmin family in Bombay in 1934 and was trained in dance as child, beginning when she was about four.[20] When she and her family moved to Madras, she trained with the *naṭṭuvaṉār* Kattumannarkoyil Muthukumara Pillai (1874–1960) and later with Vazhuvoor Ramaiah Pillai, eventually becoming a poster child for the Vazhuvoor school of Bharatanāṭyam, that was really only perpetuated by Ramaiah Pillai and his students.[21] The pairing of Kamala and Ramaiah Pillai was extremely popular on urban stages, and Ramaiah Pillai was conscious of the snowball effect that Kamala's dance had on Madras audiences. He choreographed the *pāmpu naṭaṉam* and *kuṟatti* (gypsy dance) for her, as well as the Tamil poems of the ninth-century saint and goddess Āṇṭāḷ, and her performances were consumed in large doses by urban elites. These dances were also simultaneously depicted in cinema, as we will see in chapter 5. It was this kind of new Bharatanāṭyam that created resonances between the stage and screen and made dance form popular among middle-class women.

In 1947, the same year that India became independent, Kamala acted in a film titled *Nam Iruvar* (mentioned above in this chapter). Among other things, this film celebrated the independence movement, and the figure of Gandhi in particular. Indeed, the marketing for the film, as seen in the rare image reproduced here as figure 3.4a, prominently displayed the scene in which Kamala garlands a statue of Gandhi while dancing (see also figure 3.4b).

The song *Makāṉ kāntiyē makāṉ* (Gandhi is great!) remains one of the most popular sequences in the entire film—it is regularly broadcast on Tamil television channels, especially on occasions such as Independence Day and Republic Day. The sequence opens with a shot of a framed painting of Bhārat Mātā (Mother India, or the nation as goddess)—a ubiquitous visual symbol that makes the link between women, religion, and nation concrete and ever-present in the popular imagination (Ramaswamy 2010). The camera then pans to an image of Kamala, who holds a garland in her hand and hums a tune. Like the poster for the film we saw above, this clip speaks to several registers: nation, gender, caste, class, and aesthetics. Kamala, seen in the midst of middle-class domestic markers

Figure 3.4 a, b. Advertisements for the film Nam Iruvar *(We two; 1947). Courtesy of the Roja Muthiah Research Library.*

(a spacious home, Western-style furniture, and a radio) adds a garland to a home shrine dedicated to Gandhi, while interpreting a patriotic song through *abhinaya*. By this point, dance has already been brought into the home. It has become a symbol of what Partha Chatterjee describes as the "inner world," or the home (*ghar*), the space of the ideal female citizen in nationalist rhetoric (1993, 119; see also 120–21).

The film *Nam Iruvar* also includes a song by Subramania Bharati, *Āṭuvōmē paḷḷu pāṭuvōmē* (Let's dance, let's sing, proclaiming that we have achieved ever-blissful freedom!), perhaps one of the most spectacular moments in the film. This sequence mobilizes the visual and symbolic vocabulary of Gandhian nationalism in unprecedented ways, and Kamala—literally dancing on, in, and through this semiotic world—weaves Bharatanāṭyam into its fabric. The sequence is unique in that a doubling technology makes it appear that there are twin Kamalas dancing throughout the song. The "two Kamalas" dance to backdrops consisting images of the early Indian flag (marked with Gandhi's spinning wheel); the map of India with an image of Bhārat Mātā in the middle; a map made of glowing oil lamps; and then finally the god Śiva-Naṭarāja, who symbolizes both nation and religion (figure 3.5).

Figure 3.5. Kamala dances Āṭuvōmē paḷḷu pāṭuvōmē *against the backdrop of the map and Bhārat Mātā in* Nam Iruvar *(1947). Collection of Davesh Soneji.*

Through a number of other films, Kamala traverses the full spectrum of cultural nationalisms in South India. While the sequences in *Nam Iruvar* actualize a Bharati-Gandhi nationalist matrix, other sequences explicitly foreground the Tamilness of the arts in an attempt to offer commentary on Tamil populist politics. In the film *Manthirikumari* (The minister's daughter; 1950), the last Tamil film directed by Dungan, Kamala dances to the song *Icai tamiḻē initāṉa* (There is no joy greater than that of Tamil music).[22] The film stars M. G. Ramachandran in the lead and was written by M. Karunanidhi, both of whom would become chief minister of Tamilnadu in the 1970s and 1980s. The film is loosely based on the fifth-century Tamil Buddhist epic text *Kuṇṭalakēci* and had what Randor Guy described as a "strong political slant" in its explicit celebration of the Tamil past (2007). Kamala's dance to the song *Icai tamiḻē initāṉa* (figure 3.6) also enables Bharatanāṭyam to be incorporated into an emerging new generation of Dravidianist politics in the 1950s.

Much more could be said about Kamala and her associations with bourgeois nationalist representations of Bharatanāṭyam through the 1940s and early 1950s. However, I now turn to a film that was made long after Kamala had become a celebrity, acted in Hindi films, and had a very successful career as a Bharatanāṭyam dancer. One of Lakshman's most memorable films was the big-budget Tamil film *Konjum Salangai*

Figure 3.6. Kamala performs the song Icai tamiḻē initāṉa *in the film* Manthirikumari *(1950)* (Kuṇṭūci, *July 1950, 26). Courtesy of the Roja Muthiah Research Library.*

(A little kingle of the dancing bells; 1962). This film is effectively the last product of Kamala's career—namely, a complete and nearly watertight rescripting of Bharatanāṭyam's history, a radical reformation of its aesthetics, and more generally a new and explicitly religious spirit that has dominated the dance's representation up to the present.

Set in nineteenth-century South India, *Konjum Salangai* presents a kind of fantasy world of temple dance and music in resplendent technicolor. The film was directed by M. V. Raman (b. 1913, death date unknown) and the music was composed by M. S. Subbaiah Naidu (1914–79). The narrative of the film revolved around the love triangle between a handsome young musician (played by the actor Gemini Ganesan [1920–2005]), a temple singer (played by the actress Savitri [1937–81]) and a temple dancer (played by Kamala). All three characters represented professional artists from the *devadāsī* community, which by then had reinvented itself as the politically mobile *icai vēḷāḷar* caste.

Figure 3.7 a, b. Screenshot of Kamala (left) and Kuchalakumari (right) in the dance competition sequence from Konjum Salangai *(1962).*

Kamala plays a *devadāsī* in this film. A woman really from a *devadāsī* background, Kuchalakumari (discussed in chapter 1), plays her nemesis. In one scene in the film, Kamala and Kuchalakumari, who are rivals, are pitted against each other in a dance competition set in an elaborate palace ornamented with giant images of the dancing Śiva-Naṭarāja (figures 3.7a and 3.7b). After a long sequence that includes both dancers drawing images of animals with their feet dipped in colored powder, there is a long, somewhat boisterous rhythmic sequence in which Kuchalakumari loses the competition and Kamala is celebrated for her dancing prowess, perhaps a fitting evocation of Bharatanāṭyam's social history. Indeed, Kamala's vigorous and athletic dancing (discussed in greater detail in chapter 4) was unmatched by that of any dancer before her, and the point I wish to make here is that this kind of dancing did not exist before her appearance on screen.

In addition to a new kind of virtuosity, sequences from *Konjum Salangai* also provide audiences with commentary on Bharatanāṭyam's pasts. Arguably the most popular song sequence in the film is *Kāṇa kaṇ kōṭi vēṇṭum* (You need a million eyes to see) (figures 3.8a and 3.8b). The lyrics of the song and the choreography are in praise of localized Hindu deities (Śiva at the Chidambaram temple, Viṣṇu at the Srirangam temple, the goddess Mīnākṣī at the Madurai temple, Murukaṉ at the Thiruchendur temple, and finally the apotheosized female saint Āṇṭāḷ at Srivilliputtur and Srirangam). In the last of these sequences, Kamala dresses as Āṇṭāḷ—which by this time was already an established feature of her stage performances of Bharatanāṭyam.[23] The sequence was choreographed by another popular *naṭṭuvaṉār*, Karaikkal Dandayudhapani Pillai (1923–74), a contemporary of Kamala's teacher Ramaiah Pillai.

Figure 3.8 a, b. Kamala in two scenes from the song Kāṇa kaṇ kōṭi vēṇṭum *in the film* Konjum Salangai. *On the left, she plays a* devadāsī *with her music troupe, and on the right, she is dressed as the apotheosized saint Āṇṭāḷ.*

This song dramatizes a particular narrativization of Bharatanāṭyam's pasts that had already occurred by the 1950s. The song and scene present Bharatanāṭyam as essentially religious. The scene portrays a transhistorical temple dance, projecting it away from its uncomfortable social history in local *devadāsī* communities. This rendition of the dance allies it closely with nationalist reinventions and historicizations that occurred in the 1930s and 1940s. The cinematography—particularly the use of new camera techniques and quick-paced edits—accentuated the visual appeal of the dance. Audiences were now shown sets that resembled the local temple shrines of various Hindu deities. In fact, this dance sequence could be read as a kind of a virtual temple pilgrimage. Tamil audiences had a sacred vision (*darśana*) of a pure, golden age of dance that was once associated with temples.[24] The refrain of the song (*Kāṇa kaṇ kōṭi vēṇṭum* [You need a million eyes to see]) implies not just seeing the god but also beholding the dance in the nation's Hindu imaginary, an imaginary populated by the local shrines of Hindu deities and temple dancing.

The film also comments on the aesthetics of *devadāsī* dance by strategically deploying satirical representations of the older conventions of dance. The scene depicts the *mēḷam* style of presentation, in which the *devadāsī* performed in front of her musicians, who stood at the back of the performance space. This convention was employed by *devadāsī* troupes until the time of Kandappa Pillai (1899–1942), T. Balasaraswati's teacher, who had the orchestra sit on the side of the performance space. The *mēḷam*-style presentation was meant for temple or court environments, in which the audience was gathered around the dancer—who, in the course of her performance, would rotate a full 360 degrees. Mimicking this convention, in this sequence, the film shows the audience the exaggerated facial expressions and body language of the musicians. These caricatures represented the *devadāsī* community as fundamentally unsophisticated and crude, and ultimately as unfit citizens of the modern nation. However, Kamala, who the audience knows is simply playing a *devadāsī*, stands apart. Her virtuosic movements, the religious nature of her dancing, and her public persona as a top Bharatanāṭyam dancer all enforce this idea. This reading is clear when we think about it in relation to our previous clip: Kuchalakumari, the loser in the dance competition sequence, *is* one of them.

The hybridity that affected transformations of Bharatanāṭyam dance at that time was also seen in the film. These transformations were part of a new way of thinking about Bharatanāṭyam as a malleable form that was not limited to non-Brahmin castes or the *devadāsī* community. The dance and music sequences in *Konjum Salangai* enabled elite audiences to claim Bharatanāṭyam for themselves: the dance was read as a sign of a transhistorical religious past. Even if there *were devadāsīs* and *naṭṭuvaṉārs* in that past, like the dancer Kuchalakumari and choreographer Dandayudhapani Pillai, they are clearly not the focus. In contrast, Kamala represents the reclaimed Bharatanāṭyam. Many of the songs from movies such as *Konjum Salangai* became extremely popular on stage and continue to be presented as signs of cultural nostalgia on television game shows featuring classical dance.[25] Indeed, Bharatanāṭyam's domestic avatar was part of a larger world of Indian nationalism that brought women, religion, and patriotism together. It is at this intersection of modernity and mythology that Kamala's performance of hybridized Bharatanāṭyam has to be situated.

Kamala's role in the recasting of Bharatanāṭyam as a nationalist and religious art form in the twentieth century runs deep. On stage, she danced to and popularized a number of devotional songs that went on to become popular numbers in modern Bharatanāṭyam such as *Tāyē yacotā* (Oh mother of Kṛṣṇa!) for example, at her performance in the Tambaram Sangeeta Sabha in Madras on January 14, 1951.[26] In an interview she gave to a popular South Indian entertainment website (Aruna n.d.), Kamala told the interviewer that she regularly teaches dances from her films to students at Sri Bharata Kamalalayam, her dance school in New Jersey, where she emigrated in 1980. She specifically identified the nationalistic poems of Subramaniya Bharati that she danced in the films *Nam Iruvar* (1947) and *Vedhala Ulagam* (1948), as well as the snake dance (the song *nātar muṭimēl irukkum*) from the film *Digambara Samiyar* (1950), as pieces that she teaches to her Bharatanāṭyam students in the diaspora today.

DANCING DOMESTICITY: GOOD WIVES AND DIDACTIC REPRESENTATIONS OF NATIONALIZED WOMANHOOD

According to Ramaswamy, "Mother India was partly modeled on the 'new' mother presiding over the reformed urban middle-class household hesitatingly emerging in different parts of colonial India, itself imitative of Victorian domesticity but yet not sacrificing the essential 'tradition' and 'spirituality' of an authentic (Hindu) past. This, in turn, meant more than ever as nationalism gathered strength, that the representative Indian women's dominant function was the production and reproduction of the nation itself, with her primary identity that of motherhood. It also meant that the nation's women had to remain essentially, authentically, and *visibly* 'Indian,' even Hindu" (2010, 238).

As we have already seen in the example of the poetry of Bharati, representations of women as keepers of tradition and metonyms for the nation circulated widely in Tamil cinema in the early twentieth century. Caste and class were also integral parts of this moral representation. Good women were almost always shown as being both upper caste and middle class. An obvious anxiety about morality characterized the reinvention of dance in Madras in the 1930s, and this anxiety also became entrenched in the pedagogical program of Bharatanāṭyam as a middle-class expressive form. Therefore, I would like to turn to two examples that clearly illustrate this nexus of morality, caste, and class but also foreground another dimension of dance in the cinema: its didactic or pedagogical value. The archive records the intersection of aesthetics and moral pedagogy in fragments such as the statement below, in which bourgeois brokers of culture juxtapose Arundale's "positive" reinvention of Bharatanāṭyam with the "atrocious" aesthetics of *devadāsī* dance. This is immediately followed by a recommendation that the new Bharatanāṭyam be taught to girls in Madras's public schools:

> Fortunately, Bharatanāṭyam still has some respectability. But those people who claimed that they were going to make changes have

> still not done so yet. Based on the recent Bharatanāṭyam concert of Mutturatnambal, it is clear that one can still see the atrocious dress and the overall aesthetics [of the presentation] have marred the quality of the dancer's skill. Knowledgeable dance connoisseurs and leaders should come together and make some positive changes to the costumes, design, stage decor and presentation of the dance. To this end, Smt. Rukmini Devi Arundale has been setting a great example. People should certainly follow this and take her lead. Furthermore, as the Chief Minister of Madras [C. Rajagopalachari] says, all girls should be taught dance and music, and if this happens, every home will resound with *caṅkītam* [*saṅgīta*, music and dance]. To this end, all girls should learn dance and music in their schools as part of their daily curriculum. This also will inevitably improve the mental faculties of these girls, as well the physical well-being of their bodies. (*Āṭal Pāṭal* 1938, 25)

The concerns about women's bodies, controlling them, and most importantly controlling their representation remain central to both staged and cinematic presentations of Bharatanāṭyam after the 1930s. The *devadāsī* performer who is derided in the quote above, Tirunelveli Mutturatnambal (1892–1964), ironically performed at the Madras Music Academy on December 27, 1937 (which is likely the performance referred to above), and her performance contributed to making Bharatanāṭyam a palatable dance to the middle class (figure 3.9).

Returning to the pedagogical underpinnings of the reinvented Bharatanāṭyam for women, I wish to discuss two later (1950s) Bharatanāṭyam pieces in the cinema. In both of the representations, the lyrics are meant to be deeply internalized by the audience. At least one of these songs made regular appearances in Bharatanāṭyam dance recitals in Madras in the late 1950s, showing that the moral registers of the cinema and stage versions of Bharatanāṭyam were constantly in intimate dialogue in this period.

The first example is from the film *Manamagal* (The bride; 1951).[27] It is significant that by this time, Bharatanāṭyam had been a middle-class, upper-caste expressive form for close to fifteen years, and thus it is not surprising to see that questions of upper-caste women's morality have come to occupy center stage, while such women have become role models for women from other communities. Indeed, in this sequence,

Figure 3.9. Tirunelveli Mutturatnambal. Photograph courtesy B. M. Sundaram.

the song is put into the mouth of Kuchalakumari (who, as noted above in this chapter, was from a *devadāsī* family). The song also sits alongside a poem by Subramaniya Bharati that is also featured in the film as another song, (*Cinnanciru kiḻiyē*). The song, *Nalla peṇmaṇi* (she is a jewel among women), written by the film lyricist Udumalai Narayana Kavi (1899–1981), is clearly didactic, telling young women how they should behave as citizens of the new Indian nation:

> [Listen!] She is a jewel among women
> The one who follows the customs of her Motherland,
> She is a jewel among women
> The one who awakens at the first call of the rooster,
> The one who bathes and cleanses her body of dirt, who washes her clothes,
> The one who attends school from dawn to dusk,
> The one who cultivates good habits and reads many books,

She is a jewel among women
The one who makes it a habit to help her mother and cook rice,
"First she must do her chores and only then can she rest."
She mustn't waver from these wise words uttered by her father.
The one who embodies good qualities like patience and grace
everyday,
She is a jewel among women. ("Tamil Old" n.d.)

While such didactic songs about women's morality were ubiquitous in Indian cinema across regions of the country and throughout the twentieth century, what makes this piece unique is that its relationship to Bharatanāṭyam runs deep. Not only is the text conveyed through the gestural language of *abhinaya* in Kuchalakumari's performance in the film, but the song also continues to be part of stage performances of Bharatanāṭyam. In a regular Bharatanāṭyam performance in Madras on July 12, 1959, Kumari Vasanta, a disciple of the *naṭṭuvaṉār* Sikkil Ramaswamy Pillai (1876–1972), performed this piece on stage (figure 3.10). It appeared in lieu of the erotic song genres of *padam* or *jāvaḷi* that would normally have appeared in the second part of the performance. Indeed, the erotic repertoire was almost completely absent from this performance, replaced by this piece, a gypsy dance (*kuṟatti*, which we will discuss in detail below), and the umbrella dance (*kuṭai ṭāṉcu*). The use of the film song in this context is significant. It maps the ways in which the moral registers of Bharatanāṭyam had changed by the 1950s: courtesan pieces had been replaced by those that explicitly expressed a non-courtesan sexual morality. While much of mainstream Bharatanāṭyam accomplished this by sublimating sexuality into devotion or the foregrounding of mythical female figures (such as Sītā, Draupadī, Ahalyā, and other *pativratās* [chaste women]), this song features a middle-class woman and scripts these discourses on her through a new, mediatized Bharatanāṭyam.

The second example comes from the film *Panam* (Money; 1953). This song, also written by Narayana Kavi, is titled *Kuṭumpattiṉ viḷakku* (Light of the family). Similar in tone and texture to the dance we have just discussed, this song is danced by the dancer and actress Padmini Ramachandran, who was not from the *devadāsī* community. The text of this song is also very didactic, outlining the characteristics of the ideal new Hindu woman.

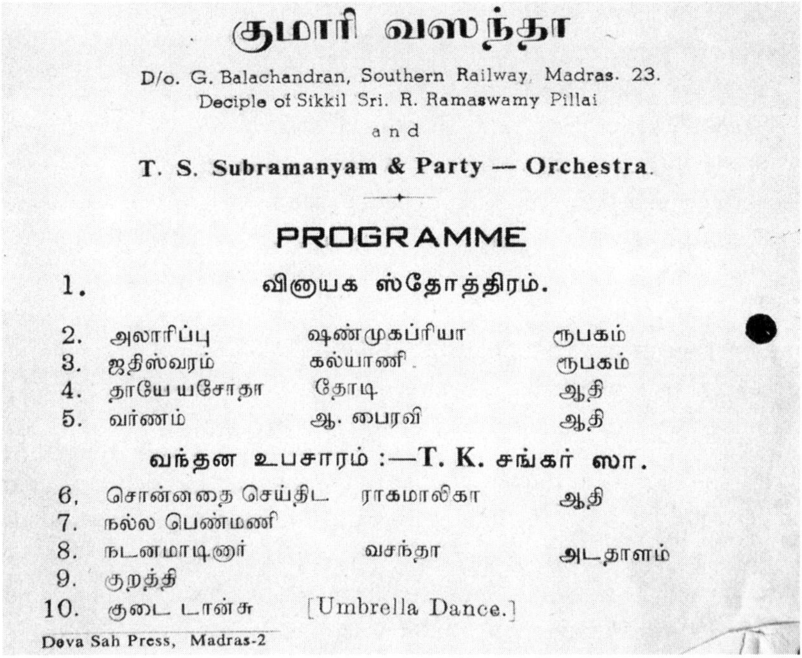

குமாரி வஸந்தா

D/o. G. Balachandran, Southern Railway, Madras. 23.
Deciple of Sikkil Sri. R. Ramaswamy Pillai

and

T. S. Subramanyam & Party — Orchestra.

PROGRAMME

1.	விநாயக ஸ்தோத்திரம்.		
2.	அலாரிப்பு	ஷண்முகப்ரியா	ரூபகம்
3.	ஜதிஸ்வரம்	கல்யாணி	ரூபகம்
4.	தாயே யசோதா	தோடி	ஆதி
5.	வர்ணம்	ஆ. பைரவி	ஆதி

வந்தன உபசாரம் :—T. K. சங்கர் ஸா.

6.	சொன்னதை செய்திட	ராகமாலிகா	ஆதி
7.	நல்ல பெண்மணி		
8.	நடனமாடினார்	வசந்தா	அடதாளம்
9.	குறத்தி		
10.	குடை டான்சு	[Umbrella Dance.]	

Deva Sah Press, Madras-2

Figure 3.10. Program notes for a stage dance performance by Kumari Vasanta in Madras on July 12, 1959, that used the film song Nalla peṇmaṇi *(item number seven). Collection of Davesh Soneji.*

The light of a good family,
She is the light of the family.
Woven into the family as a mother, just as thread is woven into a sari,
She is the light of the family.
Living in a country where women like her are praised by everyone,
She is the light of the family.
Doing her housework, no matter how busy she is,
She is the light of the family.
Intelligence quick as that of a fish,
She is the light of the family.
She doesn't gossip or spend time in others' homes,
She is the light of the family.
She never attracts negativity from others,
She is the light of the family.
Of flawless moral character, no one doubts her,

She is the light of the family.
She raises her children with the best habits,
She is the light of the family.
She is always praised by her mother-in-law,
She is the light of the family.
She always delights the heart of her husband,
She is the light of the family.
She stands, serves, and respects her husband's relatives when they come home,
She is the light of the family.
She excels in protecting her family's name and moral character,
She is the light of the family. ("Panam 1952" n.d.)

These songs push the boundaries of the function of Bharatanāṭyam in cinema. Not only does Bharatanāṭyam embody bourgeois nationalist propaganda through women's bodies, but it also becomes a medium through which the highly gendered language of what Kalyani Devaki Menon (2010) calls women's "everyday nationalism" shapes ideal upper-caste, middle-class femininity. This prescriptive nature of Bharatanāṭyam, voicing the deep patriarchy of Indian nationalism, is one key to its success as a persistent and popular form through the twentieth and twenty-first centuries.

BRAHMIN DANCER-ACTRESSES AND THE ASPIRATIONAL AESTHETICS OF BHARATANĀṬYAM

I end this chapter with some deliberations on the power of the new form of Bharatanāṭyam represented by figures like Kamala and the ways it paved the road for what I call the aspirational aesthetics of today's Bharatanāṭyam. I argue that the bourgeois cultural nationalism we have seen, embodied in and disseminated through both cinematic and stage versions of Bharatanāṭyam, shaped the national consensus about notions of the classical in the 1930s, 1940s, and 1950s. New class- and caste-based orientations and aspirations were scripted into the aesthetics of the new nationalist Bharatanāṭyam. While other scholars have referred to these new aesthetics as a kind of Brahminic taste (Soneji 2012), I would extend this idea to say that it was "Brahminic" not only in the sense that it was perpetuated and embodied almost exclusively by Brahmin women, but also in the sense that it encoded aspirations or upward mobility.

Figure 3.11. A still of T. Prabhavathi dancing in the Kannada-language film Samsāra Naukā *(The boat of existence; 1948) in "Ṭi. Pirapāvati" (1950, 71). Courtesy of the Roja Muthiah Research Library.*

Non-Brahmin women who were not *devadāsīs* and came from relatively upper-caste backgrounds (such as Tamil-speaking Mutaliyārs, Ceṭṭiyārs, and Nāyars from Kerala) not only sought to absorb the aesthetics of new Bharatanāṭyam but also worked hand in hand with Brahmin dancers to fortify Bharatanāṭyam's social exclusivity through the language of the classical, with all its religious, nationalist, and reformist aesthetic inflections.

The on-screen dancing of Kamala undoubtedly represented a kind of social intervention. Previously, Tamil Brahmin women (or women not associated with *icai nāṭakam*) very rarely had any significant presence in the performing arts. However, it would be wrong to assert that Kamala was the first Brahmin woman to be known for her dancing in films. A case in point is the little-known actress T. Prabhavathi, born in 1924 in Trichur, Kerala, to Ramanatha Iyer and Chellamal, both from the *smārta* Brahmin community (figure 3.11).

Very little information is available about Prabhavathi, but we know that she danced Bharatanāṭyam in a number of films before Kamala appeared on the scene. I have been able to find one archival source that features her. This source provides perhaps the only available biographical information about her training in dance and how she, as Brahmin actress, came to represent Bharatanāṭyam on screen before the 1950s:

When she was six years old she underwent training in Kathākālakṣepam (Harikathā) from Krishna Bhagavatar. She went to many villages [performing] under the name of "Trichur Rukmini." Her sister would accompany her on vocals. Blessed with a beautiful singing voice, Prabhavathi also leaned music from "Kaviñar" Meenakshi Sundaram Pillai and Palaghat Nataraja Vadyar. She also underwent training in Harikathā from the late S. S. Mani Bhagavatar. She has not performed Kathākālakṣepam for a long time, excepting a few performances that included *Vatsalā Kalyāṇam*. She felt incorporating *abhinaya* into Kathākālakṣepam performances would make it appealing to a wider audience and would make her work more accessible. For this, she went to study under [the *devadāsī* performer] Mylapore Gauri Ammal [1892–1971]. Noting her natural flair for *abhinaya*, her beautiful face and her supple body, Gauri Ammal encouraged her to also formally learn Bharatanāṭyam. In fact, Prabhavathi had dreamed of learning Bharatanāṭyam since she was a child. So she began learning from one Kannappa Nattuvanar [dates unknown]. After six months of arduous training, she gave her *araṅkēṟṟam* at [the] Chembur Railway Institute [in Kerala]. After this she also performed at the [Indian] Fine Arts Academy [in Madras]. She then went on to perform in many towns and people immensely appreciated her dancing.

All this praise of her dancing naturally led film producers to gravitate toward her. Will the film folk keep quiet when there is a talented girl dancing? Invitations to act in films came pouring in. Her first film was *Vipranarayana*, produced by Gopalakrishna Talkies. Incidentally it was also the first movie of [the] Telugu actress Suryakumari.... She [Prabhavathi] is currently acting in Jupiter Pictures' *Krishna Vijaya* as Radha. Because of her busy schedule in films, she was not able to dance Bharatanāṭyam much. However, recently she has returned to presenting recitals of Bharatanāṭyam again. Having lost her parents at a young age, she lives with sister in Chennai. She is fluent in Tamil and Malayalam and also knows some English. She practices very good etiquette, and the fact that she is from an upper-class family shines through in how she behaves and acts. Endowed with a beautiful face and amazing dancing and acting skills, she has acted in nine films so far. ("Ṭi. Pirapāvati" 1950, 62–63)

In this excerpt from the feature on Prabhavathi, we see very clearly a direct juxtaposition of a narrative about her training in dance, a summary of her work in the cinema, and an explicit foregrounding of her moral virtues, which are understood to be rooted in her upper-class (that is, upper-caste) background. Indeed, it was figures like Prabhavathi who, straddling the early worlds of cinematic and stage performances of Bharatanāṭyam, enabled people like Kamala to enter these professional spaces.

A chapter such as this would not be complete without a mention of the star Brahmin dancer-actress Vyjayanthimala. Like Kamala, Vyjayanthimala began her career as a dancer, training at first under Vazhuvoor Ramaiah Pillai (who had already established his presence in the Tamil cinema by the late 1930s) and then later under K. N. Dandayudhapani Pillai, who also initially involved in Arundale's Kalakshetra and started choreographing for the cinema in the late 1940s. It was during one of Vyjayanthimala's stage performances of Bharatanāṭyam that A. V. Meiyappa Chettiar, founder of AVM Studios in Madras, and the director M. V. Raman saw her for the first time in 1949, and they hired her for the Tamil film *Vazhkai* (Life; 1949). This was remade into Telugu as *Jeevitham* (Life; 1950) and Hindi as *Bahar* (Springtime; 1951). In the 1950s, Vyjayanthimala continued her dance training under K. P. Kittappa Pillai of Thanjavur, and she continued to dance Bharatanāṭyam, publish books on the subject, and produce commercial recordings of Bharatanāṭyam music as she became a superstar in the Hindi cinema from the 1950s to the 1970s.[28] Usha Iyer's work on film dance and female stardom in the Hindi cinema includes an excellent analysis of Vyjayanthimala's role in producing a particular kind of reproducible dance vocabulary for the Hindi cinema, based on her training in modern Bharatanāṭyam:

> Vyjayanthimala's training in and continued performance of the classical dance form Bharatanatyam produced a certain kind of performing body that was employed in a number of costume dramas and the courtesan film genre and led to the creation of performance spaces [in the form of sets] such as royal courts or the professional stage in order to accommodate her movement vocabulary. Vyjayanthimala's movement vocabulary produced an image markedly imbricated in popular Hindu iconography and extradiegetically, her classical dance training helped create a "clean" star text,

Figure 13.12 a, b. Screenshot of Vyjayanthimala dancing to the song Ilalō sāṭilēni bhāratadeśam *in the Telugu film* Sangham *(1953). She is framed against the iconic images of "respectable" dancing: Śiva-Naṭarāja, a map of the nation, and the Hindu temple (right).*

> more or less insured against scandal and gossip, and served to prop her up [as] an icon of national cultural heritage. (2014, 11)

As Iyer notes, Vyjayanthimala, like Prabhavathi and Kamala, straddled the worlds of screen and stage dance, as well as the South Indian and Hindi cinema industries, and like Kamala, she is "insured" against the kinds of stigma that surrounded hereditary *devadāsī* performers and female drama artists in this period. Iyer's point about Vyjayanthimala's imbrication in nationalist ideologies of "cultural heritage" and the Hindu imaginary may be most obvious in one of her earliest films, which was made in three languages: *Sangham* (Confluence; 1953) in Telugu, *Penn* (Woman; 1954) in Tamil, and *Ladki* (Girl; 1954) in Hindi. The song that in Telugu is called *Ilalō sāṭilēni bhāratadeśam* (There is no country equal to India) is danced to by Vyjayanthimala in the same manner in all three versions of the film. The dance is divided into three sequences, in which Vyjayanthimala is framed against all of the iconic images of respectable dancing: an icon of Śiva-Naṭarāja (figure 3.12a), the map of the nation, and the Hindu temple (figure 3.12b). This unquestionably harks back to Kamala's spectacular dance to the song *Āṭuvōmē paḷḷu pāṭuvōmē* in *Nam Iruvar* (1947) that we examined above.

While Kamala and Vyjayanthimala became iconic Brahmin performers who facilitated the near-exclusively Brahminic nature of the new Bharatanāṭyam in public culture, another dancer-actress may best exemplify the aspirational aspect of Bharatanāṭyam's new avatars on stage and screen. This is Padmini Ramachandran (1932–2006), who was

Figure 3.13 a, b. Left: Poster for the film Vinōtiṉi *(Vinodini; 1949), featuring dances by Padmini and Lalitha.* Kuṇṭūci *(February 1949, 7). Right: Still of Padmini from an unknown Tamil film. From the private collection of S. V. Jayababu.*

neither a Brahmin nor from a *devadāsī* background. Padmini, as she was best known, descended from members of the Nāyar caste, an upper-caste group that—in the case of Padmini's family—was in the employ of the princely state of Travancore. Padmini and her older sister, Lalitha, (1930–82), and younger sister, Ragini (1937–76), became known as the Travancore Sisters for this reason (figures 3.13a and 3.13b). They all learned Bharatanāṭyam from the *naṭṭuvaṉār* Thiruvidaimarudur Mahalingam Pillai (1917–2002) and Kathakaḷi from Perumanoor Gopinath Pillai (1908–87; also known as Guru Gopinath). Like Vyjayanthimala, Padmini became one of the most famous early South Indian dancer-actresses to perform in the Hindi cinema. In her Tamil films, she often danced to the choreography of the *naṭṭuvaṉārs* Ramaiah Pillai and K. N. Dandayudhapani Pillai.

Even though it came relatively late in her career, one of her most popular roles was in the film *Thillana Mohanambal* (Mōkaṉā who dances the *tillāṉā*; 1968), in which she played the role of a *devadāsī* named Mōkaṉā (or Mōkaṉāmpāḷ). This film was based on the Tamil novel of the same name by the Brahmin writer Kothamangalam Subbu (1910–74).[29] As Indira Peterson has demonstrated, the novel and the film offer a new public scripting of the *icai vēḷāḷar* community in which the art (*kalai*) of men in the community who play the *nāgasvaram* is valorized (2008b, 261), while the figure of the *devadāsī* remains ambiguous and is cast in a "deeply conservative and reformist (and Gandhian puritanical) spirit" (ibid., 260). The film became famous largely because of its star cast, in which Sivaji Ganesan (1928–2001) played the hero and Padmini the heroine. It was also popular because of its virtuosic *nāgasvaram* performance and Padmini's spectacular dancing, which drew on the aesthetics made popular by Kamala's new form of highly athleticized, fast-paced, and virtuosic Bharatanāṭyam.

Like Kamala and Vyjayanthimala, Padmini—often along with Lalitha and Ragini—continued to perform Bharatanāṭyam on stage even at the height of her career as a film star. Often these were performances that, like Kamala's repertoire from Ramaiah Pillai, consisted of traditional genres mixed with new or innovative pieces. In the program from their 1957 performance in Madras (figure 3.14), for example, they performed pieces like the courtly *tillāṉā* alongside the peacock dance, Śiva-Pārvati dance, and even mini dance dramas such as *Pārijātāpaharaṇam* and *Mīrā* (about the saint Mīrabāī). The themes of both of these dramas undoubtedly were chosen because they were the subjects of very popular South Indian films in the 1930s, 1940s, and 1950s. The program also featured dances to the songs *Naṭaṉam āṭiṉār* (discussed in detail in chapter 5), and the Kannada-language devotional song *Kṛṣṇa nī bēganē bārō* (made popular by the Madras-based *devadāsī* performer T. Balasaraswati). Their repertoire thus comes from what we might think of as popular Bharatanāṭyam—that is, stage versions of Bharatanāṭyam that drew upon a range of semiotic, textual, and movement registers, including that of the cinema and other imaginings of Bharatanāṭyam in Madras in the 1930s and 1940s.

In conclusion, I would like to return to the idea of the aspirational aesthetic of the dancing of Kamala, Vyjayanthimala, and Padmini that enabled Bharatanāṭyam to become a popular yet classical art form. Bharatanāṭyam's classicism was scripted and enunciated by elite figures like Arundale, Raghavan, and Krishna Iyer, and its popularity was undoubtedly supported by its representation in the cinema. However, its cinematic representations carefully kept intact elements of the dance's

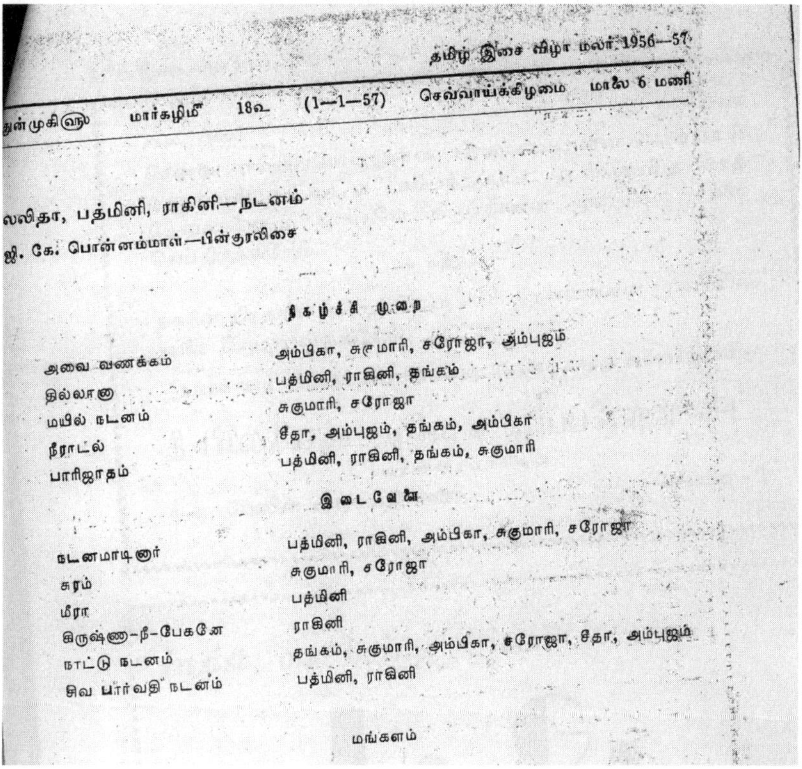

தமிழ் இசை விழா மலர் 1956—57

துன்முகி ௵ மார்கழி ௴ 18௳ (1—1—57) செவ்வாய்க்கிழமை மாலை 6 மணி

லலிதா, பத்மினி, ராகினி—நடனம்

ஜி. கே. பொன்னம்மாள்—பின்குரலிசை

நிகழ்ச்சி முறை

அவை வணக்கம்	அம்பிகா, சுகுமாரி, சரோஜா, அம்புஜம்
தில்லானா	பத்மினி, ராகினி, தங்கம்
மயில் நடனம்	சுகுமாரி, சரோஜா
நீராட்டல்	சீதா, அம்புஜம், தங்கம், அம்பிகா
பாரிஜாதம்	பத்மினி, ராகினி, தங்கம், சுகுமாரி

இடைவேளை

நடனமாடினார்	பத்மினி, ராகினி, அம்பிகா, சுகுமாரி, சரோஜா
சுரம்	சுகுமாரி, சரோஜா
மீரா	பத்மினி
கிருஷ்ணா—நீ—பேகனே	ராகினி
நாட்டு நடனம்	தங்கம், சுகுமாரி, அம்பிகா, சரோஜா, சீதா, அம்புஜம்
சிவ பார்வதி நடனம்	பத்மினி, ராகினி

மங்களம்

Figure 3.14. The program for a Bharatanāṭyam performance by Padmini, Lalitha, and Ragini in Madras on January 1, 1957, sponsored by the Tamil Isai Sangam. Collection of the author.

discursive and symbolic classicism by invoking its ties to religion and nationalism and by generally avoiding or deriding its social and historical roots in courtesan communities. These two actions allowed Bharatanāṭyam to travel into new communities and granted it an aspirational quality in social terms. This is why, despite Brahminic claims to its custodianship in the present, it is also practiced by range of upper-caste and/or upper-class groups throughout India. The complex signs and signals of modern Bharatanāṭyam—which blend Brahminic stewardship of the arts with devotional forms of religion and counternarratives about the dance's social roots—cannot be understood without reference to cinematic reinforcement of this coded world. Indeed, I would suggest that Bharatanāṭyam's claim to classicism can be understood only if we think of it as celluloid classicism. The persistent signposts of its classicism were created not only in the hermetic space of the imaginary of the nation's bourgeoisie, but also through its interface with the popular as it came into being in the age of celluloid. Today's Bharatanāṭyam continues to revere and use these signposts, even as much of contemporary Tamil cinema has moved beyond them in today's transnational, postliberalization India.

[4]

THE EMERGENCE OF THE CHOREOGRAPHER AND A NEW ENVISIONING OF DANCE

Today, Bharatanāṭyam is a fully choreographed art form. Repertoire is constructed and taught in preset formats, and often every phrase of gestural interpretation, the number of times each line is repeated, and the placements of each foot and every finger are predetermined by a guru who has set the pieces herself or learned them in this manner from her own teacher. How can we determine the history of this choreographic turn in the making of modern Bharatanāṭyam? The complex answers to this question require us to shift our focus to men of the *devadāsī* community who commonly took on the professional or semiprofessional role of *naṭṭuvaṉār* and to the early Tamil cinema. Both cinema and the reinvented Bharatanāṭyam afforded financial opportunities to men from this community at a time when professional opportunities for women were fast disappearing. As early as the late 1930s, the increased demand for dance sequences in South Indian films required dance directors, and some men from the *naṭṭuvaṉār* community benefited tremendously from this, breaking into new modes of livelihood. Moreover, the popularity of their contributions to dance in the cinema enabled these men to participate in the world of modern, urban performances of Bharatanāṭyam on Madras's stages. This chapter tracks the participation of *naṭṭuvaṉārs* in the early Tamil cinema in a prosopographic way but also reads it in terms of the politics of labor, financial gain and loss, and celebrity.

A large portion of this chapter is devoted to the life and work of Vazhuvoor Ramaiah Pillai, an iconic choreographer for the early cinema and

Madras's stage performances of the new Bharatanāṭyam from the 1930s to the 1960s. Ramaiah Pillai's aesthetic sensibilities not only set the standard for representations of Bharatanāṭyam-style dances on screen, but these filtered back into stage performances in Madras. Indeed, one of his prime disciples, Kamala, whom we discussed at length in the previous chapter, seamlessly moved between stage and screen, and the dynamism of Ramaiah Pillai's choreographies for her was appreciated and deeply internalized by audiences for decades. In addition to Ramaiah Pillai, the chapter also discusses five other men from the *naṭṭuvaṉār* community who became renowned choreographers in the cinema and attracted students, many from abroad, who wanted to learn Bharatanāṭyam from them. The chapter concludes with an ethnographic portrait of one of the earliest nonhereditary dance masters of the South Indian cinema, Udupi Laxminarayan, whose work began in the 1940s, and whose legacy as a choreographer and teacher was represented on the global stage by one of his male students, the award-winning film dancer and choreographer Prabhu Deva (b. 1973).

NON-BRAHMIN POLITICS AND *ICAI VĒḶĀḶAR* MEN

Before the mid-1920s, men who belonged to communities of professional performing artists were usually referred to in Tamil as *mēḷakkārar* ("performers in the *mēḷam* [troupe]"). However, the Tamil term functioned as a broad marker that could include male musicians who accompanied *devadāsīs* (known by terms such as *pāṭuvār* ["singer"] and *muṭṭukārar* ["player of the *muṭṭu* drum"]) but also could include *naṭṭuvaṉārs* and ritual musicians who played the *nāgasvaram* and its accompanying drum, the *tavil*. As Davesh Soneji has shown, these men were also sometimes semiprofessional artists who were also sometimes identified with the barber community (*ampattaṉ*) (Soneji 2012, 145–46). This association with the traditionally low-caste status of the barber meant that men from this community were sometimes identified, albeit rather amorphously, with the lower end of the spectrum of the caste hierarchy in Tamil South India. Marriages within their caste were the norm for such men. It is important to remember that *devadāsīs* most often had intimate relationships with upper-caste men, and thus the community was necessarily mixed-caste.

The mature phase of Tamil Dravidian politics (discussed in chapter 3) began in the 1920s, as did the work of the radical anticaste ideologue

E. V. Ramasami Naicker (1879–1973; also known as Periyar). The galvanization of anticaste sentiment under Periyar represented a new social force in Tamilnadu. By the 1930s, this idea had transformed itself into a powerful political presence in the region that offered an alternative to the Gandhian nationalism of the Indian National Congress. Dravidian politics quickly aligned itself with a number of reform projects, and the antinautch movement was no exception. Periyar wrote extensively about his own anti-*devadāsī* stance, and certainly his successors, including the architects of the Dravida Munnetra Kazhagam (DMK) party, were largely men from the *mēḷakkārar* community (Soneji 2012, 151–52).

This political mobility of men in this community occurred precisely because of the reinvention of *mēḷakkārar* caste identity under the influence of both anti-Brahmin politics and the antinautch movement in the late 1920s and early 1930s. In this period, men from this community strategically entered politics by claiming a new caste identity for themselves, one that allowed them to move out of the supposedly morally dubious category of *mēḷakkārar*. As Soneji (2012, 143) has shown, the archive of Muthulakshmi Reddy preserves a number of documents from 1927 onward in which we see the use of *icai vēḷāḷar* as a name men from the *devadāsī* community used for themselves. It is not clear when or by whom this term was invented, but it was in use as early as 1927. This term enabled men to move away from the earlier stigmatized barber status and insert themselves into the larger caste group known as *vēḷāḷar* ("agriculturalists" or "cultivators"), who very clearly occupy a higher status among Tamilnadu's non-Brahmin groups. Thus, in identifying themselves as *icai vēḷāḷars*, men—including traditional *naṭṭuvaṉārs*—reinvented themselves in a new, modern social mold, one that moved them away from the stigma that remained attached to women in this community. By escaping their identification with *devadāsīs*, *naṭṭuvaṉārs* were able to enter the new forces of cultural production in new and very powerful ways, while almost none of these opportunities were afforded to *devadāsī* women.

SHIFTING REPRESENTATIONS OF MASCULINITY IN BHARATANĀṬYAM

In an essay titled "From Gynemimesis to Hypermasculinity: The Shifting Orientations of Male Performers of South Indian Court Dance" (Krishnan 2009), I have mapped various representations of masculinity that were at work in the production of the nineteenth-century courtly dance form known as Bharatanāṭyam today. These included not only the *naṭṭuvaṉār*, who was understood to be the leader of the courtesan dance troupe, but also male performers of courtesan dance who performed in a gynemimetic mode, following all the conventions of traditional courtesan performance.[1] Men's participation in the cultural production of dance before the twentieth century was thus not limited, as is commonly believed, to the role played by the *naṭṭuvaṉār* as pedagogue and conductor of performances. Gynemimetic courtly performances were desired in Tanjore in their own right, and thus dancing by men, albeit dressed and dancing as women, was also a key marker of Bharatanāṭyam before its emergence in Madras as an urban, upper-caste, and socially and aesthetically reinvented cultural practice.

As I argue in that essay, the third decade of the twentieth century marks a distinct break in these older representations of men in relation to Bharatanāṭyam (Krishnan 2009, 383–85). The emergence of the new nationalized form of dance in the 1930s reflected not only a concern about sexual and aesthetic propriety on the part of its upper-class women performers (A. Srinivasan 1984; Meduri 1996; Natarajan 1997; Weidman 2006, 111–49) but also a concern about the nurturing of a new masculine identity for male performers. This new masculinity, a reaction to colonial constructions of South Asian men as "effeminate" (Sinha 1995), was also affected by Gandhian nationalism that was rooted in the ideas of self-control, discipline, and sexual abstinence (Katrak 1992; Alter 2000). The new dance and its complex modernity has been commented upon by several scholars (Meduri 1996; Allen 1997; O'Shea 2007; Soneji 2010a), but what is important to note here is that in addition to resignification and reconstitution of the dance and its social order, the transformation of the *devadāsī* dance into Bharatanāṭyam also involved a restructuring of gender roles and expectations. Indeed, the emphasis on devotional, narrative, and nonerotic repertoire that characterized the popularization of the art form may well have been designed to provide space for the male performer. The new male performers of the 1930s such as Ram Gopal (1912–2003) became famous for their dances in which they represented the hypermasculine icon of the god Śiva-Naṭarāja, (Allen 1997). As Anne-Marie Gaston (1991), Matthew Allen (1997), and Padma Kaimal (1999) have pointed out, the popularization of this image of the dancing Śiva was the direct result of early-twentieth-century Orientalist writings on Indian art, and the linkage of the icon to the repertoire and presentation of Bharatanāṭyam dance clearly reflected the emerging Indian middle class's nationalistic pride in its past.

I would argue that cinema also played a major role in the creation of these new representations of the masculinity of the dancing body. Early cinematic representations from South India are also tinted by the politics of Orientalism, class, and caste, which I have discussed above in relation to staged versions of Bharatanāṭyam. Take, for example, one of the earliest extant appearances of a solo male dancer in South Indian cinema, a short performance in the Telugu film *Raitu Bidda* (The farmer's son; 1939) by Vedantam Raghaviah (1919–71), which Rumya Sree Putcha (2011) discusses in her dissertation on the reinvention of Kūcipūḍi dance. In this sequence, a male performer dances to a song called *Daśāvatāraśabdam* (Song of the ten incarnations [of the god Viṣṇu]") and is a dressed in a manner that almost exactly mirrors the costumes conceived and popularized by the Oriental dancer Uday Shankar (1900–77), including the large headdresses he wore when enacting the role of the dancing Śiva.[2] Putcha concludes her analysis by stating that "this scene [in the film *Raitu Bidda*] is reminiscent of the Orientalist aesthetic Uday Shankar was popularizing in the early twentieth century. In other words, the Kuchipudi dance Raghavayya performs in *Raitu Bidda* is explicitly theatrical and Hindu" (ibid., 116). Gynemimetic modes of dancing for men, which were the norm in the community of male Brahmin Kūcipūḍi performers that Vedantam Raghaviah represents, became nearly invisible by the third decade of the twentieth century, and when they were showcased, they were always constructed as signs of an archaic, undesirable past (Soneji 2004; Krishnan 2009). They were replaced instead by new modes of figuring the male dancing body that were inseparably linked to larger, metropolitan discourses about Hinduism understood through the lens of Orientalism and the transnational nature of such Orientalism, embodied in the European and North American performances of figures such as Shankar and later Gopal. Shankar produced and directed a Hindi film called *Kalpana* (Imagination; 1948), the production of which was backed by S. S. Vasan of Gemini Studios in Madras, showcasing dance technique as part of the modern pan-Indian nationalist heritage, and the vernacular press in South India publicized this a landmark cultural accomplishment (figure 4.1).

Indeed, the participation of the vernacular press in the dissemination of new forms of dance was tremendously important. The Tamil press

Figure 4.1. A still from Uday Shankar's film Kalpana *(1948) in* Kuṇṭūci, *February 1949, 23. Courtesy of the Roja Muthiah Research Library.*

in Madras shaped popular understandings of new cultural forms and helped audiences understand the purport of new medial phenomena. By the 1940s, when the social and aesthetic norms of both cinema dance and stage performances of the reinvented Bharatanāṭyam had crystallized in the popular imagination, *Kuṇṭūci* published a four-page essay titled "Paratamum Āṇkaḷum" (Bharatam and men). While the essay does not directly address the relationship between men dancing Bharatanāṭyam and the cinema, it clearly signals the fact that cinema audiences were interested in the new phenomenon of the male dancer:

> It seems that it was only twenty years ago that Bharatanāṭyam spread to family women. Until then, the art was preserved by only certain *devadāsīs* and *naṭṭuvaṉārs*. These days mainly girls perform Bharatanāṭyam. Men learning this art form are very few and far between. One wonders, despite the existence of a few men [in this art

form] if there any men capable of giving a full performance. Until now, I would say there are no men who have ever performed a full-length dance recital or had an *araṅkēṟṟam*. I wouldn't say this is because they have no interest in this art. It seems to be general public opinion that a man's Bharatanāṭyam recital may not be very attractive. . . . For the performance of *abhinaya*, the *padams* are usually songs about [the gods] Kṛṣṇa and Murukaṉ and they are just love songs (*kātal pāṭṭu*). The lyrics and meanings of the pieces imply that there is a special distinction in a woman performing the *padam*. But this does not mean a man is unable to transform himself metaphorically into a woman and perform the appropriate *abhinaya* for the *padam*!

Around two thousand years ago, when Bharata Muni wrote his *Nāṭyaśāstra* there were also rules and regulations written in great detail about cross-dressing where men played women (*stiri vēcam*) and women played men. We saw the flourishing of these traditions in Vedic and Purāṇic times, when both men and women were highly skilled in dancing and scaled great heights [in dance]. Because dancing leads to spiritual liberation (*mōṭcam*), there have also been many great [male] sages who were also skilled in dancing. The sages Taṇḍu, Bharata, his hundred sons, and sage Nārada are sufficient examples. Even male Purāṇic characters (*purāṇa purucarkaḷ*) like Kṛṣṇa and Arjuna were skilled in dancing. The dance's original source, [the god Śiva as] Naṭarāja, is of course, the one whom we always invoke [in dance]. . . . (Kiruṣṇamūrtti 1949, 101–3)

The essay, of course, builds on widely circulating modes of writing Bharatanāṭyam's history. The author invokes the idea of the erotic elements of courtesan dance as a malleable allegory, one that can easily be appropriated by male performers. In doing so, he erases the interpretive possibilities of the queer nature of gynemimetic performance traditions, which certainly would not have been visible or readily available to his readers. In addition, as in most writings on Indian dance in this period, the essay's default position is to refer back to Hindu mythology to explain aspects of the dance to his audiences. Thus not only is the mythical author of the Sanskrit text *Nāṭyaśāstra* mentioned, but a whole cast of figures from mythology (crowned of course by the figure of Śiva-Naṭarāja), are put to use in historicizing the male presence in the production of Bharatanāṭyam.

NAṬṬUVAṈĀRS MAKE IT BIG: CINEMA, FINANCIAL OPPORTUNITY, AND THE PEDAGOGY OF THE NEW CLASSICAL DANCE

As we have seen above, the anti-*devadāsī* movement in the Madras Presidency created new opportunities and social spaces for men who had been tangentially involved in the production of dance and music, even as it ironically left huge lacunae in the lives of professional female performers. Although many members of the community had already shifted their activities from smaller towns and villages to Madras—the new center of cultural patronage—by the last decades of the nineteenth century (Soneji 2012, 59), the shifts brought on by the legal interventions of *devadāsī* reform were of a different nature. These of course broadly coincided with the reinvention of dance in Madras, and many traditional *naṭṭuvaṉār* families saw tremendous financial opportunity in moving their families to the city. A case in point is the family of Kuppaiah Pillai (1895–1981), one of the most important *naṭṭuvaṉār* lineages that was employed by the Tanjore court in the eighteenth and nineteenth centuries.[3] In 1945, the son-in-law of Kuppaiah Pillai, Govindaraj Pillai (1914–84), founded the Rajarajeswari Bharatha Natya Kala Mandir in Bombay, and shortly thereafter this entire extended family—including its patriarch, Kuppaiah Pillai—moved to Bombay, where they trained thousands of middle-class students in Bharatanāṭyam The students included the Hindi film stars Kamini Kaushal (b. 1927) and Waheeda Rehman (b. 1938), as well as other choreographers for film dance such as Gopi Krishna (1935–94).[4] The stories of *naṭṭuvaṉārs* who moved to Madras like Vazhuvoor Ramiah Pillai and K. N. Dandayudhapani Pillai are the foci of this chapter, and they will demonstrate the remarkable demand for *naṭṭuvaṉārs* in the new cultural practices of urban Bharatanāṭyam and the Tamil cinema during the period between approximately 1937 and 1960. These stories also set into high relief the fact that such opportunities were next to nonexistent for women from *devadāsī* communities, who were often relatives of these iconic *naṭṭuvaṉārs*.

From the standpoint of the social organization of the choreography for the Tamil cinema, it is also important to highlight the fact that *naṭṭuvaṉārs* were not the only men who were engaged in this work, despite this chapter's focus on this community. As we have seen above, beginning in the late 1930s, Telugu-speaking Brahmin men from the village of Kūcipūḍi were involved in films produced in Madras. Thus, figures like Vedantam Raghaviah (1919–71) choreographed independently and alongside *naṭṭuvaṉārs* in Tamil cinema in the 1940s and 1950s. But unlike the *naṭṭuvaṉārs*, Raghaviah largely abandoned performing on stage and did not start teaching dance in Madras, but instead focused on a career as a film director. Later, three other men from the same community—Vempati Pedda Satyam (1922–82), Pasumarti Krishnamurthy (1922–2004), and Vempati Chinna Satyam (1929–2012)—also choreographed intermittently for both the Tamil and Telugu cinema. However, unlike Raghaviah, all three maintained primary careers as teachers of the newly invented Kūcipūḍi dance in Madras and Hyderabad. Putcha (2011) and Katyayani Thota (2016) have provided critical interventions in the history of Kūcipūḍi dance, arguing in part that the cinematic imagining of dance in Telugu films cannot be severed from the production of the aesthetic vocabulary of classical Kūcipūḍi.

Apart from these figures from the village of Kūcipūḍi, a slightly later family of choreographers in the Tamil cinema consists of men from northern India who settled in Madras—the family of the choreographer B. Sohanlal (c. 1920–80). Sohanlal and his three brothers, B. Hiralal, B. Chinnilal, and B. Radheshyam, were born in Jaipur, Rajasthan, and studied Kathak dance there. In the late 1940s or early 1950s, they moved from Jaipur to Madras, and Sohanlal and Hiralal quickly became integrated into the Tamil film industry. However, because of the presence of *naṭṭuvaṉārs*, they were rarely invited to choreograph classical-type dances in Tamil films. This separation of dance genres (Western versus classical, South Indian, and Bharatanāṭyam) in the cinema explains why Tamil films often had two or more choreographers, and this was particularly true by the late 1940s. By the 1950s, Sohanlal and later Hiralal were also choreographing for Hindi films. Their influence on both Tamil and Hindi cinema dance from the 1950s through the 1970s is undeniable, and Sohanlal was the mentor and husband of today's most famous Bollywood choreographer, Saroj Khan (b. 1948).[5]

THE COMICAL TROPE OF THE *NAṬṬUVAṈĀR*

By the 1940s, comedy had become a mainstay of Tamil cinema. Somewhat ironically, even as *naṭṭuvaṉārs* were being brought into the Tamil film industry to legitimate the presence of dance on screen, depictions of *naṭṭuvaṉārs* in film narratives were almost always morally ambiguous at best. Comedy became a subtle and seemingly always open space in which caste hierarchy and class-based prejudice could be playfully inserted into the celluloid world without much thought about social consequences.[6] *Naṭṭuvaṉārs* thus became, rather systemically, the targets of mockery in the early Tamil cinema. This parodic representation continued throughout the 1950s and reached its pinnacle in films such as *Thillana Mohanambal* (Mōkaṉā who dances the *tillāṉā*; 1968), in which strongly caricatured representations of the *naṭṭuvaṉār* provoked responses even from *naṭṭuvaṉārs* who were involved in the cinema. Udupi Laxminarayan (discussed at the end of this chapter) remembered going to watch the film with his guru, Kanchipuram Ellappa Pillai, a *naṭṭuvaṉār* who also choreographed for the cinema: "The next day after we saw the film, I asked what he thought of the movie. He spat on the floor and [said], 'the respect and dignity of the *naṭṭuvaṉār* has been lost! '*Naṭṭuvaṉār*' is such an honored title ... why did they have to do this and make a comedy of the *naṭṭuvaṉār*?'" (pers. comm., Chennai, August 20, 2012).

In the early cinematic context, the 1942 film *Manonmani* (Jewel of the mind) features a similar scene that merits some discussion. In the scene, a *naṭṭuvaṉār* and *devadāsī* perform at the court of a local king, in the presence of the son of the court's minister (figure 4.2). The pair chosen to play the role of *naṭṭuvaṉār* and *devadāsī* were a real-life couple, both known for their comedic acting abilities. The *naṭṭuvaṉār* ws played by Kali N. Ratnam, a former actor with the Tamil drama troupe called the Madurai Original Boys' Company, and the *devadāsī* character, Kōmati, was played by his real-life partner, C. T. Rajakantam, a woman who also joined the company and whose caste background is unknown (Guy 2015).

The bulk of the scene was in the form of a courtesan song type known as *svara padam*, in which lines of love poetry are interspersed with passages of solfa syllables (*svaras*). The lyrics were composed by Papnasam Rajagopala Iyer and Velsami Kavi, and the music was by Kalyanam Mahadevan. The scene unfolds as follows:

Minister's son (played by T. S. Balaiya): Don't be afraid take this [flower in his hand].

[Cuppa (the *naṭṭuvaṉār*, played by Ratnam) nudges the *devadāsī* Kōmati (played by Rajakantam) to take the flower]

Figure 4.2. Photograph taken on the set of the film Manonmani *(1942) in which the trope of the comical* naṭṭuvaṉār *is invoked. From the private collection of S. V. Jayababu.*

Cuppa: Respect! Respect! [He signals Kōmati to be thankful for the gift. She offers the minister's son some fruit.]

Minister's son: Cuppa, you told me our Kōmati is able to dance very well.

Cuppa: Yes, sir. She dances with such clarity. What steps! What tempo! What vibrancy! Shall I ask to dance her to dance [for you]? Hey, little one (*kuṭṭi*)!

Kōmati: Keep quiet. Don't tease me.

Cuppa: This is exactly what you shouldn't do. When a rich man asks you to dance with such great enthusiasm . . . [sigh] . . . and he isn't just anybody! Hurry, go dance now!

Kōmati [looking at the minister's son]: You shouldn't tease me [either], okay?

Minister's son: Never.

Cuppa: Come on!

[Kōmati begins to perform the *svara padam*. A *svara* passage starts, to which she performs abstract movement, while the *naṭṭuvaṉār* makes exaggerated movements and comically keeps the rhythm with his hands.]

Padam: Oh sweet fruit, is he verily the king of gods, Indra?

Cuppa: Use your neck [the sideways movement of the neck traditionally marks beauty]!

Padam: If I joyously seduced him with my eyes, would he still reject me?

Cuppa: Can't you seduce more with your eyes?

Padam: If I seduced him with unbridled passion, would he still reject me? In this sea of infatuation, tinged with the sweet nectar of love—

Cuppa: Move your hip a little more.

Padam: [My love!] feed me this ecstasy, embrace me, and show me pleasure. My breasts are swelling with desire. Since the day [I first saw you], my love has been growing ever stronger—

Cuppa: Yes! That's it!

Padam: The flowery arrows thrown by the god of love [Manmatha]—

Cuppa: Not like that. Here, watch me [performs the *abhinaya* in an exaggerated manner].

Padam: —land precisely on me and make me think of you all the time.

[The *padam* ends with a series of *jatis* to which Kōmati dances using abstract movements. The *naṭṭuvaṉār* is reciting but gets slapped in the face by the dancer's arms and begins to cry and pout as he continues to recite.]

Minister's son: Wonderful [looks at Kōmati with desire in his eyes]!

Cuppa: She's my student. You don't have to even ask. It's late. Hey, Kōmati, take care of Sir [winks at her].

This scene is meant to be comical on several registers. First, the audience is meant to understand, right away, the low moral standing of the *devadāsī* or *naṭṭuvaṉār* community. It is clear that although the *devadāsī* and *naṭṭuvaṉār* have an intimate relationship, he is selling her into sex work. Second, the whole aesthetic of the performance is laughable. The text of the *padam* is not taken seriously; it is only a pretense for sexual innuendos. The technique of *abhinaya* similarly is not taken seriously. The *naṭṭuvaṉār* constantly pushes Kōmati into performing exaggerated, highly sexualized *abhinaya*, again because the seduction of the minister's son supersedes the value of any aesthetic labor. Finally, and most

Figure 4.3. Vazhuvoor Ramaiah Pillai with his orchestra, c. 1950 ("Natyacharya Vazhuvoor Ramaiah Pillai" 1986, 24).

importantly for our current discussion, the *naṭṭuvaṉār* is morally and aesthetically bankrupt. In some senses, then, this scene reveals of the kind of moral stigma that followed *devadāsī* women into the cinema and affected the representations of *naṭṭuvaṉārs* on screen. The difference—which will be brought into sharp relief in the following section—is that while representations of *naṭṭuvaṉārs* may have become comical tropes in the cinema, unlike *devadāsīs, naṭṭuvaṉārs* were central to the early phase of the reinvention and repopulation of Bharatanāṭyam as a classical dance form. Thus, men from *naṭṭuvaṉār* communities found abundant employment opportunities in the emergent marking of middle-class dance in Tamil-speaking South India, unlike their female (*devadāsī*) counterparts, who for the most part could not succeed as dance teachers in the new moral economy of modern Bharatanāṭyam.

THE CASE OF VAZHUVOOR RAMAIAH PILLAI

One of the most important figures in the narrative of Bharatanāṭyam's interface with the world of Tamil cinema is Ramaiah Pillai (figure 4.3). His work is exemplary of the fluidity and symbiosis that is at the heart of this project. His choreographies flowed seamlessly between screen and stage. He singlehandedly invented a new technique for Bharatanāṭyam, a style that came to be popularly known as the "Vazhuvoor lineage" (*vaḻuvūr pāṇi*).[7] He was one of the earliest *naṭṭuvaṉār*-choreographers for the South Indian cinema, and later—through the choreographies he devised for his disciple Kamala on and off screen—he transformed the aesthetic, repertoire, and technique of Bharatanāṭyam; he made it into a popular middle-class cultural artifact. This section maps the trajectory of Ramaiah Pillai's life, especially with reference to the cinema, and discusses the debates about aesthetics and dance making that Ramaiah Pillai was at the center of from the late 1930s to the late 1950s.

The tradition of dance in the small village of Vazhuvoor (Vaḻuvūr, in the Kuthalam taluk of today's Nagapattinam district) can be traced to a man named Vaḻuvūr Cāmu Naṭṭuvaṉār (1844–1903). Initially a vocalist (*pāṭuvār*) for *devadāsī* dance performances, he later composed music for dances and taught a handful of students, among whom the *devadāsī* Vazhuvoor Nāgammal (dates unknown) was the most famous.[8] Cāmu Naṭṭuvaṉār had several children, including a son named Māṇikka Naṭṭuvaṉār (1867–1949) and a daughter named Bhagyammal (dates unknown). Bhagyammal had a relationship with man named Parthiban, and they had six children, one of whom was Ramaiah Pillai. Ramaiah Pillai's early life is a bit of a mystery, and there are some conflicting narratives about his career before he moved to Madras around 1938. In an interview published in *Sruti* in 1986, he recalled his early life: "My grandfather Samu Naṭṭuvaṉār died when my mother Bhagyamma was only six years old. My father died young. My uncle Manikka Naṭṭuvaṉār was my guru from childhood. He was famous as a dance-master and it was he who trained a leading Ceylonese dancer of those times known as Ranjana.... Before [coming to Madras] ... I had spent some time in Mayavaram [known today as Mayiladuthurai, in the Nagapattinam district]. I assisted my uncle in teaching there. As long as he was alive, I never taught anything on my own"("Natyacharya Vazhuvoor Ramaiah Pillai" 1986, 23). He traveled from the small town of Mayavaram to Madras's film world:

> I came to Madras [from the town of Mayavaram] in 1938 all of a sudden. I started [teaching or choreographing] on my own only after coming to Madras. Raja Chandrasekhar [1904–71, also known as Raja C. Sekhar], the film director I mentioned before [the producer of *Raja Desingh*, in which Arundale performed dance] invited me to Madras [to] teach dance to those who performed in films. Apparently no one else was forthcoming. My elders permitted me to go and I agreed. It was then that I started in films. There was no studio in Madras then. Films had to be shot in Calcutta. Later the Newtone Studios opened in Madras. Films were shot there too. Whenever there was a dance sequence in films, I was called in. (ibid.)

B. M. Sundaram provides a slightly different account:

> [Ramaiah Pillai] owned a little sundries store (*poṭṭikaṭai*) near Mayiladuthurai. . . . His sister Radha was hired to act in a film, and the shooting was to take place in Calcutta. Her family, fearing to send her alone, sent Ramaiah Pillai as her chaperone. During the shooting, the producers felt a dance sequence would be appropriate but due to budget and time limitations, bringing in a *naṭṭuvaṉār* [to choreograph the dance] was out of the question. Ramaiah Pillai volunteered to choreograph [it]. [He] choreographed [the sequence] with whatever little dance he knew at that time. This incident ignited a fire [in the heart of] Ramaiah Pillai, and he dreamed of becoming a [professional] *naṭṭuvaṉār*. (Sundaram 2002, 234)

These somewhat conflicting accounts of Ramaiah Pillai's life speak to the complexities of presenting the story of this now iconic figure. In my interview with Sundaram in 2012, he named the film in which Ramaiah Pillai's sister, Radha, performed (figures 4.4a and 4.4b):

> There was a movie called *Adrishtam* (Luck; 1939). There was an actress Radha, from Mayiladuthurai, who was playing a [small] supporting role. When the directors found out she came from a family of dancers, they thought, "Why not include a dance sequence?" They asked her immediately to dance, and she agreed. There was no choreographer, but Radha's brother, Vazhuvoor Ramaiah Pillai, was chaperoning her at that time. When approached about the dance, he volunteered immediately and began "choreographing" for the first time on the film set, teaching a gesture or so. He had seen dancers learning from his uncle Māṇikka Naṭṭuvaṉār. (interview by the author, Chennai, August 27, 2012)

That same year, Ramaiah Pillai choreographed a court dance sequence for the film *Prahlada* (Prahlāda [a child devotee]; 1939), directed by B. N. Rao.[9] In this sequence, we can see how Ramaiah Pillai filled in a gap by repurposing existing *devadāsī* dance repertoire when he was asked to create a court dance sequence. The scene takes place when the film's mythological antihero, Hiraṇyakaśipu, is entertained by courtesan dancers in the assembly hall. For this sequence, Ramaiah Pillai chose to insert excerpts from a composition that was very popular among courtesan dancers at the turn of the century, the *svarajati* in the *rāga* Khamās, *Māmōkalākiri mīrutē* (My passion is ever-increasing), composed by the

Figure 4.4 a, b. The cover (left) and synopsis page (right) from the songbook for Adrishtam *(1939), featuring a photo of a dancer—probably Radha, Ramaiah Pillai's sister. This may be the only surviving visual artifact from his first choreography for film. Private collection of S. V. Jayababu.*

Brahmin musician Subbarāma Dīkṣitulu (1839–1906). In the sequence, six young dancers perform two sequences to vocalized rhythms (*jatis*—recited by Ramaiah Pillai) plus two lines of *svaras* (solfa syllables) that are part of the latter half of the *svarajati* composition. Unlike in Ramaiah Pillai's later cinematic choreographies, the sequences were not distributed among the six dancers, nor were there shots that focused on the *abhinaya* or *aṭavus* (rhythmic units of movement) of the individual dancers. The identities of these dancers is unknown—like Ramaiah Pillai, they were not acknowledged in the credits of the film.

According to Sundaram, Ramaiah Pillai's first formal student was T. M. Pattammal (described in chapter 3 as dancing to the nationalist songs of Subramaniya Bharati), from a *devadāsī* family of Thirukkazhukundram (Sundaram 2002, 235). She had initially studied dance with Ramaiah Pillai's own teacher, Thirukkazhukundram Turaicāmi Naṭṭuvaṉār. Ramaiah

Pillai talked about this in 1986: "I was so busy in films, I had no time for tuition [private dance classes] really. One of the first [people] I took as a Bharatanāṭyam student was a girl called T. M. Pattammal. She was sent to me by a genius of a *naṭṭuvaṉār* named Thirukkazhukundram Doraiswamy. He had taught Pattammal and when he couldn't do it any longer because of old age, he sent her to me. I conducted rehearsals and then recitals for her. I taught her some items of my own. She danced in some films too—in *Maya Macchindra* and *DakshaYagnam* I think" ("Natyacharya Vazhuvoor Ramaiah Pillai," 25). Around this time, he also taught at least one other woman from the *devadāsī* community, Viralimalai Ramani (c. 1938–2010). She was a disciple of Kalaiyarkovil Chellaiya Naṭṭuvaṉār, who could not continue to train her due to a stroke. Ramaiah Pillai undertook the task of having Ramani perform an *araṅkēṟṟam* (debut performance) (Sundaram 2003, 279–81). It should be noted that at this early stage of his career, Ramaiah Pillai did not receive much public recognition. Neither Pattammal nor Ramani were part of Madras's emerging middle-class dance scene.

After these somewhat improvised encounters with dance in the cinema in 1939, Ramaiah Pillai won the support of Chandrasekhar, and in 1941 he choreographed for the film *Ashok Kumar*, in which the actress Pasupuleti Kannamba (1911–64, from the Telugu-speaking *kalāvantula* courtesan community) danced to a *padam* (love lyric) specially composed for the film by Papanasam Sivan.[10] Ramaiah Pillai's choreography for this piece, in which passages of abstract dance were inserted between the verses of the *padam* and accompanied by instrumental music, received critical attention and seems to have been the model for a number of his choreographies for film actresses in the 1940s.

In the early 1940s, Ramaiah Pillai was largely producing choreographies for actresses who were from the *devadāsī* or *kalāvantula* courtesan communities but who had not received extensive training in dance. For example, in 1942 he choreographed *Kannagi* (1942), about the heroine of the Tamil epic *Cilappatikāram*. The actress N. S. Saroja (dates unknown), who played the courtesan figure Mātavi, dances to a song in the *rāga* Kāmbodhi. In both structure and lyrical content, the song, *Mālākiṉāḷ svāmi maṅkaiyum uṉ mēlē* (This girl became a bride for you, Lord!), resembles the old courtesan genre of the Tamil *padam*, and Ramaiah Pillai's only innovations consisted of inserting small passages of abstract

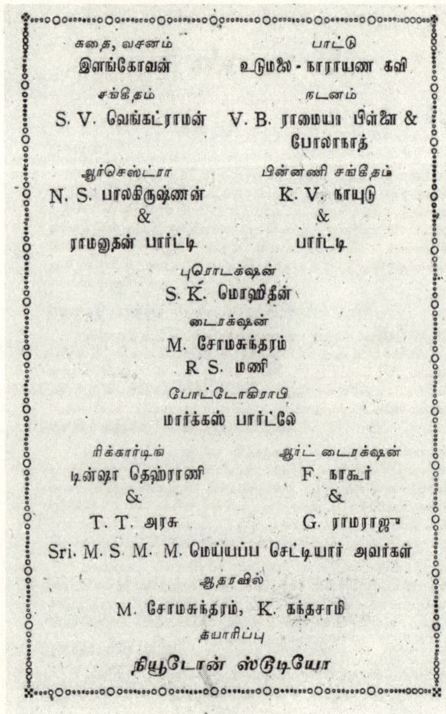
கதை, வசனம்
இளங்கோவன்

பாட்டு
உடுமலை - நாராயண கவி

சங்கீதம்
S. V. வெங்கட்ராமன்

நடனம்
V. B. ராமையா பிள்ளை &
போலாநாத்

ஆர்செஸ்ட்ரா
N. S. பாலகிருஷ்ணன்
&
ராமனாதன் பார்ட்டி

பின்னணி சங்கீதம்
K. V. நாயுடு
&
பார்ட்டி

புரொடக்ஷன்
S. K. மோஹிதீன்

டைரக்ஷன்
M. சோமசுந்தரம்
R S. மணி

போட்டோகிராபி
மார்க்கஸ் பார்ட்லே

ரிக்கார்டிங்
டின்ஷா தெஹ்ராணி
&
T. T. அரசு

ஆர்ட் டைரக்ஷன்
F. நாகூர்
&
G. ராமராஜு

Sri. M. S M. M. மெய்யப்ப செட்டியார் அவர்கள்
ஆதரவில்
M. சோமசுந்தரம், K. கந்தசாமி
தயாரிப்பு
நியூடோன் ஸ்டுடியோ

Figure 4.5 a, b. The cover (left) and credits page (right) of the songbook for Kannagi *(1942), with Ramaiah Pillai's name credited for dance (*naṭaṉam*). Private collection of S. V. Jayababu.*

dance to punctuate the space between the verses of the song.[11] Ramaiah Pillai's name appears among the very first credits in the songbook for the film (figures 4.5a and 4.5b).[12]

Ramaiah Pillai choreographed one of the earliest songs in praise of dance in the Tamil cinema, a dance in the film *Sivakavi* (1943) performed by the actress T. R. Rajakumari. In the following year, she danced in another film, the highly successful landmark film *Haridas* (1944), in which she played the role of a courtesan dancer. There is a strong possibility that Ramaiah Pillai also choreographed part of this film, although no credits are listed for "dance" in the title sequence.

Until around 1946, Ramaiah Pillai's dance remained largely straightforward, in the sense that he was fixing gestural interpretation (*abhinaya*) to songs that were similar in content to those in the traditional dance repertoire. He also created very basic passages of abstract dance when they were necessary. These were usually performed to instrumental musical passages, either between verses of songs (as in the *padam*-like songs of *Kannagi* and *Haridas*) or at the end of songs as a kind of finale. The sequences in films like *Sivakavi* and *Haridas* reflect this early stage in his choreographic trajectory.

However, in 1944 a new kind of theatricality was injected into cinema dance. In the film *Jagathalapratapan* (Lord of the world; 1944), Ramaiah Pillai choreographed a performance for a young girl to whom he had recently started teaching Bharatanāṭyam in Madras. This was Kamala (then known as Baby Kamala, as explained in chapter 3). In this fantasy film, the hero journeys to the nether regions of the world, also known in Hindu cosmology as *nāgaloka*, the abode of serpents. Kamala plays one of the serpents residing in *nāgaloka* and dances to a song that became emblematic of Ramaiah Pillai's contribution to Bharatanāṭyam We will discuss this snake dance in detail in chapter 5, but for now it is important to place the piece in the context of Ramaiah Pillai's career as a film dance choreographer. This pairing of Ramaiah Pillai and Kamala was very significant. Over the next five years, the choreographer and dancer, would radically and irrevocably alter the landscape of Bharatanāṭyam dance in South India. In 1945, Ramaiah Pillai choreographed the film *Sri Valli* (Vaḷḷi [consort of the god Murukaṉ]), in which Kamala played the double role of the god Murukaṉ as a child and his consort Vaḷḷi as a child. She danced Bharatanāṭyam in a new mode that can perhaps be best described as dramatic, in contrast to the earlier sequences by performers like Rajakumari in *Sivakavi* just two years earlier.[13]

But the real aesthetic and conceptual radicalism represented by the Ramaiah Pillai–Kamala pairing is best seen in dances in *Nam Iruvar* (We two; 1947). As explained in chapter 3, this film introduced audiences to the idea that the nationalist songs of Subramaniya Bharati could be interpreted and visualized through dance, but more importantly it cast dance as a middle-class art. Kamala performed a new kind of Bharatanāṭyam in the drawing room of a middle-class home, surrounded by a gramophone, radio, and other accoutrements of middle-class modernity in the early twentieth century. I would argue that this new staging of Bharatanāṭyam was mirrored in the new somatic approach to Bharatanāṭyam that was envisioned and used by Ramaiah Pillai. Indeed, Kamala's dance looks almost nothing like the dance of Saroja in *Kannagi* or Rajakumari in *Sivakavi*. What changed was that Kamala, unlike the hereditary dancers Saroja and Rajakumari, was a product of the so-called dance revival. Her exposure to dance (initially Kathak dance in Bombay) and Bharatanāṭyam in particular in Madras after Arundale's presentations, certainly made her body and its movement differ from those of Saroja and Rajakumari. Kamala's investments in the dance ran deep. She invented herself as a dancer to stand out among actresses, whereas *devadāsī* women such as Rajakumari invented themselves as actresses to move away from the stigma of a history associated with dance.

Ramaiah Pillai also choreographed the film *Kannika* (The virgin; 1947), which featured a version of the popular *Naṭaṉam āṭiṉār* (discussed in detail in chapter 5). This was danced by Hemamalini Arni, a Brahmin student of Pillai's, and the film also included a mini dance drama that marked the filmic debut of the Travancore Sisters (Padmini and Lalitha, later to be joined by Ragini) and was performed entirely to instrumental music. In both sequences, Ramaiah Pillai created a distinctly new kind of Bharatanāṭyam, rooted in athleticism and the layering of fast-paced, agile movements that were clearly designed for the quick cuts of the cinematic lens. Indeed, Bharatanāṭyam would not look the same after these innovations, and its aesthetic yardsticks would never be the same. These kinds of choreographies catapulted Bharatanāṭyam into new somatic spaces. The fast-paced and extremely dynamic movements became the norm for stage performances of Bharatanāṭyam in this period, and audiences who watched Bharatanāṭyam both on stage and in the cinema wanted to see them. Ramaiah Pillai's interventions in the 1940s thus mark a distinct shift in tastes related to the consumption and production of Bharatanāṭyam, much as Arundale's interventions did in the late 1930s.

Throughout the 1950s, Ramaiah Pillai choreographed a number of Tamil films, and his pairing with Kamala attained iconic status in the public imagination. His involvement in the cinema began to decrease in the late 1950s. At that time, he began to focus instead on training students for stage performances of Bharatanāṭyam, and undoubtedly students continued to come to him after hearing about and seeing his cinema dances. During the 1950s, a number of upper- and middle-class women, including the film director K. Subrahmanyam's daughter Padma started to learn dance from Ramaiah Pillai. His Bharatanāṭyam students included the dancers L. Vijayalakshmi, Kanaka Srinivasan (also known as S. Kanaka), Chitra Visweswaran, and Komala Varadan. Interestingly, the hereditary professional dancing women of the famous Kuchalambal family of Tanjore, who by the 1950s were all settled in Madras, also learned from him. Thus, T. D. Kuchalakumari (b. 1937; discussed in great detail in chapter 1), and her adopted cousin T. Jyothilakshmi were also students of Ramaiah Pillai.

By the 1950s, the circulation of Ramaiah Pillai's cinema Bharatanāṭyam had come full circle. There was a massive flow from his cinematic creations to stage performances of Bharatanāṭyam that he presented. The *vaḻuvūr pāṇi* ("Vazhuvoor style") was thus a bricolage that brought Bharatanāṭyam technique into conversation with cinematic modes of seeing and thus moving the body. This was combined with Ramaiah Pillai's own unique choreographic imagination, which included new pieces such as the famous *pāmpu naṭaṉam* in the 1944 film *Jagathalapratapan*—which became a staple in Bharatanāṭyam performances in Madras in the 1950s. In a stage performance of Bharatanāṭyam given by Ramaiah Pillai's students Kamala and Radha [Viswanathan], the daughter of M. S. Subbulakshmi, the centerpieces were a devotional *varṇam* composed by Papanasam Sivan (who composed extensively for the cinema) and, more importantly, three of Pillai's most memorable contributions to modern Bharatanāṭyam: the snake dance, the *Naṭaṉam āṭiṉār*, and the dance drama (in this case, the *kuṟavañci* drama *Kuṟṟāla Kuṟavañci*, discussed in greater detail in chapter 5), as shown in the repertoire list (figure 4.6). Documents such as these enable us to track the flows not only of dance repertoire from the cinema to stage performances (mainly due to Ramaiah Pillai), but also inevitably of technique, mannerisms in the performance of *abhinaya*, and the cult of celebrity (for example, Kamala was a star on both stage and screen). Most importantly, such documents suggest that by this time, cinematic Bharatanāṭyam and its stage versions attracted the same audiences, who had the same aesthetic expectations of both types of performance.

In 1954, the Tamil film magazine *Citrā* published a piece by Ramaiah Pillai about the state of dance, both on screen and on the stage, with the provocative title "Nāṭṭiyam Āṭiyum Payaṉillai" (There is no point to dancing). In the article—which was written at a time when other Bharatanāṭyam choreographers were beginning to surface in the cinema, and other forms of dance (largely Western-inspired forms) were becoming the norm in that world—Ramaiah Pillai writes about how his choreographies were classical (*śāstric*) and reflected traditional codified forms of knowledge about dance that were fast disappearing. He creates a narrative of the degeneration of Bharatanāṭyam in the cinema in which he

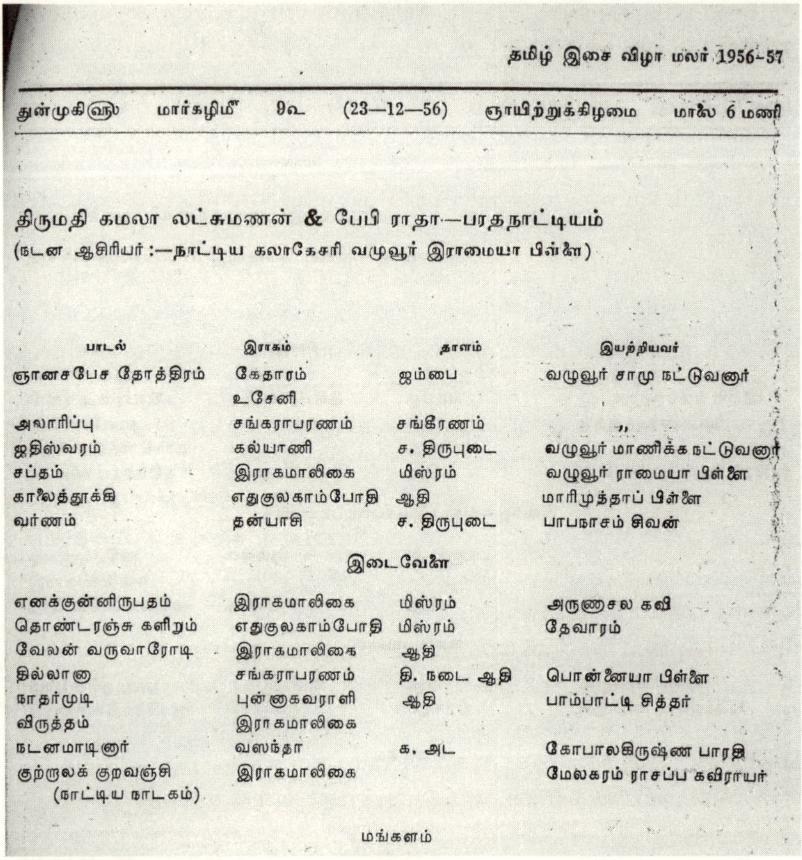

தமிழ் இசை விழா மலர் 1956–57

துன்முகி௵ மார்கழி௴ 9௳ (23—12—56) ஞாயிற்றுக்கிழமை மாலை 6 மணி

திருமதி கமலா லட்சுமணன் & பேபி ராதா—பரதநாட்டியம்
(நடன ஆசிரியர் :—நாட்டிய கலாகேசரி வழுவூர் இராமையா பிள்ளை)

பாடல்	இராகம்	தாளம்	இயற்றியவர்
ஞானசபேச தோத்திரம்	கேதாரம்	ஜம்பை	வழுவூர் சாமு நட்டுவனார்
	உசேனி		
அலாரிப்பு	சங்கராபரணம்	சங்கீரணம்	,,
ஜதிஸ்வரம்	கல்யாணி	ச. திருபுடை	வழுவூர் மாணிக்க நட்டுவனார்
சப்தம்	இராகமாலிகை	மிஸ்ரம்	வழுவூர் ராமையா பிள்ளை
காலைத்தூக்கி	எதுகுலகாம்போதி	ஆதி	மாரிமுத்தாப் பிள்ளை
வர்ணம்	தன்யாசி	ச. திருபுடை	பாபநாசம் சிவன்
	இடைவேளை		
எனக்குன்னிருபதம்	இராகமாலிகை	மிஸ்ரம்	அருணாசல கவி
தொண்டரஞ்சு களிறும்	எதுகுலகாம்போதி	மிஸ்ரம்	தேவாரம்
வேலன் வருவாரோடி	இராகமாலிகை	ஆதி	
தில்லானா	சங்கராபரணம்	தி. நடை ஆதி	பொன்னையா பிள்ளை
நாதர்முடி	புன்னாகவராளி	ஆதி	பாம்பாட்டி சித்தர்
விருத்தம்	இராகமாலிகை		
நடனமாடினார்	வஸந்தா	க. அட	கோபாலகிருஷ்ண பாரதி
குற்றாலக் குறவஞ்சி (நாட்டிய நாடகம்)	இராகமாலிகை		மேலகரம் ராசப்ப கவிராயர்

மங்களம்

Figure 4.6. The repertoire list for a stage Bharatanāṭyam performance by Kamala and Radha, conducted by Ramaiah Pillai as naṭṭuvaṉār *at the Tamil Isai Sangam's annual festival in Madras, December 23, 1956. Collection of the author.*

stood for a purely classical representation of Bharatanāṭyam as cinema dance:

> The narrow-minded idea that dancing is for only certain people, from certain communities has disappeared and now the floodgates have opened for anyone to participate in the culture of dancing. So we are seeing dancing everywhere. Wherever one goes, one can hear the jingling sounds of ankle bells. Whether on stage, in theatrical plays, or in the cinema, dance is given a prominent place.... The world is in awe of India's contributions to dance. However, there is also a trend of outsiders [Westerners] learning this art in a half-

> baked manner, and they receive great acclaim for this. I wonder if they were to see the accomplished dances of Kamala, Vyjayanthimala, and the Travancore Sisters [all film stars who had studied with him], would these same people ever [leave India to] go back to their own countries? . . . We realize that people from other countries are in awe of our dance, especially the divine aspects of our dance, aspects that are very special to India. However, I am saddened that our films do not realize [the divine nature of dance] and recently have introduced all kinds of [non-Bharatanāṭyam-based] dances. This grieves people like me. Not all movement can be considered dance. [Bharatanāṭyam] dance has many rules, traditions, and hereditary connections, all of which are steeped in history. The sage Bharata is the one who created the art form we now call "Bharatanāṭyam." The combination of expression (*bhāva*), melody (*rāga*) and rhythm (*tāḷa*) constitute Bharatam. This is a well-known fact. . . . There are specific codifications for movements of the head, eyes, feet, and torso in addition to various facial expressions. However, in films today, those who are dancing are unaware of these particularities. The heroines perform in such a half-baked manner, moving their body parts unnecessarily. Nowadays there are dances for everything, and sometimes the heroine is surrounded by ten friends doing a dance. In the house, even the servants dance. When the heroine's lover half opens a door, there is a dance. Then there are group dances. There are strip[tease] dances [a reference to the growing number of what are called cabaret dances in Tamil films]. What dances are there not? [I would say that] if even these dances are taught properly and performed properly, there is no one in the world who would admire them more than me. That's why I've given this article such a title, [I want people to know that] it is important to learn the [*śāstric*] grammar (*laṭcaṇa*) of dance. . . . My opinion is that if one takes the time to learn the rules and understand dance traditions, then film dances will become much better, and only then can we truly take pride in these Indian dances, which the entire world admires. (Ramaiah Pillai 1954, 28)

In naming Kamala, Vyjayanthimala, and the Travancore Sisters, Ramaiah Pillai endorses the dancing of non-*devadāsī*, urban, upper-caste women as iconic, *śāstric*, and therefore legitimate. In doing so he also positions himself as the preeminent aesthetic yardstick according to which cinema dance should be measured. This is significant because the emerging forms of dance that he derides (such as the cabaret dance) are forms of dance that women from traditional *devadāsī* backgrounds performed after upper-caste women such as Vyjayanthimala entered the world of cinema as heroines. The classic case is that of T. Jyothilakshmi, the adopted daughter of S. P. L. Dhanalakshmi. Even though she was a student of Ramaiah Pillai in Bharatanāṭyam, she took on the roles of a cabaret dancer and vamp in the South Indian cinema and effectively created the image of the modern South Indian "item dancer."

One of Ramaiah Pillai's final major works in the cinema was for a film about dance called *Konjum Salangai* (A little jingle of the ankle bells; 1962), starring Kamala in the lead (discussed in chapter 3). By this time, his Bharatanāṭyam had morphed into something almost completely unrecognizable from his choreographies in films from the 1940s, like *Sivakavi* and *Kannagi*. This was the new Bharatanāṭyam, full of cinematic glamour and with the now fully fleshed out narrative of its supposed temple origins and religious essence and the nearly acrobatic athleticism and virtuosity of the Ramaiah Pillai–Kamala pairing.

Ramaiah Pillai died on December 12, 1991, in Chennai. In the 1940s, he had married Gnanasundaram Ammal, a woman from the town of Tirumalairajanpattinam (in today's Karaikkal district). They had five children, Jayalakshmi, Samaraj, Gurumurthy, Manikkavinayagam, and Bhagyam. Samaraj became a fairly successful dance teacher in Chennai and passed away in 2004. Ramaiah Pillai's only surviving son, Vazhuvoor Manikkavinayagam, became a composer of what is known as light or semiclassical music in South India, as well as film music, beginning in 2001. Together with his two sons and daughter, he runs a school that teaches Ramaiah Pillai's innovative dance and also maintains a website about the "Vazhuvoor style" (Vazhuvoovar School of Classical Dance and Music 2018).

CONVERGENCES: FIVE *NAṬṬUVAṈĀRS* IN THE EARLY TAMIL CINEMA

We have seen above how Ramaiah Pillai's narrative makes it possible to trace a new kind of history of Bharatanāṭyam in the twentieth century, one in which seamless flows between stage and screen are central. If we are to understand Ramaiah Pillai's story as a kind of metonymic narrative for modern Bharatanāṭyam, then surely we must turn to the lives of other mid-twentieth century *naṭṭuvaṉārs* in Madras who similarly moved between stage and screen. In this section, I therefore very briefly discuss the lives and contributions of five such individuals who from the 1940s through the late 1950s all produced cinema dance and trained students to performance Bharatanāṭyam on stage. They are Vaideeswarankoyil Meenakshisundaram Naṭṭuvaṉār, K. N. Dandayudhapani Pillai, V. S. Muthuswami Pillai, Kuttalam Ganesan Pillai, and Kanchipuram Ellappa Pillai (also known as Ellappa Mudaliar). While I realize that much more could be said about each of these people, my intention here is simply to demonstrate, both quantitatively and through specific instantiations of form and repertoire, the extent to which *naṭṭuvaṉār* participation in the Tamil cinema shaped twentieth-century Bharatanāṭyam, even as women performers in their own communities were—perhaps because of these very processes—becoming increasingly invisible.

Vaideeswarankoyil Meenakshisundaram Naṭṭuvaṉār

We begin with the *naṭṭuvaṉār* about whom the least biographical information is available, although he was clearly one of the first *naṭṭuvaṉārs* credited for "dance" in a Tamil film. Vaideeswarankoyil Meenakshisundaram Naṭṭuvaṉār (figure 4.7) was the oldest son of Muttuswami Naṭṭuvaṉār I (dates unknown) and Ramatayamma in the town of Vaideeswarankoyil (in today's Nagapattinam district). He studied dance only with his father.

His local *devadāsī* students included Tirumayiladi Vijayalakshmi (1919–88) and Vaideeswarankoyil S. Susheela (c. 1928–2003). Susheela acted in three films, *Chitra* (1946), *Chandralekha* (1948), and *Idhaya Geetham* (Song of the heart; 1950), but only in brief supporting roles (figure 4.8).

It is not certain when or under what circumstances Meenakshisundaram left Vaideeswarankoyil for Madras. However, he suddenly appeared in Madras as the choreographer for two early films, *Sri Kanda Leela* (The miraculous deeds of Lord Murukaṉ; 1938) and *DakshaYagnam* (The fire sacrifice of King Dakṣa; 1938). In the songbook for *Śrī Kanta Līlā*, Meenakshisundaram's "dance troupe" (*naṭaṉa kōṣṭi*) is credited (figure 4.9), so we can assume that by that point he had been in Madras for some time, preparing dancers for this film.

He also choreographed at least two slightly later films, *Harischandra* (1944) and *Vidyapathi* (Lord of knowledge; 1946, figure 10a). He is cred-

Figure 4.7. A rare photograph of Vaideeswarankoyil Meenakshisundaram Nattuvaṉār with the film dancers Yogam and Mangalam. Pēcum Paṭam, *June 1945, 58. Roja Muthiah Research Library.*

Figure 4.8. Vaideeswarankoyil S. Susheela, one of Meenakshisundaram Nattuvaṉār's few known devadāsī students. Photo courtesy B. M. Sundaram.

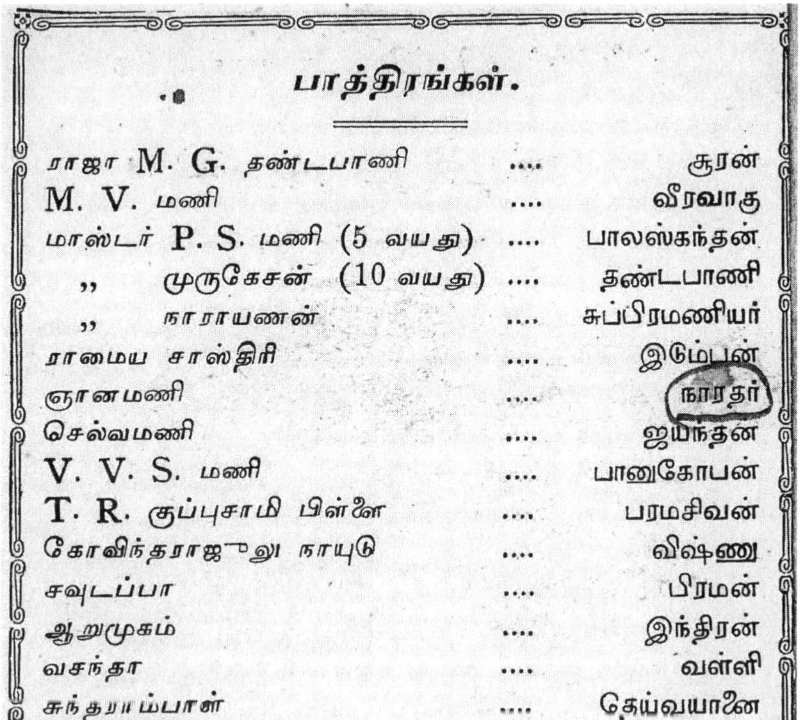

பாத்திரங்கள்.

ராஜா M. G. தண்டபாணி	....	சூரன்
M. V. மணி	....	வீரவாகு
மாஸ்டர் P. S. மணி (5 வயது)	....	பாலஸ்கந்தன்
,, முருகேசன் (10 வயது)	....	தண்டபாணி
,, நாராயணன்	....	சுப்பிரமணியர்
ராமைய சாஸ்திரி	....	இடும்பன்
ஞானமணி	....	நாரதர்
செல்வமணி	....	ஜயந்தன்
V. V. S. மணி	....	பானுகோபன்
T. R. குப்புசாமி பிள்ளை	....	பரமசிவன்
கோவிந்தராஜுலு நாயுடு	....	விஷ்ணு
சவுடப்பா	....	பிரமன்
ஆறுமுகம்	....	இந்திரன்
வசந்தா	....	வள்ளி
சுந்தராம்பாள்	....	தெய்வயானை
தனலக்ஷ்மி	....	பார்வதி
சுசீலாதேவி	....	இந்திராணி
சீதாலக்ஷ்மி	....	அசமுகி

வைதீஸ்வரன் கோயில் மீனாக்ஷிசுந்தர நட்டுவனார்
நடன கோஷ்டியார் நர்த்தனம்.

கதை, வசனம், பாட்டு : டைரெக்டர் :
L. நஞ்சப்ப செட்டியார். H. S. மேதா.

Produced by **PREMIER CINETONE,**
Coimbatore.

Figure 4.9. Credits page from the songbook for Śrī Kanta Līlā *(also* Sri Kanda Leela, *1938), in which Vaideeswarankoyil Meenakshisundaram's "dance troupe"* (naṭaṉa kōṣṭi) *is credited for dance. Private collection of S. V. Jayababu.*

ited for choreography in the songbooks for both films. *Vidyapathi* is important for a number of reasons. First, it contains dance by a *devadāsī* character named Tāci Mōkaṉāmpāḷ, played by the actress K. Thavamani Devi (1925–2001).[14] While most of the sequences were choreographed by Meenakshisundaram (and hence likely consisted of straightforward choreography, much like Ramaiah Pillai's early work), the character of Mōkaṉāmpāḷ also performs a Western-style dance in the film (figure 4.10b). The songbook for the film, which as far as I can ascertain contains the only extant visual materials, tells us that this "English dance" (*naṭaṉam-āṅkilam*) was choreographed by a woman who is credited in Tamil as "Mrs. Raiṉperṭ" (perhaps a Mrs. Reinbert). The music for this sequence was composed by "C. G. Rob and Party." The song had both Tamil and English words (figure 4.10c). The assumed cosmopolitan nature of the audience is very telling. The accompaniment of sequences of Bharatanāṭyam choreographed by Meenakshisundaram by a Western-style performance was not uncommon in films in which traditional female artists performed in Madras in the 1930s. Recall, for example, the "mixed bill" program of La Meri with the *devadāsīs* Bhanumathi and Varalakshmi that took place in Madras in 1937 was discussed in detail in chapter 2.

However, Meenakshisundaram may be best known as the teacher of the famous Brahmin film dancers Yogam and Mangalam (c. 1920–1980) (figure 4.7). We know that these sisters danced in many films in the 1940s. However, since they were never the heroines, not much is known about their background. Fortunately, two small but very important items in the Tamil film magazines *Pēcum Paṭam* ("Nāṭṭiya Mōhiṉi Maṅkaḷam 1946) and *Kuṇṭūci* ("Naṭaṉa cakōtarikaḷ Yōkam-Maṅkaḷam: Vāḻkkai varṇaṉai" 1948) furnish information about the sisters, who were very popular as film dancers and later, as stage performers of Bharatanāṭyam. I provide a translation of an abridged version of the second item here, since it may be the only written source entirely devoted to the dance careers of both these performers:

> The sisters Yogam and Mangalam were born in Thiruvaiyaru [just outside Tanjore] . . . into a Saiva Brahmin, landowning (*mirācutār*) family. Their mother, Meenakshi Ammal, came from a family of Karṇāṭak musicians. Her grandfather was Kottavasal Venkatarama Ayyar [c. 1820–80], a learned musician (*vidvān*). He had composed some *varṇams*. Meenakshi Ammal's sister's father-in-law was the

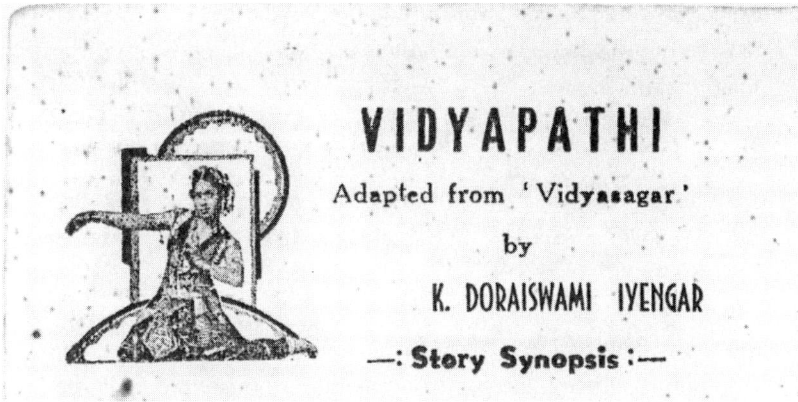

VIDYAPATHI

Adapted from 'Vidyasagar'

by

K. DORAISWAMI IYENGAR

—: Story Synopsis :—

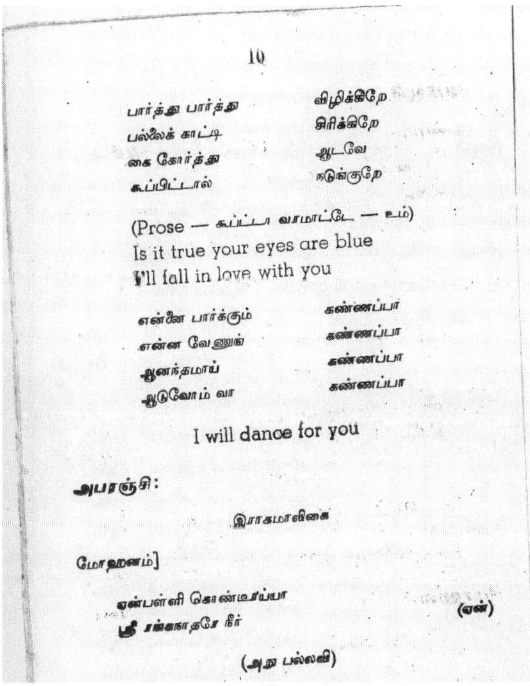

10

பார்த்து பார்த்து விழிக்கிறே
பல்லைக் காட்டி சிரிக்கிறே
கை கோர்த்து ஆடவே
கூப்பிட்டால் நடுங்குறே

(Prose — கூப்ட்டா வரமாட்டே — உம்)
Is it true your eyes are blue
I'll fall in love with you

என்னை பார்க்கும் கண்ணப்பா
என்ன வேணுங் கண்ணப்பா
ஆனந்தமாய் கண்ணப்பா
ஆடுவோம் வா கண்ணப்பா

I will dance for you

அபரஞ்சி:

இராகமாலிகை

மோஹனம்]

ஏன்பள்ளி கொண்டீரய்யா
ஸ்ரீ ரங்கநாதரே நீர் (ஏன்)

(அநு பல்லவி)

Figure 4.10 a, b, c. Excerpts from the songbook for Vidyapathi *(1946) showing the synopsis page with a photo (4.10a), the English lines in one song (4.10b), and the credits with Meenakshisundaram's name and that of "Mrs. Raiṉperṭ" (4.10c). Private collection of S. V. Jayababu.*

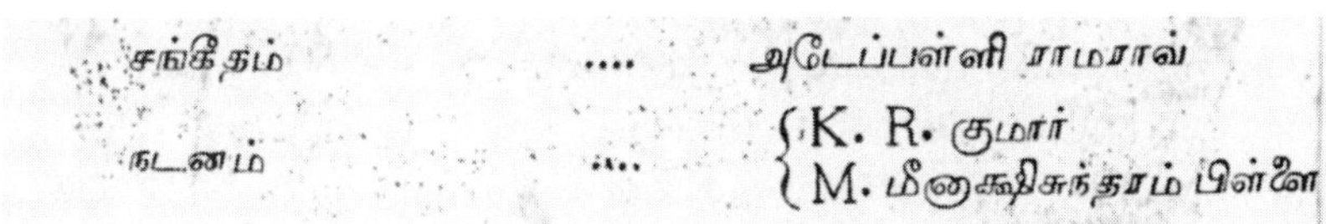

சங்கீதம் .... அடேப்பள்ளி ராமராவ்

நடனம் .... K. R. குமார்
M. மீனாக்ஷிசுந்தரம் பிள்ளை

great musician Patnam Subrahmanya Ayyar [1845–1902]. . . . Several of Yogam and Mangalam's relatives are well placed in important positions in Chennai.

When they were children, Yogam and Mangalam's father Subrahmanya Ayyar passed away. Their mother Meenakshi Ammal took them, along with their other sister, to her father's house and lived there for a while. After that, Meenakshi Ammal took her daughters to Kumbhakonam to study and lived in her sister's house. When [the film director] R. Dwarakanath wanted Baby Thangam [Yogam and Mangalam's other sister] to act [in his film], Meenakshi Ammal vehemently refused. Even the people in her household disagreed. They hated the medium of cinema. But Dwarakanath was persistent. He made a case that girls and boys from good families are now participating in cinema and that Thangam would be continuing this trend. It was then that Meenakshi Ammal had a change of heart and agreed to let Thangam act in the film. Thangam garnered some praise for this, and the following year, she acted in another film, *Chitra* [1946], produced by N. S. Krishnan.

In 1941, Meenakshi Ammal brought her other two daughters, Yogam and Mangalam, to Madras in the hope of having them act in films. . . . Both sisters acted and danced in the film, *Tamilariyum Peruman* [The lord who knows Tamil; 1942], produced by R. M. Ramanathan Chettiar of Uma Pictures, and directed by T. R. Raghunath. When that movie came out, audiences were very attracted by Yogam and Mangalam. . . . But even before their first film came out, they were already contracted for other films such as *Naveena Vikramadithyan* (The new Vikramaditya; 1942). . . . Only [one of the sisters] Yogam, acted in the film *Kannagi* (1942). The sisters also danced in the Telugu film *Patni* [The wife; 1942]. In the movie *Panchamirtham* [Sacred elixir of five substances; 1942] Mangalam acted in the lead role of the [hero's] sister, while Yogam only danced in it.

[We all know that] the [dancer] who had a beautiful swan-like gait and set an example on the stage, was T. Balasaraswati [1918–84]. After her, Mangalam is the next star [of the dance world]. She has the all the necessary attributes required for the stage, according to the *śāstras*.

Yogam and Mangalam also knew some Kathak and Manipuri. But interestingly, they didn't know Bharatanāṭyam. So when they were invited to perform *śāstric* dances, they could not accept these invitations. At that precarious time, they were taken to Vaideeswarankoyil Meenakshisundaram Pillai to learn proper Bharatanāṭyam. Pillai himself learned from the distinguished teacher from Melattur, Sri Natesa Ayyar, who also taught Mr. [E.] Krishna Iyer. . . . Pillai was thus able to teach Yogam and Mangalam very quickly and trained them to be expert and popular dancers.

Yogam and Mangalam had their *araṅkēṟṟam* on May 27, 1944, at Mayilai Sangeetha Sabha. Mrs. Ammu Swaminathan [1894–1978, mother of the Bharatanāṭyam dancer Mrinalini Sarabhai] was the chief guest at the *araṅkēṟṟam*. . . . That recital astonished the audience and created quite a stir. From that day onward, Yogam and Mangalam had no rest—they were in much demand as dancers. This is why after *Jagathalapratapan* [Lord of the world; 1944], they had to take a break from the film industry.

Their dance recitals took place in many parts of Tamilnadu. They received an immense amount of support from the public. Even the great dancer Uday Shankar, who was making the film *Kalpana*, was the chief guest for one of their recitals. Uday Shankar resided in Chennai for two or three years at that time. It must be noted that he was never chief guest at any other dance recital other than that of Yogam and Mangalam. He even invited the sisters to participate in his film *Kalpana* but for some reason they were not able to do so.

. . . After this in 1945, Yogam and Mangalam and their troupe toured Calcutta for two months and gave around fifteen dance recitals. They caused such a stir in this city and the press raved about them. . . . They performed at the most prestigious theatres. While in Calcutta, the sisters were also invited to perform at the Bengal Music Conference. ("Naṭaṉa cakōtarikaḷ Yōkam-Maṅkaḷam: Vāḻkkai varṇaṉai" 1948, 17–18)

In contrast to most women from *devadāsī* backgrounds in the cinema who had first had careers as musicians, recording artists, and theatre performers, Yogam and Mangalam left the cinema to pursue careers as popular stage performers of Bharatanāṭyam. As Brahmin women whose maternal family members were very much involved in musical production in Madras, they were able to fit rather easily into the emerging elite world of modern Bharatanāṭyam dance in the 1940s. More importantly,

Figure 4.11 a, b. Portraits of Yogam and Mangalam. Left: Pēcum Paṭam, *August 1944, 32. Right: "Naṭaṉa cakōtarikaḷ Yōkam-Maṅkaḷam: Vāḻkkai varṇaṉai" 1948, 18–19. Courtesy of the Roja Muthiah Research Library.*

for our discussion, it was Meenakshisundaram Naṭṭuvaṉār who brought about this drastic transformation in the sisters' professional lives. Like many of his contemporaries, Meenakshisundaram found success only when he began choreographing for the cinema and produced star Brahmin professional dancers (we also see this with Ramaiah Pillai and Kamala, for example). The sisters' status as Bharatanāṭyam dancers in Madras can perhaps best be gauged by the fact that they were invited to perform for the annual conference of the Madras Music Academy in 1944, the same year as their *araṅkēṟṟam* (figures 4.11a and 4.11b). The recitals of Yogam and Mangalam may be the last known activities of Meenakshisundaram Naṭṭuvaṉār. His legacy lingered in the cinema for another couple of decades because he had also trained V. S. Muthuswami Pillai (1920–92), a film choreographer and dance teacher discussed below.

K. N. Dandayudhapani Pillai

After Ramaiah Pillai, K. N. Dandayudhapani Pillai may have produced the most Bharatanāṭyam choreographies for the Tamil cinema, working from roughly 1948 to 1963 (table 4.1). He was born to Naṭēca Piḷḷai, a *nā-*

TABLE 4.1.
Films in Tamil, Telugu, and Hindi featuring choreography by K. N. Dandayudhapani Pillai, 1948–1963

YEAR	FILMS
1948	*Samasara Nauka*
1949	*Nalla Thambi* (with Vedantam Raghaviah, credited as "Taṇṭapāṇi Piḷḷai")
1951	*Manamagal* (with Hiralal); *The River*
1952	*Kalyani; Moonru Pillaigal; Panam; Valayapati*
1953	*Avvaiyar; Penn; Anbu; Kangal*
1954	*Ratha Kanneer; Ladki* (Hindi); *Sangham* (Telugu); *Sri Kalahastheeswara Mahatmyam* (Telugu); *Raja Guruvu* (Telugu); *Thuli Visham; Pehli Jhalak* (Hindi)
1955	*Chellappillai; Miss Mary; Missiamma; Gomatiyin Kadalan*
1956	*Chori Chori* (Hindi); *Bhai Bhai* (Hindi); *Ali Babavum 40 Tirudargallum; Kuladaivam; Rangoon Radha*
1957	*Vananga Mudi; Hum Pancchi Ek Daal Ke* (Hindi); *Karpukarasi*
1958	*Sarangadhara* (with Madhavan); *Illarame Nallaram; Bhookailas* (Telugu)
1959	*Sivagangai Seemai; Thilakam; Abalai Anjukam; Adhisaya Penn; Engal Kuladevi; Koodi Vaazhnthaal Kodi Nanmai; Pandithevan*
1960	*Padikkadha Medhai; Paavai Vilakku; Daivapiravi; Kaithi Kannayiram, Kalattur Kannamma; Kavalai Illatha Manithan; Kuravanji; Petra Manam; Rathinapuri Ilavarasi; Raja Desingu; Veerakanal; Bindiya* (Hindi, with A. K. Chopra and Padma)
1961	*Chhaya* (Hindi, with Chopra)
1962	*Man Mauji* (Hindi, with Chopra and Rathan Kumar)
1963	*Nan Vanangum Daivum* (with B. Chinnilal, Sampath, and Madhavan)

Note: Films with no language indicated are in Tamil.

gasvaram artist, and a woman named Cuppammāḷ in the town of Karaikkal (in today's Union Territory of Puducherry) on July 14, 1923. At a very young age, he began to study vocal music from his father and *naṭṭuvāṅkam* from Kattumannarkoyil Muthukumara Pillai. At the age of seventeen, he joined Kalakshetra and assisted Pandanallur Chokkalingam Pillai with *naṭṭuvāṅkam* and singing for Kalakshetra's dance performances. In 1943, Chockalingam Pillai left Kalakshetra, Dandayudhapani stayed on, but he too left six years later (Sundaram 2002, 45).

In 1959, Dandayudhapani Pillai established a dance school in Madras called Natyakalalayam. He felt it was necessary compose new pieces for stage versions of the new Bharatanāṭyam, and thus he focused much of his efforts in the late 1950s and early 1960s on composing new songs and

Figure 4.12. The cover of K. N. Dandayudhapani Pillai, An Evening of Bharathanatyam, *sung by M. L. Vasanthakumari, Columbia Black Label, S/33ESX 6046, 1972, 33⅓ rpm. Collection of the author.*

choreographing dances to accompany them. He composed many songs in traditional genres such as *jatisvaram*, *varṇam*, and *tillāṉā*, and eventually he released a book of these compositions in Tamil titled *Āṭalicai Amutam* (The nectar of dance music). These compositions—including some that were included in the sequences he choreographed for the cinema—became seamlessly integrated into the repertoire of traditional Bharatanāṭyam. In 1972, his compositions were recorded by vocalist M. L. Vasanthakumari (1928–90; popularly known as MLV)—also from the *devadāsī* community[15]—in an album titled *An Evening of Bharathanatyam* (figure 4.12).[16] This recording followed on the coattails of what may be the earliest commercial recording of a full suite of Bharatanāṭyam music, produced by the actress and dancer Vyjayanthimala in 1969.

Like Ramaiah Pillai, Dandayudhapani taught Bharatanāṭyam to a number of film stars, including the Travancore Sisters; Vyjayanthimala; Rajasulochana; Jayalalitha Jayaram, chief minister of Tamilnadu and former film star; and K. Srividya (1953–2006), the daughter of the vocalist M. L. Vasanthakumari). In chapter 2, we discussed how one of the key transformations that occurred in the twentieth-century reinvention of Bharatanāṭyam was the shift away from cyclical, lyrical modes of textual interpretation to linear narrative modes. Certainly, the new dance-drama idiom at it was cultivated at Kalakshetra played no small part in this transformation. Dandayudhapani, who taught there for a number of years, went on to stage his own dance dramas in Madras, and his film star students participated in these stagings of the new Bharatanāṭyam. According to Sundaram (2002, 46) these included the dance dramas *Āṇṭāḷ* (Āṇṭāḷ [a poetess], in which Vyjayanthimala played the primary role), *Civakāmiyiṉ Capatam* (The oath of Civakāmi, with the actress Chandrakantha), *Padmāvati Kalyāṇam* (The wedding of the goddess Padmāvati, with Rajasulochana), and *Kāvēri Tanta Kalaicelvi* (The goddess of arts who manifested the Kāvēri River," with Jayalalitha Jayaram).

What distinguishes Dandayudhapani's choreographic inventions in the cinema from those of Ramaiah Pillai is the incredible range of sequences he choreographed, from dances that were obviously of the Bharatanāṭyam type to those that resemble the northern Indian form Kathak and Western-style numbers that reflect a new type of dance that moved away from traditional idioms. Thus, in many of Dandayudhapani's early choreographies, such as those for English film *The River* (1951), we see only Bharatanāṭyam. In this case, the dancer—Radha Burnier, Arundale's niece—performs a *varṇam* for which he wrote the lyrics, composed the music, and choreographed the resulting number. In films such as *Penn* (1951; remade in Telugu as *Sangham* [1951] and Hindi as *Ladki* [1953], with all of the versions choreographed by Dandayudhapani), the influence of Ramaiah Pillai's style of new Bharatanāṭyamm can be seen. It is particularly evident in the deeply nationalistic dance sequences in all three versions of this film (discussed in chapter 3). A few years later, in the Hindi film *Chori Chori* (Surreptitiously; 1956; distributed by AVM Studios), there are two sequences choreographed by Dandayudhapani Pillai. The first is a *tillāṉā* performed by Kamala, sung by Vasanthakumari. As in the sequences in *Penn*, Kamala is depicted dancing in a stage Bharatanāṭyam performance, on a set that glorifies the notion of Bharatanāṭyam as the ancient temple dance of South India, complete with a large image of the god Śiva-Naṭarāja. The second sequence features the dancers Sayi and Subbulakshmi dressed in Kathak-style costumes and performing a dance at a wedding reception. The movements are loosely inspired by the Kathak dance vocabulary, and it is clear in this sequence that Bharatanāṭyam movements form the basis of the choreography. Later, in the 1958 Telugu film *Bhookailas* (Śiva's heaven on earth; 1958) Dandayudhapani choreographed the performance of the Kathak dancer Gopi Krishna—who, as we have seen above, was also trained in Bharatanāṭyam by Thiruvidaimarudur Mahalingam Pillai. Here, too, we see Kathak-type movement grafted onto a basic movement structure derived from Bharatanāṭyam. Dandayudhapani's choreographic diversity is due in no small part to his movement into the Hindi cinema in the 1950s. At this time, Bharatanāṭyam was also being introduced to northern Indian audiences, and this was facilitated by AVM Studios, one of Madras's largest production studios, which remade many successful Tamil films into Hindi. In these projects, Dandayudhapani interfaced with northern Indian dance directors such as B. Hiralal (a Kathak dancer from Jaipur who had settled in Madras) and A. K. Chopra. Some of Dandayudhapani's later work in the Hindi cinema, in films like *Bindiya* (Bindiyā [a woman]; 1960) thus creates a new vocabulary for dance in social or romantic Indian films. In *Bindiya*, for example, the heroine is played by Padmini (of the Travancore Sisters), yet most of the dance sequences have her coupled with the film's hero, and in these romantic dances, she occasionally assumes a posture reminiscent of Bharatanāṭyam. Dandayudhapani's choreographies in the Hindi cinema thus served two important functions. First, they brought Bharatanāṭyam to northern Indian cinematic audiences, as seen in films like *Ladki* and *Chori Chori*. In these films, the dancers Vyjayanthimala and Kamala brought Bharatanāṭyam genres such as *tillāṉā* to Hindi-speaking cinema audiences through the music and choreography of Dandayudhapani. Second, the emergence of social or romantic dances such as those we see in his later choreographies for Hindi films represents a new instantiation of film dance to which South Indian artists—as both dancers and choreographers—were central.

Although it would be impossible to comment on all the complexities of Dandayudhapani's major choreographies in the cinema, it is significant that he filled a void left by the slowly waning presence of Ramaiah Pillai, who by the 1950s had largely been responsible for establishing the aesthetic parameters of celluloid classicism. Dandayudhapani's Bharatanāṭyam choreography very closely resembles that of Ramaiah Pillai, and indeed it was created for dancers such as Kamala, Padmini, Vyjayanthimala, and Sayi and Subbulakshmi, all of whom had been muses for Ramaiah Pillai. Moreover, audiences had been conditioned to seeing the Ramaiah Pillai–Kamala style of cinematic Bharatanāṭyam. Dandayudhapani thus choreographs from within this aesthetic matrix, and so the classicism of the 1950s and 1960s cinematic Bharatanāṭyam appears seamlessly related to its immediate antecedents. Dandayudhapani adopted his older brother's daughter, Uma Anand, who teaches dance and has written a book in English containing a brief biography of Dandayudhapani, who died in Madras on October 12, 1974. The book also includes photographs and the musical notation for some of his Bharatanāṭyam compositions (Anand 2011).[17]

V. S. Muthuswami Pillai

V. S. Muthuswami Pillai (1921–92) was a *naṭṭuvaṉār* whose work in the cinema has already received considerable attention. Cinema Nritya, the blog run by the dance enthusiast Cassidy Behling includes a number of videos that feature his work (Behling 2015), and one of his students, the dance historian Tiziana Leucci, has written an essay about him titled "Patronage of Hereditary Performing Artists in Tamil Cinema: The Case of V. S. Muthuswamy Pillai" (forthcoming). By providing a brief sketch of his background and discussion of some of his contributions to the cinema here, I wish to highlight the similarities between his experiences and those of other hereditary dance masters who engaged with the cinema. Leucci's essay describes this engagement as "ambiguous": on the one hand, it provided a livelihood and financial stability, but on the other hand, it was both a transient and aesthetically suspect enterprise. Even though Muthuswami Pillai began his career in films as an apprentice to Vaideeswarankoyil Meenakshisundaram Pillai in the late 1940s, by the time he was recognized as a noteworthy independent choreographer in the late 1950s and 1960s, there was a growing rift between stage versions of Bharatanāṭyam (seen as the hermetic, insular space of pure and classical Indian tradition) and cinema dance (increasingly understood as a lowbrow art, even if it featured movement that was dramatically and unquestionably similar to stage Bharatanāṭyam). Leucci lived through the fallout from these understandings of dance in Madras in the 1980s, when she was studying with Muthuswami Pillai. He never quite reached the top ranks as a dance teacher in Madras, likely because of his association with the later Tamil cinema. Indeed, his most prominent Bharatanāṭyam students in Madras were Europeans (mostly from France), who did not have much of an understanding of his involvement with the cinema. In that sense, Muthuswami Pillai's story is very different from that of Ramaiah Pillai, whose cinema dance shaped the tastes of Madras audiences.

Muthuswami Pillai was a *naṭṭuvaṉār* who was born into a *devadāsī* family of artists. His grandmother was a dancer named Vaḷḷampāḷ (dates unknown), and her daughter, named Cēturāmu Ammāḷ (dates unknown), who was talented singer, gave birth to Muthuswami Pillai on October 21, 1920 (Sundaram 2002, 245). He first learned dance and *naṭṭuvāṅkam* from Vaideeswarankoyil Meenakshisundaram Naṭṭuvaṉār (discussed above in detail) and later from Kattumannarkoyil Muthukumara Pillai (1874–1960), who also had a brief stint as a choreographer for Tamil films.[18] Once again, as with Dandayudhapani Pillai, it is not clear when Muthuswami Pillai began his work in the cinema. At some point in the early 1940s he worked for Nrithyodaya, the dance school founded by the film director K. Subrahmanyam. It was likely through his exposure to Subrahmanyam's cinematic network that he began to accompany his teacher, Meenakshisundaram Naṭṭuvaṉār, as an apprentice on film sets. When he began to choreograph on his own is unknown. Speculations based on one of the few pieces written about him, an article in *Sruti* by Sujatha Vijayaraghavan (2011), have proven to be incorrect. The article lists ten films from 1939 to 1949 that Vijayaraghavan claims Muthuswami Pillai choreographed. I have been able to trace the credits of these films through songbooks, and in most cases, either Meenakshisundaram Naṭṭuvaṉār or Vazhuvoor Ramaiah Pillai is credited for "dance." However, in the 1941 film *Sabapathi* (Lord of the assembly), Muthuswami Pillai's name appears with that of Meenakshisundaram. In this film, Muthuswami Pillai is credited as a "junior" artist, indicated by the use of "Master" with his name. By the late 1940s, in films such as *Paittiyakkāraṉ* (Madman; 1947) his name appears together with those of other choreographers such as Vedantam Raghaviah (1919–71). The name is also often confusingly rendered as Muttukumāracāmi, which suggests that this instead might be Kattumannarkoyil Muthukumara Pillai, with whom Muthuswami also studied.

By this time, Muthuswami had earned a reputation as a choreographer, particularly for films produced by A. V. Meiyappan of AVM Studios. In the late 1940s, Muthuswami choreographed a number of films such as *Rukmangada* (The epic of Rukmāṅgada; 1947), *Apurva Chintamani* (Wonderous crest jewel; 1947), *Devadāsī* (1948), *Vedhala Ulagam* (Demon land; 1948), and *Inbavalli* (Affectionate woman; 1949). When he was in Salem, Tamilnadu, shooting the last of these films in 1949, he was asked by P. A. Periyanayaki to teach dance to her own niece, Sayi, and Sayi's cousin Subbulakshmi. Periyanayaki, who came from a *devadāsī* family in Panruti (today's Cuddalore district), was one of the first playback singers in the early Tamil cinema and was then recording songs for *Inbavalli*. In 1953, Muthuswami conducted an *araṅkēṟṟam* for Sayi and Subbulakshmi in Madras, and thereafter, he was almost completely identified with these star performers, who gave both stage performances of Bharatanāṭyam and danced in a number of hit films in the 1950s such as *Malaikkallan* (Mountain bandit; 1954) and *Ratthakanneer* (Tears of blood; 1954), both of which were choreographed by Muthuswami. These and other sequences, as I mentioned above, have received attention elsewhere (Behling 2015; Leucci forthcoming), so I only want to point here to Muthuswami's teaching and mentoring of Sayi and Subbulakshmi as a significant signpost in his own career. In terms of aesthetic shifts, it is very important to realize that Ramaiah Pillai's radical transformations of the aesthetic of dance in the early 1940s had deep, wide-ranging, and irrevocable effects. Thus, the work of both Muthuswami and Dandayudhapani cannot be severed from the choreographic inventions of Ramaiah Pillai.

From the 1960s onward, Muthuswami attracted number of Bharatanāṭyam students. Some of them were from India, such as Pratibha Prahalad (b. 1962) and Kalamandalam Kshemavathy (b. 1948), but there were also a number of European dancers, mainly from France, such as Dominique Delorme and Leucci. Muthuswami's son, M. Selvam, continues to teach a new generation of both Indian and European dancers in Chennai.

Kuttralam Ganesan Pillai

Kuttralam Ganesan Pillai and Kanchipuram Ellappa Pillai, the final two *naṭṭuvaṉārs* in this section, both had very brief experiences in the cinema, although they became very well known teachers of dance in Madras in the 1950s and 1960s. Kuttralam Ganesan's family was originally from the village of Pandanallur, in the Tanjore district. His father, the violinist and *naṭṭuvaṉār* Chinnaiya Pillai, relocated to the town of Kuttralam in southern Tamilnadu shortly after Kuttralam was born in 1906. After studying the *nāgasvaram* (which was played largely in temples by men from the *devadāsī* community), vocal music, and the *mṛdaṅgam* drum, Kuttralam studied *naṭṭuvāṅkam* with his father and his father's teacher, Naṭarāja Naṭṭuvaṉār (dates unknown). By the age of twenty, Ganesan had become a full-fledged *naṭṭuvaṉār*. He worked in Hyderabad for a while as a dance teacher but moved to Madras in June 1954. There he trained a number of dancers and began his engagement with the Tamil film industry, where he worked for close to a decade. As far as I can tell from the material currently available, Ganesan choreographed three films: *Rani Lalithangi* (Queen Lalitāṅgī; 1957), with Pasumarti Krishnamurthy and Thangaraju; *Ambikapathi* (Ambikāpati [a poet]; 1957); and *Kudumba Gauravam* (The family's honor; 1958). By the 1960s, he had stopped working in the cinema, and he founded a dance school called Indiya Kalachara Kazhagam in 1969. He had one daughter, named Meena, and died in Chennai on April 6, 1979.

Kanchipuram Ellappa Pillai (Ellappa Mudaliar)

The final *naṭṭuvaṉār* I discuss in this chapter is Kanchipuram Ellappa Mudaliar (1908–74) (figure 4.13). Ellappa Pillai was very marginally involved in the cinema, and only in the 1960s, at a very late stage. However, one of Ellappa Pillai's most celebrated disciples, a Brahmin man named Udupi Laxminarayan (discussed in detail below in the chapter), taught others who figure prominently in today's world of Tamil cinema dance. Ellappa's aesthetic genealogy thus consists of two generations in the cinema. And even though these instantiations of Tamil cinema dance fall outside of the historical parameters of this project, they represent significant interventions that have long-standing effects on the practice and perception of Bharatanāṭyam in this later period.

Ellappa was born in the town of Kanchipuram (near Madras) to a musician named Kurusvāmi Mutaliyār, and his wife, Kiruṣṇammāḷ—who died when Ellappa was only three years old (Sundaram 2002, 35). His older brother, Kuppuswamy Mudaliar, was the drummer for the famous dancer T. Balasaraswati. Ellappa was initially trained by his uncle, a *naṭṭuvaṉār* named Tiruvengada Pillai. He also studied music with his father and studied the *mṛdaṅgam* drum from another relative, named Varada-

Figure 4.13. Kanchipuram Ellappa Pillai. Courtesy B. M. Sundaram.

raja Mudaliar. Later, he studied with Kandappa Pillai (1899–1942), the primary teacher of Balasaraswati, and when Kandappa Pillai left for Almora (in today's Uttarakhand state) to work with Uday Shankar in the late 1930s, Ellappa became the regular conductor for Balasaraswati's orchestra. A few years later, when K. Ganesan Pillai (1923–87), Kandappa Pillai's son, joined Balasaraswati's troupe, Ellappa gave him some training and left the group in 1959. Ellappa married a woman named Varalakshmi and had a number of children. One of them was E. Gnanasundaram, who was trained by Ellappa to be a dance teacher but moved to Calcutta and died prematurely. Ellappa passed away in Madras on July 22, 1974.

As with Vaideeswarankoyil Meenakshisundaram, is not clear how or when Ellappa began to choreograph films. By the late 1940s, we know that he was teaching elite, nonhereditary dancers in Madras and giving private instruction to a number of young dancers. It is likely that he began to choreograph films in the mid-1950s. His name appeared in the

Figure 4.14. Screenshot from the credits of the film Parthiban Kanavu *(1960), mentioning both Kanchipuram G. Ellappa and Vaideeswarankoyil Meenakshisundaram.*

credits for *Valliyin Selvan* (The son of Valli; 1955), and in this film he choreographed the song *Naṭaṉam āṭiṉār* (discussed in detail in chapter 5). A few years later he recited the rhythmic syllables for the same song that he choreographed again in *Manamaalai* (Garland of the heart; 1958), and it is around this time that his students begin to include the song in their stage performances at the Madras Music Academy (discussed in chapter 5).

One of the final two films that Ellappa is associated with is *Parthiban Kanavu* (Pārttipaṉ's dream; 1960), in which his name appears together with that of Vaideeswarankoyil Meenakshisundaram (this was also one of his very last films) (figure 4.14). This fantasy film is set in the early medieval days of the Tamil Cōḻa empire, and while it mostly contains dance that is clearly not meant to look like Bharatanāṭyam, there is one long sequence of Bharatanāṭyam rhythmic dance (performed to *jatis*). This appears to be have been choreographed by Ellappa, as his voice recites the rhythmic syllables. The sequence is performed by Kamala, who plays a court dancer in the film. By this point, Kamala, and the film's heroine, Vyjayanthimala, had clearly established their presence in the world of both cinema and stage versions of Bharatanāṭyam. The choreography for this sequence is remarkably reminiscent of Ramaiah Pillai's choreographies for Kamala, which contain displays of rhythmic virtuosity, are athletic, and appear polished compared to performances by

T. R. Rajakumari and other early *devadāsī* performers before the mid-1940s.

Finally, one of the last places in which we see the name of Ellappa Pillai is in the credits for the film *Konjum Salangai*, where the names of Ramaiah Pillai and those of his students M. S. Ramasami Pillai and Thangappan also appear. Some of the content of this film was discussed in chapter 3.

In this section, I have provided a brief overview of men from traditional *naṭṭuvaṉār* families who, following the experience of Ramaiah Pillai, carved out careers for themselves that oscillated between stage and cinematic performances of Bharatanāṭyam. I end this chapter by shifting the focus to one of the earliest non-*naṭṭuvaṉār* male choreographers for the Tamil cinema, who also participated in stage performances of Bharatanāṭyam as performer, dance master, and choreographer.

NONHEREDITARY MALE DANCERS AS DANCE TEACHERS AND FILM CHOREOGRAPHERS: THE CASE OF UDUPI LAXMINARAYAN

By the 1950s, just as women from upper-caste backgrounds were entering the cinema and reducing the opportunities for *devadāsī* women there, a similar process was taking place with the emergence of non-*naṭṭuvaṉār* male choreographers. In both cases, of course, this was not a clear, linear shift. Instead, some traditional performers remained, and there were multidirectional and overlapping circulations of forms of knowledge about dance that flowed between *naṭṭuvaṉārs*, *devadāsīs*, and other male teachers and female performers. Here, I turn to the case of Udupi Laxminarayan, who was one of the first nonhereditary choreographers for the Tamil cinema to have trained under a *naṭṭuvaṉār* and also was a full-time Bharatanāṭyam dance teacher in Madras. While Laxminarayan's work in the cinema began only in the mid-1950s, his dance training took place in the late 1940s and early 1950s, the time when major transitions were taking place in the social organization of the world of Tamil cinema. Moreover, Laxminarayan represents a concrete link between the world of Bharatanāṭyam in the 1950s and the present. As we will see at the end of this section, one of his students was Prabhu Deva (b. 1973), one of the most celebrated choreographers of contemporary Indian cinema, whose father, Mugur Sundar, was also a nonhereditary film choreographer in the Kannada-language cinema. Laxminarayan thus stands at the intersection of the early cinematic dance world; the world of the dance revival (from the 1940s to the 1960s), which also includes the repopulation of the early cinema dance world by nonhereditary dancers; and the globalized, post-1980s world of Bollywood (and Tamilnadu's Kollywood) dance.

Most of my discussion of Laxminarayan's life and work comes from a series of conversations I had with him in August 2012. Here, I present excerpts from his free-flowing autobiographical narrative. Even though it is lengthy, I feel it is in important if not integral piece of the history of Bharatanāṭyam performers' lives in the Tamil cinema for the reasons I have outlined above:

> I learned dance from Kanchipuram Ellappa Pillai. I come from a very orthodox family. There was no learning dance and all that. My grandfather is a Sanskrit pandit. He taught Sanskrit to the monastic head (*maṭhādhipati*) of the monastery at Udupi. Everyone knew my grandfather in Udupi. I was taught Vedas as a child. I studied the *Sāmaveda* for four years, and then I went to the Sanskrit College [the Sri Madhva Siddhanta Prabodhini Sanskrit College in Udupi].
>
> But I was always very interested in music. My mother's father was always singing *bhajans* [devotional songs] during *pūjā* [worship at the home shrine]. My mother also sang. I also sang with my mother. . . . When I was in Sanskrit College, I studied the texts of the poet Kālīdāsa. I began to understand the importance of dance (*nāṭyam*). In one verse I read, I realized the spiritual importance of dance. So I asked myself, "why shouldn't I learn dance?"
>
> The head of the Pejavara Adokshaja Monastery in Udupi, Visveswara Tirtha Swamiji, studied [Sanskrit] with me in college. I told him my future plans, and he said he would arrange dance classes for me in Madras. I was about twenty-one then. I had finished college and graduated with a *vidvān* degree in Sanskrit (a kind of postgraduate degree). By then I had also learned a little dance from a man named Srinivas Kulkarni in Dharwad. . . . He encouraged me to go to Madras to learn more. . . . Swamiji told me to come to Madras then. He introduced me to the proprietor of Woodlands Hotel, Krishna Rao. Swamiji explained my situation to Krishna Rao, whose children were being taught by Ellappa Pillai. . . . I was

twenty-one [in 1949] when I began training with Ellappa. Now I am now eighty-five, going on eighty-six.

Ellappa Pillai was from Kanchipuram. The Kanchipuram style is very different from the Tanjore style. There was once a certain Paccamuttu Mutaliyār, who was the court *naṭṭuvaṉār* (*āsthāna vidvān*) for the Mysore maharaja. My teacher Ellappa Pillai came from that lineage. His brother Kuppuswamy Mudaliar played *mṛdaṅgam* [the drum] for Balasaraswati's performances. I had many wonderful experiences with my teacher. . . . Usually *naṭṭuvaṉārs* would teach only people from their own caste. But he taught me, a Brahmin man, everything. That is my good fortune. Whenever I had difficulty, he was always there for me. He loved me so much.

Ellappa used to sing for Balasaraswati. I used to watch her rehearsals all the time. Her *abhinaya* was my inspiration. I learned so much just by watching her. . . . Ellappa Pillai died on July 22, 1974. He had a sudden heart attack. I was in a film shooting . . . when I got the news. The director told me to finish that shot and leave [for the funeral] immediately afterward.

Ellappa Pillai had choreographed films, and I was always his assistant. He did not know film techniques, but I could understand some of them. For example, I had to always give something called the "cue movement" to mark transitions and provide continuity between shots and locations. Ellappa would always take my advice for these cue movements. So I always had to modify his choreography to suit the film, but in such a way that my master always got the credit and the praise.

While I was learning from Ellappa, I needed money to eat! So I was working at a library in Madras before I got a job at Gemini Studios. Someone from the library knew someone in Gemini Studios and recommended me. He told me to contact someone from Gemini Studios. I had to go through an audition. The first film I danced for was called *Raji En Kanmani* [Raji, the apple of my eye; 1954]. I did a group dance. I was nervous because I only knew Bharatanāṭyam, but in this film, I had to do other forms. Bhaskar Roy Chowdhury, also a student of Ellappa Pillai's, was the choreographer for that film. . . . I danced in a couple of Gemini films, such as *Valliyin Selvan* [Valli's son; 1955]. I was on contract with Gemini pictures. I did not do any Bharatanāṭyam, only cinema dance. I did not feel bad about it at all. I could separate the two. I wanted to earn money to pay Ellappa Pillai [for my ongoing study of Bharatanāṭyam]. I was very professional and kept it separate.

The first film I choreographed was *Galatta Kalyanam* [A troubled wedding; 1968] in which I did a song for [the actors] Sivaji Ganesan and Nagesh. I was not credited for this. When I was choreographing films—for example, if they gave me a love duet, it was always dignified. Not like what is going on now.[19]

In this passage, Laxminarayan talks about his training under a traditional *naṭṭuvaṉār*, Kanchipuram Ellappa Pillai. Ellappa had choreographed a number of Tamil films in the 1950s, including *Valliyin Selvan*, in which Laxminarayan performed. In this film, Ellappa choreographed a version of the song *Naṭaṉam āṭiṉār* (discussed above and discussed in greater detail in chapter 5). Laxminarayan had a productive career in the cinema of the 1960s and prided himself on his connections to the major stars of that period:

I choreographed the sequence depicting Śiva's cosmic dance (*civa tāṇṭavam*) for the hit movie *Thiruvilaiyadal* [The sacred sports of Śiva; 1968]. I knew Sivaji Ganesan [1928–2001; the actor who played the hero of the film] because I worked in his theatre company—known as Civājī Nāṭaka Maṉṟam—as a dance master, choreographing all the plays. . . . Sivaji was a big supporter of my work. He would always announce to the audience that I was the one who choreographed the *civa tāṇṭavam* sequence when he came [and gave a speech] for my stage performances. There was no Bharatanāṭyam in this, but I used my imagination of what it would be like to choreograph for an angry Śiva! In the film, I was also the man behind the mask of [the sacred bull] Nandi, playing the drum. The person playing Nandi was not up to the mark, and the director lost patience, so I stepped in.

Laxminarayan's work in the Tamil cinema extends well beyond the parameters of Bharatanāṭyam-influenced dancing. In the next passage, he talks with pride about how his knowledge of framing and spatial organization enabled him to choreograph a club dance sequence:

When I was composing the dance, I would also imagine the various shots. In a movie called *Gauravam* [Pride; 1973], [the actor] Sivaji

> [Ganesan] himself recommended that I choreograph the film. I was choreographing a club dance sequence, nothing to do with Bharatanāṭyam. Everyone on the set thought I wouldn't be able to do it. Sivaji reassured me that I could. I composed the dance for the song *Aticaya ulakam* [Wondrous world] in that film. The cameraman Vincent was the director of the film. I would offer my suggestions in terms of how I conceived of the various shots for that sequence, using just my hands to mark the movement and placement of the camera lens. The director completely agreed with me. . . . The producer said my choreography was comparable to that of the great choreographer Hiralal. . . . Because I had the basics of Bharatanāṭyam, I could easily use my imagination and create creative Western movement. That song became a hit. I was given the fee of my choice after that.
>
> Stage Bharatanāṭyam is not really the same as cinema Bharatanāṭyam. On stage we can dance whatever we want. But on film, we have to collaborate with the director, producer, music director, camera man. . . . Everyone must be satisfied in a making a film dance sequence. There are close shots, mid-shots, long shots, crane shots, rush shots, trolley shots. We have to choreograph accordingly to the type of shot. If it is a close-up, the expression has to be catered to that shot alone. In a trolley shot, the trolley follows the artist, and another trolley runs across from [perpendicular to] the artist. It's a distinct way to choreograph for films.

Laxminarayan's discourse represents one of the few articulations by a male choreographer that I have found about a certain awareness the uniqueness of cinema dance choreography—shown by his comment that "stage Bharatanāṭyam is not really the same as cinema Bharatanāṭyam." It also marks stage Bharatanāṭyam as insular (that is, classical) and sealed off from the popular.

However, Laxminarayan expressed ambiguity about the precise relationship between Bharatanāṭyam and cinema dance, and even about the relationship between traditional forms of dance and experimental dance in the late twentieth century. I would like to conclude this section with an analysis of this ambiguity and the ways in which it is clearly tied to the larger historical and social issues discussed above. For a number of years, for example, Laxminarayan collaborated with Chandralekha (1928–2006), the radical reinterpreter of Bharatanāṭyam.[20] While he was open to her early innovations, which he characterized as "something very creative," when her work began to more explicitly address themes related to sexuality, he parted company with her. His discomfort with representations of sexuality comes across in his narration of a decline in the quality of dance in contemporary Tamil cinema: "People who criticize Bharatanāṭyam dance in old [Tamil] films don't understand what Bharatanāṭyam is. I was in the cinema field for about twelve years or so. I also left the field because the old directors had changed. The new ones thought about dance differently. It became very cheap and vulgar. They were not dignified. They treated girls dancing in the 'chorus' [backup dancers] very badly. I did not like this. These days the films have become very low class. The audiences' tastes have changed. The trends have changed."

The first line of this passage captures more of Laxminarayan's ambiguous sense of Bharatanāṭyam in the cinema. For him, the "old" cinema somehow captures the true nature of Bharatanāṭyam, whereas dances in Tamil films today are not part of an aesthetic genealogy that includes classical Bharatanāṭyam, and thus they are "cheap and vulgar." Somewhat ironically, Laxminarayan speaks with great pride about one of his students, the contemporary South Indian film choreographer Prabhu Deva (b. 1973), who is known for his risqué and sexually bold cinema dance today:

> I taught my student Prabhu Deva very well. I taught him exactly how to pay attention to *Tāḷa* [rhythm], to the stage space, and to the movements. Because he had this strong foundation in the basics, he was able to adapt [to new contexts] and do all his creative choreography. He adapted my basics and made new movements from them. Nowadays people copy from him and do this very poorly. His father [Mugur Sundar, from Mysore] and I were good friends. He was a dance master for many films and was very famous. In fact, I did the *araṅkēṟṟams* of all three of his sons—Prabhu Deva, Raju Sundaram, and Nagendra Prasad—in 1986. All three are now film choreographers.

Part of this ambiguity no doubt stems from his perception of his orthodox Brahminic background, but another major part of it comes from the fact that he was also established as a Bharatanāṭyam guru in Madras. The early twentieth-century discourses of respectability and the sacred nature of Bharatanāṭyam discussed in chapters 2 and 3 remain a prominent part of his self-image. He is careful to stress both respectability and religion in his discussion on Bharatanāṭyam pedagogy in his school, Natya Manjari, which was established in Madras in 1962:

> In our school, we do not teach pieces about eroticism [*śṛṅgāra*]. Devotion [*bhakti*] alone is paramount. How can we teach young girls about love? I never do this. I do not teach *jāvaḷis* [the old courtesan genre of love lyric]. I only teach *bhakti*-based songs. My teacher Ellappa Pillai had mature women learning from him, so he taught *śṛṅgāra* pieces. But I have many young girls as students, so I do not teach this, only *bhakti*. And not just *bhakti* toward God, but guru *bhakti* [devotion toward the teacher] is equally important. Our school is a temple. Anybody who comes for our shows will feel devotion. We also do not discriminate based on caste or religion. I have taught Christians and Muslims, too.

Here we see how despite his bold statements about the aesthetic value of cinema dance above, his representations of Bharatanāṭyam's moral register lapse into the tropes of the reinvention. He points to the dichotomy between eroticism and devotion (*śṛṅgāra* and *bhakti*) that were central to debates provoked by Arundale's interventions from the late 1930s into the mid-1950s. He also speaks disparagingly of courtesan dance genres (even though in films he choreographed these).[21] He calls his school a temple, borrowing the two tropes of Bharatanāṭyam as temple dance and the sacred nature of learning and teaching Bharatanāṭyam as a religious exercise that were key to the middle-class reconfiguration of the dance. Finally, the rhetoric of the supposed caste- and religion-based inclusivity that he refers to was also a major framing device for the universalization and democratization of Bharatanāṭyam that enabled it to simultaneously inhabit regional (Tamil), national (Indian), and global spaces of representation (O'Shea 2007).

CONCLUSION

In this chapter, we mapped the complex and challenging roles played by men who were involved in the production of Bharatanāṭyam as cinema dance in the early to the mid-twentieth century. Men from *naṭṭuvaṉār* communities, in particular, not only participated in the remaking of Bharatanāṭyam as simultaneously a stage and screen art, but also to a large extent shaped its emerging aesthetics. Nowhere is this more evident than in the work of Ramaiah Pillai, and those *naṭṭuvaṉārs* such as V. S. Muthuswami Pillai and K. N. Dandayudhapani Pillai who followed the path he charted. This chapter also highlighted the close entanglement between cinema and stage representations of Bharatanāṭyam by focusing on the pedagogical lives of these *naṭṭuvaṉārs*. Teaching Bharatanāṭyam to middle-class (mostly upper-caste) women in Madras instilled new forms of so-called respectability certainly into Bharatanāṭyam, but also into the lives of these teachers. Had they remained in the world of cinema alone, they likely would not have achieved the professional success they did as celebrated gurus in modern India's dance scene. We see strains of the danger of this potential cultural marginalization in the case of Muthuswami Pillai, for example, who never quite achieved the fame of Ramaiah Pillai or Dandayudhapani because so much more of his early professional career focused on the cinema rather than the stage. Regardless, the life narratives of these figures all show the negotiations and slippages between form and discourse, between ideas about the popular and the classical, and Bharatanāṭyam and its discontents. The social and technological interventions represented by the advent of cinema dance and the consequent emergence of the dance choreographer in South India had significant consequences for stage versions of the dance as well. The idea that Bharatanāṭyam could in fact be choreographed—in terms of both its abstract dance (*aṭavukaḷ*) and textual interpretation (*abhinaya*)—evolved at the hands of these *naṭṭuvaṉārs* who moved between stage and screen. Indeed, we might even say that the idea of choreographing a composition in modern Bharatanāṭyam takes its cues from the ways in which dance was reworked by *naṭṭuvaṉārs* in the cinema—again, with Ramaiah Pillai's choreographic formulas and vocabularies at the heart of the enterprise. In the chapter that follows, we examine several such cinematic representations of choreography across Bharatanāṭyam genres in detail, to understand these shifts from generic, aesthetic, and technical standpoints.

[5]

GENRE, REPERTOIRE, AND TECHNIQUE IN CINEMA AND ON THE URBAN STAGE

This final chapter illuminates how the embodied and material significations of Bharatanāṭyam dance—in terms of its aesthetics, technique, and repertoire—were irrevocably transformed through its encounter with the cinema. The chapter traces the ways in which traditional *devadāsī* dance genres like the Tamil *padam* are revised in the cinema. It analyzes the way that tune (*meṭṭu* or *varṇameṭṭu*), gestural exegesis of poetry (*abhinaya*), and movement techniques (*aṭavu, jati,* and *kōṟvai*) are deployed in genres like *padam* as well as in other genres like *tillāṉā* and *kīrtana* that find their way into the cinema. In some sense, the early cinema also provides a window onto older dance technique and repertoire that have disappeared from today's Bharatanāṭyam but remain captured on film from the 1930s and 1940s. This chapter also examines how slippages between idioms were integral to the making of both cinema dance and stage versions of Bharatanāṭyam in this period. The chapter unpacks these slippages by pointing to the creation of new types of dance that were specifically the products of the encounter between cinema and stage, such as the *pāmpu naṭaṉam* and dances that narrativize devotion to the dancing god Śiva-Naṭarāja. These new forms breathe a different aesthetic life into the idiom of Bharatanāṭyam, and these new instantiations of the dance become representative of Bharatanāṭyam as a whole in the mid-twentieth century. Finally, in thinking about dance repertoire, it is imperative that we take seriously the idea of intermedial cultural formations in early twentieth-century Madras. In this chapter, print culture—in the form of both film songbooks and chapbook-style compilations of items in the traditional dance and music repertoire—again plays a major role, not only as a way of documenting or preserving repertoire, but also as a key site where music, dance, and cinema meet. Throughout the chapter, we will see the centrality of text in the production and dissemination of Bharatanāṭyam in its staged and cinematic iterations. Indeed, even when visual sources are available, they must be brought into dialogue with the textual archive that helps us contextualize and understand the movement that we see in celluloid representation. I argue that it is this deeply intermedial and cross-pollinizing play between text, music, the dancing body, and celluloid representation that constitutes the modern idea of the classical as it is expressed in twentieth-century Indian dance.

OLD REPERTOIRE IN NEW MEDIA: COURTESAN DANCE REPERTOIRE AND TECHNIQUE IN THE CINEMA

From the very first instantiations of dance in the South Indian cinema, it is clear that courtesan dance provided a kind of template for choreographic representation. While the reinvented Bharatanāṭyam was already clearly on the horizon as cinema was becoming a popular cultural form, the cinema of the 1930s and early 1940s also preserves a record of the residual aesthetics of the prerevival dance. As we saw in the previous chapter, the earliest choreographers to be credited in the Tamil cinema, figures like Vaideeswarankoyil Meenakshisundaram Naṭṭuvaṉār and Vazhuvoor Ramaiah Pillai, emerged from within the *devadāsī* or *icai vēḷāḷar* community and thus brought a keen awareness of courtesan dance technique and repertoire into their work in the cinema. In this section, I trace some of the ways in with traditional courtesan genres—such as *padam*, *jāvaḷi*, *svarajati*, and *tillāṉā*—that were exclusively the preserve of *devadāsī* artists in the nineteenth century become modes of performance that traveled widely through the cinema. It is also significant that genres like *padam* and *jāvaḷi* were also present in Tamil drama. While some of the published scripts for Tamil *icai nāṭakam* plays simply labeled their songs using the generic Tamil term *pāṭṭu* ("song"), others consciously used terms borrowed from earlier indigenous theatre forms, such as the term *taru* (from the Telugu *daruvu*) or terms borrowed from courtesan dance such as *padam* or *jāvaḷi*.[1] The presence of courtesan genres in the drama thus also enabled their movement into the new spaces of the early cinema. In the process of this new mobility, these genres are often repurposed and transformed, and then in their new forms they entered the world of stage performances of the reinvented Bharatanāṭyam.

Repurposed Repertoire: The Svarajati and Tillāṉā in the Cinema

One of the earliest examples of such repurposing comes from the mythological film *Prahlada* (Prahlāda [a child devotee]; 1939), produced by Salem Shankar and directed by B. N. Rao. In this film, there is a scene in which the demonic father of the child devotee Prahlāda, named Hiraṇyakaśipu, is being entertained by courtesans in his palace. This film is one of the earliest choreographic projects of Ramaiah Pillai, and for this sequence, he chose to repurpose a piece that was in wide circulation among *devadāsī* performers and *naṭṭuvaṉārs* in Madras at the time, a *svarajati* titled *Māmōkalākiri mīrutē* (My passion is ever-increasing). It is in the *rāga* Khamās and was written by the poet Kaṭikai Namaccivāya Pulavar and composed by the musician Subbarāma Dīkṣitulu, who were both associated with the court of Ettayapuram in today's Thoothukudi district.[2] The *svarajati* is a virtuosic piece in the *devadāsī* repertoire that alternates between poetic interpretation through gesture (*abhinaya*) and passages of abstract movement (*jatis* and *kōṟvais*). The text of this *svarajati*, in the *rāga* Khamās, was dedicated both to the deity Murukaṉ and raja of Ettayapuram, Rāma Kumāra Eṭṭappā Nāyakkar (r. 1868–90). In his repurposing of the song for *Prahlada*, Ramaiah Pillai deleted the textual references to the raja, so that it appears that the courtesans are performing a dance dedicated to Hiraṇyakaśipu. Thus only an excerpt of the full *svarajati* was performed, and this became a precedent for similar instances of repurposing that occurred later.

Another instance that I would like to briefly discuss here—the repurposing of a piece in the *tillāṉā* genre in the Telugu film *Suvarna Sundari* (Golden beauty; 1957), remade into the Tamil film *Manaalane Mangaiyin Bhagyam* (A husband is a woman's good fortune; 1957)—is significant for two reasons. First, the piece was composed by K. Ponnaiya Pillai (1888–1945), a descendant of the famous Tanjore Quartet of the nineteenth century. This is significant because this family had no other involvement with dance in the cinema, despite being at the forefront of the reinvention of Bharatanāṭyam for the stage (Rukmini Arundale's teacher, Pandanallur Meenakshisundaram Pillai, was also a descendant of this family). Unlike other *naṭṭuvaṉārs* such as Ramaiah Pillai and K. N. Dandayudhapani Pillai, members of this family did not choreograph for the

South Indian cinema. The second reason is linked to the first: the repurposing of the piece and its presence in the film became a point of contention for this family. The piece was used in the film without the family's permission, and a legal battle ensued between the film's producers and K. Sivanandam Pillai (1913–2003), son of the composer K. Ponnaiya Pillai. B. M. Sundaram, a close associate of the family who was apparently involved in the legal process, told me what happened:

> At the time of filming both the Telugu and Tamil versions, Sivananadam was very upset and asked me why they would have used his family's *tillāṉā* in the films without acknowledging them. Immediately, at his request, the advocate Sarangapani, who was also a patron of this family, issued a lawyer's notice to the producer [and the star of the film], Anjali Devi, requesting one lakh rupees [approximately $1,500 today] as compensation. The judge in this case, named Seshagiri Rao, asked Sivanandam if the rather abstract sounding vocalized drum syllables like "*udana*," "*tom*," and "*tanana*" [which are used in the composition] have any meaning. Sivanandam looked at me, and I said, "Yes, they have meanings." The judge then gave him fifteen days to come up with what these mean [arguing that Sivanandam could claim copyright infringement of the text of the song itself]. I went to the Sarasvati Mahal Library in Thanjavur and researched their meanings as they appeared in some old manuscripts and gave these to Sivanandam in Madras, who in turn immediately gave [them] to the judge. The judge passed the judgment, and Sivanandam was awarded the one lakh rupees. (interview by the author, Chennai, August 27, 2012)

The *tillāṉā* was composed in the *rāga* Aṭhānā and ends with a Telugu benediction to the goddess Veṇubhujāmbikā, consort of Śiva-Paśupatīśvara in the town of Pandanallur. It was a popular composition in this family's repertoire, and several students (both from courtesan and noncourtesan families) performed this piece in the early decades of the twentieth century. The Telugu version ends:

Ī vasudhalo nīku sāṭi daivamu ledanucu nā madini dalaci ninu
On this earth, there is no deity comparable to you, this is what I believe in my heart,
mari mariyĕnto balkitinamma paśupateśvaruni rāṇi kŏmma

Figure 5.1. Screenshot of Rajasulochana and Girija in Suvarna Sundari *(1957).*

I've entreated you time and time again, queen of Śiva-Paśupatīśvara. (Suvarna Sundari Full-Length Telugu Movie n.d.)

For the Tamil version of the film, the lyrics were rewritten, in a slightly altered form, in Tamil:

Pārainilē uṉ pātāmpujamelil karula uṉ malarē caraṇākati
On this earth, I surrender to your lotus-like, most beautiful feet
paṇintuṉai nane makiḻtiṭuvēṉē pacupatē makilum lōkanāyaki
I worship you with joy, mother of the world, celebrated by Paśupati [Śiva]. (Manalane Mangayin Bagyam n.d.)

In both films, the choreography is by Vempati Pedda Satyam (1922–82), a Brahmin dancer from Kuchipudi village whose life and work in the Telugu cinema has been traced extensively by Katyayani Thota (2016). P. Adinarayana Rao is credited with composing the music for the film, and Tanjai Ramaiah Das and Kosaraju are credited with writing the lyrics. In both films, the *tillāṉā* is sung by P. Leela (1934–2005) and A. P. Komala (b.1934). In the films' narrative, the court dancer Jayantī (played by Rajasulochana) teaches this *tillāṉā* to the young Princess Pratimā Devī (played by Girija) (figure 5.1). This lesson takes place in a royal dance hall in a mythological palace. While the film is set an unspecified ancient time, the court dancers perform a piece that was only composed by Ponnaiya Pillai in the twentieth century. The scene is slightly longer than two minutes, but it contains all three sections of the composition (*pallavi, anupallavi* and *caraṇam*). Interspersed between these sections are *jatis*, and the choreography of these oscillates between recognizably Kūcipūḍi and Bharatanāṭyam movement, a pattern that was characteristic of dance in the Telugu cinema of this period (Putcha 2011; Thota 2016).

Love Recast: The Tamil Padam in the Cinema

The Tamil *padam* may be one of the most frequent, amorphous, and complex representations of *devadāsī* repertoire in the Tamil cinema. It is a genre of usually erotic love poetry in the tripartite structure of *pallavi, anupallavi*, and *caraṇam* that dates back to the late seventeenth century. As the ethnomusicologist Matthew Allen (1992) has shown, the earliest compositions in the *padam* genre were likely in Telugu, but very soon *padams* were also composed in Tamil and later even in Marathi.[3] Among the earliest Tamil *padam* poets were Muttutāṇṭavar (c. early seventeenth century) and Mārimuttā Piḷḷai (1712–87), both *icai vēḷāḷar* poets in whose hands the genre acquired some of its most characteristic features. However, but it is perhaps most closely identified with a prolific nineteenth-century Brahmin composer named Vaitīcuvaraṉkōyil (or Pikṣāṇṭarkōyil] Cupparāma Aiyar (c. 1829–80). Aiyar's *padams* became emblematic of the genre and traveled throughout *devadāsī* and *naṭṭuvaṉār* communities all over the Tamil-speaking regions of the Madras Presidency. In terms of content, the *padam*, like most pieces in the courtesan dance repertoire, almost always revolves around three heavily stylized narrative presences: the heroine (*nāyikā*), her female confidante (*sakhī*), and the hero (*nāyaka*). Most commonly, the *padam* is in the voice of either the heroine, who has been estranged from her beloved, or in the voice of the confidante, who has been entrusted with the task of bringing the hero back to the heroine.

Allen (1992 and 1998) also discusses another aspect of the *padam*—namely the genre's highly malleable status, based on the interchangeability of tune and text that seems to be at the very heart of its performative life. Allen calls this the phenomenon of "the common tune," noting that *padams* are often characterized by "fuzzy boundaries" both textually and musically (Allen 1992, 358 and 368). He notes that a large number of Tamil *padams* have the same tunes but alternative texts, or the same texts may have alternative tunes. This flexibility and adaptability is clearly also at the center of the repurposing of *padams* in films. Two of the best known examples of this come from songs that were originally Telugu *jāvaḷis,* a genre closely related to the *padam,* but were reworked as explicitly devotional Tamil *padams* in their filmic iterations.[4] These come from the films *Meera* (1945) and *Chandralekha* (1948). In both films the tunes of nineteenth-century Telugu *jāvaḷis* are used with lyrics that are completely unrelated in content to the original *jāvaḷis*—which essentially become Tamil *padams* in their new form. Thus, in *Meera,* a Telugu *jāvaḷi* in the *rāga* Paras, attributed to the poet Tiruppanandal Pattabhiramayya (b. c. 1863), *Celi neneṭlu sahintune* (Friend, I can't bear this agony) is transformed into a devotional *padam* in Tamil, beginning with the words *Maravēnē eṉṉālilumē* (I will never forget your grace, Kṛṣṇa), simply by using the new words. In *Chandralekha,* the Telugu *jāvaḷi* in the *rāga* Yaman Kalyāṇī, attributed to the poet Dharmapuri Subbarāya Ayyar (c. 1864–1927), *Adi nīpai marulu kŏnnadirā* (That girl is deeply in love with you) is changed into the Tamil devotional song to the child Kṛṣṇa, beginning with the words *Pālaṉ karuṇai purivāy* (Child god, please bestow your compassion). In both cases, we see the sublimation of the erotic qualities of the *jāvaḷi* in favor of a more devotional composition, which indicates the new audiences for both the cinema and the reinvented Bharatanāṭyam by the 1940s.

While the early Tamil cinema can provide many examples of the repurposing of *padams,* in the section that follows, I want to briefly focus on two types of representations of *padams*: one in which a traditional *padam* is used as is from within the courtesan repertoire, by way of two examples from 1940s films; and another in which new songs are composed in the *padam* framework to make them feel like *padams*.[5] In both contexts, I hope to demonstrate how filmic mediation recasts the genre as suitable for representation on stage.

Representations of Older *Padams*

In this section I wish to examine two *padams,* one from the social drama *Sabhapathy* (Lord of the assembly; 1941) and the other from the film *Jagathalapratapan* (Lord of the world; 1944)—both of whose choreographers were among the earliest *naṭṭuvaṉārs* in the cinema, Vaideeswarankoyil Meenakshisundaram Naṭṭuvaṉār and Ramaiah Pillai, respectively.

Sabhapathy contains one of Aiyar's best-known *padams,* which appears in print sources that are almost contemporaneous with the com-

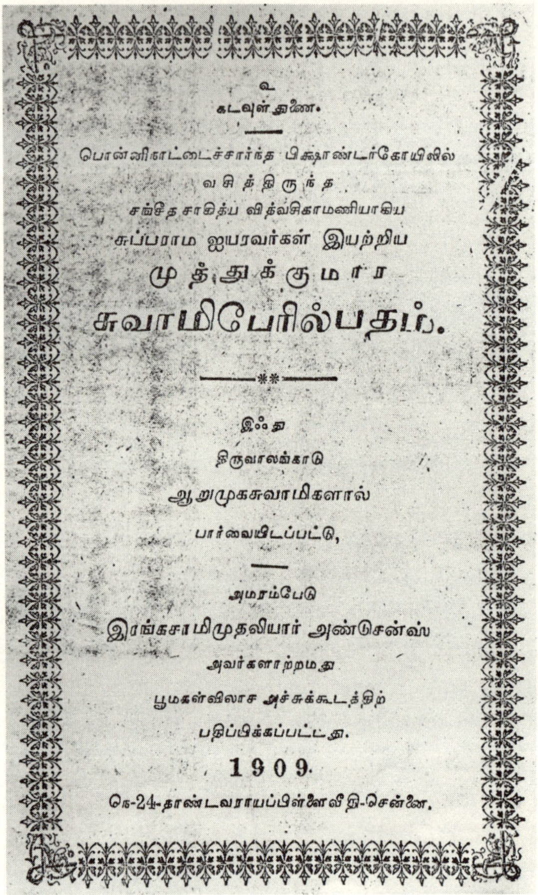

உ
கடவுள் துணை.
பொன்னிநாட்டைச்சார்ந்த பிக்ஷாண்டார்கோயிலில்
வசித்திருந்த
சங்கீத சாகித்ய வித்வசிகாமணியாகிய
சுப்பராம ஐயரவர்கள் இயற்றிய
முத்துக்குமார
சுவாமிபேரில்பதம்.
இஃது
திருவாலங்காடு
ஆறுமுகசுவாமிகளால்
பார்வையிடப்பட்டு,
அமரம்பேடு
இரங்கசாமிமுதலியார் அண்டுசன்ஸ்
அவர்களாற்றமது
பூமகள்விலாச அச்சுக்கூடத்திற்
பதிப்பிக்கப்பட்டது.
1909.
நெ-24-தாண்டவராயப்பிள்ளைவீதி-சென்னை.

Figure 5.2. The cover of a 1909 compilation of the Tamil padams *of the poet Aiyar titled* Cupparāma Aiyaravarkaḷ iyaṟṟiya Muttukkumāra Cuvāmipēril Patam *(Padams composed by Cupparāma Aiyar dedicated to the god Muttukkumāra [Murukaṉ]). Collection of the author.*

poser's lifetime (figure 5.2).[6] The *padam* in the film is *Nāṉ aṅkē varuvēṉō* (Should I go there?), which appears in almost all of the early print compilations of Cupparāma Aiyar's *padams* and is usually among the first five *padams* lin these sources.[7]

In the film, the *padam* is performed by R. Padma, who was from a *devadāsī* background and was the mother-in-law of the dancer Sayi of the famous duo Sayi and Subbulakshmi (discussed in the previous chapter).[8] The piece was choreographed by Vaideeswarankoyil Meenakshisundaram Naṭṭuvaṉār, assisted by his disciple V. S. Muthuswami Pillai. Padma plays the character of Sivakami, a young (non-*devadāsī*) middle-class woman who is to marry the hero of the film, Sabhapathy (played T. R. Ramachandran). The scene for this dance is typical of many social dramas

Figure 5.3. Screenshot of the performance of the padam Nāṉ aṅkē varuvēṉō *by R. Padma in the film* Sabhapathy *(1941).*

of the time: a young woman is dancing for relatives and potential in-laws to demonstrate her cultural accomplishments and thus her eligibility for marriage. Bharatanāṭyam dance and Karṇāṭak music figure in this scene, demonstrating that by 1941, dance had already become a respectable and almost fully domesticated art (Weidman 2006; Soneji 2010a). Moreover, Padma performs in front of her mother and future mother-in-law in a clearly domestic setting of a living room with colonial furniture, flower-pots, and picture frames (and a picture of a woman—perhaps Jean Harlow—who is obviously a Hollywood star, holding a cigarette). She wears a modern stitched Bharatanāṭyam costume, very similar to that designed for Arundale by Mary Elmore and "Madame Cazan" (discussed in chapter 2) (figure 5.3).

The *padam Nāṉ aṅkē varuvēṉō* has been discussed at length by Allen (1992, 260–61). It is significant that the last line of the *padam* in the film (*utukai uṉavatum vērukutē caki aṭikkaṭi virakam perukutē*) does not appear in any of the early print editions of Aiyar's songs and appears to have been composed for the film. Here is an abridged translation of the *padam*:[9]

Pallavi:
Nāṉ aṅkē varuvēṉō turai tāṉ iṅkē varuvārō eṉṟu?
Should I go there, or will my Lord come here?
Nayantu pēci maṉatai aṟintu vāṭi.
Go speak to him gently and understand his feelings.
Anupallavi:
Vāṇavar paṇiyum vēḷūr taṉil vaḷar muttukumarēcar mītu.
He is Muttukumāra [Murukaṉ] of Vēḷūr, worshipped by the celestials.
Maiyal akutu iṉi tāḷātu māṉē aṭi tēṉē.
I fell in love with him and cannot bear this separation, my sweet gazelle!
Caraṇam:
Paṭukkai vīṭu jōṭittu vaḷi pārttu viḻiyum pūrttutē.
My eyes are increasingly exhausted as I look for him from my bedroom.
Pāti jāmam āccutē ūrpaṭaiyum oṭuṅkip pōccutē.
It's beyond midnight, and the people of the town are fast asleep.
Utukai uṉavatum vērukutē caki aṭikkaṭi virakam perukutē.
I abhor ornaments and cannot eat, my friend, I am constantly longing. (Sabapathy n.d.)

In the film, there is clear a displacement of the erotic by situating it in the controlled and tempered space of the home, with the primary audience being not male spectators but elderly women. Although the choreography by Vaideeswarankoyil Meenakshisundaram Naṭṭuvaṉār uses the typical gestural language for a *padam*, the emphasis on the use of erotic or suggestive gestures for such a song has clearly been lessened. For example, the interpretation of many *padams* about longing make use of erotic gestures known as *rati mudrās* ("passion gestures") to depict memories of lovemaking and erotic desire.[10] In contrast, Padma's character, Sivakami, is supposed to be a student who has learned the dance in school. The choreography thus deliberately makes her appear student-like and uses no metaphoric elaboration or improvisation. This kind of straightforward representation of courtesan dances like the *padam* and *jāvaḷi* become the normative, erotically neutral mode in which these genres reappeared on stages in Madras in the 1940s. Finally, while the presentation of this *padam* avoids the erotic dimensions of courtesan performance, it cannot escape other elements. As with most representations of *padams* and *jāvaḷis* in both Tamil and Telugu cinema, passages of instrumental music are interspersed between the sections of the song (*pallavi, anupallavi,* and *caraṇam*). At the end of the sequence, Padma performs a courtesan technique known in Telugu as *gaptuvarusa* ("string of movement"), a kind of improvised rhythmic flourish performed only to instrumental music that brings an upbeat closure to the textual interpretation through *abhinaya* that has just preceded it.

The second example of an old *padam* representation comes from the film *Jagathalapratapan*, produced and directed by Sriramulu Naidu for Pakshiraja Studios. The film catapulted Pudukottai Ulanganatha Chinnappa (1916–51), a non-Brahmin singer, to stardom. The mythic narrative of the film was "about a prince [played by Chinnappa] who incurs the wrath of his father [P. B. Rangachari] when he expresses his heartfelt desire to spend his life in the company of four angelic women, Indrani [M. S. Sarojini), Nagakumari [U. R. Jeevaratnam], Agnikumari [S. Varalakshmi] and Varunakumari [T. A. Jayalakshmi], princesses of [the celestial realms] Indraloka, Nagaloka, Agniloka, and Varunaloka respectively" (Guy 2010). The songbook for the film (figures 5.4a and 5.4b) also contains an elaborate synopsis of the film in English, along with the texts for the two *padams* that appear in the film, both titled *naṭaṉam* ("dance").

Among a host of other dance pieces (which includes another Tamil *padam*),[11] the film features the Tamil *padam Ētukkittaṇai* (Why this indifference?) in the *rāga* Curuṭṭi, composed by Mārimuttā Piḷḷai (1712–87) and performed extensively by members of courtesan communities throughout the late nineteenth and early twentieth centuries. The song also appears in what I believe is the earliest print edition of *padams* by this composer, with the songs of another early Tamil *padam* composer, Muttutāṇṭavar (figure 5.5). This *padam* is composed in a particular register of poetry known in Tamil as *ēcal* ("abuse" or "slander") and in Sanskrit as *nindā-stuti* ("blame praise"). In this register, the heroine rebukes the hero by insulting and abusing him, but this is all understood to be a form of praise that indicates the deep intimacy that exists between the two. Here is a translation of the song:

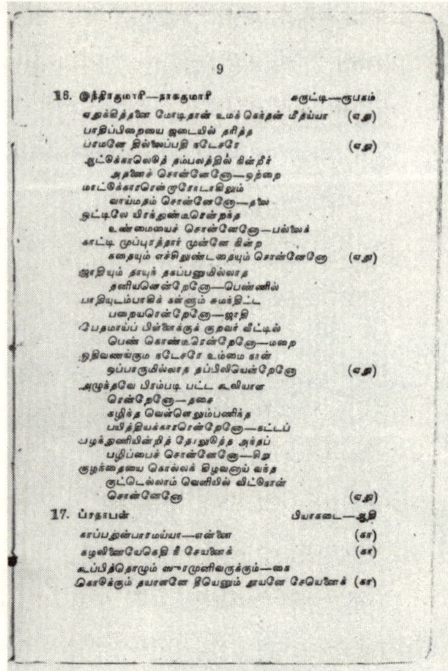

Figure 5.4 a, b. Left: The cover of the songbook for Jakatalapratāpaṉ *(1944). Right: The text for the Tamil* padam Ētukkittaṉai *from the songbook. Private collection of S. V. Jayababu.*

Pallavi:
Why this indifference toward me, Lord?
Anupallavi:
You wear the half-moon [in] the locks of your hair,
And you are the king of dance in the city of Cidambaram.
Caraṇam 1:
Did I say anything when you danced on a single leg in the dancing hall, Lord?
Did the astrologer announce out loud that you ride upon a bull?
Did I expose the truth when you begged with a bowl made from a skull and ate from it?
Did I complain even when you smirked in front of everyone, after contaminating food with your saliva?
Caraṇam 2:
Did I announce that you don't have a father, mother, or caste?
Did I ever say you had a woman on one half of your body, or call you an untouchable, even though you consumed alcohol?
Did I call you out when you accepted a daughter-in-law from a different caste for your son?
And did I not refer to you as peerless, flawless, and praised in the holy scriptures?

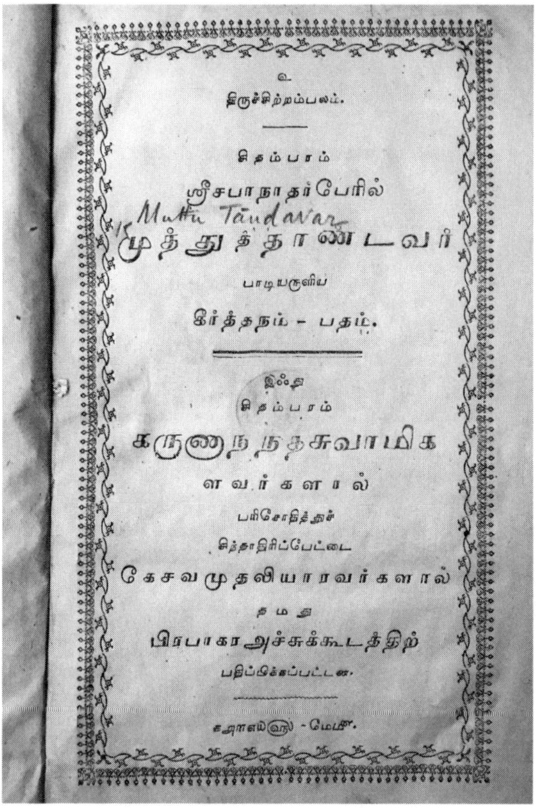

Figure 5.5. The cover of an early compilation of the Tamil padams *of Muttutāṇṭavar and Mārimuttā Piḷḷai, dated 1870. This edition contains what may be the earliest appearance in print of the* padam Ētukkittaṇai. © *British Library Board (pTam 14170.k.20).*

Caraṇam 3:

Did I announce that you were once forcefully beaten with a cane, like a commoner?

Did I refer to you as the madman worshipped by the poor?

Did I embarrass you by saying you have no clothes and so have to wear a tiger's skin?

Did I say anything even when you came as an old man to slay the dwarf-demon?

In the film *Jagathalapratapan*, the *padam* does not further the narrative of the film. It is inserted into the film in a scene where King Pratāpaṉ, played by Chinnappa, is bring entertained by his wives. The king is sitting on his throne in the company of three of his wives, Intirakumāri, Nākakumāri, and Varuṇakumāri. Each of them perform a section of the *padam*. The first and fifth section (the *pallavi* and the third *caraṇam*)

Figure 5.6. Screenshot of the performance of the Tamil padam Ētukkittaṉai *in* Jagathalapratapan *(1944). The dancer is M. S. Sarojini.*

are performed by Sarojini, the second c*araṇam* is performed by Jayalakshmi and the first c*araṇam* is performed by Jeevaratnam. According to Theodore Baskaran, except for Jeevaratnam, these actresses (in addition to the hero's fourth wife, played by Varalakshmi, who does not participate in this song) were all from the *devadāsī* community (pers. comm., Chennai, May 3, 2016). The sequence was choreographed by Ramaiah Pillai.

Here, too, we see a repurposing of the *padam*. The lyric clearly has the god Śiva as the hero (all of the coded references—such as the moon in his hair, his residence in Cidambaram, the tiger's skin and the dwarf-demon, for example—clearly establish this). But in the film, the women perform the *padam* as if these references are to Pratāpaṉ, collapsing the difference between the king and the god.

Each dancer performs the gestural interpretation or *abhinaya* in a conventional manner, matching each lyric to a specific gesture (figure 5.6). The *abhinaya* is quite subtle and not overly theatrical, as we see in Ramaiah Pillai's choreographies from the 1960s. Each dancer interprets each word of the song with a particular gesture and then walks back for another line of music, reminiscent of a technique in courtesan dance that serves to signal the change to the next line of text. Ramaiah Pillai strategically inserts the popular pose of the "dancing Śiva-Naṭarāja" (with the left leg raised) during the words *tillai pati naṭēcaṉē* ("Naṭeśa, Lord of Cidambaram") and *ampalattiṉ niṉṟu* ("standing in the dancing hall"), words for which the obvious reference would be the icon of Naṭarāja. This choreographic motif of creating a chain of poses also signals a change from the lyrical and cyclical mode of courtesan *abhinaya* to the more popular style of choreography seen in Bharatanāṭyam today.

A final version of this song is performed by Kamala Lakshman in *Sarangadhara* (Wielder of the bow, 1958), choreographed by K. N. Dandayudhapani Pillai. While the lyrics remain stable, the tune has been composed by G. Ramanathan in multiple *rāgas* (the *pallavi, anupallavi,* and first *caraṇam* are in the original *rāga* Curuṭṭi, while the second *caraṇam* is in the *rāga* Ṣaṇmukhapriyā, and the final *caraṇam* is in the *rāga* Durgā). The choreography is framed as a kind of mini "dance-drama," with Kamala taking on multiple roles as a court dancer, the god Śiva, and the dual "social" roles of a tyrannical overlord beating a peasant (indexing one of the Śaiva myths referenced in the song). This final iteration dramatizes the ways in which even the most intimate solo dance repertoire itself was being refracted through the new idiom of the "dance-drama," which by the 1950s had become a regular feature of stage performances of Bharatanāṭyam.

New Iterations of the *Padam*

In this section, I wish to turn to new *padams*—that is, songs that were scripted to resemble the older *padams* that were performed by *devadāsī* artists. Each of these examples, however, has an element of newness in that is not simply a representation of an old song on film, but a constitutive process in which a new aesthetic canon for dance (understood as "classical dance") is being created through communication between the reinvented Bharatanāṭyam and the Tamil cinema. It is important to note that in both the examples discussed below, the choreography was by Ramaiah Pillai—which shows that the idea of innovations in the repertoire simultaneously becomes entrenched in the world of Madras's stage performances of Bharatanāṭyam and inextricably linked to his aesthetic vision as early as the late 1930s. Indeed, it would not be an exaggeration

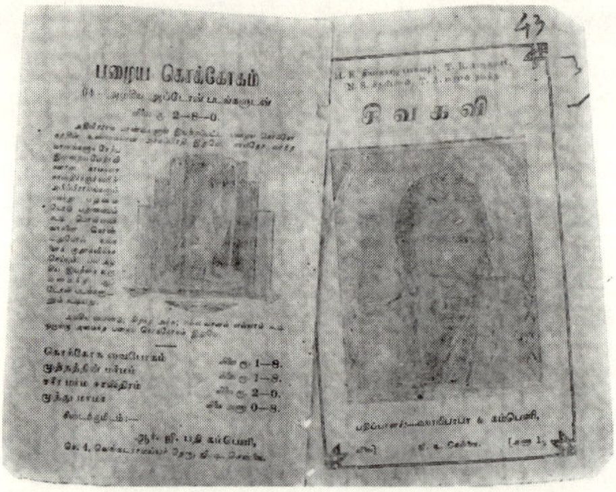

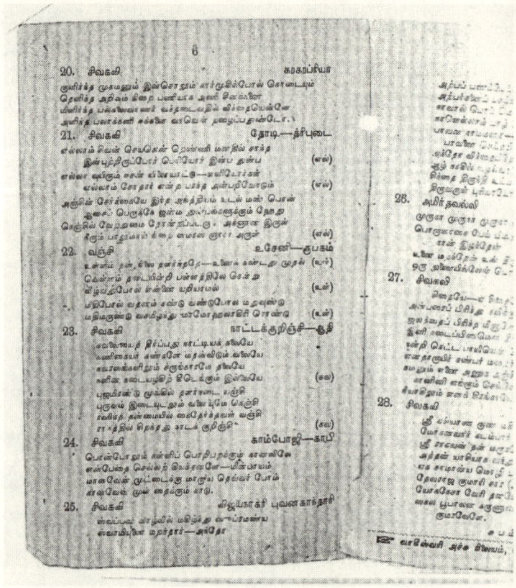

Figure 5.7 a, b. The front and back covers (left) and page 6 (right) of the songbook for Sivakavi *(1943), containing the* padam Nāṭṭiya kalaiyē. *Private collection of S. V. Jayababu.*

to say that innovation in modern Bharatanāṭyam owes most of its existence to his early filmic experiments.

The first example comes from the film *Sivakavi* (Śiva's poet; 1943), produced by Pakshiraja Film Studios and directed by S. M. Sriramulu Naidu. The story revolves around the life of a mythical poet named Poyyamoḻi Pulavar. This role was played by M. K. Thyagaraja Bhagavathar, and T. R. Rajakumari plays the role of Vañciyammai, an arrogant court dancer. The music was composed by Papanasam Sivan. The *padam* here appears in a scene in which the character played by Bhagavathar is requested to improvise a new composition, a song about the greatness of dance. Bhagavathar insists that his song should be accompanied by a dance interpretation. Rajakumari acquiesces to his request and dances to the song. Here is a translation based on the Tamil transcription of the song as it appears on page six of the film's songbook (figures 5.7a and 5.7b):

Pallavi:
Kavalaiyait tīrppatu nāṭṭiyak kalaiyē.
The art of dance removes all suffering.
Kaṇikaiyar kaṇkaḷē mataṉviṭum valaiyē.
The net of the god of desire is cast from the eyes of the courtesan.
Anupallavi:
Navarasaṅkaḷilum cruṅkāramē talaiyē.

The erotic sentiment is king among all the nine emotions.
Naḷiṉa naṭaiyaḻakiṟ kīṭeṅkum illaiyē.
So there is no harm in appreciating the beauty of a graceful walk.
Caraṇam:
Pujamiraṇṭu mūṅkil taḷarnaṭai yañci,
A hypnotic walk emerges from the swaying of both arms,
puruvam iṭaiyuṭalum vaḷaiyumē keñci.
And an ideal body is borne of beautiful eyebrows and curvaceous frame.
Rasikat taṉmaiyil kaitōntavaḷ vañci,
Such a dancing woman is also a supreme connoisseur of art,
rākattil ciṟantatu nāṭak kuṟiñci.
Just as Nāṭakkuṟiñci is supreme among all the *rāgas*. (*Sivakavi* songbook, 6)

A trace of the traditional *padam* survives here in the form of the allegorical references to women's beauty, but perhaps more importantly, it is an early example of a song that is actually about dance. As we saw in chapter 2, Tamil films like *Jalaja* (1938) were very early examples of this phenomenon of songs in praise of dance, but this example is significant because by 1943 reinvented Bharatanāṭyam had reached its maturity as a civilizational symbol, a cultural metonym for nation, religion, and identity. The lyrics of this *padam*, therefore, seem to be more about a new notion of art than about love and eroticism.

In this early choreography by Ramaiah Pillai, a choreographic structure and his calculated use of space are obvious. The set for the sequence includes a circular floor pattern, and he used this to frame the way he represented the song. During the first half of all the musical interludes between the stanzas, Rajakumari dances in the outer portion of the circle, and each musical interlude ends with a performance of a threefold flourish known as *aruti*. When the text for each stanza begins, Rajakumari makes her way to the center of the space and begins her *abhinaya*. In addition to this interesting spatial separation between rhythmic movement and *abhinaya*, Rajakumari also walks forward and backward, always facing the king, as she performs the *abhinaya* portions. For the most part, this convention of walking up and down through the performance space while performing *abhinaya* (which was very common among *devadāsī* performers) had been excised from reinvented Bharatanāṭyam, so this might be a coded reference to older practices, given that the scene takes place in an imagined courtly context.

The second example of a new *padam* comes from just a year after *Sivakavi*, in the film *Haridas* (Servant of God; 1944) which played continuously for a record three years in Madras theatres.[12] In the film, which we have already briefly discussed in chapter 1, Rajakumari plays a courtesan named Rambhā, who at one point performs at a salon concert in the house of a patron named Hari, played by Bhagavathar. The dance piece here is meant to be a song of seduction between Rambhā and Hari. The song, *Ma<u>n</u>mata līlaiyai ve<u>nr</u>āruṇṭō* (Have you ever won at the games of the god of love?") is set to the *rāga* Cārukeśī and was choreographed by Ramaiah Pillai (whose voice can be heard on the soundtrack as he recites a cluster of vocalized dance rhythms or *jati*).[13] In many ways, the text of the song captures how courtesan dance performance morphed into the romantic cinema song that became the staple of later Indian popular cinema. In Tamil cinema, a number of early romantic songs cannot be understood without reference to the erotic framework of the Tamil *padam*, and this song in particular brings into sharp relief the "slippery slope" between the Tamil *padam* of the courtesan repertoire and the early romantic film song. Here is a translation based on the Tamil transcription of the song as it appears on page 6 of the film's songbook (figures 5.8a and 5.8b):

Pallavi:
Ma<u>n</u>mata līlaiyai ve<u>nr</u>āruṇṭō?
Have you ever won at the games of the god of love?
E<u>n</u>mēl u<u>n</u>akkē<u>n</u>ō parāmukam?
Why do you show such indifference toward me?
Anupallavi:
Ni<u>n</u> mati vata<u>n</u>amum nī<u>l</u> vi<u>l</u>iyum kaṇṭu
Your face bright as the moon and fish-shaped eyes
e<u>n</u> mati mayaṅki<u>n</u>ē<u>n</u> mū<u>nr</u>u ulakilum.
Have cast a spell upon me in these three worlds.
Caraṇam:
E<u>nn</u>uṭa<u>n</u>ē nī pēci<u>n</u>āl vāy muttutirntu viṭumō?
I wonder, if you spoke to me, would pearls would fall from your
tongue?
U<u>n</u>ai ennēramum ni<u>n</u>ainturukum e<u>nn</u>iṭam vantāl me<u>n</u>ak keṭumō?

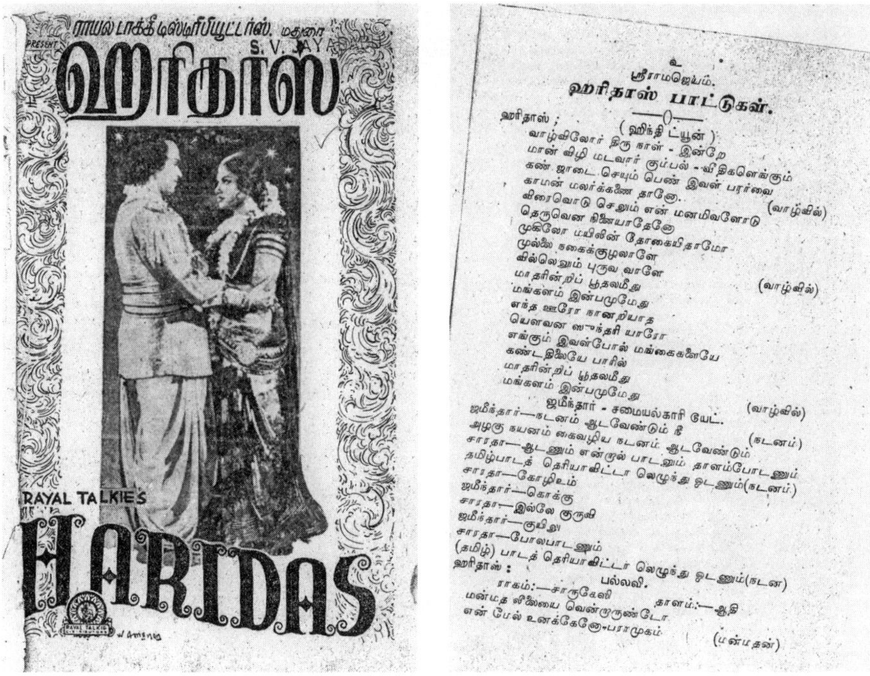

Figure 5.8 a, b. The cover (left) and page 6 (right) of the songbook for Haridas *(1944), containing the text of the song* Ma<u>n</u>mata līlaiyai ve<u>nr</u>āruṇṭō. *Private collection of S. V. Jayababu.*

I think of you all the time. Would it be so difficult for you to come to me?
U<u>nn</u>ai nayantu nā<u>n</u> vēṇṭiyumōrmuttam tantā ku<u>r</u>aintiṭumō?
I'm just asking you for a kiss. Would this belittle you?
Orupilai ya<u>r</u>iyā e<u>n</u>ma<u>n</u>am malarkkaṇai pāyntu allalpaṭumō?
I haven't committed but one sin, yet the flowery arrows [of the god of love]
pierce my heart. Won't my heart suffer? (*Haridas* songbook, 6)

The song is set in a kind of private salon context, which as Davesh Soneji (2012) has shown, was a primary site for *devadāsī* performance at the beginning of the twentieth century. As the sequence unfolds, we see Bhagavathar dressed in a king's costume (*rājā pārṭ* or *rājā vēcam*) used in *icai nāṭakam*, followed by a very brief shot showing his character's Brahmin wife, played by the actor and singer N. C. Vasanthakokilam (1919–51) and wearing a typical nine-yard sari (*maṭicār*) that unquestionably marks her

Figure 5.9. Screenshot from Haridas, *with T. R. Rajakumari dressed as the god of desire, in the song* Maṉmata līlaiyai veṉṟāruṇṭō?>>maṉmata līlaiyai.

as a Brahmin character. As the music begins, Rajakumari appears against a backdrop of the rising sun, dressed like the god of desire (Manmatha) and holding a bow and the five flowery arrows of desire (figure 5.9). She shoots an arrow toward Bhagavathar, and it punctures a piñata-type object that hangs above him. Flower petals fall from the piñata and are strewn all over his body. He appears to be in ecstasy. Rajakumari dashes toward Bhagavathar as he begins to sing the main line of the song, "Have you ever won at the games of the god of love?" One of the main conceptual links between the song and a traditional courtesan *padam* is the invocation of the god of desire, who often torments either the hero or heroine of a *padam* and whose flowery arrows are a constant motif in Tamil *padams* throughout the eighteenth and nineteenth centuries.

The choreography follows the conventions of courtesan dance, in which the lyrics and the gestures resonate with one another. However, the film dance differs from courtesan dance in that there is a clear lack of the improvisation that is so characteristic of *devadāsī abhinaya* for *padams*. In such improvisations, the courtesan performer moves beyond a literal gestural interpretation of the text, with her gestures operating on the metaphoric and allegorical registers. By contrast, in the film dance, the choreography is set, even though there are spaces that create the illusion of an impending improvisation. For example, after a few lines of *abhinaya*, when the line is repeated, Rajakumari walks backward, a move typical of courtesan performance that allows the dancer to think about her gestural improvisation for the next repetition of the line of text. The choreography for postreinvention Bharatanāṭyam had thus become structured by the early 1940s, and this was clearly reflected in cinematic representations of the dance from this decade.

Interspersed between the various lines of text are passages of instrumental music at a slightly faster pace, a musical technique that became popular in the early cinema and eventually entered a range of popular cultures of music in South Asia. These instrumental musical passages, as we have already seen, mark the differences between the major sections of the composition (*pallavi*, *anupallavi*, and *caraṇam*), but they also break the monotony of *abhinaya* through the insertion of a dynamic, usually rhythmic, interlude in both music and dance. I would thus argue that it was Bharatanāṭyam choreography in the cinema that established the importance of fast-paced, energetic movement sequences as attractive hallmarks of the dance in its stage versions. This sequence from *Haridas* is thus crucial in mapping the disappearance of courtesan dance technique from the public sphere in favor of a distinctly modern version of Bharatanāṭyam for new audiences. The sequence is a kind of transitory moment, for in it we see elements of the old-style courtesan *abhinaya* as well as some of the earliest configurations of new modes of approaching choreography for a dance accompanying a *padam*-like song.

Moreover, inextricably linked to these shifts in representation is the question of the morality of the dancing body, and again this *padam* reveals the ever-changing definitions of propriety for women and morality. In this sequence, Rajakumari performs typical courtesan-style movements during the instrumental passages, which include movements of the hips and waist. Movements in the courtesan dance style (such as stamping the feet in rhythm while performing *abhinaya*, known as *taṭṭumeṭṭu* in the courtesan tradition from Pudukkottai) relied on movements in which the hips move from side to side. For the most part, such movements had been eliminated in Bharatanāṭyam on the stage by the 1940s. Somewhat ironically, such movements continued to be made in the less respectable spaces of the early cinema. This created a fundamental moral tension that characterized the relationship between Bharatanāṭyam's new middle-class gurus and the world of cinema. Movements of the hips and waist were eliminated in favor of an exaggerated geometry of the angular use of line inspired by the Russian ballet—seen most clearly in Arundale's conception of Bharatanāṭyam technique, in which this new austere body represented the outer manifestation of a spiritual body shaped by both Theosophical occultism and new urban assertions of Brahminic orthodoxy in 1930s Madras.[14]

Finally, deeply implicated in the moral uneasiness about the sequence is a passage at the end of the song. This passage features Rajakumari blowing a kiss to Bhagavathar in close proximity, complete with the sound of a kiss dropped in. This was very controversial at the time, and it is significant that it was part of a Bharatanāṭyam dance sequence—indicating that filmic Bharatanāṭyam was a morally ambiguous space. Indeed, it would be hard for such a scene to have appeared anywhere else in an early Tamil film, except perhaps in a scene about courtesans. It thus also marked a kind of moral *diglossia* related to the primary sites of Bharatanāṭyam performance. In contrast to the morally ambiguous cinematic Bharatanāṭyam, a space of potential sensual and erotic excess, stage Bharatanāṭyam represented moral propriety, asceticism, and the sublimation of desire.

OTHERNESS, OCULARITY, AND ORIENTALISM: THE SNAKE DANCE IN CINEMA AND ON STAGE

In a fascinating essay titled "Domesticating Otherness: The Snake Charmer in Popular American Culture" (2016), the ethnomusicologist A. J. Racy traces the expressive complexities of the motif of snake charming in popular Western culture. He argues that the notion of the "otherness" triggered by the snake charmer and embedded in the contemporary popular American imagination represents a kind of experiential bricolage, drawing from sources ranging from Rudyard Kipling to Indiana Jones. While the American experience clearly draws on modes of Orientalist and imperial power that are felt and negotiated very differently in South Asia, Racy's observations about the multiplicity of influences that fuel popular representations of the snake charmer are certainly relevant for our next discussion of repertoire, which focuses on the *pāmpu naṭaṉam*. As Racy's work makes clear, the Indian snake dance was a key part of the Orientalist filmic imagination in the early twentieth century. The German film *Das indische Grabmal* (The Indian tomb; 1921) and its remakes in 1938 and 1959 all feature a snake dance performed by a temple dancer before images that supposedly represent Hindu deities. In the last remake (*The Indian Tomb*, directed by Fritz Lang), the American actress Debra Paget's iconic snake dance remains a landmark sequence in the genre of the modern adventure film (Plass 2009). This section thus explores the history and aesthetics of the *pāmpu naṭaṉam* as it appeared in the early Tamil cinema and posits its hybridity as metonymic of the hybridity inherent in cinematic representations of Bharatanāṭyam. It also explores the unique classical yet popular status of Bharatanāṭyam as an art form that it occupies in the imaginary of its modern practitioners. The *pāmpu naṭaṉam* is seen as a lowbrow expressive form (invoking the "otherness" of the figure of the low-caste snake charmer in Tamil society, for example), while being firmly embedded in the classical idiom of Bharatanāṭyam—illustrating one of the many contradictions and anxieties that are at the center of the notion of the classical in the world of Indian dance.

The *pāmpu naṭaṉam*, as we will see, was a piece invented for the cinema. But before we discuss this piece, it is important to note that serpent symbolism and the image of the snake charmer (*pāmpāṭṭi*) both have a long and complex history in Tamil culture, and specifically in the courtesan dance repertoire. A number of *devadāsī* families (and the family of my teacher, R. Muttukkannammal of Viralimalai), preserve a dance piece called *mōṭi-etukkiṟatu* or simply *mōṭi*, which is about a quarrel between a snake charmer and his female lover. Soneji (2012, 181–84) has written extensively about this piece, based on his observation of my training in it with Muttukkannammal. Soneji has traced this dance back to the time of King Serfoji II of Tanjore (1777–1832), through a Marathi court document dated 1820 (ibid., 181), and notes its persistence in a range of documents through the nineteenth century. In the version as it survives in the family of Muttukkannammal, it is a romantic quarrel, and the word *mōṭi* here has a double entendre. It is a reference both to the pipe played by the snake charmer (normally known as *makuṭi* in Tamil), and to a kind of magic of illusion practiced by both the snake charmer and his lover. The song that accompanies this dance is in Tamil and sung in the *rāga* Punnāgavarāḷi, a *rāga* associated with serpents and the one used in the cinematic *pāmpu naṭaṉam*.

Moreover, in Tamil-speaking regions reverence for serpents has had an intimate connection to goddess worship (Allocco 2009), and often the *rāga* Punnāgavarāḷi is played on the *nāgasvaram* to induce goddess possession among both men and women in a range of religious contexts. In addition to these contexts, and perhaps more directly relevant to our discussion of the filmic iteration of the *pāmpu naṭaṉam*, is the fact that a major esoteric presence in medieval Tamil religion is that of the quasi-mythical poet-alchemists known as *cittar* (from the Sanskrit *siddha*, "accomplished ones"), and one of the most popular Tamil *cittars* is the fifteenth-century figure known as Pāmpāṭṭi Cittar ("the snake-charmer *cittar*").[15] One of his surviving poems forms the textual basis of the *pāmpu naṭaṉam*, and this is the poem called *Nātar muṭimēl irukkum* (Snake, you reside atop the head of Śiva), which is also sung in the *rāga* Punnāgavarāḷi (Buck 1976).

Having set the stage, we can now explore the formation, through the influence of the cinema, of a distinctly new genre in Bharatanāṭyam, the *pāmpu naṭaṉam*. As we have noted above, the textual basis for the dance is Pāmpāṭṭi Cittar's poem *Nātar muṭimēl irukkum*, which had been sung in the same *rāga* long before its appearance in the Tamil cinema. Here is a composite text of the poem as it appears in various filmic renditions, with my translation:

Nātar muṭimēl irukkum nākapāmpē.
Snake, you reside atop the head of Śiva.
Naccuppaiyai vaittirukkum nallapāmpē.
Cobra, you hold poison in your mouth.
Pātalattiṟ kuṭipukum paikoḷ pāmpē.
Snake, you dwell in the netherworld.
Pāṭippāṭi niṉṟu vilayāṭu pāmpē!
Snake, sing and play!
Kuṟṟamaṟṟa civaṉukkuk kuṇṭalamāṉāy.
You are the earrings worn by the flawless Śiva.
Kuṟun tirumāliṉukkuk kuṭaiyumāṉay.
Your hood provides shelter for the head of Viṣṇu.
Kaṟṟaikkuḻal pārvatikkuṅ kaṅkaṇamāṉay.
You are the bangles worn by Pārvati with curled locks of hair.
Karavāmal uḷaṅkaḷittāṭu pāmpē.
Dancing snake, you move with a fearless gait.
Āṭu pāmpē vilayāṭu pāmpē![16]
Dance, snake! Dance!

Figure 5.10. Screenshot from Jagathalaprathapan *of Kamala Lakshman performing the snake dance.*

The *pāmpu naṭaṉam*'s earliest instantiations in the Tamil cinema are associated with Ramaiah Pillai, so in the absence of evidence to the contrary, it seems that he identified this poem and was the first to choreograph it in the twentieth century. It is also significant that its first appearance, in *Jagathalaprathapan*, is also linked to Kamala, then ten years old, who performs the sequence in this film (figure 5.10). Indeed, her presence enforces the argument I made in chapter 3: that Kamala—in her role as muse for Ramaiah Pillai's choreographic experiments—was the harbinger of a distinctly new movement vocabulary for Bharatanāṭyam in the twentieth century. Her association with the *pāmpu naṭaṉam* makes the innovative dimensions of the new Bharatanāṭyam obvious.

Kamala performs the *pāmpu naṭaṉam* to solely instrumental music, played by various Indian and Western wind instruments—there are no lyrics used in this sequence. Ramaiah Pillai's choreography takes advantage of the extreme flexibility of the youthful and energetic Kamala through an explicitly acrobatic dance. She begins the sequence by taking on the role of a snake charmer, using gestures to simulate playing the pipe he uses. Kamala was initially trained in Kathak dance, and Ramaiah Pillai incorporates this movement vocabulary into his choreography, along with the free movements he has invented. This kind of hybridity—in which Kathak's fast spins and heavily rhythmic foot work fuse with the *aṭavus* (basic units of movement) of Bharatanāṭyam in the context of a markedly innovative piece of dance—becomes a kind of choreographic norm in both the cinema and other popular representations of twentieth-century Bharatanāṭyam.[17] Next, Kamala performs the role of the snake, and the choreography becomes fluid as the waving of her arms and shoulders mimic serpentine movement. But overall, in this initial instantiation, we see more Kathak and Bharatanāṭyam phrasing, and this may have been meant to showcase Kamala's classical dance prowess, rather than to emphasize realism in the representation.

By contrast, in the 1947 film *Kannika*, realism is much more important. Here, we see a snake dance again set to the melody of Pāmpāṭṭi Cittar's poem in the *rāga* Punnāgavarāḷi. Even though Ramaiah Pillai is credited as the choreographer of this film, the performer of this dance seems to be Caucasian, perhaps a contortionist from a touring circus company. In a kind of inversion of the South Asian performer at American circuses in this period that promulgated "a racial hierarchy in which South Asians were depicted to be static, and unable to keep pace with the Anglo-American 'race'" (Davis 1993, 121), this performer—dressed in a rather revealing black unitard—represents the excess and "otherness" of the Western dancing body (figure 5.11). However, here it is indigenized and made into a palatable spectacle through both the plot of the film as well as the use of Pāmpāṭṭi Cittar's poem. Unfortunately, the performer's name is not in the credits of the film.

The sequence is embedded in the fantasy-adventure plot of *Kannika*. It begins when a demon king (played by D. Balasubramaniam) commands the celestial dancer Tilottamā (played by an unknown actress), whom he has abducted, to perform for him. Tilottamā tells the demon king that she must transform herself to be able to perform. She morphs into the Caucasian contortionist, dressed in a tigh black unitard, with large open patches throughout the side of her costume. As the dancer performs a series of highly acrobatic movements that develop from simple configurations to more complex ones, she turns her body upside down, flips back and forth, and puts herself into various poses that are meant to replicate the shapes of a serpent. She performs the entire se-

Figure 5.11. Screenshot from Kannika *(1947) of an unknown Caucasian female performing the snake dance.*

quence against a background of music played on the *veṇu* (South Indian flute) and *vīṇā* (a stringed and fretted instrument), the pulse and count of which has little if anything to do with the choreography. The disjuncture between dance and music is somewhat jarring, given that in this period (as we have seen above) there was normally a direct correspondence between text, music, and gestural movement.

The last appearance of the *pāmpu naṭaṉam* occurred three years later, when a teenage Kamala performs this dance as a full-fledged Bharatanāṭyam repertory number in *Digambara Samiyar* (The naked sage; 1950), directed by T. R. Sundaram (1907–63) and produced by Modern Theaters (figure 5.12). Kamala's *pāmpu naṭaṉam* appears toward the end of the film, in which she plays a courtesan dancer named Duraikannu. She performs the dance as a kind of ploy to trick the villain of the movie, a corrupt lawyer named Cattanātaṉ. The choreography is by Ramaiah Pillai and consists of three dances: the snake dance; a modern double-act duet in which Kamala plays both the young male lover and his female love interest; and a Rajasthani-inspired folk dance about love and seduction.

Kamala performs the tripartite piece in a kind of makeshift theater in Cattanātaṉ's home, which is full of Western furniture. The constant visual of the moving hands of a clock suggests that Kamala has been dancing for him for several hours. She performs the snake dance against a backdrop of a forest full of anthills, simulating the shrines of snake

Figure 5.12. Screenshot from Digambara Samiyar *(1950) of Kamala Lakshman performing the snake dance.*

deities in rural South India. Her modern Bharatanāṭyam dance costume is dotted with textures and colors meant to represent a snake. Her hairstyle is also unusual: the high bun is meant to invoke the matted locks of the god Śiva, where, according to the poem of Pāmpāṭṭi Cittar, the snake rests. The text for the piece is the poem, but this time it was set two *rāgas*, Ābheri and Punnāgavarāḷi, by the composers G. Ramanathan (d. 1963) and S. M. Subbaiah Naidu (1914–79). Kamala performs the dance, lip-synching the text of the poem to the playback vocals of the singer P. Leela. Kamala begins the sequence with an instrumental passage and performs the *abhinaya* to the lyrics of the song, matching each word with a gesture. During the chorus of the song (the line *Āṭu pāmpē vilayāṭu pāmpē* [Dance, snake! Dance!]), Kamala strikes a series of acrobatic poses—not to be compared with those of the Caucasian performer in *Kannika*, of course—but nevertheless serpentine poses created by Ramaiah Pillai that are suited for a Bharatanāṭyam-trained body.

These three filmic iterations of the *pāmpu naṭaṉam* gave rise to stage performances of the dance by Bharatanāṭyam dancers. According to Anne-Marie Gaston (1996, 308), the dance was first performed on stage in 1955 by Kamala at the Madras Music Academy, choreographed by Ramaiah Pillai. The persistence of the *pāmpu naṭaṉam* and its incorporation into the body of work understood and accepted as classical Bharatanāṭyam shows how the category of the classical in Indian dance cannot be separated from the world of the Tamil cinema. The example of the *pāmpu naṭaṉam* ultimately demonstrates how cinematic representations of Bharatanāṭyam were constitutive spaces in which new genres and forms were created for the cinema and then traveled, through the dancing bodies of figures like Kamala, through the various spaces that modern Bharatanāṭyam came to occupy as the twentieth century progressed.

SONGS TO THE DANCING ŚIVA-NAṬARĀJA

By now scholars have established that a major dimension of the so-called revival or reinvention of Bharatanāṭyam in the 1930s was the replacement of the traditional *devadāsī* repertoire with new genres and compositions that enabled the middle-class dancer and dance teacher to transform Bharatanāṭyam into a (Hindu) religious expressive form. Devotional dance compositions drawing from musical genres such as *kīrtana* and liturgical verses for domestic prayers (*stotra*) were thus consciously incorporated into the performance practice of Bharatanāṭyam, eclipsing traditional genres of courtesan performance such as the *padam*.[18] This shift in repertoire as it was performed on stage has been documented quite thoroughly (see, for example, Allen 1997; Gaston 1996; Meduri 1996). In the section that follows, I focus on representations of the mythology and iconography of the dancing Śiva-Naṭarāja by foregrounding cinematic versions of dances to the Tamil song *Naṭaṉam āṭiṉār* (He danced . . .), a *kīrtana* composed by the poet Kōpālakiruṣṇa Pārati (1810–96):

Pallavi:
Naṭaṉam āṭiṉār veku nākarīkamākavē kaṉaka capaiyil āṉanta.
He danced so beautifully, so artfully, a blissful dance in the golden
hall of Cidambaram.
Anupallavi:
Vaṭa kayilaiyil muṉṉāḷ māmuṉikku aruḷceytapaṭi
tavaṟāmal tillai patiyil vantu taimātattil kuru pūcattil pakal
nēratattil.
Long ago on Mount Kailasa in the north,

Keeping his promise to the great sages
Without fail, he came to the city of Cidambaram
In the month of Tai, on the full moon anniversary of the guru.
Jati:
Tām takiṭa taka jam taka ṇam. [...]
And he danced: "*tām takiṭa taka jam taka ṇam.*"
Caraṇam:
Aṣṭa ticaiyum kiṭukiṭuṅka cēṭaṉ talai naṭuṅka
aṇṭamatira kaṅkai tuḷicitaṟa poṉṉāṭarum koṇṭāṭa
iṣṭamuṭaṉē kōpālakiruṣṇaṉ pāṭa caṭaiyāṭa aravampaṭamāṭa
atilum naṭamāṭa tontōmeṉṟu patavikaḷ tantōmeṉṟu.
He danced, and all the eight directions shook "gidu gidunga."
The head of the cosmic snake trembled, the whole earth shivered.
Water drops from the Ganges splashed over the land, and the gods celebrated.
Krishna sang lovingly for his [Nataraja's] dance.
Siva's matted locks swayed in the air while the cobra danced with its hood spread.
He danced about, giving all assembled his blessings with the sound of "tontom tantom." (Allen 1997, 81)

This song is brought into the dance repertoire at the moment of the dance's reinvention in Madras in the 1930s (Allen 1997), with a range of performers claiming that they were the first to perform it through choreography composed by Pandanallur Meenakshisundaram Pillai. For example, the male dancer Ram Gopal (1912–2003), one of the first non-*devadāsī* performers of Bharatanāṭyam, claims that "*Nadanam Adinar* was composed specially for me by Minakshisundaram. I was the first to perform it. Now they don't do it properly. It should be danced by a man" (quoted in Gaston 1996, 103). By contrast, as Allen (1997, 80–81) has demonstrated, the first documented performance of the dance at the Madras Music Academy was in 1939, by Lakshmi Sastri (later known as the Hindustani vocalist Lakshmi Shankar, 1926–2013), a disciple of Pandanallur Chokkalingam Pillai (1893–1968, son of Pandanallur Meenakshisundaram Pillai). There is also anecdotal reference to *naṭaṉam āṭiṉār* having been choreographed for Arundale, together with another composition on Śiva-Naṭarāja by her teacher, Meenakshisundaram Pillai.[19] The dance was performed by a number of *devadāsī* and non-*devadāsī* performers in Madras in the 1940s and 1950s and, as Gaston observes (1996, 275), was often performed as a finale at dance recitals, replacing the *tillāṉā* that traditionally functioned in this capacity.[20] Regardless of who first performed it in Madras, by the early 1940s the dance had become the crowning (albeit definitively new) piece of the modern Bharatanāṭyam dance repertoire.

Before we discuss the appearance of this song on stage and then in the cinema, it is significant that along with the insertion of new songs such as *Naṭaṉam āṭiṉār*, representations of the dancing Śiva on stage circulated in the imperial world from America (with Ted Shawn's famous "Cosmic Dance of Shiva" [1925]) to Paris (with the Calcutta-born Uday Shankar's performances of "Tandava Nrittya" and "Shiva-Parvati Nrittya Dwandva" in 1931).[21] As Allen (1997, 83) has shown, a key influence on the insertion of the figure of Śiva-Naṭarāja into the public sphere was the 1912 publication of an essay titled "The Dance of Śiva," by Ananda Kentish Coomaraswamy. The effect of this text on emerging forms of cultural nationalism that gave rise to new, fundamentally religious interpretations of Indian art has been observed by many scholars. Suffice it to say that dance and its metaphysical interpretations lie at the heart of such reformulations.

These early stage representations of the dance of Śiva also made their way into the world of the early South Indian cinema, with one of the earliest documentable instances occurring in the Tamil film *Karaikkal Ammaiyar* (Mother of Kāraikkāl; 1943). The film featured the dancers Nataraj and Shakuntala (dates unknown) (figures 5.13a and 5.13b), who are dressed in costumes that almost exactly mirror the ones worn by Shankar and his partners. The film *Sri Murugan* (The God Murukaṉ; 1946) featured a similar dance performed by the rising star M. G. Ramachandran (who became chief minister of Tamilnadu) dancing as Śiva and an actress named Malathi, a Telugu performer from the *kalāvantula* courtesan community in Kakinada, performing as Pārvatī (figure 5.14a). A Tamil film called *Ciyāmalā* (Śyāmalā; 1952) featured another such dance, choreographed by the Telugu choreographer Pasumarti Krishnamurthy (1927–2004) and performed by unknown dancers also dressed in similar costumes (figure 5.14b). As we have noted above, Shankar's film *Kalpana* was also released in Madras in the 1940s, but his Oriental dance aesthetic was circulating in South India long before this and influenced representations of both Bharatanāṭyam and Kuchipudi throughout the 1940s and 1950s (Thota 2016, 92–95).

Figure 5.13 a, b. Left: Cover of the songbook of the Tamil film Kāraikkāl Ammaiyār *(1943). The film featured a Śiva-Pārvatī dance performed by Nataraj and Shakuntala (right). Private collection of S. V. Jayababu.*

By the late 1940s, when the dance *Naṭaṉam āṭiṉār* had firmly established a space for itself in the repertoire of the new classical Bharatanāṭyam, Shankar's aesthetic legacy of the Śiva-Pārvatī dance, was alive and well and continued to circulate with renderings of *Naṭaṉam āṭiṉār*, in the form of his film *Kalpana*. Almost all of the advertisements for the film in Madras featured Shankar's iconic costume for the Śiva-Pārvatī dance (figure 5.15).

Taken together, these representations illustrate how like the textual and stage performances of the mythology and iconography of the dancing Śiva, filmic renditions also served to enforce the links between religion, esotericism, and cultural nationalism that were being forged through the reinvention of India's classical dances. Aligning the courtesan dance traditions of Bharatanāṭyam with a new, transcendental interpretation of dance as a kind of spiritual, ascetic, and otherworldly practice was a way in which the dance became an iconic marker of India's national culture.[22] In the final pages of this chapter, I would like to turn to the song *Naṭaṉam āṭiṉār* to demonstrate how a single composition flows

Figure 5.14 a, b. Left: Still from the film Sri Murugan *(1946), with MGR as Śiva and Malathi as Pārvatī. Private collection of S. V. Jayababu. Right: Note about the Śiva-Pārvatī dance from the film* Ciyāmalā *(1952), choreographed by Pasumarti Krishnamurthy (dancers unknown).* Kuṇṭūci, *December 1952, 38. Courtesy of the Roja Muthiah Research Library.*

through the various spaces of textual discourse, stage performance, and cinema. The song's rich history of performance enables us to track both the constitution and legitimization of the category of the classical as metaphysical and spiritual.

NAṬAṈAM ĀṬIṈĀR: THE DANCE OF ŚIVA ON SCREEN

Naṭaṉam āṭiṉār thus became increasingly popular on the stage and in the early Tamil cinema. In this section I discuss the dance as it appears in three early films: *Kannika* (1947); *Valliyin Selvan* (1955); and *Manamalai* (1958). Perhaps due to the popularity of this song on the emerging Bharatanāṭyam stage, an excerpt from it had already appeared in the 1945 film *Sri Valli*, about the the deity Murukaṉ's marriage to the forest-dwelling woman Vaḷḷi. The film was directed by A. V. Meyappan and A. T. Krishnaswamy, with music by T. M. Rajagoplala Sharma and R. Sudarsanam and lyrics by Papanasam Sivan and Rajagopala Iyer (Guy 2007). Kamala was the young Vaḷḷi, and in the dance sequence toward the beginning of the film, she performed a devotional song written for the film, *Yār*

Figure 5.15. A Tamil advertisement for Kalpana *(1948) with Uday Shankar as Śiva and Amala Shankar as Pārvatī. Private collection of S. V. Jayababu.*

uṉkalaippōl aṟṟaipavar ārumuka aracē (None other than you can protect us, six-faced lord!). The choreography by Ramaiah Pillai took advantage of Kamala's initial dance training in Kathak for the first instrumental sequence and then used Bharatanāṭyam choreography. Between the first section (*pallavi*) and the second section (*anupallavi*) of the song, there is a sung rhythmic passage, called *colkaṭṭu svara*. This passage was clearly adapted from the *jati* passage in the song *Naṭaṉam āṭiṉār.* While the *rāga* and rhythmic cycle (*tāla*) have been changed for this film, the individual drum syllables (*colkaṭṭu*) and their sequencing remain identical to those in *Naṭaṉam āṭiṉār.* Ramaiah Pillai's choreography is also similar to what he later produced for *Kannika* (discussed below). The first instance of the appearance of an element of *Naṭaṉam āṭiṉār* in the cinema thus also used musical and textual repurposing.

Kannika, the first film in which *Naṭaṉam āṭiṉār* appeared in its entirety, was produced by S. M. Sriramulu Naidu, (1910–76) of Pakshiraja Studios. The fantasy story revolves around a demon (played by Bala-

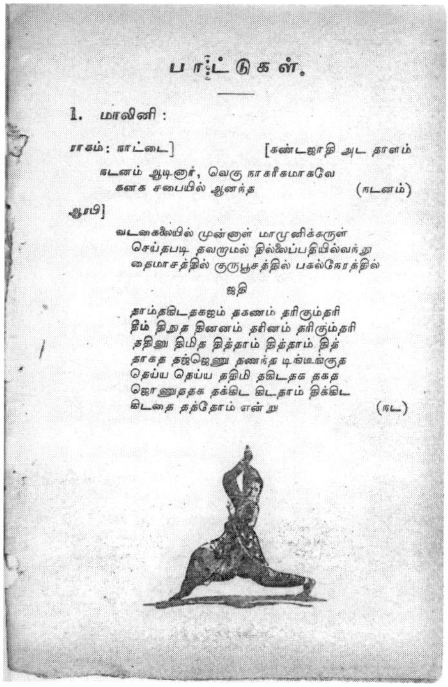

பாட்டுகள்.

1. மாலினி :

ராகம் : நாட்டை] [கண்டஜாதி அட தாளம்

நடனம் ஆடினார், வெகு நாகரீகமாகவே
கனக சபையில் ஆனந்த (நடனம்)

ஆரபி]

வடகைலையில் முன்னாள் மாமுனிக்கருள்
செய்தபடி தவறாமல் தில்லைப்பதியில்வந்து
தைமாசத்தில் குருபூசத்தில் பகல்நேரத்தில்

ஜதி

தாம்தகிடதகஜம் தகணம் தரிகும்தரி
தீம் திறுத தினனம் தரினம் தரிகும்தரி
ததினு திமித தித்தாம் தித்தாம் தித்
தாகத தஜ்ஜெனு தணந்த டிங்டிங்குத
தெய்ய தெய்ய ததிமி தகிடதக தகத
ஜொணுததக தக்கிட கிடதாம் திக்கிட
கிடதை தத்தோம் என்று (நட)

Figure 5.16 a, b. The front and back covers (left) of the songbook for Kannika *(1947), with the page providing the lyrics for* Naṭaṉam āṭiṉār *(right). Private collection of S. V. Jayababu.*

subramaniam) whose spirit is imprisoned in a pigeon. In the climax, a young man (played by T. E. Varadan) destroys the demon and marries his daughter, Kannika (played by Sarojini). Ramaiah Pillai choreographed most of the dance sequences, although (as discussed in chapter 4) Kattumannarkoyil Muttukumara Pillai made an appearance in the film and was said to have choreographed other dance sequences in it. One of these was a mini dance drama, "Siva-Mohini," performed by Lalitha and Padmini, marking the very first time they performed in a Tamil film (B. M. Sundaram, interview by the author,Chennai, August 27, 2012). The other sequence was the *pāmpu naṭaṉam* that we have already discussed (figures 5.16a and 5.16b).

Naṭaṉam āṭiṉār is performed at the beginning of the film, when the young Kannika (the demon princess and heroine of the film) dances at the court of the demon king (figure 5.17). The role of Kannika was played by Hemamalini Arni (b. 1934; also known as Hemamalini Vijayaraghavan). She was one the foremost students of Ramaiah Pillai and was from the Tamil Brahmin community. Her father, C. K. Vijayaraghavan (d. 1950) was India's first inspector seneral and later became home secretary in

Figure 5.17. Screenshot of Hemamalini Arni performing Naṭaṉam āṭiṉār *in* Kannika.

the Government of Madras. Her mother was an amateur vocalist. Hemamalini and her sister Padmini were taught dance and music starting at a young age, and Hemamalini also sang the vocals in the soundtrack for *Naṭaṉam āṭiṉār* in *Kannika*. On her website, Hemamalini describes her experiences dancing in *Kannika*: "Around 1947/48 Mr. S. M. Sreeramulu Naidu, the famous Film Producer and Director approached my father and wanted me to act in a film 'Kannika' in a role portraying Kannika in her youth. He agreed and we made about 4 to 5 trips from our home in Adyar, Madras to his Pakshiraja Studios in Coimbatore where the film was shot. My role required dancing and some singing too. I danced 'Natanam Adinaar' and sung [*sic*] a prayer composed by the famous Papanasam Sivan. One of the presents given to me was a . . . car" (Arni n.d.).

The dance sequence contains passages of instrumental music that break up the verses of text. The original *rāga* of *Naṭaṉam āṭiṉār* is Vasantā, but in the film, the the second and third sections are in other *rāgas* such as Ārabhi and Madhyamāvatī. This indicates that the original song was so popular that it would have been recognized by audiences, and perhaps to showcase his innovation, the composer changed the *rāga*.

This kind of experimentation became a norm in staged performances of Bharatanāṭyam in the later decades of the twentieth century. Another feature of this scene is the presence of the *naṭṭuvaṉār* Kattumannarkoyil Muttukumara Pillai as one of the courtiers in the royal assembly. According to B. M. Sundaram, "When he [Muttukumara Pillai] was in Kovai [the producer] Srimulu Naidu of Pakshiraja Pictures was preparing to produce his film *Kannika*, [and] he contracted Muttukumaran to appear in the film" (2002, 43).[23]

At the commencement of the dance, Hemamalini salutes the king by bowing to him, holding the folded-hands gesture known as *añjali*. The music for this is an instrumental passage in the *rāga* Vasantā. After that she begins the interpretation of the text of the song through *abhinaya*. The choreography is filled with poses of Śiva-Naṭarāja. The idea of combining movement with static poses that resemble images on Hindu temples, a hallmark of Ramaiah Pillai's choreography, became a choreographic norm in most staged performances of twentieth-century Bharatanāṭyam.[24] Hemamalini performs the *abhinaya* to the text as a word-for-word interpretation in this dance, aligning each gesture with the the rhythm of the song. In this rendition of *Naṭaṉam āṭiṉār* there are also no passages of *jatis* (clusters of vocalized drum syllables recited by the *naṭṭuvaṉār*). This apparent lack of the rhythmic force of the song is captured in the next appearance of *Naṭaṉam āṭiṉār* in the film *Valliyin Selvan*.

As *Naṭaṉam āṭiṉār* became more popular on the stage, later films used a more speedy and showier version of this dance. A clear example occurs in *Valliyin Selvan* (Valli's Son; 1955). Directed by Kothamangalam Subbu (who wrote the novel *Tillāṉā Mōkaṉāmpāḷ* discussed in chapter 3) and produced by United Film Arts, a subsidiary of Gemini Studios. The music was composed by P. S. Anantharaman; the dance was choreographed by Bhaskar Roy Chowdhury (1930–2003), an actor and dancer who studied with Kanchipuram Ellappa Pillai; and the singer was Seerkazhi Govindarajan (1933–88).[25] It is thus highly likely that the choreography for *Naṭaṉam āṭiṉār* in the film was greatly influenced by Ellappa Pillai's interpretation of this piece for stage performances (a version of which we will discuss in our final example). The dancer in *Valliyin Selvan* was an actress named Vanaja. Unlike the previous rendition of *Naṭaṉam āṭiṉār* that was set in a mythological court, this version was set in what is clearly a middle-class living room in Madras (figure 5.18). The dancer is dressed in a modern kurta pajama and is depicted as practicing her

Figure 5.18. Screenshot from Valliyin Selvan *(1955) of* Naṭaṉam āṭiṉār, *performed by Vanaja.*

dance in the comfort of her own home. This marks a major intervention in the history of Bharatanāṭyam, as we saw in chapter 4 with Kamala's performance in *Nam Iruvar* (1947): the dance is now consciously brought into the domestic setting. The dancer performs amidst a number of visual signposts of middle-class modernity in South India—colonial furniture such as a cupboard, picture frames, curtains, carpets, and most importantly the gramophone (which plays the music she rehearses to)—and markers of Indian heritage such as a statue of Śiva-Naṭarāja, musical instruments (such as the *vīṇā*), and brass oil lamps. Along with the shift in the location of the dance to the domestic space comes the amateurization of its practice, as a hobby. The young woman in the scene compartmentalizes dance as one small part of her life, a point made clear when she very intentionally turns the gramophone player on and off before and after her rehearsal. Unlike in the earlier *Kannika,* in this version of *Naṭaṉam āṭiṉār,* there are additional passages of rhythmic syllables recited to further enhance the dynamism of the song. The dancer speeds up her movements and creates a more counterintuitive response to the song. The dancer is constantly moving, and the pace of the choreography is very quick.

Three years after *Valliyin Selvan*, *Naṭaṉam āṭiṉār* was performed once again, in the film *Manamalai* (Garland of the heart; 1958), directed by Chitrapu Narayana Rao (1913–85) and produced by Janatha Pictures. Unfortunately, I have not had access to the film, but I do have the audio track of its version of *Naṭaṉam āṭiṉār*, as well as the songbook from the film. In the songbook, choreography for the film is attributed to the *naṭṭuvaṉār* P. S. Gopalakrishnan (a student of Ramaiah Pillai), although in the audio track, it is Ellappa Pillai who recites the drum syllables (*jatis*). The dancers are Ragini of the Travancore Sisters and her cousin Sukumari (1940–2013). The vocals are by the popular Brahmin singers Radha (b. 1932, date of death unknown), Jayalakshmi (d. 2014) and the Malayali singer P. Leela. The music for the film was composed by S. Vedha. In this version of *Naṭaṉam āṭiṉār*, the composition is reimagined to include several layers of rhythms and orchestration. The main chorus line is in several different *rāgas*. An extended recited drum syllabic sequence begins the composition. Perhaps due to Ellappa Pillai's connection to T. Balasaraswati, for whose performances he was often the *naṭṭuvaṉār*, one can detect obvious similarities to her very personal dance style in the composition and arrangement of the drum syllables, illustrating once again how echoes of the styles of stage performances of Bharatanāṭyam resonate in the Tamil cinema. This version of *Naṭaṉam āṭiṉār* also ends with a phrase of solfa syllables (known in Karṇāṭak vocal music as *svarakalpanā*), which is reminiscent of a concert. Perhaps because composers for the cinema were becoming increasingly distanced from the older musical forms that constituted the traditional genres of courtesan performers, starting in the early 1950s more and more elements of Karṇāṭak vocal concert music were inserted into music for dance.

These examples have demonstrated the broad cross-fertilization of dance on stage and on screen through a discussion of the flow of repertoire in both directions. In many ways repertoire provides insights into many of the larger issues represented by the reformation and repopulation of dance that resulted from the so-called dance revival of the 1930s. As we have seen, Bharatanāṭyam's domestication and the ameteurization of its practice as a hobby, as well as its links to middle-class cultural identity and of course to religion, are all dramatized through representations of *Naṭaṉam āṭiṉār* in the cinema. By contrast, the *pāmpu naṭaṉam* demonstrates the ways in which choreographic innovation recast Bharatanāṭyam at the crossroads of a revived notion of Tamil tradition and Orientalism. Finally, the *padam*'s ever-shifting and malleable presence in the Tamil cinema highlights the ways in which modern Bharatanāṭyam was constituted as a plastic and unstable form, through the repurposing of textual, musical, and choreographic materials. As a complex combination of intermedial materials, Bharatanāṭyam's new post-1930s significations produced a surplus of choreographic forms—in terms of repertoire, technique, and semiotics—that constitute the basis of the dance's life for the remainder of the twentieth century and beyond.

CODA

The Enduring Pedagogical Afterlives of Bharatanāṭyam's Celluloid Classicism

In October 2001, JAYA TV—the television channel founded by the former dancer-actress and chief minister of Tamilnadu, Jayalalitha Jayaram—broadcast the first television reality show centered on Bharatanāṭyam (figure C.1). It was called *TakaDhimiTa* after the individual vocalized rhythms (*colkaṭṭu*) of South Indian music that accompany Bharatanāṭyam. This radically new venture, which brought the new postliberalization private TV networks into conversation with the classical arts and new forms of corporate sponsorship, heralded a new beginning. In many ways, it represented the catapulting of Bharatanāṭyam into the fully globalized twenty-first century. Integral to this new life of the dance was an acknowledgment—indeed, a foregrounding—of the relationship between stage forms of Bharatanāṭyam and its cinematic iterations. The televised experience of Bharatanāṭyam, as mediated by this program, was an extension of the intermedial lives of Bharatanāṭyam and its representations, which have formed the heart of this book. Indeed, on television, Bharatanāṭyam was suitably repackaged to resonate with the new aesthetic economy of satellite television.

The show's creator and producer, Radhika Shurajit, is a Bharatanāṭyam dancer who has been bridging the worlds of Bharatanāṭyam stage and cinema dance for well over two decades. She has choreographed Bharatanāṭyam sequences for a number of Tamil films; is vice president of the Association of Bharatanāṭyam Artists of India; and runs her own dance school, the Thrayee School of Bharatanāṭyam.[1] The show is hosted by contemporary celebrity actresses who are also classical dancers—including Bhanupriya (b. 1967), Shobana (b. 1970; niece of Padmini),

Figure C.1. A still from a TV advertisement for the show TakaDhimiTa.

and Sukanya (b. 1969)—and it has also featured guest appearances by dancer-actresses of an older generation such as Vyjayanthimala and Padmini (discussed above). The show initially functioned as a straightforward dance competition judged by prominent Bharatanāṭyam dancers, mostly from Chennai. However, in 2004, the show introduced a mandatory "film song" round in which contestants had to interpret a film song using Bharatanāṭyam technique. In an interview I conducted with Radhika in 2012, just as *TakaDhimiTa* was about to complete filming its 425th episode, she shared her thoughts about the show in relation to Bharatanāṭyam's recent history:

> I had to glamorize Bharatanāṭyam. So what? I reached people [through the show]. To "glamorize" means using captivating shots, having a set, exciting edits. . . .
>
> As a dancer, I think the cinema songs of that [earlier] period [the 1950s, 1960s, and 1970s] are eternal. I would say the poetry of [the film lyricist] Kannadasan [1927–81] is equal to that of the Tanjore Quartet. . . . The films' songs about love give me the same feeling as dancing to a *padam* does. The great masters like Vazhuvoor Ramaiah Pillai and K. N. Dandayudhapani Pillai understood the old-world logic of Bharatanāṭyam very well, and that lent itself very

easily to choreography in films. Hence the logic of film, the logic of the camera, and the logic of Bharatanāṭyam choreography blended so beautifully together.

[For *TakaDhimiTa*] We brought in judges who were all the superstars of dance. I must thank all these artists for trusting me. Eventually [appearing on] *TakaDhimiTa* became a status symbol, and everyone came from all over the world not only to participate in the dancing, but also to judge. *TakaDhimiTa* is about bringing the old-world charm of Bharatanāṭyam into people's living rooms. . . . It is a marriage of electronic and visual art.[2]

Radhika's notions represent what Usha Iyer calls "somatic nostalgia" about the embeddedness of Indian dance in the cinema, a "citationary" revival of older sequences of song and dance (Iyer 2014, 224–25). However, it may be important to ask how such projects of revival and embodied nostalgia are generated and transmitted. In other words, what are the afterlives of the issues addressed in this book? More specifically, how could some of the ideas presented in this project be used to explain current trends in the world of today's Bharatanāṭyam? From innovative pedagogical methods and the proliferation of urban film dance schools, to the creation of celebrity dancers modeled after the paradigmatic celebrities of cinema in South India, to the performance of contemporary film songs in stage and television performance of Bharatanāṭyam, the idea of celluloid classicism that undergirds the form thrives well beyond its earliest instantiations.

CELLULOID CLASSICISM AS A PEDAGOGICAL IMPERATIVE

Print material from the 1940s and 1950s tirelessly foregrounded pedagogical ideas; articles in film magazines about training and accomplishment in Bharatanāṭyam dance were easily aligned with gossip about stars, film and vinyl record advertisements, and other cinematic paraphernalia. For example, in April 1953, *Kunṭūci* magazine published an article in a series titled "Nāṭṭiya Muttiraikaḷ" ("Gestures of Dance") (figure C.2). These articles were meant to educate film audiences about the meanings of Bharatanāṭyam gestures and to introduce their Sanskrit names and applications (*prayogas*). This is an older practice that was brought into modern Bharatanāṭyam pedagogy through the work of Rukmini Arundale and Kalakshetra.

Figure C.2. An article titled "Nāṭṭiya Muttiraikaḷ" (A. Kiruṣṇamūrtti 1953).

It is clear from this example that modern Bharatanāṭyam practice is comfortably positioned in the same optic world as the cinema, and it is assumed that dance and the cinema have the same audiences and consumers. Moreover, teaching audiences about Bharatanāṭyam—and the notion of education about the classical arts more generally—seems to be a preoccupation in the world of cinema. For example, consider the statement below from an article titled "Nāṭṭiyam Paṭum Pāṭu" (The hardship dance is facing") by a woman named Malavika that was published in *Kuṇṭūci* in August 1950. When speaking about the modern challenges facing Bharatanāṭyam, she invoked the idea of a deep institutionalization of the dance and state-sponsored competitive training:

> Given the state of affairs today, the government can play an important role and make arrangements. The government should go through a rigorous selection process [for funding dance training]. Even if [the government] is unable to have a separate university-like educational institution dedicated to dance, it should set up proficiency tests (*pariccaikaḷ*). [The government should] conduct yearly exams [for dancers], and issue certificates as they do for typewriting, playing the *vīṇā*, tailoring, vocal music, and playing

the fiddle. They should focus on the most proficient dancers and have them take exams. They can extract the best dancers in this process. These dancers should be invited by cultural organizations (*sabhās*) to give recitals. In this process, the true essence of Bharatanāṭyam will come shining through. The government need not spend any money on this. The revenue can be earned by the fees the students will pay. (Mālavikā 1950)

Why should a cinema magazine discuss such issues at all? Part of the answer is that the elements of modern Bharatanāṭyam construed as classical are dependent upon the visual and symbolic world of the cinema and the movement between media of dance teachers and star performers. Indeed, it seems as though audiences gravitate toward Bharatanāṭyam through a language of dance that circulates almost exclusively via the cinema. Certainly the movement of cinematic songs into stage performances of classical Bharatanāṭyam confirms this.

I have already discussed how Kalakshetra's classicizing project remained an extremely elite one and that it was really figures like Kamala and Ramaiah Pillai who brought the idea of classical dance to the masses through cinema. Similarly, the pedagogical experiments of Kalakshetra, although paradigmatic (as demonstrated by the hand gestures discussed above), remained elite projects. At the popular level, it was later provincial institutions such as Saraswathi Gana Nilayam (established in 1939 by the dancer K. Lalitha), the film director K. Subrahmanyam's Nrithyodaya (established as Natana Kala Seva in 1941), and Sri Sai Natyalayam in Madras (established in 1950 by J. Vijayamohana, the daughter of M. S. Ramaswamy Pillai, who was the first student of Ramaiah Pillai) that began to include songs from the films of the 1930s through the 1950s in their teaching repertoire. In another example, two young dancers named P. Chandra and R. Lila (students of the dance teacher and actress Neela Balasubramaniam, who directed a school called Nataraja Natya Nilayam) performed at the Sanatana Marga Sabha in Madras, among other things, the Marwadi dance (a dance set to the song *Naṉtakōpālaṉoṭu nāṉ āṭuvēṉē* [I'll dance with Kṛṣṇa]) from the Tamil film *Vazhkai* (1949; discussed in chapter 4), which was originally danced by Vyjayanthimala (figure C.3).

Their performance of a dance made popular by Vyjayanthimala also indicates the celebrity that many dancer-actresses had accrued by the

சிறிய மேடையில் பெரிய விருந்து

“ஆடத் தெரியாத நடன மாது கூடம் கோணல் என்று குறை சொல்வான்” — என்று ஒரு பழமொழி உண்டு. ஆடத் தெரிந்த பெண், கூடம் கோணலாயிருந்தாலும், இடம் குறைவானாலும் அழகாக ஆடிவிடுவாள் என்ற உண்மையை ஊர்ஜிதப்படுத்திக் காட்டுவதேபோல் இருந்தது—சென்ற மாதம் 24-ந் தேதியன்று கோடம்பாக்கம், சனாதன மார்க்க சபாவில் நடைபெற்ற பி. சந்திரா, ஆர். லீலா—ஆகிய சிறுமிகளின் நடனக் கச்சேரி.

கோடம்பாக்கத்தில், ஒரு சிறிய வீட்டின் மேல் தளத்தில் இக்கச்சேரிக்கு மேடை அமைக்கப் பட்டிருந்தது. பனிரண்டடி சதுரமே உள்ள மேடையில் பக்க வாத்யக்காரர்கள், நடன ஆசிரியை —பின்பாட்டுக்காரர்கள் அத்தனைபேரும் ஒரு ஓரத்தில், அமர்ந்திருக்க இரு சிறுமிகள் ஏககாலத்தில் நன்கு ஆடிக்காட்டியது ஆச்சரியமாயிருந்தது!

பழைய மாம்பலத்தில் நடராஜ நாட்டிய நிகேதனத்தை நடத்திவரும் நாட்டிய நடிக திலகம் ஸ்ரீமதி நீலா பாலசுப்ரமண்யத்தின் சிஷ்யைகளே இந்த சிறுமியர். குமாரி சந்திரா அவருடைய சொந்த புத்திரி. குமாரி லீலா, ஸ்டாண்டர்டு வேக்கூம் ஆயில் கம்பெனி என்ஜினீயர் ஸ்ரீ. ஏ. கே. ராவின் புத்திரி ஆவார். இச்சிறுமிகளுக்கு நல்ல பயிற்சி அளித்திருப்பதோடு, அன்றையக் கச்சேரியில் ஆசிரியையே இனிமையாகவும் ஸ்பஷ்டமாகவும் பாடி, நட்டுவாங்கமும் செய்து, கச்சேரியை நன்கு சோபிக்கச் செய்தார்.

சந்திராவும், லீலாவும், சேர்ந்து ஆடிய போது சில குறைகள் தென்பட்டன. இருந்த போதிலும், தனித்தனியே ஆடிய போது இக் குறைகள் தென்படவில்லை. சந்திரா ஆடிய “நந்த கோபாலன்” (மார்வாரி) நடனமும், இருவரும் ஆடிய நாடோடி நடனமும் பிரமாதமாய் இருந்தன. சந்திராவின் விறுவிறுப்பான அங்க அசைவுகளும், கண் வீச்சும் சபையோரின் மனதைக் கவர்ந்தன. லீலா “நடனம் ஆடினார்” பாட்டிற்கு நன்கு பதாபிநயம் செய்தார்.

அன்றையக் கச்சேரிக்கு “குண்டூசி”யின் நடன ஆசிரியர் “நந்தி” தலைமை வகித்தார். அவர் இந்தக் குமாரிகளின் ஆட்டத்தைப் பாராட்டிவிட்டு, சபையின் சார்பாக குமாரிகளுக்கு இரு மெடல்களை பரிசளித்தார்.

கச்சேரிக்கு விஜயம் செய்திருந்த “குண்டூசி” ஆசிரியர் பி. ஆர். எஸ். கோபால் இந்த சபையின் சன்மார்க்க சேவையைப் பாராட்டி விட்டு, கோடம்பாக்கம் வாசிகளுக்கு பெரிய அளவில் நல்ல பொழுது போக்கை அளிக்கக்கூடிய பெரிய சபையாக இது வளர்ச்சி பெற வேண்டும் என்று ஆசி கூறினார். “ஜதி”

பி. சந்திரா

ஆர். லீலா

Figure C.3. A magazine article about two dancers—P. Chandra and R. Lila—who perform the Marwadi dance from the film Vazhkai *(1949) in a stage performance at the Sanatana Marga Sabha, in Madras (“Ciṟiya mēṭaiyil periya viruntu” 1953). Courtesy of the Roja Muthiah Research Library.*

1950s; this point will be addressed in more detail below. For now, it is sufficient to note that ideas of the classical—fully inflected with all its pedagogical, moral, religious, caste-bound, and aesthetic implications—were thriving in a middle-class world in which Bharatanāṭyam had become almost completely amateurized, and where the culture of the cinema was both accessible and affectively efficacious. In its new urban avatar, Bharatanāṭyam was a hobby. It was morally, religiously, and culturally loaded, of course, but it was an amateur practice nonetheless. Perhaps one of the clearest illustrations of Bharatanāṭyam's amateurization in the period after the 1930s is the culture of the *araṅkēṟṟam*. As Janet O'Shea points out, "The *arangetram*, for many young women, marks their entry into a middle-class . . . community rather than into the performance milieu, often terminating a period of dance study instead of inaugurating a dance career" (2007, 3).[3] To be sure, publicity for the *araṅkēṟṟam* existed even during the 1940s and 1950s, when film magazines like *Kuṇṭūci* carried announcements for *araṅkēṟṟams* taking place in Madras side by side with advertisements for new film releases and gossip about film stars. One such announcement from *Kuṇṭūci* in December 1952 reads:

> On the 12th of last month [November], Kumari Ramani had her Bharatanāṭyam *araṅkēṟṟam* at Mylapore Rasika Ranjani Sabha. For that *araṅkēṟṟam*, the respected minister Krishna Rao was the chief guest. Ramani is the student of Saraswati, who herself is a student of Vazhuvoor Ramaiah Pillai.
>
> The *araṅkēṟṟam* of the "Kochi sisters" (Kumari N. Saroja and Kumari N. Shakuntala) took place on the 14th of November at Mylapore Rasika Ranjani Sabha. They are students of M. S. Ramasami Pillai, who is a student of Ramaiah Pillai. On that occasion, respected judge M. S. P. Iyer was the chief guest. (*Kuṇṭūci* 1952)

Indeed, the *araṅkēṟṟams* of dancer-actresses were announced and publicized with great pomp even into the 1970s. For example, Ramaiah Pillai and his son Samaraj conducted the *araṅkēṟṟam* of the Malayalam film star Jayabharathi (b. 1954) in 1974 in Ettumanoor, Kerala. On the invitation card (figure C.4), Jayabharathi is very prominently shown performing a cinematic yet classical dance, the Āṇṭāḷ dance, which was created for Kamala by Ramaiah Pillai.

Figure C.4. Invitation card to the August 1974 Bharatanāṭyam araṅkēṟṟam *of the Malayalam actress Jayabharathi, at which she performed the Āṇṭāḷ dance. Private collection of S. V. Jayababu.*

CELLULOID CLASSICISM AND CELEBRITY IN THE WORLD OF BHARATANĀṬYAM

The example of Jayabharathi takes us to another point I wish to make about the pedagogical and didactic nature of the idea of the classical as it was constituted through the always-already cross-pollinated space of cinema and stage Bharatanāṭyam. This point has to do with cults of celebrity in Bharatanāṭyam, which evolved from stardom as it was imagined and lived in the cinema. As Iyer (2014) has so eloquently shown, classical dance became a key aspect of female celebrity in the Hindi cinema. For example, dancer-actresses such as Vyjayanthimala were celebrated largely because of their dancing ability, which had a number of moral, cultural, and sexual significations. However, I am interested in how the cinema consequently enabled a cult of stardom in the realm of the classical arts. Today, generations of classical Bharatanāṭyam dancers (for example, Padma Subrahmanyam) surely have star status, which they

Figure C.5. The dancer Tara Chaudhri, a student of Pandanallur Meenakshisundaram Pillai, performs in the Tamil film Parijatam *(1950) (*Kuṇṭūci, *December 1949, 34). Courtesy of the Roja Muthiah Research Library.*

acquired through a range of opportunities, including innovative pedagogy. In an earlier time, these opportunities largely revolved around state sponsorship and international touring through organizations such as the Indian Council for Cultural Relations. Today, wide-scale transnational connections, globalized Indian classical dance schools, and online pedagogy enable such stardom.

In turning back to the primary sources, we can see that the archive contains some early iterations of the star Bharatanāṭyam dancer. On the one hand, dancers who achieved star status may have performed in the cinema, as figures like Kamala, Padmini, and Vyjayanthimala did. A lesser-known example is the dancer-actress Tara Chaudhri (d. 2013).[4] Chaudhri was born in Punjab and initially trained in Kathak together with her sister. In 1943, she moved to the south to train in Bharatanāṭyam and Kathakali. She studied Bharatanāṭyam with Pandanallur Meenakshisundaram Pillai, the same *naṭṭuvaṉār* who trained Arundale. For a brief time, while she lived in Madras, Chaudhri was part of the world of the Tamil cinema. She performed dances in Tamil films such as *Vedhala Ulagam* (Demon world; 1948) and *Parijatam* (The wish-fulfilling tree; 1950) (figure C.5). Although Chaudhri was primarily a stage performer, in a pattern quite opposite to that of the figures discussed by Iyer, her presence in the cinema contributed to her popularity as a stage performer. Publicity and star status enabled not only dancers but also Bharatanāṭyam to be accepted by the middle and upper classes. Indeed, the accoutrements of the modern Bharatanāṭyam dancer—expensive saris, jewels, international travel, the management of dance institutions, and so on—are signs of class status. In a sense, they function as gatekeepers for the class-based insularity of the dance (Soneji 2010a). For many dancers of the 1940s and 1950s, their presence in popular magazines and other forms of publicity that were allied with the film world enabled them to unquestionably garner a certain class identity.

The archive also shows that celebrity dancers who had nothing to do with the cinema became part of cinematic discourse as keepers of classical tradition. This argument complements the work of Neepa Majumdar (2009) and Iyer (2014), who have argued that moral anxieties related to tradition and idealized forms of womanhood are at the center of Indian configurations of female celebrity and stardom more generally. The dancer Mrinalini Sarabhai (1918–2016)—who was raised in Madras, educated in Switzerland, and married a leading scientist in Gujarat while maintaining a career as a Bharatanāṭyam dancer after being trained by Meenakshisundaram Pillai—had no involvement in the cinema, unlike Chaudhri (who was marginally involved in it) or Kamala and Vyjayanthimala (who were film stars). However, Sarabhai still became an iconic figure whose dancing images and life narrative circulated as part of the discursive construction of the star Bharatanāṭyam dancer. A 1949 article in *Kuṇṭūci* called her work in the field of dance a "service" (*cēvai*), locating the classicism of dance on the moral high ground (figure C.6). Indeed, the term *cēvai* (from the Sanskrit *sevā*, "service") is most frequently used to depict selfless acts of piety or devotion. The stars of the dance world are covered in publications like *Kuṇṭūci* in a manner that is strikingly similar to those of the cinema world. Indeed, the article on Sarabhai has a tone very similar to that of the feature on the actress T. R. Rajakumari that was discussed in chapter 2. In the intertwined world of Bharatanāṭyam and the early Tamil cinema, stardom thus represented another mode of positioning and representing women actors and dancers in the vernacular press.

....

While this book has been limited to the 1930s, 1940s, and 1950s, Bharatanāṭyam and the Tamil cinema have continued their cross-polination into

மிருணளினியின் அரிய சேவை

வலதுபுறம்

1. மிருணளினியும், அவரது கணவர் டாக்டர் விக்ரம் ஏ. சாராபாயும்.

*

2. மிருணளினியின் ஒரு நடனத் தோற்றம்.

*

3. பண்டித ஜவஹர்லாலும், மிருணளினியும்.

Figure C.6. An article about Mrinalini Sarabhai (1918–2016) ("Miruṇāḷiṉiyiṉ Ariya Cēvai" 1949). Private collection of S. V. Jayababu.

the twenty-first century. I conclude, therefore, with some examples of the enduring ways in which the links I have attempted to foreground between Bharatanāṭyam and the Tamil cinema thrive in today's globalized economic and cultural industries. One of my interviewees, the dancer Radhika Shurajit, continues to create full-length Bharatanāṭyam performances using only Tamil film songs. On December 2, 2011, as part of a major dance festival in Chennai presented by the cultural organization Kartik Fine Arts, she created a full suite of Bharatanāṭyam dances drawn from Tamil cinematic songs from the 1950s to the present. She had titled this production "G. Ramanathan Mutal A. R. Rahman Varai" (From [the composer] G. Ramanathan to [the composer] A. R. Rahman") ("Radhika Shurajit's Dance Show Based on Evergreen Tamil Film Songs," 2012). The production focused on an iconic film music composer from each decade and showcased their most popular film songs interpreted through Bharatanāṭyam choreography by Shurajit. The composers were G. Ramanathan from the 1950s, Vishwanathan Ramamurthy from the 1960s, Illayaraja from the 1970s and 1980s, and the Oscar award winner A. R. Rahman from the 1990s. As Shurajit told me, "this is my attempt to bring the art of Bharatanāṭyam to the common people in India via the medium of Tamil cinema" (interview by the author, Chennai, August 13, 2012). Clearly, this is an explicit continuation of the complex yoking of Bharatanāṭyam and the cinema that began in the 1930s, albeit in a highly systemized, structured, and professional manner that foregrounds the hybid aesthetic of celluloid classicism.

Another example of this type of sustained performance of celluloid classicism comes from another celebrity performer, the dancer Padma Subrahmanyam. In November 2001, she created a new dance work titled "Nāṭṭiya Cāstiramum Naṭikar Tilakamum" (The *Nāṭyaśāstra* and the crest jewel of acting) in which she integrated parts of fifty films by the iconic Tamil actor Sivaji Ganesan (1928–2001) and demonstrated how his various facial expressions from these films were congruous to that of the facial expressions of Bharatanāṭyam dancers as laid out in the Sanskrit text, the *Nāṭyaśāstra*. Here, we see how the juxtapositioning of the Sanskrit *Nāṭyaśāstra*, which was a key tool in giving Bharatanāṭyam its perceived classical status at the time of its reinvention, and the performances of a celebrity actor of the modern Tamil cinema constitutes a narrative that can best be understood by invoking the idea of celluloid classicism. In other words, for Subrahmanyam, Ganesan's performance on the screen is wholly compatible with the aesthetic parameters of the ancient and classical idiom of Bharatanāṭyam, represented here by the *Nāṭyaśāstra*. Bharatanāṭyam's essential aesthetic characteristics cannot be understood outside the frameworks instantiated and actualized in the cinema.

On the one hand, the politics of the dance revival of the 1930s created a perceived dichotomy in the dance world of modern South India of the classical (represented by stage versions of Bharatanāṭyam) and the popular (represented by dance in cinema). On the other hand, as cinema became a more respectable idiom and was repopulated by women from upper-caste and upper-class urban backgrounds, it became increasingly possible for flows between stage and screen to exist, in a process that both simultaneously celebrated and broke down the supposed insularity of the pure and sacred idiom of the postrevival Bharatanāṭyam. The rhetoric of breaking down the barriers between the two became so ubiquitous in the 1980s and 1990s that it became routine to see crossover performances (such as those by Shurajit discussed above) even in the Indian diaspora. Today, Bharatanāṭyam dancers all over the world choreograph the latest Tamil blockbuster film songs through the idiom of Bharatanāṭyam, and these circulate widely through a range of social media, most commonly on YouTube.

Finally, repertoire items made popular in Tamil cinema, such as the snake dance performed by Kamala since the 1940s, continue to have afterlives on the stage today. For example, in August 2016, the California-based Bharatanāṭyam dancer Surabhi Bharadwaj performed the famous *pāmpu naṭaṉam* at Wagner Park in New York as part of the Erasing Borders Festival of Indian Dance. Like Kamala, Bharadwaj performs a very acrobatic version of Bharatanāṭyam, and her appearance in New York met with popular acclaim. However, unlike Kamala's cinematic version, Bharadwaj's live performance expanded the physicality of the serpentine movements, in a kind of intense dramatization that pushed the limits of the physical endurance of the twenty-first century Bharatanāṭyam dancer. In a future project, I hope to be able to map with more precision and deeper analysis the enduring presence of the relationship between classical dance and the Tamil cinema of the period after the 1960s, paying particular attention to the ironies of India's economic liberalization and cultural conservativism, and the new class formations and identities they enable.

This book has attempted to trace the relationships of dependency and cultures of commingling that are at the heart of the emergence of South India's most visible cultural forms. It has done so by reading historical data through a prism of intermediality in which the worlds of cinema and the emerging classical dance are not so far apart. Indeed, each evolved in direct contact with the other.[5] As a modern practice, Bharatanāṭyam is heavily mediated by notions of social organization, morality, nationhood, and aesthetics as they emerged in the early cinema. Far from being a hermetically sealed off cultural space of an unsullied and timeless classicism, its aesthetic self-perception (as timeless, religious, national, and upper caste) cannot be understood without reference to the cinema. This dynamic, in which one form actually constitutes the other through refraction, representation, and reprisal, forces us to reconsider the modern social and aesthetic history of Bharatanāṭyam. Its interface with the cinema produces a kind of aesthetic, a somatic habitus, and a social world that exceeds the categories—such as the classical—through which it represents itself.[6] In widening our lens and placing cinema at the heart of Bharatanāṭyam's life in the modern world, we push the limits of understanding all modern cultural forms as always more than monomedial. In this intermedial, hybridized space of Bharatanāṭyam *in* and *as* cinema, the aesthetics of movement simultaneously live on several registers, each a valid dimension of the spectacle, speaking to real and imagined ideas about the pasts of Indian dance.

APPENDIX

Synopsis of Jalaja *(1938)*

It is the hour of midnight worship in the temple, in the Rangamangalam village, Tanjore District. The bell tolls twelve; with the last stroke fading away into a tremble, Jalaja dances in the Mantapa [pavilion] before Lord Nataraja, to the rhythmic beat of the drum and to the tinkle of little cymbals.

Rajagopalan, a lover of art and one specially devoted to dance enters the scene and recognizes in Jalaja the perfect Bharata Natya artist he has been in long and arduous search of. It is a miracle of a chance. And then and there he decides to take Jalaja to Madras to present her genius to a wider and more artistic public. For this he seeks the help of the temple priest and with him talks it out with Doraikannu, Jalaja's mother who has high ambitions for her daughter.

Rajagopalan is rich, handsome and young—not a bad catch, decides Doraikannu. The Mudaliar, the local Mirasdar and Temple trustee who is amorously keen on Jalaja can be a permanent patron; and so with Jalaja she leaves the village for Madras. Coming to know that the priest had helped them in their decision, the Mudaliar dismisses him from the temple service. His next act is to set his agent to track out Jalaja and bring her back to the village.

In the city, events in Rajagopalan's house move fast, scandal growing to its full outside, that undercover of regenerating Art, Rajagopalan is living a companionate life with Jalaja. Rajagopalan himself has purified Jalaja, inculcating in her the supreme idea that her Dance is greater than herself—this the public never knows nor cares to know; he brings about a meeting of his wife Lalita with Jalaja, on purpose of Jalaja learning a song from Lalita; the two quarrel. Rajagopalan's home begins rapidly to disintegrate. Kittu a gentleman vagabond making good in scandal-mongering what he could not in lawyering, [carries] tales to Sivarama

Iyer, Rajagopalan's father, setting his wife Pankajam to do the same with Lalita. It crashes when Sivarama Iyer sees his son sit publicly with Jalaja in the course of her dance recital in a public hall, challenge the dancer and proclaim that Jalaja is the only genuine Bharaya Natya artist. The crowd hoots, cat-calls and disperses in a general stampede. Sivarama Iyer comes home, a vessel of shame and wrath ready at any moment to burst.

It is twelve o'clock in the night. Lalita is anxiously [a]waiting the arrival of Rajagopalan. Sivarama Iyer enters. Lalita is taken aback at the anger which glitters unmistakably on her father-in-law's face; soon Rajagopalan steps in and Sivarama Iyer confronts him, talks heatedly and throws the ultimatum before him: "Either live in my house as behoves [*sic*] a decent man or get out of it altogether." The rest of the night is full of terrible conflict for both Jalaja and Lalita; and in the small hours of the morning after coaxing Lalita to sleep, Raja leaves the house, taking a final sorrowful glance of the sleeping wife.

The publicity of the first appearance of Jalaja at Madras is in full swing. Meanwhile the Mudaliar has been quick. He sets his minions to kidnap Jalaja; his agent and Kittu have ably planned it. Things go very badly with Lalita. Raja's leaving the house badly unhinges her mind. A sudden yearning for a child makes her pathetically [sing a] lullaby [to] a toy and [there] is a strange obsession trip over dance phrases and bits of dance technique. The doctor in attendance prescribes a dance cure for her at which Sivarama Iyer is shocked: A family woman to become a dancer!

The evening, two days prior to the performance, Jalaja accompanied by Doraikannu, Alagappan: and her little sister Rukmini go to the temple for the matin [morning] worship. Worship over, Jalaja walks swiftly out of the temple at the appearance of the disgusting agent. Doraikannu and the Agent exchange whispered words; now the sound of the car starting is heard from outside; they smile significantly. Their own driver who has been previously bribed is rapidly whisking along Jalaja in the car to the Mudaliar's riverside bungalow at Rangamangalam.

The Mudaliar is wild with happiness at having Jalaja at first within his Juandom. But fond love-sick fool that he is, he does not reckon with: "shut the door on a woman's wit; she will be up at the casement." Jalaja vamps him; leading him into the garden dancing, and there with the help of the priest ties the Mudaliar fastly [*sic*] to a tree, and makes her escape to Madras.

In the meantime, obsessed with the idea that it was Jalaja's dance which drew her husband to her, Lalita tries to learn some steps, fails; and the obsession grows upon her day by day, making her queerer and queerer.

Rajagopalan is happy that Jalaja has returned safe in time for her big dance recital for which he has made the whole town expectant. But he wants at the same time, to book the Mudaliar for his villanies. The Mudaliar, not to be outwitted, [makes] a complaint to the village Police that Jalaja had stolen five thousand rupees worth of jewels from his house and run away to Madras; while Rajagopalan in his turn [makes] a complaint to the Police in the City against the Mudaliar for the kidnapping and wrongful confinement of Jalaja. The police complaints move briskly. Jalaja is indescribably happy. Unaware of the presence of Rajagopalan, she dances the dance ecstatic in the garden under the smiling "moon and the peeping eyes of the stars; lulled by the flower-laden breezes; and her song grows lyrical with a soft shower of the playing fountain." It is a Chopin-like Nocturne. Doraikannu disturbs her trance, calls her in, and giving her a flask of milk asks her to take it to Rajagopalan. Jalaja does so and just when Rajagopalan is about to drink, Rukmini who has followed unseen dashes it out of his hands. She explains to the astounded Rajagopalan that her mother and Alagappan have drugged the milk. It is now the turn of Jalaja to be astounded; the seed of a faint suspicion takes root in Rajagolapan's mind but quite discreetly he hushes up the matter, as Jalaja's great dance-recital is to come off on the morrow night. The midnight hour strikes its doleful twelve. The owl hoots. The night-bird shrieks and a distant dog wails. Lalita sleep-walks her chambers, recollecting sad and sweet memories of old. The next day night. It is the theatre. The dance-hour is about to strike. The audience sits expectant. The Mudaliar with the village Sub-Inspector and a couple of constables enters by the wing to arrest Jalaja, only to find himself smartly arrested by the City Police who had followed him quickly, silently. The curtain parts. The dance begins. Jalaja does an item. The audience cheers. Lalita, at home, is attempting to learn some dance-poses. She fails, she seems to hear the dance-music, coming sweetly, plaintively; she becomes agitated. Jalaja does another item. The excited Lalita comes crashing to the theatre in a car driven by herself.

The curtain is rung down. Interval.

Lalita jumps out of her car and dashes through the crowd of audience, elbowing her way madly. Jalaja sits before a mirror, against the make-up table in the green room. Rajagopalan stands near her, congratulating her on the glory of her performance. The last word is still on his lips when the two are startled by a hysterical laughter. They see Lalita, haggard, disheveled, advancing towards them. Lalita violently accuses Jalaja for having bewitched her husband away from her through thousand disgusting viles and base strategems. Jalaja meets all her mad actions and madder words with absolute calmness. And Jalaja dances the Tillana as her reply. Lalita's ruffled features soften with every foot-beat of the dance measure; finally she reaches her normality [returns to normal]. The transformation is miraculous. Lalita praises Jalaja lyrically. Rajagoplan leads Lalita out. Jalaja stands in adoration before the image of Lord Nataraja, her hands folded, her face a light of beatitude. (*Jalaja* songbook, 1938, 2–4 [from the private collection of S. V. Jayababu])

NOTES

INTRODUCTION: ON CONVERGENT HISTORIES

1. The interrelated histories of Bharatanāṭyam and the early Tamil cinema have received hardly any critical attention by cultural historians of South India. A notable exception is M. S. S. Pandian's short but insightful essay "Tamil Cultural Elites and Cinema" (1996), which locates both contemporary Bharatanāṭyam and popular cinema along a continuum of class- and caste-bound tastes among South Indian cultural elites. A recent essay by Sundar Kaali (2013) discusses the Tamil film *Chintamani* ("The wish-fulfilling gem," 1931) in relation to discourses on *devadāsī* reform in the Madras Presidency.

2. Ravi Varma has been discussed extensively by scholars of visual culture in South Asia. For more on his work and the afterlives of his paintings and their chromolithographic reproductions, see Guha-Thakurta 1986, Kapur 2000, Jain 2007, Neumayer and Schelberger 2003 and 2005, and Pinney 2004.

3. A significant amount of work has been done on the unique ideological axes that come together to constitute the political and cultural world of the Madras Presidency in the early twentieth century. For example, the historical anthropologists and historians Bernard Bate (2009), Eugene Irschick (1986), Sumathi Ramaswamy (1997), M. S. S. Pandian (1996 and 2007) and Ravi Vaithees (2015) trace the emergence of Dravidian politics and describe its implications for various aspects of South India's cultural history.

4. Davesh Soneji is working on a project that extensively documents the ways in which musical cultures in South India were transformed by the advent of the Parsi theatre and its offshoot, *icai nāṭakam*, in Tamil-speaking South India. Much of the material in this section of the book—especially the idea of *rāga*-based music—is indebted to his unpublished paper titled "*Indra's Court* in Madras: The Urdu Theatre and the Cosmopolitan Origins of Modern Tamil Musical Drama." (2017). For more on the circulation of the Parsi theatre in Southeast Asia via South India, see Hansen 2018.

5. As Soneji (2017) describes, many of the scripts for the modern Tamil theatre were written by Brahmins but funded and published by upper-caste non-Brahmins such as Mutaliyārs, Ceṭṭiyārs, and Vēḷāḷars. The performers came from a range of lower-caste backgrounds, although even here upper-caste people were marginally involved. The relatively inclusive cosmopolitan nature of the new drama may have been one of the reasons for its tremendous appeal and financial success in the late nineteenth and early twentieth centuries.

6. This is a reference to a performance of the Tamil play *Ṭampācārivilācam* (Dalliances of a dandy) by Caitāpuram Kācivicuvanāta Mutaliyār (1806–71) that will be discussed in greater detail in chapter 1. I am grateful to Davesh Soneji for the following reference, from the *Madras Mail* of August 24, 1876: "Native Female Amateurs—A number of wealthy Hindus of Madras are about getting up a drama entitled 'Dumbacharri Velasam,' the principal actors in which are to be Nautch, or Dancing Girls, who are undergoing a course of lessons in a house in Black Town. The performance will take place in the early part of next month."

7. The film *Kalidas* was produced by Ardeshir Irani (1886–1969)—who was also responsible for *Alam Ara* (1931), India's first talkie—and directed by his former assistant, H. M. Reddy, for the Imperial Movi-Tone Studios. While it may be fair to say that *Kalidas* was the first talkie to contain Tamil, it was in reality a multilingual film with characters speaking in Tamil, Telugu, and Hindi. However, all of its songs were *rāga*-based, in the mold of what is considered classical Karṇāṭak music today. For example, it contained Rajalakshmi's rendition of the devotional song (*kīrtana*) by the composer Tyāgarāja, *ĕnta nercina* ("no matter how erudite . . ."), in *rāga* Śuddha Dhanyāsi. This of course has a parallel with the ways in which song genres such as *kīrtanas, padams*, and *jāvaḷis* flowed through the early Tamil drama in a slightly earlier period. It indicates the dialectical relationship between these cultural forms, as well as the malleability and flexibility of the genres—a theme that is discussed in greater detail in chapter 5.

8. Early works included anecdotal and celebratory writings by a number of Indian scholars. See, for example, Ranga Rao 1995.

9. The recent history of Kūcipūḍi is highly contested. At first glance it appears very similar to Bharatanāṭyam, largely because it was refashioned after the reinvention of Bharatanāṭyam in the 1950s. Critical rereadings of Kūcipūḍi's recent history began with the work of Anuradha Jonnalagadda (1996) and Davesh Soneji (2004) and have continued with reference to the Telugu cinema in the works of Putcha and Thota.

10. Some of the major earlier works on Tamil cinema include Baskaran 1996 and 2009; Dickey 2009; Gopalan 2002; Guy 1997; Hardgrave 1975; Hariharan 1995; Lakshmi 1995 and 2008; M.S.S. Pandian 1996; and Velayutham 2008. Important works that discuss the relationship between Tamil cinema and regional politics include Barnett 1976; Baskaran 1981; Hardgrave 1975 and 2008; Jacob 1997 and 2008; M. S. S. Pandian 1992; Sivathamby 1981; and Vaasanthi 2006.

11. Venkatachalapathy dedicated a whole chapter of his brilliant book to this class of Tamil publications and traces the origin of the term *gujili* (*kucili*) to an area of Madras near the central railway station known as Gujili Bazaar, after the large numbers of Gujarati people who lived in this area (2012, 134–35).

12. A detailed account of S. S. Vasan and Gemini Studio is found in Guy 1997, 236–51. A more critical account of Gemini Studios is found in Pillai 2015, 99–189.

13. This magazine was named after the pen name of the film journalist P. R. S. Gopal, who became famous writing for another film magazine, *Silver Screen*. *Kuṇṭūci* was owned and edited by a man who came to be known as "Gundoosi" Radhakrishnan. The contemporary writer Vāmaṉaṉ has published a biography of Gopal (2013).

14. Other important early Tamil film magazines include *Ciṉimā Ulakam* (The world of cinema) and *Hanumāṉ* (named after the monkey god, Hanuman), which became popular because it regularly featured the work of the Tamil writer Ka. Na. Subramanyam (1912–88). *Silver Screen*, the other popular early film magazine with content in English, was founded by a man named Ramaratnam in the late 1930s.

15. In 1954, a few years after the release of this film, the Kannada writer G. V. Iyer wrote a novel titled *Śāntalā* that tells the quasi-historical story of Viṣṇuvardhana, a king of the Hoysala dynasty who reigned 1108–52, and his love for a court dancer named Śāntalā, whom he apparently married. In the novel, she cannot produce a male heir for the kingdom and so tragically ends her own life. The novel may have been inspired in part by the film.

16. The title of *Āṭal Pāṭal* comes from the title of a column on music and dance by the famous Gandhian writer "Kalki" R. Krishnamurthy (1899–1954) that had appeared in the magazine *Āṉanta Vikaṭaṉ*. Krishnamurthy eventually founded the tremendously popular Tamil magazine *Kalki* in 1941 (discussed in chapter 3).

17. Ironically in most writing in English on Bharatanāṭyam in the 1930s and 1940s, *devadāsī* dancers who performed in the cinema are mentioned only in passing, if at all. Many of these women (discussed in detail in chapter 1) played critical roles in presenting Bharatanāṭyam as a legitimate artistic practice in the film industry. It is only in the vernacular archive that we hear about them in detail.

1: THE *DEVADĀSĪ* COMMUNITY AND THE CINEMATIC IMAGINATION

1. I base my invocation of prosopography on the historian Lawrence Stone's classic essay titled "Prosopography" (1971). The essay offers perspectives on the epistemic value of collective biography. Of course, I use this term only as a point of reference, in the sense that I am not attempting to create a database, nor am I using the term in a social-scientific sense, as a sociologist might. I simply want to highlight the importance of recovering, juxtaposing, and combining life narratives that have otherwise eluded critical historicization.

2. Davesh Soneji has recently pointed to the colonial discursive formation and political mobilization of the Sanskrit term "*devadāsī*." Following Leslie Orr (2000), Soneji argues that *devadāsī* as an "umbrella term" came to signify various local communities of unrelated women, who were brought together under this term for the purposes of colonial bureaucracy and administration (2012, 6).

3. On civic (Brahmin) elites and colonial bureaucracy, see Hancock 1999; Fuller and Narasimhan 2014.

4. Outside the Madras Presidency, there were a number of interventions aimed at other courtesan communities and communities of professional performers such as the Marathi- and Konkani-speaking *kaḷāvant* communities of Bombay (see Arondekar 2012; Cabral e Sa 1990; Perez 2005), and the *tawā'if* and *bāījī* courtesans of northern India and Bengal (see, for example, du Perron 2007; Maciszewski 1998, 2006, and 2007; Qureshi 2006; Sachdeva 2008). Some the earliest attempts to take legal action against professional female performers occurred in the Bombay Presidency in 1912 (Jordan 2003, 75–86).

5. Of course there are notable exceptions, such as the famous dancer T. Balasaraswati and the singer M. S. Subbulakshmi (discussed below in this chapter). However, as Soneji points out, it is significant that these women were exceptions in the sense that they engaged with the structures of the state and elite politics in Madras in a way that was not possible for the majority of women from *devadāsī* backgrounds who neither lived in Madras nor received patronage from urban elites and emerging cultural institutions (Soneji 2012, 22–23).

6. Scholarly work in English on the Self-Respect Movement is meager. Major texts on the subject include Irschick 1986, Geetha and Rajadurai 1998, and M. S. S. Pandian 2007. For an excellent work on gender and sexuality in the Self-Respect Movement, see Srilata 2003.

7. On the linkages between Tamil politics in the 1920s and 1930s and the cinema, see Irschick 1986, Baskaran 1981, Dickey 1993, and Jacob 2008. The work of Eugene Irschick in particular focuses on the participation of men from the *devadāsī* community (such as C. N. Annadurai and M. Karunanidhi) in modern Tamil politics.

8. In fact, subsection 3.2 of the act uses only Telugu words (other than the Sanskrit "*devadāsī*") to refer to these women: "Any custom or usage in the Hindu community such as the Bogum [*bhogam*, in Telugu], Kalavanthula [Telugu], Sani [Telugu], Nagavasulu [Telugu], Devadāsī, and Kurmapulu [Telugu] . . . are hereby declared unlawful and void" (quoted in Soneji 2012, 236).

9. In a brilliant essay titled "What Is Tamil about Tamil Cinema?" (2010), Stephen Hughes addresses the question of language in the early talkies. He argues that the issue of Tamilness and linguistic differentiation in the South Indian cinema cannot be read outside the context of the emergence of Dravidian politics and the increasing number of films produced in Madras.

10. *Kalidas* starred T. P. Rajakumari (1911–64) as the heroine, and she was not from the *devadāsī* community. Her life was rather exceptional in that she was a Brahmin who joined a drama troupe at the age of eleven to support herself and her mother (Guy 1997, 53–54). There is almost nothing known about the actress who performed in the first silent film made in South India, *Keechaka Vadham* (1918). We know only that her name was Jeevarathnam and she had acted in the theatre before the cinema, so she may have been from a *devadāsī* background.

11. For more on early Telugu women playback singers, see Indraganti 2016.

12. Following the model of the Parsi theatre, and like the modern Tamil theatre, the Telugu theatre was organized into professional guilds called "companies," the most famous of which was the Surabhi Drama Company, founded by the actor Vanarasa Govinda Rao in 1885 in Surabhi, a village in the Kadapa District. The company was the first to encourage women to play female roles in the modern Telugu theatre (Indraganti 2016, 39). The female lead in the first Telugu film, *Bhakta Prahlada* (The devotee Prahlada; 1931), was the actress Surabhi Kamalabai (1913–77), who was not from the courtesan community. But it is significant that the company also enabled a number of women from the *kalāvantula* community to enter the professional world of theatre and cinema. The most famous of these women *kalāvantula* artists who started with

Surabhi and went on to act in both Telugu and Tamil films from the 1940s to early 1960s was Surabhi Balasaraswati (dates unknown).

13. The Parsi theatre is a distinctly modern theatrical form that integrated older forms of Indian theatre with aesthetic modes and narratives drawn from traveling Shakespearean theatre troupes that moved through colonial South Asia. In the Bombay Presidency, many of these plays were initially translated into Gujarati and Hindi or Urdu and were staged in these languages, using staging techniques, costumes, and narratives drawn from the traveling troupes. This hybrid type of theatre eventually came to be known as Parsi theatre because it was patronized by the upwardly mobile Parsi or Zoroastrian community in Bombay. The Bombay Presidency Parsi theatre troupes eventually toured South India and affected local theatre traditions. The development of *icai nāṭakam* thus owes a great deal to the Parsi theatre. On the Parsi theatre, see Hansen (1999, 2001, 2003, 2009, 2011, 2018).

14. The term "boys' company" was likely borrowed from British theatre companies that staged performances with the cooperation of semiprofessional or amateur actors, who were often involved in the military and hence were referred to using phrases like "our boys' company." Sometimes these productions—such as that of *H.M.S. Pinafore* in Madras in April 1880—would have military-inspired themes. Newspapers such as the *Madras Mail* are full of advertisements for such theatrical productions. *Our Boys* (1875) was also the title of a very popular comedic drama by Henry James Byron that was staged across India in the 1880s and 1890s.

15. Work on Cuvāmikaḷ in English is meager. However, there is a sizable amount of work on him and his plays in Tamil, some of the most important of which is by the music scholar Arimaḷam Patmanāpaṉ (2000, 2002, and 2008).

16. Pi. Vi. Irāmacāmi Rāju, the author of this drama, also wrote an English play titled *Urjoon Sing, or the Princess Regained* (c. 1875); a Tamil translation of Shakespeare's Romeo and Juliet titled *Rōmiyō Jūliyaṭṭu Eṉpavarkaḷuṭulyu Katai* (1877), commissioned by the Madras Vernacular Literature Society; a children's book called *Indian Fables* (1889); and *Sreemat Rajangala Mahodayam* (1894), a set of Sanskrit verses about the rise of the British Empire (this also contains a long piece called *Sreemat Pandita Rajatarangini*, an account of the life of Ishwar Chandra Vidyasagar, the prominent Bengali social reformer and writer).

17. Soneji has also shown how *devadāsīs* writing in the early twentieth century connected themselves to such mythical *devadāsī* figures to provide themselves with a genealogy at the height of the anti-*devadāsī* movement. He notes this in the case of the Tamil book titled *Uruttirakaṇikaiyar* (Śiva's courtesans), written by the *devadāsī* K. Añcukam in 1911 (Soneji 2010) and in the context of letters written by *devadāsīs* opposing the legal interventions of Muthulakshmi Reddy (Soneji 2012).

18. The name Ceṅkamalam was also used later to refer to a *devadāsī* character—in the novel *Pāvaiviḷakku* (Votive lamp), by the Tamil writer Akilaṉ (1922–88). The novel was made into a film with the same title (*Pavai Vilakku*; 1960), starring the Brahmin dancer Kamala and Sivaji Ganesan.

19. Contemporary sources on Rukmani such as her Wikipedia page and an obitu-

ary that appeared in the *Hindu* on September 5, 2007, do not mention anything about her early years or about her mother's professional engagement with dance and music.

20. In this section I draw from two major anonymous archival sources from the film magazines *Kuṇṭūci* and *Āṭal Pāṭal*, "Es. Ṭi. Cuppulakṣmi" 1952 and "Kuḻantaikaḷē Periyavarkaḷāka Ākiṟārkaḷ" 1936.

21. *Harikathā* or *kathākālakṣepam* is derived from the Marathi devotional practice known as *kīrtan*, which combines song, storytelling about the lives of Vaiṣṇava saints, and commentary (Schultz 2012). In the eighteenth century, Marathi traditions of *kīrtan* were brought to Tanjore, and by the late nineteenth century, these forms had been appropriated and transformed by Tamil Brahmin musicians and given the name *kathākālakṣepam*. For more on this form, see Gurumurthy 1994 and Soneji 2013. This was originally performed only by male Brahmins, but by the early twentieth century, women from *devadāsī* communities began to perform it, and by the 1930s, Brahmin women were performing it (Soneji 2013).

22. The film had approximately fifty-five songs in it, and the music was composed by Papanasam Sivan (discuss in more detail in chapter 2).

23. This was Meenakshi Iyer, the granddaughter of Rao Bahadur K. S. Venkatarama Iyer of Nagapattinam. She married Subrahmanyam in 1920, when she was nine and he was sixteen (Kannan and Kannan 2004, 28).

24. Padma Subrahmanyam, interviewed by the author, Chennai, December 23, 2012.

25. One of her famous recordings is of a Tamil *padam* in the *rāga* Kāmbodhi, *Uṉakkō maṉamillai* (Don't you have a heart?"), by an unknown composer. She also recorded the Telugu *kīrtana Bhajana seya rādā* (Shouldn't we sing [his] praises?) in the *rāga* Aṭhānā, by the composer Tyāgarāja (1767–1847) and the Sanskrit *kīrtana* in the *rāga* Bhairavī titled *Cintaya makanda mūlakandam* (Meditate upon the lord who is at the base of the mango tree), by Muddusvāmi Dīkṣitulu (1775–1835). This is in addition to at least one song in the *tillāṉā* genre in the *rāga* Kāpi, various verses from the Tamil Śaiva canonical hymns known as *Tēvāram*, and one piece simply labeled "Comic Song." For a complete list according to the gramophone labels, see Kinnear (1994).

26. This is likely because it was done with other photographs that have been incorporated into the Konerirajapuram murals. The most famous image in these murals is that of the *tavil* (drum) player Ammapettai Pakkiri Pillai (1874–1920), whose image was copied into the murals from a photograph (Sundaram 2001, 259–62).

27. Almost nothing is known about Kunnakkudi Venkatarama Ayyar, except for a list of films for which he composed music. These included *Krishna Bhakthi* (Devotion to Kṛṣṇa; 1949), in which Rajakumari acted.

28. The plot of *Kacha Devayani* is taken from the epic *Mahābhārata* and is about the illicit love between Kaca, the son of Bṛhaspati, a priest of the gods, and Devayāni, the daughter of a priest of the demons, Śukrācārya. The story was the subject of three silent films made in 1919, 1926, and 1929 in Bombay. The 1929 version was made by Dhundiraj Govind Phalke.

29. The song was written by Papanasam Sivan in the *rāga* Nāṭakuṟañci, and sung by MKT in the film.

30. The song was written by Sivan in the *rāga* Cārukeśī, and sung by MKT in the film. Its popularity has been commented upon by Guy (1997, 257), and the refrain *manmatalīlai* ("glories of the god of love") was also the title of a 1976 Tamil film starring Kamala Haasan. The refrain was also incorporated into a song for another of Haasan's films, *Panchathantiram* (2002).

31. Between the production of *Haridas* and *Chandralekha*, we know that Rajakumari acted in at least two other films, *Vikatayogi* (The crooked yogi; 1946), directed by Subrahmanyam, and *Pankajavalli* (Lady of the lotus; 1947), directed by S. Soundararajan Ayyangar.

32. Rajakumari's brother married the actress B. S. Saroja (b. 1922) in 1949. Saroja was born into a Malayali family and initially entered films as a chorus singer, since both her parents were musicians. She acted and danced in many Tamil (and later Malayalam) films, including *Nattiyarani* (Queen of dance; 1949).

33. Their bungalow was named Kanyakumari Bhavanam ("abode of the virgin goddess") and was on Habibullah Street in T. Nagar, Madras (Sampath Kumar 1951, 57).

34. For more on the *katti kalyāṇam* and its wider courtly and social meanings, see Sreenivas 2008. For details on the practice in Tanjore, see Soneji 2012, 34–36.

35. We spoke in Tamil in Kuchalakumari's home in Chennai on December 17, 2012. All of the quotes from Kuchalakumari that follow are from this conversation.

36. The local goddess has a temple in the town of Thiruvidaimarudur and is named Bṛhat Sundara Kucāmbā ("the mother with beautiful large breasts") in Sanskrit and Naṉmulaināyaki or Perum Mulaināyaki ("the lady with full breasts") in Tamil.

37. Pragathi Studios was owned by Avichi Meiyappa Chettiar (also known as A. V. M. Chettiar, 1907–79), and because of the war eventually moved south of Madras to Karaikkudi (S. Pillai 2015, 59).

38. This song and its gendered and nationalist implications are discussed in detail in chapter 3.

39. Kameswaran was born to a *naṭṭuvaṉār* family in the city of Madurai. He initially trained under a *naṭṭuvaṉār* named Vaideeswarankoyil Mahadeva Pillai (1904–65). When Kameswaran moved to Madras in 1945, he became an assistant to Vazhuvoor Ramaiah Pillai and ran a school called Mahalakshmi Natyalaya. His daughter, K. Mahalakshmi, is a professional dancer.

2: THE OCULAR POLITICS OF MAKING MODERN BHARATANĀṬYAM

1. One of the most interesting new works of scholarship to address the complex intersections between religion and Indian nationalism that unfolded under the aegis of the Theosophical Society is Lubelsky 2012.

2. On the cosmopolitan identities of urban Tamil Brahmins in the early twentieth century, see Hancock 1999; Fuller and Narasimhan 2014.

3. Of course, it is important to note that Arundale was not offended by northern Indian dance and music per se, only when it was performed by hereditary professional artists. Later, she choreographed a dance drama called *Meera of Mewar* (1985) about the late medieval northern Indian mystic poetess Mīrābāī, with music tuned by the Bengali musician Falguni Mitra. Toward the end of her life, she also expressed a

desire to choreograph the canonical Hindi version of the *Rāmāyaṇa* known as *Rāmcaritmānas* as a dance drama (Ramani 2003). However, it was because of the religious content (particularly in its nationalized form as part of a pan-Indian devotional Hinduism) that Hindustani music appealed to Arundale. That is, unlike the Parsi theatre-inspired Hindi songs that were performed by *devadāsīs* (which were invariably constructed as lowbrow art by figures like Arundale), it was the spirituality and nationalist unity represented by the devotional works of Mīrābāī or the *Rāmcaritmānas* that made their presence acceptable in the new institutions of classical dance and music in South India.

4. Not only do the major ocular interventions characterize staged performances of Bharatanāṭyam, but contemporary Bharatanāṭyam dancers also celebrate the revival history through productions that dramatize their perceptions of this period of history. See, for example, Janet O'Shea's fascinating study of historical representation in the dance production titled *Vata Vriksha* or *The Banyan Tree*, about Arundale's rediscovery of Bharatanāṭyam, staged in Chennai in January 1996 (2006, 139–44).

5. For example, we know that they regularly performed a piece from the Tanjore court called *malaippu [jati]*, a piece that no longer exists in today's Bharatanāṭyam but was danced by courtesans in Tanjore and is also found in Telugu manuscripts in the Tanjore Sarasvati Mahal Library (Davesh Soneji, pers. comm., October 11, 2015).

6. Examples of such representations include the French *ballet de cour* titled *Le triomphe de l'amour* (The triumph of love; 1681); operas *La vestale* (The vestal virgin; 1807) and *Les bayadères* (1810), both with librettos by Etienne de Jouy (1764–1846); and the very popular opera ballet *Le dieu et la bayadère, ou la courtisane amoureuse* (The god and the bayadere, or the amourous courtesan; 1830), which was known in England as *The Maid of Cashmere*. Each of these included temple backdrops and highly romanticized, fantastical depictions of Hindu temple dancers. The most famous post-1838 production was of course Marius Petipa's *Bayaderka* (1877), which is still very much a staple in the Russian ballet repertoire. For details on these and many other such European representations, see Leucci 2005 and 2009.

7. Rayon was extremely popular at this time. A short Tamil drama entitled *Tācikaḷ Vēcam eṉṉum Imiṭēṣaṉ Kalar Cilku* (The dāsīs' guises or imitation color silk; 1930) uses imitation silk as a metaphor for the imitational love of the *devadāsī*-courtesan. This drama, published in Madras, was likely performed by local *icai nāṭakam* companies.

8. Arundale's first dramatization of a narrative work was the staging of a Tamil text, *Kuṟṟāla Kuṟavañci* (The Kuṟa fortune teller from Kuṟṟālam), a literary work composed in 1715 by the poet Mēlakaram Tirikūṭarācappak Kavirāyar. *Kuṟavañci* (fortune teller) dramas were often performed by *devadāsīs* as part of special festivals in local temples in Tamilnadu, particularly in the Kaveri delta region. However, unlike the very popular *Carapēntira Pūpāla Kuṟavañci* or the *Virālimalai Kuṟavañci* dramas that were still being performed in temples by *devadāsīs* until the 1940s, Arundale chose *Kuṟṟāla Kuṟavañci*, which had no living performance tradition associated with it but was dedicated to the god Śiva. The other dramas mentioned above were in honor of King Serfoji II (r. 1798–1832) and Cuppiramaṇiya Mutaliyār, a minister of King Vijaya

Raghunātha Rāya Toṇḍaimān (r. 1807–25), respectively. Arundale considered traditional repertoire in praise of humans to be of a lower class and hence chose to dramatize *Kuṟṟāla Kuṟavañci*. Her choreography of this text was first staged in Madras, then Bombay, and then inside the temple in the town of Kuṟṟālam (known today as Courtallam or Kutralam) itself. For more on the *Kuṟavañci* genre, see Muilwijk 1996; Peterson 1998 and 2008a. For a full translation of *Kuṟṟāla Kuṟavañci*, see Buck 2005.

9. Details about Sivan's early life and the dates cited here can be found in Veṅkaṭarāmaṉ 2001, 15–25.

10. Arundale's dance drama was based on a musical play in Sanskrit written by Maharaja Svāti Tirunāl of Travancore (1813–46). The play was first published in Devanagari script in Trivandrum in 1932.

11. Sivan is also listed as a cocomposer (with Bhagavatula Seetharama Sarma and Turaiyur Rajagopala Sarma) for the dance dramas *Krishnamari Kuravanji* (1971) and *Matsya Kurma Avataram* (1974) (Samson 2010, 234).

12. A case in point is his *kīrtana* in Tamil, *Āṉanta naṭamiṭum pātaṉ* ("the foot that performed the dance of bliss"), in the *rāga* Kedāragaula. This became a staple song about Śiva-Naṭarāja in Bharatanāṭyam concerts from the early 1940s onward, but its first appearance was in the opening credits of the Tamil film *Nandanar* (1942).

13. About Kurucāmitās's work, Soneji writes:

"K. Kurucāmitās was a fairly prolific writer who composed several such poems. He published his own work from 1943–45, and it spans a range of subjects, from murders in the Presidency, to cattle markets in the suburbs of Kumbhakonam, to the British victory over Tunisia during World War I. Another significant work is *Kumpakoṇam Kaikkāṭṭi Maratteruvil Naṭanta Rāmacāmi Kolaiccintu* ("Collection of Songs about the Murder Committed by Rāmacāmi in Kumbhakonam," 1943) which describes the case of Rāmacāmi from Kumbhakonam who murdered a prostitute named Sītālaṭcumi for jilting him" (2012, 253, n. 19).

14. *Raja Desingh* was later remade as *Raja Desingu* (1960) by the director T. R. Raghunath, with the iconic stars M. G. Ramachandran and the dancer-actress Padmini. In this version, instead of the *padam Putaṟi varukutu* (see below in the text), Padmini's dance number *Pāṟkaṭal alaimēlē* is featured. This is a new devotional song composed for the film that describes the god Viṣṇu at Srirangam, a move that furthers the scripting of Bharatanāṭyam as an essentially devotional art form. The song was written by the film lyricist Udumalai Narayana (1899–1981), set to music by G. Ramanathan (c. 1899–1963), and sung in playback by M. L. Vasanthakumari (1928–90), a very famous twentieth-century concert vocalist from the *devadāsī* community.

15. On the folk narrative about Tēciṅkurājaṉ (Tej Singh) in Tamilnadu, see S. Subrahmanyam 1999.

16. This Tamil *padam* has a long and complex performance history. It was likely composed in the mid-nineteenth century by either Kaṉam Kiruṣṇa Ayyar (c. 1790–1854) or Vaitīcuvaraṉkōyil Cupparāma Ayyar (c. 1829–67), and it was quite popular in the traditional courtesan community. In the 1920s and 1930s, *devadāsī* artists such as T. S. Rangammal and Bangalore Thayee recorded the piece on 78 RPM phonograph records. See Allen 1992, 208–10.

17. Adapted from the translation in Allen 1992, 210.

18. Jagadambal was a famous *devadāsī* who lived in Madras until 1929 and was a disciple of the dance master Vazhuvoor Samu Nattuvanar (1844–1903). Later, Krishna Iyer trained with a Brahmin dance master named A. P. Natesa Ayyar from the village of Melattur, who practiced a form of dance theatre called Bhāgavata Mēḷa Nāṭaka. Natesa Ayyar also taught *abhinaya* to several *devadāsīs* in Madras.

19. Vadivelu Pillai was a disciple of Thanjavur Kannuswami Nattuvanar (1864–1923), the grandfather of my own teacher, Thanjavur K. P. Kittappa Pillai. Vadivelu Pillai was the son of a well-known *naṭṭuvaṉār* named Svaminatha Pillai, and he died on September 9, 1937, very soon after La Meri's performance in Madras (Sundaram 2002, 220–21).

20. The Renaissance Theatre was inaugurated in September 1932 and first produced two Shakespearean plays. This was followed by Seshagiri's forays into the cinematic world, in which the Renaissance Theatre financially backed the talkies *Sita Kalyanam* (The marriage of Sita; 1934) and *Chandrasena* (1935). Both of these films were made in Marathi and Hindi, and they were directed by the Marathi filmmakers Baburao Phendarkar and V. Shantaram (1901–90), respectively. The Renaissance Theatre went on to produce a Tamil play titled *Kaṭṭaivaṇṭi* (The bullock cart), an adaptation of Gilbert and Sullivan's Savoy opera *The Gondoliers; or, The King of Barataria* (1889). In the souvenir program of the performance by La Meri in Madras, the Renaissance Theatre takes credit for revitalizing Bharatanāṭyam dance: "In the meantime, a morass was expanding, sucking into its foul bosom Bharata Natya, the Indian Dance with a tradition extending to centuries. . . . The Renaissance Theatre group of dance-critics and enthusiasts came to the rescue, did discriminating propaganda for preserving the purity of Bharata Natya as a great and noble art with a status of its own in the scheme of our life, discovered artists, brought them from the temple percincts [*sic*] to the platform of the music hall, cheered them, footlighted them; and to-day that much-maligned "Nautch" smiles with a dignity [like] that of the gods" (*The Celebrated International Dancer La Meri* 1937).

21. Untitled souvenir program for a performance by La Meri, Varalakshmi, and Bhanumathi, the Renaissance Theatre, Madras, 1937; Performing Arts Collections [Dance] *MGZB (*The Celebrated International Dancer La Meri* 1937).

22. The films advertised in the program include the Telugu *Sarangadhara* (1937); the Tamil *Sethu Bandhan*, *Chintamani*, *Sati Anusuya*, *Miss Sundari* (advertised as featuring "Azuri's dagger dance, a speciality"), and *Sati Ahalya* (all 1937); and the bilingual *Bala Yogini* (1937) (ibid.).

23. Ibid.

24. The following Bharatanāṭyam compositions are listed in the sections of the program describing Varalakshmi and Bhanumathi's performance: *alārippu* (no *tāla* listed), *jatisvaram* (*rāga* Kalyāṇī), *padam* (*Dāri jūcucunnadi* in the *rāga* Śaṅkarābharanam), *svarajati* (*Ēmāyalāḍirā* in the *rāga* Huseni), *śabdam* (*Veṇyuḍa* in the *rāga* Kāmbhoji), *padam* (*Uṉṉai tūtaṉuppiṉēṉ* in the *rāga* Sāveri), *padam* (*Pataṟi varukutu* in the *rāga* Kāmbhoji), and *tillāṉā* (in the *rāga* Kāpi).

25. Raghavan (1908–79) was head of the Sanskrit Department at Madras Univer-

sity from 1935 to 1968. He was secretary of the Madras Music Academy for over four decades and the editor of the *Journal of the Music Academy* (1935–79). He authored a number of articles on Bharatanāṭyam in the formative period of its reinvention in Madras in the 1930s, sometimes using the pen names Bhava-Raga-Tala and Bhavuka. He also edited and published several important Sanskrit texts related to dance in medieval South India, such as Akbar Shah's seventeenth-century *Śṛṅgāramañjarī* (1951) and Jāyappa Senāpati's thirteenth-cenutry *Nṛttaratnāvali* (1965). He was very close to the family of the famous dancer T. Balasaraswati, and his daughters became her first students at the Balasaraswati School of Indian Music and Dance, a short-lived dance school on the grounds of the Madras Music Academy, in 1953 (Knight 2010, 146). He also collaborated with Balasaraswati on a small book in Tamil titled *Paratanāṭṭiyam* (Bharatanāṭyam; Balasaraswati and Raghavan 1959). In addition to co-writing the story for *Jalaja*, he also wrote compositions for Bharatanāṭyam in Sanskrit that were choreographed by Balasaraswati.

26. The short story was first published with eleven others in a volume with the same name, *No Ankletbells for Her* (Isvaran 1949). The foreword to the book was by the British novelist John Hampson (1901–55). The four-page-long story, the first in the collection, recalls the fantasy of a young girl who desires to perform in Madras, a theme that is at the centre of the film *Jalaja*. Amid lengthy poetic descriptions of Hillman Minx cars, the concrete urban landscape of the city (presumably Madras in the 1930s and 1940s), and members of the upper class, the reader meets a young woman who dreams of dancing on stage. At the climax of her fantasy, her mother calls out to her, and the spell is broken. The girl, it turns out, is a scavenger who collects sticks with her mother. The story highlights modern Bharatanāṭyam's embeddedness in a deeply classist economy and the unevenness that underwrites access to dance even in the period immediately following its reinvention in Madras.

27. The couple had two sons and a daughter, Mallika. She married Murasoli Maran (1935–2003), a prominent politician who was the nephew of the chief minister of Tamilnadu, M. Karunanidhi. This indicates the continued participation of men from *devadāsī* communities in the civic life of South India and the caste endogamous marriage that define life for most women in this community today.

28. *Jalaja* songbook, 1938, 4, from the private collection of S. V. Jayababu.

29. *Silver Screen, Āṇṭu Malar* 1938, n.p.

30. The other two vocalists mentioned were named Shakuntala and Kokilam. Kokilam also appears in the list of credits in the songbook as appearing in the film in the role of "Singer."

31. Like the handful of other women from this community who were active in Madras's cultural scene in the 1930s, such as T. Balasaraswati and M. S. Subbulakshmi, Bhanumathi had an unusual career trajectory. She continued giving performances of Bharatanāṭyam even after the release of *Jalaja*, until around 1954 (Pattabhi Raman 1992, 28). As Soneji has shown, the lives of these "exceptional" women obfuscate the lives of thousands of other women from courtesan communities who could not "make it" in the new world (2012, 22–23). Perhaps unintentionally, the story of *Jalaja* captures the spirit of such failure.

32. The piece she performs is the Tamil *padam* in the *rāga* Khamās, *Nāṉ aṅkē varuvēnō* ("Should I go to him?"), attributed to the nineteenth-century poet Vaitīcuvaraṉkōyil Cupparāma Aiyar. The representations of Tamil *padams* in the cinema are discussed in greater detail in chapter 5.

33. *Tēvaṭiyāl kaccēri* was frequently used to describe *devadāsī* dance performances in the early Tamil cinema—for example, in the films *Dambachari* (1935; discussed in detail in chapter 1), *Tiruneelakandar* (1939), *Dasi Aparanji* (1944), and *Devadasi* (1948; also discussed in chapter 1).

3: CINEMA, DANCE, AND BOURGEOIS NATIONALISM

1. See, for example, the PhD dissertations of Amrit Srinivasan (1984) and Avanthi Meduri (1996). For later work, see Allen 1997; Chakravorty 1998; O'Shea 2007; Soneji 2010a.

2. For details on the foundation, inauguration, and early years of the Madras Music Academy, see Sriram 2009; Subramanian 2006.

3. For example, in 1905, Bharati translated Bankim Chandra Chatterjee's 1882 anticolonial Sanskrit anthem to Mother India, titled *Vande mātaram* (Salutations to the motherland) into Tamil and published it in the magazine he founded called *Cakkravartaṉi*.

4. Details on Bharati's life and work are found in Tamil in the excellent work of Venkatachalapathy (2004 and 2008). For English-language scholarship on Bharati, see, for example, Frost 2007; P. Srinivasan 2014; Sundara Rajan 2001; Venkatachalapathy 2018.

5. For a brief history of the dissemination of Bharati's works in print after his death and a discussion of the copyright issues that ensued, see Sundara Rajan 2001; Venkatachapathy 2018.

6. For example, *Thyagabhoomi* (1939), discussed above, featured patriotic Gandhian songs written by Kalki. The film *Mathrubhoomi* (Motherland; 1939) featured deeply nationalistic songs whose lyrics and music both were written by Papanasam Sivan, including those that dwelled on the nation as mother—such as *Namatu janmapūmi* (Our birthland), *Aṉṉaiyiṉ kālil vilaṅkukalō* (Are the mother's feet in shackles?), and *He pārata vīrarkaḷē* (O heroes of India!). For a lengthy discussion on nationalist songs in the early Tamil cinema, see Baskaran 1981, 69–83.

7. The 1932 version of *Maya Macchindra* was produced by Prabhat Films and directed by the very famous filmmaker V. Shantaram). Both versions of the film were based on the story of the tenth-century Nātha yogi Matsyendranātha and his disciple Gorakhanātha.

8. The early issues of *Kalki* contained a separate section for the discussion of issues related to dance and music, called "Āṭal-Pāṭal" (Dance and music). It is noteworthy that these early issues combined reviews of and opinions about cinema, dance, and music in this section. Later, this section became an independent (but short-lived) magazine called *Āṭal-Pāṭal*, exclusively devoted to the performing arts, both on stage and in film.

9. The film version of Kalki's novel, *Thyagabhoomi* (1939), juxtaposed representa-

tions of Brahmins and Dalits marching together with real clips of Gandhi's speeches. For this reason, it was generally understood to be a propaganda film for the INC (Baskaran 1981, 135).

10. The historical figure of Mīrābāī is shrouded in uncertainty. Scholars such as Mukta (1994), Martin-Kershaw (1997), and Hawley (2012) have created some critical awareness of the historical Mīrābāī and her songs. It is significant, however, that her story likely came to twentieth-century Tamilnadu through the writings of Besant. Her book, *Children of the Motherland* (1906), which features the story of Mīrābāī, inspired the first Tamil drama about Mīrābāī, written by R. Srinivasan (1919). In his preface, Srinivasan talks about how Besant's narration of Mīrābāī's story first inspired him to perform *kathākālakṣēpam* or *harikathā* centred on the theme of her life, and he later transformed this into a formal play (ibid., 1). The play first appeared in serialized form in the Tamil magazine *Pūrṇacantrōtayam* (ibid., 2). Though we cannot be certain, this play could explain why there may have been an interest in presenting the life story of Mīrābāī through the idiom of a Tamil film in 1940s Madras.

11. Kalki's investments in cultural nationalism ran deep and wide. With C. Rajagopalachari and the Tamil scholar T. K. Chidambaranatan, he even coined the modern, widely used Tamil word for "culture," *paṇpāṭu* (A. Ramnarayan 2006, 76).

12. The novel is the subject of the PhD dissertation of Akhila Ramnarayan (2006), Kalki's great-granddaughter. Details about its narrative, politics, publication, circulation, and reception are found in her work, so I will not repeat them here.

13. An iconic filmmaker whose life and work has been memorialized by the nation, Subrahmanyam has also been the subject of a recent English-language biography by M. R. Rangarajan, titled *K. Subrahmanyam: A Biography* (2005).

14. The Bhāgavata Mēḷa Nāṭaka is a Telugu-language theatre form that originated in the seventeenth century, and it had a symbiotic relationship with *devadāsī* dance until the early part of the twentieth century (Inoue 2008; Soneji 2012, 48). Today it is performed in only three villages in the Thanjavur region: Melattur, Saliyamangalam, and Teppperumanallur. Subrahmanyam's relationship with this form is mentioned in Kannan and Kannan (2004, 28) and was also conveyed to me in conversation with his daughter, the dancer Padma Subrahmanyam—who mentioned that he studied this form under a "guru from [the village of] Melattur by the name of Kinjin Kodandarama Aiyyar" (Padma Subrahmanyam, interviewed by the author, Chennai, December 23, 2012).

15. The novel *Sevāsadan* was originally titled *Bāzār-e-Husn* (Marketplace of beauty) and was published in Calcutta in Hindi in 1919, then in Urdu in Lahore in 1924. It was the first major novel of the author, whose real name was Dhanpat Rai Srivastava (1880–1936). A full English translation of the novel has been produced by Snehal Shingavi and published with a critical introduction by Vasudha Dalmia (Premchand 2005).

16. Subrahmanyam was offered, but declined, the position of minister of information and broadcasting by Jawaharlal Nehru (Kannan and Kannan 2004, 31).

17. He was also the first vice-chairman of one of the earliest state-funded arts organizations in Tamilnadu, the Tamilnadu State Sangeetha Nataka Sangam (now re-

named the Tamilnadu Eyal Isai Nataka Manram), and in that capacity he was involved in the establishment of policy related to the arts within the Tamilnadu State Government (Kannan and Kannan 2004, 31).

18. References to these ideas can be seen in her documentary film, *Bharatiya Natyashastra* (The Indian *Nāṭyaśāstra*; 1992, produced by Doordarshan, the state-run TV channel), and her book *Nāṭyaśāstra and National Unity* (1997).

19. Kamala has been long-celebrated as an iconic figure who bridged the worlds of Bharatanāṭyam dance and the cinema. See, for example, Ranga Rao 1988.

20. Kamala was known by various names during her career. She was initially identified as Baby Kamala and then as Kumari ["maiden"] Kamala. As a young woman she married Rasipuram Krishnaswami Iyer Laxman (1921–2015), who went on to become one of India's most famous cartoonists. Thus, for a number of decades when she was at the peak of her dance career, she was known as Kamala Laxman or Kamala Lakshman, the name I use throughout this book. In 1960, she divorced Laxman. She later married T. V. Lakshminarayanan and eventually moved to New Jersey. In the later part of her life, she used the name Kamala Narayan or Kamala Narayanan, a surname drawn from her second husband's name.

21. Kamala had her *araṅkēṟṟam* in 1941. She also studied Kathak in Bombay under Pandit Sundar Prasad (birthdate unknown, d. 1970) and Lacchu Maharaj (1907–78).

22. The choreography in this film was jointly done by three non-*naṭṭuvaṉārs*, Krishnamurti, Hiralal, and Madhavan.

23. As noted above, her stage performances often included an Āṇṭāḷ dance, which was choreographed by her teacher Ramaiah Pillai, in which she would dress like the Vaiṣṇava saint and poet Āṇṭāḷ and dance to one or two verses from the Tamil poems attributed to her. Āṇṭāḷ's enduring popularity among Tamil-speaking Brahmins has been noted in Archana Venkatesan's recent work on the interpretation of Āṇṭāḷ's poetry and its reception (Venkatesan 2010; Venkatesan and Branfoot 2016).

24. *Darśana* generally refers to a central act of Hindu temple ritual—namely, seeing and being seen by the sacred icon of the deity (Eck 1981). The invocation of this logic of visual transaction in Indian cinema has been commented upon by a number of scholars (see, for example, Dwyer 2006; Taylor 2002).

25. The song *Ciṅkāra vēlaṇē* in the *rāga* Ābheri from *Konjum Salangai*, for example, is regularly featured in Tamil game shows on the cable network Vijay TV and is also frequently played by *nāgasvaram* artists in rituals to the god Murukaṉ at Tamil temples in India and the diaspora.

26. The song *Tāyē yacotā* is a musical composition in the devotional singing style known as *bhajana saṃpradāya* in the Tanjore region. It is a composition of the poet Uttukkadu Veṅkaṭa Kavi (c. 1700–65), and was brought into the dance repertoire during the reinvention in the 1930s.

27. This film was based on a popular Malayalam-language play titled *Suprabha*, written by the noted playwright Munshi Paramu Pillai (1902–62). The dialogues for the film were written by M. Karunanidhi, from the *icai vēḷāḷar* community, who later became chief minister of Tamilnadu.

28. For example, a program for her performance hosted by the organization called Tamil Isai Sangam in Madras on January 2, 1954, mentions her performing Bharatanāṭyam repertoire (including *alārippu*, *jatisvaram*, and the song *Naṭaṉam āṭiṉār*) as she learned it from the *naṭṭuvaṉār* Dandayudhapani Pillai (*Tamiḻ Icai Caṅkam Tamiḻicai Malar* 1954, 67).

29. Subbu directed a number of important early Tamil films, including *Kannamma en kadhali* (Kaṇṇammā is my love; 1945) and *Avvaiyar* (Avvaiyār [a poetess]; 1953). He also acted in a number of films, including *Miss Malini* (1947) and *Valliyin selvan* ("Son of Vaḷḷi; 1955), both which he also directed. He was a close associate of S. S. Vasan, who owned Gemini Studios and *Āṉanta Vikaṭaṉ*, in which the novel *Tillāṉā Mōkaṉāmpāḷ* first appeared in serialized form in 1956–57.

4: THE EMERGENCE OF THE CHOREOGRAPHER AND A NEW ENVISIONING OF DANCE

1. The essay discusses traditional *naṭṭuvaṉār* figures such as Tañjāvūr Ciṉṉaiyā (1802–56), one of the famous Tanjore Quartet that engaged in gynemimetic forms of dance, as did various other men at the Marāṭhā court in Tanjore in the nineteenth century—including the Brahmin court musician Muvālūr Sabhāpatayya (c. early nineteenth century) and the Marāṭhā noble named Kṛṣṇasvāmi Rāv Jādav (c. 1820–70) (Krishnan 2009).

2. Shankar and his performances have been the subjects of a number of scholarly works. See, for example, Abrahams 2007; Erdman 1987 and 1996; Purkayastha 2012. I do not wish to rehearse their arguments here, except to draw attention to the fact that the new forms of vocabulary and symbol that Shankar created as Oriental dance were in fact reincorporated into the new dance culture of urban South India. Thus, Shankar had a lasting influence on the choreographic presentations of figures like Vedantam Lakshminarayana Sastri (c. 1886–1956), who reinvented Kūcipuḍi dance in Madras (Putcha 2011, 99–101). He also inevitably influenced male dancers who performed and represented Bharatanāṭyam in the period immediately following its reinvention, such as Gopal, Bhaskar Roy Chowdhury (1930–2003), and a host of others who would follow by the middle of the twentieth century.

3. This family's involvement with the court of Tanjore can be traced to the figure of Veṅkaṭakṛṣṇa Naṭṭuvaṉār (dates unknown), who was chief *naṭṭuvaṉār* at the court of King Serfoji II (1777–1832). Veṅkaṭakṛṣṇa Naṭṭuvaṉār's son was Vīrācāmi Naṭṭuvaṉār (dates unknown), and his son was Pañcāpakēca Naṭṭuvaṉār (1842–1902). Kuppiah Pillai was the only son of Pañcāpakēca Naṭṭuvaṉār. For details, see Sundaram 2002; Sri Rajarajeswari Bharatha Natya Kala Mandir 2010.

4. Gopi Krishna was the grandson of Sukhdev Maharaj, a male teacher of Kathak dance. Krishna attracted national attention as the main actor in the Hindi film *Jhanak Jhanak Payal Baje* (The ankle bells make the sound "jhanak"; 1955), directed by V. Shantaram. This film tells the story of a courtesan who is reformed by being initiated into the classical (*śāstric*) traditions of Kathak by male gurus, one of whom becomes her dancing partner and lover. Following the tremendous success of this

film, Krishna went on to choreograph over sixty Hindi films and various South Indian films. He trained in Bharatanāṭyam with Thiruvidaimarudur Mahalingam Pillai and Govindaraj Pillai (1914–84) at Rajarajeswari Bharatha Natya Kala Mandir in Bombay.

5. Considering their influence on Hindi cinema, it is surprising that very little scholarly attention has been paid to Sohanlal and his family. Works such as that of Kishore and Kerrigan (2016) that seek to analyze the rise of the Bollywood dance director mention them only in passing.

6. Kristen Rudisill (2007) has made this argument as well, but in the context of popular urban Tamil theatre of post-1940s Madras.

7. Ramaiah Pillai's family and students sometimes claim that this distinct style of Bharatanāṭyam, which was separate from the Tanjore courtly tradition, existed in the time his ancestors, such as Vaḻuvūr Cāmu Naṭṭuvaṉār (1844–1903). However, this is simply not the case. The *naṭṭuvaṉārs* who lived in the towns of Vazhuvoor and Thirukkazhukundram where Ramaiah Pillai's ancestors and teachers lived were all aware of the Tanjore traditions, and repertoire and technique from Tanjore were certainly at the heart of their practices in the late nineteenth century. The distinction arose only when Ramaiah Pillai and his students began to use a distinct dance style, in part to set Ramaiah Pillai's dance apart from that of the Tanjorean *naṭṭuvaṉār* families (such as that of Pandanallur Meenakshisundaram Pillai) who were involved with the reinvention of Bharatanāṭyam in Madras, and in part to legitimate Ramaiah Pillai's aesthetic innovations as tradition in this moment of great aesthetic flux, transformation, and competition for men from *naṭṭuvaṉār* families.

8. Nāgammal, about whom almost nothing is known, apparently danced at the Mysore court, at which time one of Cāmu Naṭṭuvaṉār's only surviving musical compositions (a *tillāṉā* in the *rāga* Curuṭṭi) was composed in honor of the king of Mysore, Cāmarājendra Wodeyar IX (r. 1881–94). This is mentioned in "Natyacharya Vaḻuvūr Ramaiah Pillai" 1986, 21.

9. The story of Prahlāda, a child devotee of Viṣṇu, is a popular Hindu narrative whose most popular representation is the tenth-century Sanskrit text known as the *Bhāgavata Purāṇa*. The narrative is also popular in certain localized South Indian theatre forms such as the Bhāgavata Mēḷa Nāṭaka of the Tanjore region (Inoue 2008). According to the story, Prahlāda was born to a wicked and tyrannical demon, named Hiraṇyakaśipu. After torturing Prahlāda for his devotion to Viṣṇu, Hiraṇyakaśipu is slain by Viṣṇu, who descends to the earth (*avatāra*) in a half-man, half-lion form known as Narasiṃha.

10. This is the *padam Uṉṉai kaṇṭu* in the *rāga* Bhairavi.

11. Another instance in the film in which Saroja performs traditional *abhinaya* is the song *Vantaṉaṉ oru cuntari* (A beauty has arrived.), tuned to a so-called folk melody (*tēcikac cintu*). The words for this song are found on page 11 of the songbook (*Kaṇṇaki* songbook, 1942, 11).

12. Listed with Ramaiah Pillai is a man named Pōlānāt. This is Pandit Bholanath Sharma, a Kashmiri who lived in Madras for some time and likely choreographed the sequence depicting the god Śiva dancing at the very beginning of the film, which appears very much to be in the vein of Oriental dancing.

13. Interestingly, in the same film, Ramaiah Pillai choreographed a *tillāṉā* in the *rāga* Khamās for Kumari Rukmani, the heroine of the film. Rukmani, unlike Kamala, was from the *devadāsī* community (she was the daughter of the dancer Nungambakkam Janaki, who eventually became the "second wife" to the filmmaker Y. V. Rao). The *tillāṉā* also bordered on looking like the new kind of athleticized and fast-paced Bharatanāṭyam that Ramaiah Pillai had fully developed by the early 1950s. This was also the case with another *padam*-like sequence that Rukmini performed to the song *Cintai aṟintu vāṭi* (Friend, go figure out his intentions) in the *rāga* Ṣaṇmukhapriyā, in which Ramaiah Pillai narrativized the love lyrics through flashback sequences, making the *padam*-like lyric into a kind of dance drama. This song was so popular that it was repeated and performed with *abhinaya* by the star male actor Sivaji Ganesan (1928–2001) in the film *Kaveri* (The Kāvēri River; 1955).

14. Thavamani Devi (1925–2001) was born in Jaffna, Sri Lanka (formerly Ceylon). She acted in a number of films produced in Madras in the 1940s. It is unclear how or from whom she learned dance and music, but she was famous for her rendition of vocals for the songs her characters sang in the period before the advent of playback singing. She also acted with M. S. Subbulakshmi in *Shakuntalai* (The story of Śakuntalā; 1940), directed by Ellis Dungan.

15. Vasanthakumari was a highly accomplished musician who worked largely in Madras in the early twentieth century. She was the daughter of Madras Lalithangi (c. 1910–55; a noted singer and gramophone artist from the *devadāsī* community) and the Brahmin musician Kutthanur Ayyasvami Ayyar. In addition to being one of the few highly regarded hereditary female musicians to thrive in the new world of twentieth-century Karṇāṭak music in Madras, Vasanthakumari also provided playback vocals for Tamil films between roughly 1946 and 1970. Her daughter, K. Srividya (1953–2006) was a Bharatanāṭyam dancer who studied under Dandayudhapani Pillai and was a very prominent Tamil and Malayalam film star from the 1970s to the mid-1990s. Srividya, the daughter of Vasanthakumari, became the muse for the choreography for the dance music on the record *An Evening of Bharathanatyam*. She is also credited on the cover of the record.

16. The record featured the following compositions: a *jatisvaram* in the *rāga* Haṃsānandi, a *varṇam* in the *rāga* Śaṅkarābharaṇam, and a *tillāṉā* in the *rāga* Hindolam.

17. Uma Anand's 2011 book is titled *Natyakala Chakravarthy K. N. Dandayudapani Pillai: Life and Contribution.*

18. Muthukumara Pillai was born on October 27, 1874. He had connections with most of the major figures in the world of early twentieth century Bharatanāṭyam. He moved from his native village of Kattumannarkoyil (in today's Cuddalore district) to Madras in 1936, where he taught at Kalakshetra for less than a year before joining the troupe of Ram Gopal in Bangalore. He was the first Bharatanāṭyam teacher of Kamala, and when he could no longer teach her, he sent her to learn from Ramaiah Pillai. He also trained V. S. Muthuswami Pillai and K. N. Dandayudhapani Pillai in *naṭṭuvāṅkam*. His involvement with the cinema was minor, even though photography was his hobby. He is known to have choreographed one film, *Kannika* (The virgin; 1947), in which he made a brief appearance as a *naṭṭuvaṉār*. Much has been written about

this on the blog run by Cassidy Behling (2015), and we will also refer to it again in the section on the song *Naṭaṉam āṭiṉār* in chapter 5. Sundaram explains how Muthukumara Pillai became involved with the cinema: "The T. K. Shanmukha brothers (TKS Brothers) had their drama group in the town of Coimbatore. They were seeking for a talented teacher who could teach dance to their actors. When Muthukumaran was returning back to his village from Madanapalli [in Andhra Pradesh, where he stayed for a brief time], the TKS brothers invited him to come to teach in their company. Thus by the end of 1944, Muthukumaran became the dance teacher for the troupe.... When he was in Kovai [Coimbatore], Sriramulu Naidu who was in charge of Pakshi Raja Pictures was preparing to produce his film *Kannika*. He contracted Muthukumaran to be the choreographer for the film" (2002, 43). One of Muthukumaran's chief students, M. K. Saroja, also performed in a couple of films such as *Paittiyakkāraṉ* (Madman; 1947), choreographed by Muthuswami Pillai, and *Nalla Thambi* (The good younger brother; 1949), choreographed by Vedantam Raghaviah and Dandayudhapani Pillai.

19. Udupi Laxminarayan, interviewed by the author, Chennai, August 20, 2012. All quotes from Laxminarayan are from this interview.

20. Chandralekha was a Bharatanāṭyam dancer and choreographer who, like Laxminarayan, was a student of Kanchipuram Ellappa Pillai. She is best remembered as a radical choreographer who broke out of traditional presentations of Bharatanāṭyam, and created a new approach to the dancing body in India by bringing Bharatanāṭyam into conversation with bodily practices such as yoga and indigenous martial arts. For more on Chandralekha, see Bharucha 1995; Chatterjea 2004.

21. For example, in the 1956 Telugu film *Muddu Bidda* (Darling child), Laxminarayan performed the role of the *naṭṭuvaṉār* for a performance by the actress Krishnajyoti, from the *kalāvantula* community, set to a *jāvaḷi* (Soneji 2012, 108–10).

5: GENRE, REPERTOIRE, AND TECHNIQUE IN CINEMA AND ON THE URBAN STAGE

1. For example, the published plays of Caṅkaratās Cuvāmikaḷ who is often considered to be the father of modern Tamil drama, used the term *pāṭṭu* to refer to the songs. However, other plays, such as the *Periya Intiracapā* (date unknown) by the earlier dramaturge T. T. Appāvupiḷḷai (c. 1860–1930) used the term *jāvaḷi* in strategic places to refer to certain kinds of romantic or erotic songs. Davesh Soneji's work on the Parsi theatre in South India (2017) discusses these differences in detail. The term *taru* is also sometimes used, and this comes from the Tamil *kūttu* theatre tradition, in which songs are called *taru*. The term *taru* is also used in *devadāsī kuṟavañci* dramas and the Telugu dramatic tradition in Thanjavur known as Bhāgavata Mēḷa Nāṭaka.

2. The popularity of this composition among traditional performers cannot be understated. It was first published in the Telugu text written by the song's composer, Dīkṣitulu, titled *Saṅgīta Saṃpradāya Pradarśini* (An illumination of the tradition of music) in 1904. It is often claimed that Dīkṣitulu and Pulavar also collaborated on a Tamil drama called *Vaḷḷi Paratam* (Dance of Murukaṉ's consort Vaḷḷi), and that this *svarajati* was initially part of that drama. A version of the drama was staged in the postrevival period by T. Balasaraswati, but printed editions of the text are rare. The

Saṅgīta Saṃpradāya Pradarśini was republished in Tamil script by the Madras Music Academy under the direction of V. Raghavan in 1961–77.

3. The *padam* is generally thought to have its origin in the late seventeenth-century Telugu compositions of a poet referred to as Kṣetrayya, who may or may not have been a real historical figure (see Ramanujan, Narayana Rao, and Shulman 1994). Nevertheless, a group of songs called *kṣetrayya padamulu* (*padams* of Kṣetrayya) first appear in manuscript sources from the early eighteenth century (Davesh Soneji, pers, comm., June 8, 2017). These early Telugu compositions may have formed the basis of the early Tamil *padams* by people such as Cupparāma Aiyar (see the text).

4. For more on the relationship between the *padam* and the *jāvaḷi*, and for a similar argument about the fundamental flexibility and malleability of the *jāvaḷi* as a genre that crosses medial boundaries, see Soneji 2012, 95–111.

5. A slightly later but important example of the malleability of the *padam* genre in cinema comes from the film *Mangayarkarasi* (Queen among women; 1949) in which a *padam* titled *Kātal kaṉiracamē* (You are the sweet essence of love) was written for the film. The dancer was Anjali Devi (discussed in chapter 1), and the choreographer was Vedantam Raghaviah. Here, the new lyrics were grafted onto the tune (*meṭṭu*) of the Sanskrit devotional song (*kīrtana*) *Nāda tanumaniśaṃ śaṅkaram* (Śiva, the embodiment of all sound), composed by Tyāgarāja (1767–1847) in the *rāga* Cittarañjanī. In the new lyric, the devotional register is transformed into an erotic one, yet there is an emphasis on repeating the name of the *rāga*, as if to remind the audience that the piece is thoroughly classical (through its relationship to the original song) despite being a courtesan piece.

6. Aiyar's *padams* were among the most frequently published Tamil songs in the late nineteenth century. I have been able to trace more than twenty editions of collections of them, with the earliest dated 1876 and the latest 1912. Their contents are almost identical. The coherence and consistency with which these songs are represented in print demonstrates how remarkably popular and well-circulated these songs must have been in this period.

7. Aiyar's Tamil *padams* appear in a number of places in the early Tamil cinema, sometimes in a highly coded form. For example, the opening credits of the film *Kalamegam* (Kālamegham [a poet]; 1940), directed by Ellis Dungan, feature the *padam Kaiyil paṇam illāmal* (If you don't have money in hand), but no lyrics are sung—the tune is played on range of instruments.

8. Padma is also briefly discussed in Behling 2013b.

9. As Allen shows, the *padam* seems to have had three *caraṇams*, but there is only one in the film—the one that appears as the second *caraṇam* in most early print editions.

10. *Rati mudrās* were deliberately excised from modern representations of courtesan dance forms throughout South India during the process of their reinvention as classical dance. For more on the use of *rati mudrās* in courtesan performance in coastal Andhra Pradesh, see Soneji 2012, 105 and 217.

11. Page eight of the songbook of the film also contains the text of the Tamil *padam Vēlavarē umait tēṭi oru maṭantai* (Murukaṉ, a young woman has been searching for

you) in the *rāga* Bhairavī, attributed to the composer Kaṉam Kiruṣṇaiyar (c. 1790–1854). This is another example of a Tamil *padam* that very widely circulated among *devadāsīs* and *naṭṭuvaṉārs*. For details on this *padam* in performance, see Allen 1992, 211–12.

12. According to Randor Guy (2008a), the film played at both the Broadway Cinema and Sun Cinema in Madras, beginning on the day of the Hindu festival of Dīpāvalī in 1944, and ran uninterruptedly for 114 weeks until the day of the same festival in 1946—a record for any regional-language film in India.

13. This is one of the earliest available recordings of Ramaiah Pillai's voice. Moreover, the song was apparently a crowd pleaser for a number of reasons—including the fact that in one segment, Rajakumari blows Bhagavathar a kiss. Guy writes: "One particular song celebrating erotic love, "Manmathan leelayai . . . ," drove people crazy and became an all-time hit. Indeed, this song became part of Tamil colloquial idiom! The melody, the simple but effective orchestration, the lyrics, Bhagavathar's sensuous rendering . . . everything was perfect, making the song memorable. . . . In this song, Rajakumari gives Bhagavathar a flying kiss which was considered revolutionary in those days!" (2008a).

14. The Russian ballet dimension comes from Arundale's training with Cleo Nordi. In the 1930s, when Arundale established the International Academy for the Arts (later renamed Kalakshetra), she instituted mandatory ballet classes that she felt would "make the adavus [*aṭavus*] accurate in form" (Sarada 1985, 20–21). This requirement was later dropped.

15. For a translation of Pāmpāṭṭi Cittar's surviving poems, see Buck 1976. On the tradition of the Tamil *cittars* and the encounter of this tradition with modernity in Tamilnadu, see Weiss 2009; Little 2004.

16. The transliteration for the Tamil text of Pāmpāṭṭi Cittar's poem here follows the version found in a popular modern compilation of *cittar* poems (Murukēcaṉ 2004, 189–90).

17. Iyer's work (2014) contains extensive information about the fusion of multiple Indian classical dance styles in the Hindi cinema of the twentieth century.

18. For an excellent discussion of the production, circulation, and consumption of popular devotional music in South India, see Hughes 2014.

19. The other piece is the *kīrtana Ānanda naṭana prakāśam* (Illuminator of the blissful dance), composed in the *rāga* Kedāram by Muddusvāmi Dīkṣitulu (1775–1835). The reference to Meenakashisundaram Pillai's choreographing this piece for Arundale is from G. Ramnarayan 1984, 19.

20. Gaston notes that in the dance performances at the Madras Music Academy's annual conferences, a number of dancers performed *Naṭaṉam āṭiṉār*. Her list for 1944–60 is as follows (including *Naṭṭuvaṉār* names, with VRP for Vazhuvoor Ramaiah Pillai and KND for K. N. Dandayudhapani; the bracketed text is Gaston's): "1944 (P. Jayalakshmi); 1945 (Hemamalini Vijayaraghavan-VRP); 1948 (Anandi, Radha-VRP and Kamala-VRP [twice]); 1949 (Hemamalini Vijayaraghavan-VRP); 1952 (Kamala-VRP); 1953 (Hemamalini Vijayaraghavan-VRP); 1954 (Nirmala Ramachandran-T. Swaminathan); 1955 (Kamala-VRP); 1956 (Chandralekha-K. Ellappa); 1956

(R. K. Jivaratnam-P. M. Mutthaiya and P. C. Subbarayan); 1956 (Kamala-VRP); 1957 (Sarala-Gopalakrishnan [VRP's student]); 1957 (Kamala-VRP); 1957 (Chitralekha [*sic* Chandralekha]-K. Ellappa); 1958 (Kamala, Radha-VRP); 1958 (Vyjayantimala-KND); 1960 (Vyjayantimala-Adyar Lakshman)" (1996, 307).

21. For more on Shankar's use of the image of the dancing Śiva-Naṭarāja, see Brenscheidt gen. Jost 2011.

22. Although Arundale's project under the aegis of the Theosophical Society could be seen as the best example of the alignment of Bharatanāṭyam with a new occultism and the agenda of cultural nationalism, many other such examples followed. Gopal clearly interpreted the dance *naṭaṉam āṭiṉār* as reflecting the otherworldly nature of Bharatanāṭyam. For example, he said, "At the very beginning of the dance, I often preferred to do a few Siva poses and get into a sort of a trance" (quoted in Gaston 1996, 275).

23. For a lengthy discussion of Muttukumara Pillai's appearance in the cinema, see Behling 2015.

24. "Poses" were a feature of modern Bharatanāṭyam choreography that many dancers I interviewed commented upon. For example, the dancer and teacher Nandini Ramani told me: "The problem was, Ramaiah Pillai's style in the films shifted onto the stage. Poses, additional scintillating embellishments . . . made Bharatanāṭyam look attractive and spectacular [on screen]. All this was shifted onto Bharatanāṭyam as it was performed on stage. In earlier days, the dancer on stage would move only forward and backward. Ramaiah Pillai imbued his choreography with sideways and angular walks, and various kinds of walks to cover the stage. Unfortunately, today, the poses [introduced by him] have become Bharatanāṭyam now, directly because of the films. . . . These techniques stemming from cinema are . . . the mainstay of staged versions of Bharatanāṭyam now" (Nandini Ramani, interviewed by the author, Chennai, August 25, 2012). The dancer and teacher Sudharani Raghupathy noted, "Whatever Ramaiah Pillai did was very big [in terms of scale], such as all those massive poses in *Naṭaṉam āṭiṉār*" (Sudharani Raghupathy, interviewed by the author, Chennai, August 19, 2012).

25. Bhaskar Roy Chowdhury (often credited in films as simply "Roy Chowdhury") moved to the United States in 1955. Before that, he worked at Gemini Studio in Madras, where he acted in Gemini's Hindi films such as *Bahut Din Huwe* (Many days have passed; 1954) and *Insaniyat* (Humanity; 1955), in which he was credited as dance director, as well as in Gemini's Tamil films *Kanavane Kankanda Deivam* (One's husband alone is the living god; 1955) and *Rajee En Kanmani* (Rājī my darling: 1954, which was remade in Telugu the same year under the title *Rājī Nā Prāṇam*). He trained in Bharatanāṭyam under Kanchipuram Ellappa Pillai and Pandanallur Chokkalingam Pillai in Madras and had his *araṅkēṟṟam* at Victoria Public Hall in Madras.

CODA: THE ENDURING PEDAGOGICAL AFTERLIVES OF BHARATANĀṬYAM'S CELLULOID CLASSICISM

1. Radhika had a rather extensive performing career as a Bharatanāṭyam dancer. With her sisters Gayathri Krishnamurthy and Shobana Bhalchandra, she gave perfor-

mances as a trio, which earned them the professional nickname "Trio Sisters." They trained for a number of years under V. P. Dhananjayan and his wife, Shanta, a couple who had trained at Kalakshetra. For more than a decade and half, Radhika's career has focused on connecting classical Bharatanāṭyam with the Tamil cinema. She has hosted a number of dance events and stage shows at which old Tamil film songs are reinterpreted in Bharatanāṭyam. For her major contributions, including detailed facts about the TV show *TakaDhimiTa*, see Shurajit n.d.

2. Interviewed by the author, Chennai, August 13, 2012.

3. A middle-class girl's giving an *araṅkēṟṟam* was a necessary element in the new pedagogy of the classical. The *araṅkēṟṟam*—originally a *devadāsī* artist's professional public debut—is transformed into a rite of passage that is a show of a dancer's completion of a basic course in dance. Indeed, the *araṅkēṟṟam* is often translated into English as "dance graduation," especially in the global Indian diaspora. For more on the *araṅkēṟṟam*, see Gaston 1991, 155–56, and 1996. For more about the *araṅkēṟṟam* in the context of *devadāsī* lives, see A. Srinivasan 1984; Kersenboom 1987.

4. For more on Chaudhri's life, see Behling 2013a.

5. For an excellent recent study that discusses the tensions between the perceived monomedial nature of literature and its interface with performance (specifically dance) in eighteenth- and nineteenth-century Britain, see Marcsek-Fuchs 2015.

6. In their extended discussion of the emergence of an idea of the classical in South India, Indira Peterson and Soneji refer to the distinctly classical imperative that governs the reinvention of the performing arts in this region. Not only is the classical an invention of tradition, but it is also a new bourgeois formulation that is inextricably linked to ideas relating to nation, heritage, and civilizational greatness on the one hand, as well as science, theoretical knowledge, and intellectual hegemony on the other hand (Peterson and Soneji 2008, 1–40).

BIBLIOGRAPHY

Abrahams, Ruth. 2007. "Uday Shankar: The Early Years, 1900–1938." *Dance Chronicle* 30 (3): 363–426.

Allen, Matthew Harp. 1992. "The Tamil 'Padam': A Dance Music Genre of South India." PhD diss., Wesleyan University.

———. 1997. "Rewriting the Script for South Indian Dance." *Drama Review* 41 (3): 63–100.

———. 1998. "Tales Tunes Tell: Deepening the Dialogue between 'Classical' and 'Non-Classical' in the Music of India." *Yearbook for Traditional Music* 30:22–52.

Allocco, Amy. 2009. "Snake Goddesses and Anthills: Modern Challenges and Women's Ritual Responses in Contemporary South India." PhD diss., Emory University.

Alter, Joseph. 2000. *Gandhi's Body: Sex, Diet and the Politics of Nationalism*. Philadelphia: University of Pennsylvania Press.

Anand, Uma. 2011. *Natyakala Chakravarthy K. N. Dandayudapani Pillai: Life and Contribution*. Chennai: Subatra Dandayudapani and Uma Anand.

Āṉanta Vikaṭaṉ. 1937. January 31, 17.

Anderson, Benedict. 1983. *Imagined Communities: Reflections on the Origins and Spread of Nationalism*. London: Verso.

Appadurai, Arjun, and Carol A. Breckenridge. 1995. "Public Modernity in India." In *Consuming Modernity: Public Culture in a South Asian World*, edited by Carol A. Breckenridge, 1–22. Minneapolis: University of Minnesota Press.

Araṅkacāmi, Paḻaṉi. 1989. *Tamiḻ Nāṭakam: Toṟṟamum Vaḷarciyum*. Thanjavur: Tamil University.

Arni, Chandra. "Reflections: Foray into Film Land." N.d. Hemamalini. Accessed November 11, 2018. http://www.hemamaliniarni.com/.

Arondekar, Anjali. 2009. *For the Record: On Sexuality and the Colonial Archive in India*. Durham, NC: Duke University Press.

———. 2012. "A Small History of the Gomantak Maratha Samaj." In *South Asian Feminisms: Contemporary Interventions*, edited by Ania Loomba and Ritty A. Lukose, 244–66. Durham, NC: Duke University Press.

Aruna, S. N.d. "'Kumari' Kamala: Bharatanatyam Dancer." Kutcheribuzz.com. Accessed September 4, 2017. http://www.kutcheribuzz.com/features/interviews/kkamala.asp.

Arundale, Rukmini. n.d.a. "Bharata Natya, The Complete Art." In *Some Selected*

Speeches and Writings of Rukmini Devi Arundale, edited by Shakuntala Ramani, 22–29. Chennai: Kalakshetra Foundation.

———. n.d.b. "Handwritten Manuscript on Dance." In *Some Selected Speeches and Writings of Rukmini Devi Arundale*, edited by Shakuntala Ramani, 13–16. Chennai: Kalakshetra Foundation.

———. 1948. "Bhava, Raga, Tala." In *Some Selected Speeches and Writings of Rukmini Devi Arundale*, edited by Shakuntala Ramani, 1:17–21. Chennai: Kalakshetra Foundation.

———. 1958a. "My Experiments with Dance." In *Some Selected Speeches and Writings of Rukmini Devi Arundale*, edited by Shakuntala Ramani, 1:59–66. Chennai: Kalakshetra Foundation.

———. 1958b. "Theatre in India Now." In *Some Selected Speeches and Writings of Rukmini Devi Arundale*, edited by Shakuntala Ramani, 1:85–89. Chennai: Kalakshetra Foundation.

———. 1959. "Indian Dance Today." In *Some Selected Speeches and Writings of Rukmini Devi Arundale*, edited by Shakuntala Ramani, 39–43. Chennai: Kalakshetra Foundation.

Bakhle, Janaki. 2005. *Two Men and Music: Nationalism in the Making of an Indian Classical Tradition*. New York: Oxford University Press.

Balakrishnan, Suresh. 2010. *Bagavather: His Life and Times*. Chennai: Sumithra Balakrishnan.

Balasaraswati, T., and V. Raghavan. 1959. *Paratanāṭṭiyam*. Ceṉṉai: Auvai Nūlakam.

Barnett, Marguerite Ross. 1976. *The Politics of Cultural Nationalism in South India*. Princeton, NJ: Princeton University Press.

Baskaran, Theodore. 1981. *The Message Bearers: The Nationalist Politics and the Entertainment Media in South India, 1880–1945*. Madras: Cre-A.

———. 1996. *The Eye of the Serpent: An Introduction to Tamil Cinema*. Madras: East West Books.

———. 2001. "Persistence of Conventions: 'Company Drama' and the Tamil Cinema." *Seagull Theatre Quarterly* 31:75–88.

———. 2009. *History through the Lens: Perspectives on South Indian Cinema*. Hyderabad: Orient Blackswan.

Bate, Bernard. 2009. *Tamil Oratory and the Dravidian Aesthetic: Democratic Practice in South India*. New York: Columbia University Press.

Behling, Cassidy. 2013a. "Remembering the Late Tara Chaudhri." Cinema Nritya, September 28. cinemanrityagharana.blogspot.com/2013/09/remembering-late-tara-chaudhri.html.

———. 2013b. "Sayee and Subbulakshmi's Film-Industry Relatives: R. Padma, P. A. Perianayaki, and Others (Part 3)." Cinema Nritya, October 5. cinemanrityagharana.blogspot.ca/2013/10/sayee-and-subbulakshmis-film-industry.html.

———. 2015. "Muthukumara Pillai on Screen in *Kannika* (1947), and Other Nattuvanars in Indian Cinema." Cinema Nritya, November 28. cinemanrityagharana.blogspot.com/2015/11/muthukumara-pillai-on-screen-in-kannika.html.

Besant, Annie. 1906. *Children of the Motherland*. Benares: Central Hindu College.

Bharucha, Rustom. 1995. *Chandralekha: Woman, Dance, Resistance*. New Delhi: Indus.

Bhrugubanda, Uma Maheswari. *Deities and Devotees: Cinema, Religion, and Politics in South India*. New Delhi: Oxford University Press, 2018.

Bor, Joep. 2007. "Mamia, Ammani and Other Bayaderes: Europe's Portrayal of India's Temple Dancers." In *Music and Orientalism in the British Empire, 1780s–1940s*, edited by Martin Clayton and Bennett Zon, 39–70. London: Ashgate.

Brannigan, Erin. 2011. *DanceFilm: Choreography and the Moving Image*. New York: Oxford University Press.

Brenscheidt gen. Jost, Diana. 2011. *Shiva Onstage: Uday Shankar's Company of Dancers and Musicians in Europe and the United States, 1931–38*. Berlin: LIT Verlag.

Buck, David C. 1976. *Dance, Snake! Dance! A Translation with Comments of the Song of Pāmpāṭṭi Cittar*. Calcutta: Writers Workshop.

———. 2005. *A Kuravanji in Kuttralam: A Tamil Tale of Love and Fortunes Told*. Chennai: Institute of Asian Studies.

Cabral e Sa, Mario. 1990. "The Evolution of a Community: Devadasis of Goa." *Manushi* 56 (January–February): 25–27.

The Celebrated International Dancer La Meri and the Brilliant Bharatanatya Artists of South India Varalakshmi and Bhanumani. 1937. Madras: Devi Press.

Chakravarthy, N. Manu. 2016. "Dancing with Body and Being." *Hindu*, August 18.

Chakravorty, Pallabi. 1998. "Hegemony, Dance and the Nation: The Construction of the Classical Dance in India." *South Asia* 21 (2): 107–20.

———. 2017. *This Is How We Dance Now: Performance in the Age of Bollywood and Reality Shows*. New Delhi: Oxford University Press.

Chatterjea, Ananya. 2004. *Butting Out: Reading Resistive Choreographies through Willa Jo Zollar and Chandralekha*. Middletown, CT: Wesleyan University Press.

Chatterjee, Partha. 1993. *The Nation and Its Fragments: Colonial and Postcolonial Histories*. Princeton, NJ: Princeton University Press.

"Ciṟiya mēṭaiyil periya viruntu." 1953. *Kuṇṭūci*, April, 4.

Coomaraswamy, Ananda. 1918. *The Dance of Siva: Fourteen Indian Essays*. New York: Sunwise Turn.

Cupparāma Aiyaravarkaḷ Iyaṟṟiya Muttukumāracuvāmipēril Patam [Padam songs composed by Cupparāma Aiyar, Dedicated to Murukaṉ as Muttukumāra]. 1909. Ceṉṉai: Pūmakaḷvilāca Accukkūṭam.

"Dance in the Talkies." 1936. *Silver Screen*, April 4, 2.

David, Ann. 2007. "Beyond the Silver Screen: Bollywood and Filmi Dance in the UK." *South Asia Research* 27 (1): 5–24.

———. 2010. "Dancing the Diasporic Dream? Embodied Desires and the Changing Audiences for Bollywood Film Dance." *Participations* 7 (2). http://www.participations.org/Volume%207/Issue%202/PDF/david.pdf.

Davis, Janet. 1993. "Spectacles of South Asia at the American Circus, 1890–1940." *Visual Anthropology* 6 (2): 121–38.

De Bruin, Hanne. 1999. *Kaṭṭaikkūttu: The Flexibility of a South Indian Theatre Tradition*. Groningen, the Netherlands: Egbert Forsten.

Deleuze, Gilles. 1989. *Cinema 2: The Time-Image*. Trans. Hugh Tomlinson and Robert Galeta. Minneapolis: University of Minnesota Press.

Dhananjayan, G. 2014. *Pride of Tamil Cinema: 1931–2013*. Chennai: Blue Ocean Publishers.

Dickey, Sara. 2009. *Cinema and the Urban Poor in South India*. Cambridge: Cambridge University Press.

Dīkṣitula, Subbarāma. 1904. *Saṅgīta Saṃpradāya Pradarśini*. Ettayapuram: Vidya Vilasini Press.

Dodd, Sherril. 2001. *Dance on Screen: Genres and Media from Hollywood to Experimental Art*. New York: Palgrave Macmillan.

Du Perron, Lalita. 2007. *Hindi Poetry in a Musical Genre: Thumri Lyrics*. London: Routledge.

Dwyer, Rachel. 2006. *Filming the Gods: Religion and Indian Cinema*. London: Routledge.

———. 2011. "The Case of the Missing Mahatma: Gandhi and the Hindi Cinema." *Public Culture* 23 (2): 349–76.

Ebeling, Sascha. Forthcoming. "The Scandal of the Devadāsī in Nineteenth-Century Tamil Theater: Caitapuram Kacivicuvanata Mutaliyar's Drama *Tampacari Vilacam*." In *Dance and the Early South Indian Cinema*, edited by Hari Krishnan, Davesh Soneji, and Tiziana Leucci. New Delhi: Oxford University Press.

Eck, Diana. 1981. *Darśan: Seeing the Divine Image in India*. Chambersburg, PA: Anima Books.

Erdman, Joan L. 1987. "Performance as Translation: Uday Shankar in the West." *Drama Review* 31 (1): 64–88.

———. 1996. "Dance Discourses: Rethinking the History of the 'Oriental Dance.'" In *Moving Words: Rewriting Dance*, edited by Gay Morris, 288–305. London: Routledge.

"Es. Ṭi. Cuppulakṣmi: Vāḻkkai Varṇaṉai." 1952. *Kuṇṭūci*, 13–16 and 66–71.

Fernandez, Jean. 2005. "Graven Images: The Woman Writer, the Indian Poetess, and Imperial Aesthetics in L. E. L.'s *Hindoo Temples and Palaces at Madura*." *Victorian Poetry* 43 (1): 35–52.

Frost, Christine Mangala. 2007. "Bhakti and Nationalism in the Poetry of Subramania Bharati." *International Journal of Hindu Studies* 10 (2): 151–67.

Fuller, C. J., and Haripriya Narasimhan. 2014. *Tamil Brahmans: The Making of a Middle-Class Caste*. Chicago: University of Chicago Press.

Gaston, Anne-Marie. 1991. "Dance and the Hindu Woman: Bharatanatyam Re-Ritualized." In *Roles and Rituals for Hindu Women*, edited by Julia Leslie, 149–72. Rutherford, NJ: Fairleigh Dickinson University Press.

———. 1996. *Bharata Natyam: From Temple to Theatre*. New Delhi: Manohar Publications.

Geetha, V., and S. V. Rajadurai. 1998. *Towards a Non-Brahmin Millennium: From Iyothee Thass to Periyar*. Calcutta: Samya Books.

Gopal, Sangita, and Sujata Moorti, eds. 2008. *Global Bollywood: Travels of Hindi Song and Dance*. Minneapolis: University of Minnesota Press.

Gopalan, Lalitha. 2002. *Cinema of Interruptions: Action Genres in Contemporary Indian Cinema*. London: British Film Institute.

Guha-Thakurta, Tapati. 1986. "Westernization and Tradition in South Indian Painting in the Nineteenth Century: The Case of Raja Ravi Varma (1848–1906)." *Studies in History* 2 (2): 165–95.

Gupt, Somnath. 2005. *The Parsi Theatre: Its Origin and Development*. Translated by Kathryn Hansen. Calcutta: Seagull Books.

Gurumurthy, Prameela. 1994. *Kalakalakshepa: A Study*. Madras: International Society for the Investigation of Ancient Civilizations.

Guy, Randor. 1997. *Starlight, Starbright: The Early Tamil Cinema*. Madras: Amra Publishers.

———. 2007. "Sri Valli—1945." *Hindu*, December 28. thehindu.com/todays-paper/tp-features/tp-cinemaplus/sri-valli-1945/article3024163.ece.

———. 2008a. "Haridas 1944." *Hindu*, July 11. thehindu.com/todays-paper/tp-features/tp-cinemaplus/haridas-1944/article3023110.ece.

———. 2008b. "Krishna Bhakthi 1948." *Hindu*, February 15. thehindu.com/todays-paper/tp-features/tp-cinemaplus/krishna-bhakthi-1948/article3022555.ece.

———. 2010. "Jagathalaprathapan 1944." *Hindu*, August 14. thehindu.com/todays paper/tp-features/tp-metroplus/Jagathalaprathapan-1944/article16130728.ece.

———. 2013. "Devadasi (1948)." *Hindu*, June 8. thehindu.com/features/cinema/cinema-columns/devadasi-1948/article4794918.ece.

———. 2015. "The Ratnam Brand of Comedy." *Hindu*, February 5. http://www.thehindu.com/features/friday-review/in-lighter-vein-column-kali-n-ratnam-ct-rajakantham/article6860504.ece.

Hancock, Mary. 1999. *Womanhood in the Making: Domestic Ritual and Public Culture in Urban South India*. Boulder, CO: Westview Press.

Hansen, Kathryn. 1999. "Making Women Visible: Gender and Race Cross-Dressing in the Parsi Theatre." *Theatre Journal* 51 (2): 127–47.

———. 2001. "Theatrical Transvestism in the Parsi, Gujarati and Marathi Theatres (1850–1940)." *South Asia* 24 (supplement 1): 59–73.

———. 2003. "Languages on Stage: Linguistic Pluralism and Community Formation in the Nineteenth-Century Parsi Theatre." *Modern Asian Studies* 37 (2): 381–405.

———. 2009. "Staging Composite Culture: Nautanki and Parsi Theatre in Recent Revivals." *South Asia Research* 29 (2): 151–68.

———. 2011. *Stages of Life: Indian Theatre Autobiographies*. New Delhi: Permanent Black.

———. 2018. "Parsi Theatrical Networks in Southeast Asia: The Contrary Case of Burma." *Journal of Southeast Asian Studies* 49 (1): 4–33.

Hardgrave, R. L. 1975. "When Stars Displace the Gods: The Folk Culture of Cinema in Tamil Nadu." Occasional Paper No. 3, Center for Asian Studies, University of Texas at Austin.

———. 2008. "Politics and the Film in Tamil Nadu: The Stars and the DMK." In

Tamil Cinema: The Cultural Politics of India's Other Film Industry, edited by Selvaraj Velayutham, 59–76. London: Routledge.

Hariharan, K. 1995. "Who Is the Bad Guy? Commercial Cinema in the South." In *Frames of Mind: Reflections on Indian Cinema*, edited by Aruna Vasudev, 191–96. New Delhi: UBS Publishers.

Hawley, John Stratton. 2012. *Three Bhakti Voices: Mirabai, Surdas, and Kabir in Their Times and Ours*. New Delhi: Oxford University Press.

Hughes, Stephen Putnam. 1996. "Is There Anyone out There? Exhibition and Formation of Silent Film Audiences in South India." PhD diss., University of Chicago.

———. 2002. "The 'Music Boom' in Tamil South India: Gramophone, Radio, and the Making of Mass Culture." *Historical Journal of Film, Radio and Television* 22 (4): 445–73.

———. 2007. "Music in the Age of Mechanical Reproduction: Drama, Gramophone, and the Beginnings of Tamil Cinema." *Journal of Asian Studies* 66 (1): 3–34.

———. 2010a. "What Is Tamil about Tamil Cinema?" *South Asian Popular Culture* 8 (3): 213–29.

———. 2010b. "When Film Came to Madras." *Bioscope* 1 (2): 147–68.

———. 2014. "Play It Again, Saraswathi: Gramophone, Religion and Devotional Music in South India." In *More Than Bollywood: Studies in Indian Popular Music*, edited by Gregory D. Booth and Bradley Shope, 114–41. New York: Oxford University Press, 2014.

———. Forthcoming. "Intermediaries on Stage and Screen: Cinema Stage-Dance and the Making of Tamil Cinema." In *Dance and the Early South Indian Cinema*, edited by Hari Krishnan, Davesh Soneji, and Tiziana Leucci. New Delhi: Oxford University Press.

Indraganti, Kiranmayi. 2016. *Her Majestic Voice: South Indian Female Playback Singers and Stardom, 1945–1955*. New Delhi: Oxford University Press.

Inoue, Takako. 2008. "Between Art and Religion: Bhagavata Mela in Thanjavur." In *Music and Society in South Asia*, edited by Yoshitaka Terada, 103–36. Osaka, Japan: National Museum of Ethnology.

Irschick, Eugene F. 1986. *Tamil Revivalism in the 1930s*. Madras: Cre-A.

Isvaran, Manjeri S. 1949. *No Ankletbells for Her*. Madras: Mitra.

Iyer, Usha. 2014. "Film Dance, Female Stardom, and the Production of Gender in Popular Hindi Cinema." PhD diss., University of Pittsburgh.

Jacob, Preminda. 1997. "From Co-Star to Deity: Popular Representations of Jayalalitha Jayaram." In *Representing the Body: Gender Issues in Indian Art*, edited by Vidya Dehejia, 140–65. New Delhi: Kali for Women.

———. 2008. *Celluloid Deities: The Visual Culture of Cinema and Politics in South India*. Lanham, MD: Lexington Books.

Jain, Kajri. 2005. "Figures of Locality and Tradition: Commercial Cinema and the Networks of Visual Print Capitalism in Maharashtra." In *Bollywood: Popular Indian Cinema Through a Transnational Lens*, edited by Raminder Kaur and Ajay J. Sinha, 70–89. New Delhi: Sage Publications.

———. 2007. *Gods in the Bazaar: The Economies of Indian Calendar Art*. Durham, NC: Duke University Press.

Jonnalagadda, Anuradha. 1996. "Tradition and Innovations in Kuchipudi Dance." PhD diss., University of Hyderabad.

Jordan, Kay. 2003. *From Sacred Servant to Profane Prostitute: A History of the Changing Legal Status of the Devadasis in India, 1857–1947*. New Delhi: Manohar.

Kaali, Sundar. 2013. "Disciplining the Dasi: *Chintamani* and the Politics of a New Sexual Economy." *Bioscope* 4 (1): 51–69.

Kaimal, Padma. 1999. "Shiva-Nataraja: Shifting Meanings of an Icon." *Art Bulletin* 81 (3): 390–419.

Kannan, B., and Gayatri Kannan. 2004. *Nrithyodaya Jubilee Commemoration Volume*. Chennai: Nrithyodaya.

Kapur, Geeta. 2000. *When Was Modernism? Essays on Contemporary Cultural Practice in India*. New Delhi: Tulika Books.

Katrak, Ketu H. 1992. "Indian Nationalism, Gandhian "Satyagraha,' and Representations of Female Sexuality." In *Nationalisms and Sexualities*, edited by Andrew Parker, Mary Russo, Doris Summer, and Patricia Yaeger, 395–406. New York: Routledge.

Kersenboom, Saskia. 1987. *Nityasumangali: Devadasi Tradition in South India*. New Delhi: Motilal Banarsidass, 1987.

Kinnear, Michael S. 1994. *The Gramophone Company's First Indian Recordings, 1899–1908*. New Delhi: Popular Prakashan.

Kiruṣṇamūrtti. 1949. "Paratamum Āṇkaḷum." *Kuṇṭūcī, Āṇṭu Malar*, 100–103.

Kiruṣṇamūrtti, A. Rā. 1953. "Nāṭṭiya Muttiraikaḷ [Gestures of dance]." *Kuṇṭūci*, April, 26–27.

Kiruṣṇamūrtti, Ku. Cā. 1979. *Tamiḻ Nāṭaka Varalāṟu*. Ceṉṉai: Vāṉati Patippakam.

Kishore, Vikrant, and Susan Kerrigan. 2016. "Designing the Song and Dance Sequences: Exploring Bollywood's Cinematic Creativity." In *Salaam Bollywood: Representations and Interpretations*, edited by Vikrant Kishore, Amit Sarwal, and Parichay Patra, 112–36. New Delhi: Routledge India.

Knight, Douglas M. 2010. *Balasaraswati: Her Life and Art*. Middletown, CT: Wesleyan University Press.

Krishna Iyer, E. 1932. "A Reply to Dr. Muthulakshmi Reddy." *Madras Mail*, December 17.

———. 1948. "Renaissance of Indian Dance and Its Architects." In *Souvenir of the Sixteenth South Indian Music Conference*, 20–25. Madras: Indian Fine Arts Society.

Krishnan, Hari. 2008. "Inscribing Practice: Reconfigurations and Textualizations of Devadasi Repertoire in Nineteenth and Early Twentieth Century South India." In *Performing Pasts: Reinventing the Arts in Modern South India*, edited by Indira Viswanathan Peterson and Davesh Soneji, 71–89. New Delhi: Oxford University Press.

———. 2009. "From Gynemimesis to Hypermasculinity: The Shifting Orientations of Male Performers of South Indian Court Dance." In *When Men Dance:*

Choreographing Masculinities Across Borders, edited by Jennifer Fisher and Anthony Shay, 378–91. New York: Oxford University Press.

"Kuḻantaikaḷē Periyavarkaḷāka Ākiṟārkaḷ [The one who has grown from being a child to an adult]." 1936. *Āṭal Pāṭal, Āṇṭu Malar*, 51.

Kuṇṭūci. 1952. December, 76.

Kurucāmitās, Ke. 1937. *Kaliyukattil Naṭaṉamiṭum Ṭākkīs Paritāpac Cintu*. Self-published.

"Kuṭumpa Stirikaḷum Ciṉimāvum [Family women and cinema]." 1938. *Āṭal Pāṭal*, year-end issue, 43.

La Meri. 1941. *The Gesture Language of the Hindu Dance*. New York: Columbia University Press Press.

Lakshmi, C. S. 1995. "Seduction, Speeches and Lullaby: Gender and Cultural Identity in a Tamil Film." *Economic and Political Weekly* 30 (6): 309–11.

———. 2008. "A Good Woman, a Very Good Woman: Tamil Cinema's Women." In *Tamil Cinema: The Cultural Politics of India's Other Film Industry*, edited by Selvaraj Velayutham, 16–28. London: Routledge.

Lal, Vinay, and Ashis Nandy. 2007. "Introduction: Popular Cinema and the Culture of Indian Politics." In *Fingerprinting Popular Culture: The Mythic and Iconic in Indian Cinema*, edited by Vinay Lal and Ashis Nandy, i–xxvii. New Delhi: Oxford University Press.

Leucci, Tiziana. 2005. *Devadasi e Bayaderes: Tra storia e leggenda*. Bologna, Italy: Cooperativa Libraria Universitaria Editrice Bologna.

———. 2009. "Du Dasi Attam au Bharata Natyam: Ethno-histoire d'une Tradition Chorégraphique et de sa Moralisation et Nationalisation dans l'Inde Coloniale et Post-coloniale." PhD diss., École des Hautes Études en Sciences Sociales.

———. Forthcoming. "Patronage of Hereditary Performing Artists in Tamil Cinema: The Case of V. S. Muthuswamy Pillai." In *Dance and the Early South Indian Cinema*, edited by Hari Krishnan, Davesh Soneji, and Tiziana Leucci. New Delhi: Oxford University Press.

Little, Layne Ross. 2004. "Bowl Full of Sky: Story-Making and the Many Lives of the Siddha Bhogar." PhD diss., University of California, Berkeley.

Lubelsky, Isaac. 2012. *Celestial India: Madame Blavatsky and the Birth of Indian Nationalism*. Sheffield, UK: Equinox Publishing.

Maciszewski, Amelia. 1998. "Gendered Stories, Gendered Styles: Contemporary Hindusthani Music as Discourse, Attitudes, and Practice." PhD diss., University of Texas.

———. 2006. "Tawa'if, Tourism, and Tales: The Problematics of Twenty-First-Century Musical Patronage for North India's Courtesans." In *The Courtesan's Arts: Cross-Cultural Perspectives*, edited by Martha Feldman and Bonnie Gordon, 332–52. New York: Oxford University Press.

———. 2007. "Texts, Tunes, and Talking Heads: Discourses about Socially Marginal North Indian Musicians." *Twentieth Century Music* 3 (1): 121–44.

Majumdar, Neepa. 2009. *Wanted, Cultured Ladies Only: Female Stardom and Cinema in India, 1930s–1950s*. Champaign: University of Illinois Press, 2009.

Mālavikā. 1950. "Nāṭṭiyam Paṭum Pāṭu [The hardship dance is facing]." *Kuṇṭūci*, August, 44.
Manalane Mangayin Bhagyam—Tom Tana Na Tana—classic Tamil song. N.d. Accessed November 11, 2018. https://www.youtube.com/watch?v=pRMxoeftPB8.
Mangai, A., and V. Arasu. 2009. "Ushering Changes: Constructing the History of Tamil Theatre during Colonial Times through Drama Notices." In *Theatre in Colonial India: Play-House of Power*, edited by Lata Singh, 105–31. New Delhi: Oxford University Press.
Marcsek-Fuchs, Maria. 2015. *Dance and British Literature: An Intermedial Encounter*. Leiden, the Netherlands: Brill Rodopi.
Martin-Kershaw, Nancy. 1997. "Dyed Deep in the Color of Her Lord: Multiple Representations of Mirabai." PhD diss., Graduate Theological Union.
Meduri, Avanthi. 1996. "Nation, Woman, Representation: The Sutured History of the Devadasi and Her Dance." PhD diss., New York University.
———. 2008. "Temple Stage as Historical Allegory in Bharatanāṭyam." In *Performing Pasts: Reinventing the Arts in Modern South India*, edited by Indira Viswanathan Peterson and Davesh Soneji, 133–64. New Delhi: Oxford University Press.
Menon, Kalyani Devaki. 2010. *Everyday Nationalism: Women of the Hindu Right in India*. Philadelphia: University of Pennsylvania Press.
"Miruṇāḷiṉiyiṉ Ariya Cēvai." 1949. *Kuṇṭūci*, August, 6–7.
Morcom, Anna. 2013. *Illicit Worlds of Indian Dance: Cultures of Exclusion*. London: Hurst.
Mudaliar, Preeti, and Joyojeet Pal. 2016. "Watching from an Arm's Length: The Foreign Hand in Tamil Cinema." *Communication, Culture and Critique* 9 (2): 231–49.
Muilwijk, Marina. 1996. *The Divine Kura Tribe: Kuravanci and Other Tamil Prabandhas*. Groningen, the Netherlands: Egbert Forsten.
Mukhopadhyay, Urvi. 2011. "Addressing the Masses: Gandhi's Notion of 'The People' and Indian Cinema's Popular Market." *South Asian History and Culture* 2 (3): 417–30.
Mukta, Parita. 1994. *Upholding the Common Life: The Community of Mirabai*. New Delhi: Oxford University Press.
Murukēcaṉ, Ci. Es., editor. 2004. *Cittar Pāṭalkaḷ (Periya Ñāṉakkōvai)*. Ceṉṉai: Caṅkar Patippakam.
Nakassis, Constantine. 2016. *Doing Style: Youth and Mass Mediation in South India*. Chicago: University of Chicago Press.
"Naṭaṉa cakōtarikal Yōkam-Maṅkaḷam: Vāḻkkai varṇaṉai [The dancing sisters Yogam Mangalam: A description of their lives]." 1948. *Kuṇṭūci*, February, 16–21.
Natarajan, Srividya. 1997. "Another Stage in the Life of the Nation: Sadir, Bharatanatyam, Feminist Theory." PhD diss., University of Hyderabad.
"Nāṭṭiya Mōhiṉi Maṅkaḷam [The dancing enchantress Mangalam]." 1946. *Pēcum Paṭam*, June, 3–6.
"Natyacharya Vazhuvoor Ramaiah Pillai: A Creative Master in the Traditional

Mould." 1986. Translated from Tamil by Sujatha Vijayaraghavan. *Sruti*, November, 17–28.
Neumayer, Erwin, and Christine Schelberger. 2003. *Popular Indian Art: Raja Ravi Varma and the Printed Gods of India*. New Delhi: Oxford University Press.
———. 2005. *Portrait of an Artist: The Diary of C. Raja Raja Varma*. New Delhi: Oxford University Press.
Nijhawan, Amita. 2009. "Excusing the Female Dancer: Tradition and Transgression in Bollywood Dancing." *South Asian Popular Culture* 7 (2): 99–112.
Orr, Leslie. 2000. *Donors, Devotees, and Daughters of God: Temple Women in Medieval Tamil Nadu*. New York: Oxford University Press.
O'Shea, Janet. 2006. "Dancing through History and Ethnography: Indian Classical Dance and the Performance of the Past." In *Dancing from Past to Present: Nation, Culture, Identities*, edited by Theresa Jill Buckland, 123–52. Madison: University of Wisconsin Press.
———. 2007. *At Home in the World: Bharata Natyam on the Global Stage*. Middletown, CT: Wesleyan University Press.
Panam. 1952. "Kudumbathin Vilakku." N.d. Accessed November 11, 2018. https://www.youtube.com/watch?v=10mi4RoFReE.
Pande, Mrinal. 2006. "Moving beyond Themselves: Women in Hindustani Parsi Theatre and Early Indian Cinema." *Economic and Political Weekly* 41 (17): 1646–53.
Pandian, Anand. 2015. *Reel World: An Anthropology of Creation*. Durham, NC: Duke University Press.
Pandian, M. S. S. 1992. *The Image Trap: M. G. Ramachandran in Film and Politics*. New Delhi: Sage Publications.
———. 1996. "Tamil Cultural Elites and Cinema: Outline of an Argument." *Economic and Political Weekly* 13 (15): 950–55.
———. 2007. *Brahmin and Non-Brahmin: Genealogies of the Tamil Political Present*. New Delhi: Permanent Black.
"*Pārati nāṭṭiyam*." 1939. *Hanumāṉ*, year-end issue, 44–47.
Parekh, Bhikhu. 1991. "Nehru and the National Philosophy of India." *Economic and Political Weekly* 26 (1–2): 35–39.
Patmanāpaṉ, Arimaḷam Cu. 2000. *Tavattiru Caṅkaratās Cuvāmikaliṉ Nāṭakaṅkaḷil Icaikkūrukal*. Putuccēri: Icait Teral.
———. 2002. *Caṅkaratās Cuvāmikaliṉ Cantaṅkaḷ*. Putuccēri: Icait Teral.
———. 2008. *Caṅkaratās Cuvāmikaliṉ Nāṭakak Kalañciyam*. Ceṉṉai: Kāvyā.
Pattabhi Raman, N. 1992. "Bharatanatyam Artist K. Bhanumathi: A True Exponent of the Art." *Sruti*, winter bumper issue, 25–29.
"Pēcum Paṭaṅkaḷil Naṭaṉam." *1936. Silver Screen*, April 4, 1.
Perez, Rosa Maria. 2005. "The Rhetoric of Empire: Gender Representations in Portuguese India." *Portuguese Studies* 21 (1): 126–41.
Perumal, A. N. 1977. *Tamiḻ Nāṭakattiṉ Tōṟṟamum Vaḷarcciyum*. Ceṉṉai: Aṇiyakam.
———. 1981. *Tamil Drama: Origin and Development*. Madras: International Institute of Tamil Studies.
———. 1988. *Irupatām Nūṟṟāṇṭatil Tamiḻ Nāṭakam*. Ceṉṉai: Tēṉmaḻaip Patippakam.

Peterson, Indira Viswanathan. 1998. "The Evolution of the Kuravanci Dance-Drama in Tamil Nadu: Negotiating the 'Folk' and the 'Classical' in the Bharata Natyam Canon." *South Asia Research* 18 (1):. 39–72.

———. 2008a. "The Drama of the Kuravanci Fortune-Teller: Land, Landscape and Social Relations in an Eighteenth Century Tamil Genre." In *Tamil Geographies: Cultural Constructions of Space and Place in South India*, edited by Indira V. Peterson and Martha Ann Selby, 59–86. Albany: State University of New York Press.

———. 2008b. "Rewriting Cultural History through the Novel: Kalaimani's *Tillana Mohanambal*." In *Performing Pasts: Reinventing the Arts in Modern South India*, edited by Indira Viswanathan Peterson and Davesh Soneji, 252–80. New Delhi: Oxford University Press.

Peterson, Indira Viswanathan, and Davesh Soneji. 2008. Introduction to *Performing Pasts: Reinventing the Arts in Modern South India*, edited by Indira Viswanathan Peterson and Davesh Soneji, 1–42. New Delhi: Oxford University Press.

Pillai, Swarnavel Eswaran. 2015. *Madras Studios: Narrative, Genre, and Ideology in Tamil Cinema*. New Delhi: Sage Publications.

Pinney, Christopher. 2004. *Photos of the Gods: The Printed Image and Political Struggle in India*. New Delhi: Oxford University Press.

———. 2014. "The Look of History: The Power of the Aesthetic." In *New Cultural Histories of India: Materiality and Practices*, edited by Partha Chatterjee, Tapati Guha-Thakurta, and Bodhisattva Kar, 115–38. New Delhi: Oxford University Press.

Plass, Ulrich. 2009. "Dialectic of Regression: Theodor W. Adorno and Fritz Lang." *Telos* 149 (winter): 127–50.

Premchand, Munshi. 2005. *Sevasadan*. Translated by Snehal Shingavi. New Delhi: Oxford University Press.

Purkayastha, Prarthana. 2012. "Dancing Otherness: Nationalism, Transnationalism and the Work of Uday Shankar." *Dance Research Journal* 44 (1): 69–92.

Putcha, Rumya Sree. 2011. "Revisiting the Classical: A Critical History of Kuchipudi Dance." PhD diss., University of Chicago.

Qureshi, Regula. 2006. "Female Agency and Patrilineal Constraints: Situating Courtesans in Twentieth-Century India." In *The Courtesan's Arts: Cross-Cultural Perspectives*, edited by Martha Feldman and Bonnie Gordon, 312–31. New York: Oxford University Press, 2006.

Racy, A. J. 2016. "Domesticating Otherness: The Snake Charmer in Popular American Culture." *Ethnomusicology* 60 (2): 197–232.

"Radhika Shurajit's Dance Show Based on Evergreen Tamil Film Songs." 2012. YouTube. November 2. www.youtube.com/watch?v=HskmkUFyHoo.

Rāju, Pi. Vi. Irāmacāmi. 1877. *Piratāpacantira Vilācam*. Madras: C. Foster.

Ramani, Shakuntala. 2003. *Rukmini Devi Arundale: Birth Centenary Volume*. Chennai: Kalakshetra Foundation.

Ramanujan, A. K, Velcheru Narayana Rao, and David Shulman. 1994. *When God Is a Customer: Telugu Courtesan Songs by Ksetrayya and Others*. Berkeley: University of California Press.

Ramaswamy, Sumathi. 1997. *Passions of the Tongue: Language Devotion in Tamil India, 1891–1970*. Berkeley: University of California Press.

———. 2010. *The Goddess and the Nation: Mapping Mother India*. Durham, NC: Duke University Press.

Ramaiah Pillai, Vazhuvoor. 1954. "Nāṭṭiyam Āṭiyum Payaṉillai [There is no point to dancing]," *Citrā, Āṇṭu Malar*, 27–28.

Ramnarayan, Akhila. 2006. "Kalki's Avatars: Writing Nation, History, Region, and Culture in the Tamil Public Sphere." PhD diss., Ohio State University.

Ramnarayan, Gowri. 1984. "Rukmini Devi: Dancer and a Reformer (Part 2)." *Sruti*, July, 17–29.

Ranga Rao, V. A. K. 1988. "Excellence on the Filmic Grid." *Sruti*, July, 35–36.

———. 1995. "Dance in Indian Cinema." In *Rasa: The Indian Performing Arts in the Last Twenty-Five Years*, edited by Sunil Kothari and Bimal Mukherjee, 87–92. Calcutta: Anamika Kala Sangam.

Rangarajan, M. R. 2005. *K. Subrahmanyam: A Biography*. Madras: East-West Books.

Rogers, Martyn. 2009. "Between Fantasy and 'Reality': Tamil Film Star Fan Club Networks and the Political Economy of Film Fandom." *South Asia* 32 (1): 63–85.

Rosenberg, Douglas. 2012. *Screendance: Inscribing the Ephemeral Image*. New York: Oxford University Press.

Rudisill, Kristen. 2007. "Brahmin Humor: Chennai's Sabha Theater and the Creation of Middle-Class Indian Taste from the 1950s to the Present." PhD diss., University of Texas.

Sabapathy—Naan Angae Song. N.d. Accessed November 11, 2018. https://www.youtube.com/watch?v=TWGUuXjOKo8.

Sachdeva, Shweta. 2008. "In Search of the Tawa'if in History: Courtesans, Nautch Girls and Celebrity Entertainers in India (1720s–1920s)." PhD diss., SOAS–University of London.

Sampath Kumar. 1951. "Ṭi. Ār. Rājakumāri Vāḻkkaic Cittiram." *Pēcum Paṭam*, 1951, 44–57.

Samson, Leela. 2010. *Rukmini Devi: A Life*. New Delhi: Penguin Books India.

Sarada, S. 1985. *Kalakshetra Rukmini Devi: Reminiscences*. Madras: Kala Mandir Trust.

Schultz, Anna. 2012. *Singing a Hindu Nation: Marathi Devotional Performance and Nationalism*. New York: Oxford University Press.

Seizer, Susan. 2005. *Stigmas of the Tamil Stage: An Ethnography of Special Drama Artists in South India*. Durham, NC: Duke University Press.

Shresthova, Sangita. 2011. *Is It All about Hips? Around the World with Bollywood Dance*. New Delhi: Sage.

Shurajit, Radhika. n.d. Radhika Shurajit: Dancer, Teacher, Choreographer. Accessed September 23, 2018. radhikashurajit.com.

Sinha, Mrinalini. 1995. *Colonial Masculinity: The "Many Englishman" and the "Effeminate Bengali" in the Late Nineteenth Century*. Manchester, UK: Manchester University Press.

Sivathamby, Karthigesu. 1981. *The Tamil Film as a Medium of Political Communication*. Madras: New Century Book House.

Soneji, Davesh. 2004. "Performing Satyabhāmā: Text, Context, Memory and Mimesis in Telugu-Speaking South India." PhD diss., McGill University.

———. ed. 2010a. *Bharatanāṭyam: A Reader*. New Delhi: Oxford University Press.

———. 2010b. "Śiva's Courtesans: Religion, Rhetoric and Self-Representation in Early Twentieth-Century Writing by Devadāsīs." *International Journal of Hindu Studies* 14 (1): 31–70.

———. 2012. *Unfinished Gestures: Devadāsīs, Memory, and Modernity in South India*. Chicago: University of Chicago Press.

———. 2013. "The Powers of Polyglossia: Marathi Kīrtan, Multilingualism and the Making of a South Indian Devotional Tradition." *International Journal of Hindu Studies* 17 (3): 339–69.

———. 2017. "*Indra's Court* in Madras: The Urdu Theatre and the Cosmopolitan Origins of Modern Tamil 'Musical Drama.'" Paper presented at the 46th Annual Conference on South Asia at University of Wisconsin, Madison, October 28.

Sreenivas, Mytheli. 2003. "Emotion, Identity, and the Female Subject: Tamil Women's Magazines in Colonial India, 1890–1940." *Journal of Women's History* 14 (4): 59–82.

———. 2008. *Wives, Widows, and Concubines: The Conjugal Family Ideal in Colonial India*. Bloomington: Indiana University Press.

Sri Rajarajeswari Bharatha Natya Kala Mandir. 2010. http://www.bharathanatyam.com/raj.html.

Srilata, K. 2003. *The Other Half of the Coconut: Women Writing Self-Respect History*. New Delhi: Kali for Women.

Srinivas, Lakshmi. 2016. *House Full: Indian Cinema and the Active Audience*. Chicago: University of Chicago Press.

Srinivas, S. V. 2013. *Politics as Performance: A Social History of the Telugu Cinema*. New Delhi: Permanent Black

Srinivasan, Amrit. 1984. "Temple 'Prostitution' and Community Reform: An Examination of the Ethnographic, Historical and Textual Context of the Devadasi of Tamil Nadu, South India." PhD diss., Cambridge University.

Srinivasan, Perundevi. 2014. "Nationalist Fabric, Gendering Threads: Notes on Subramaniya Bharati's Draupadi." *International Journal of Hindu Studies* 18 (1): 1–31.

Srinivasan, R. 1919. *Mīrāpāy, Meerabai: An Interesting and Instructive Tamil Drama*. Madurai: Kalvi Publishing House.

Sriram, V. 2009. *Four Score and More: A History of the Madras Music Academy*. Chennai: Madras Music Academy.

Stone, Lawrence. 1971. "Proposography." *Daedalus* 100 (1): 46–79.

Subrahmanyam, Padma. 1997. *Nāṭyaśāstra and National Unity*. Tripunithura: Sri Ramavarma Government Sanskrit College.

Subrahmanyam, Sanjay. 1999. "Friday's Child: Or How Tej Singh Became Tecinkurajan." *Indian Economic and Social History Review* 36 (1): 69–113.

Subramanian, Lakshmi. 2006. *From the Tanjore Court to the Madras Music Academy: A Social History of Music in South India*. New Delhi: Oxford University Press.
Sugimoto, Yoshio. 2008. "'Boys Be Ambitious': Popular Theatre, Popular Cinema and Tamil Nationalism." In *Music and Society in South Asia: Perspectives from Japan*, edited by Yoshitaka Terada, 229–40. Osaka, Japan: National Museum of Ethnology.
Sundara Rajan, Mira T. 2001. "Moral Rights in the Public Domain: Copyright Matters in the Works of Indian National Poet C. Subramania Bharati." *Singapore Journal of Legal Studies* 2001:161–95.
Sundaram, B. M. 2001. *Maṅkaḷa Icai Maṉṉarkaḷ*. Citamparam: Meyappaṉ Patipakkam.
———. 2002. *Marapu Vaḻi Paratap Pērācāṉkaḷ*. Citamparam: Meyappaṉ Tamiḻāyvakam.
———. 2003. *Marapu Tanta Māṇikkaṅkaḷ*. Chennai: Raghavan Centre for the Performing Arts.
Suvarna Sundari Full-Length Telugu Movie. N.d. Accessed November 11, 2018. https://www.youtube.com/watch?v=Lk5wkoepTLY.
"Tamil Old—Nalla penmani miga nalla penmani (vMv)—MANAMAGAL 1951." N.d. Accesssed November 18, 2018. https://www.youtube.com/watch?v=yqPl-mhMyFM.
Tamiḻ Icai Caṅkam Tamiḻ Icai Malar. 1954. Ceṉṉai: Tamiḻ Icai Caṅkam.
Taylor, Woodman. 2002. "Penetrating Gazes: The Poetics of Sight and Visual Display in Popular Indian Cinema." *Contributions to Indian Sociology* 36 (1–2): 297–322.
Thapar, Romila. 2011. *Śakuntalā: Texts, Readings, Histories*. New York: Columbia University Press.
Thota, Sree Katyayani. 2016. "Stage to Screen, and Back: A Study of the Dialogue between Kuchipudi and Telugu Cinema." PhD diss., University of Hyderabad.
"Ṭi. Pirapāvati." 1950. *Kuṇṭūci*, January, 58–73.
Trautmann, Thomas. 2006. *Languages and Nations: The Dravidian Proof in Colonial Madras*. Berkeley: University of California Press.
———. ed. 2009. *The Madras School of Orientalism: Producing Knowledge in Colonial South India*. New Delhi: Oxford University Press.
Vaasanthi, S. *Cut-Outs, Caste and Cine Stars: The World of Tamil Politics*. New Delhi: Viking.
Vaithees, Ravi V. 2015. *Religion, Caste, and Nation in South India: Maraimalai Adigal, the Neo-Saivite Movement, and Tamil Nationalism, 1876–1950*. New Delhi: Oxford University Press.
Vāmaṉaṉ. 2013. *Pi. Ār. Es. Kōpāliṉ Kuṇṭūci*. Ceṉṉai: Māṇikkavācakar Patippakam.
Vazhuvoovar School of Classical Dance and Music. 2018. www.vazhuvoorars.com.
Velayutham, Selvaraj, ed. 2008. *Tamil Cinema: The Cultural Politics of India's Other Film Industry*. Routledge.
Venkatachalam, G. *Dance in India*. Bombay: Nalanda Publications, 1947.
Venkatachalapathy, A. R. 2004. *Pāratiyiṉ "Vijaya" Katturaikaḷ* [Uncollected writings of Bharati from the journal *Vijaya*]. Nagercoil: Kalācuvaṭu Patippakam.

———. 2008. *Pārati Kaṟuvūlam: Hindu Nalittalil Pāratiyiṉ Eḻuttukaḷ* [Uncollected writings of Bharati from the *Hindu* newspaper]. Nagercoil: Kalācuvaṭu Patippakam.
———. 2012. *The Province of the Book: Scholars, Scribes, and Scribblers in Colonial Tamilnadu*. New Delhi: Permanent Black.
———. 2018. *Who Owns That Song: The Battle for Subramania Bharati's Copyright*. New Delhi: Juggernaut Publications.
Veṅkaṭarāmaṉ, Caṅkar. 2001. *Tiraiyulakil Icaik Kalaiñarkaḷ*. Ceṉṉai: Sarigamapadhani Foundation.
Venkatesan, Archana. 2010. *The Secret Garland: Antal's Tiruppavai and Nacciyar Tirumoli*. New York: Oxford University Press.
Venkatesan, Archana, and Crispin Branfoot. 2016. *In Andal's Garden*. Mumbai: Marg.
Venkateswaran, Usha. 2005. *The Life and Times of La Meri: The Queen of Ethnic Dance*. New Delhi: Indira Gandhi Centre for the Arts.
Vijayaraghavan, Sujatha. 2011. "A Marvel of Tradition and Talent." *Sruti*, April, 9–14.
Weidman, Amanda. 2006. *Singing the Classical, Voicing the Modern: The Postcolonial Politics of Music in South India*. Durham, NC: Duke University Press.
———. 2012a. "Musical Genres and National Identity." In *The Cambridge Companion to Modern Indian Culture*, edited by Vasudha Dalmia and Rashmi Sadana, 247–63. Cambridge: Cambridge University Press.
———. 2012b. "Voices of Meenakumari: Sound, Meaning, and Self-Fashioning in Performances of an Item Number." *South Asian Popular Culture* 10 (3): 307–18.
Weiss, Richard S. 2009. *Recipes for Immortality: Medicine, Religion and Community in South India*. New York: Oxford University Press.

SONGBOOKS

Adrishtam. Madras, 1939.
Ekampavaṇaṉ. Vellore: Prabhat Press, 1947.
Haridas. Madurai: Chandira Press, 1944.
Jakatalapratāpaṉ. Madras, 1944.
Jalaja. Madras: Devi Press, 1938.
Kalidas. Madras, 1931.
Kaṉṉaki. Madras, 1942.
Kannika. Madras: Chakravarthy Press, 1947.
Karaikkāl Ammaiyār. Madras, 1943.
Kiruṣṇapakti. Madras: Muttukumaraṉ Accakam, 1948.
Kīta Kānti. Madras: Krishna Printing Works, 1949.
Raja Desingh. Madras: Devi Press, 1936.
Sivakavi. Madras: Saibaba and Company, 1943.
Śrī Kanta Līlā. Madras: Caxton Press, 1938.
Vidyapathi. Madras, 1941.

INDEX

Note: Page numbers in *italics* refer to illustrations and tables.

ABOUT THE AUTHOR

Hari Krishnan is associate professor of dance at Wesleyan University. His research areas include queer identities in South Asian and global dance performance, colonialism, postcolonialism and Indian dance, Bharatanāṭyam in Tamil cinema, and the history of *devadāsī*-courtesan dance traditions in southern India. He is also the artistic director of inDANCE, a Toronto-based dance company, and as an award-winning dance maker receives international commissions for his bold and transgressive contemporary dance choreography.